Assessing Young Language Learners

THE CAMBRIDGE LANGUAGE ASSESSMENT SERIES

Series editors: J. Charles Alderson and Lyle F. Bachman

In this series:

Assessing Grammar by James E. Purpura
Assessing Language for Specific Purposes by Dan Douglas
Assessing Language Through Computer Technology by Carol A. Chapelle
and Dan Douglas
Assessing Listening by Gary Buck
Assessing Reading by J. Charles Alderson
Assessing Speaking by Sari Luoma
Assessing Vocabulary by John Read
Assessing Writing by Sara Cushing Weigle
Statistical Analyses for Language Assessment by Lyle F. Bachman
Statistical Analyses for Language Assessment Workbook by Lyle F.
Bachman and Antony J. Kunnan

Assessing Young Language Learners

Penny McKay

CAMBRIDGE
UNIVERSITY PRESS

CAMBRIDGE UNIVERSITY PRESS
Cambridge, New York, Melbourne, Madrid, Cape Town, Singapore, São Paulo

Cambridge University Press
The Edinburgh Building, Cambridge CB2 8RU, UK

www.cambridge.org
Information on this title: www.cambridge.org/9780521601238

First published 2006
Reprinted 2007

Printed in the United Kingdom at the University Press, Cambridge

A catalogue record for this publication is available from the British Library

Library of Congress Cataloguing in Publicaton data
McKay, Penny.
  Assessing young language learners / Penny McKay.
    p.   cm. – (Cambridge language assessment series)
  Includes bibliographical references and index.
  ISBN 0-521-60123-1 – ISBN 0-521-84138-0
  1. Language and languages – Ability testing. I. Title. II. Series.

P53.4.M356 2005
407.6–dc22   2005031299

ISBN 978-0-521-84138-2 hardback
ISBN 978-0-521-60123-8 paperback

*To Lauren, Dana, Alicia, Tayla, Maddison and Chelsee:
look for the possibilities!*

And to all the family, especially to Andy, Paul and Chris.

Contents

Series editors' preface

Recent years have seen considerable growth in the number of children learning a second or foreign language, as the importance of being able to use a language other than one's first language has become recognized in an increasingly globalized world. In Asia and Europe in particular, there has been a tendency to lower the age at which school children begin to learn a foreign language, since it is believed that the earlier a child starts to learn a foreign language, the greater the ultimate achievement will be. In addition, in many regions of the world, vast numbers of children attend schools in which the language of instruction is not the same as their native or mother tongue. In many African countries, for instance, the language of education is not the same as the language of the home for the majority of children. In many settings, the children of immigrants must not only deal with the same subject matter as their classmates for whom the language of instruction is their native language, but also acquire that language as a second, sometimes as a third, language. Such children are variously referred to as 'bilingual students', 'foreign language (FL) learners', 'second language (SL) learners', 'pupils having English as an additional language (EAL)', 'students of non-English-speaking background (NESB)' or 'English language learners (ELLs)'. In many countries, these 'young language learners' comprise a sizeable proportion of the school-age population. In the USA, for example, it has recently been estimated that well over 3 million children, or nearly 12 per cent of all children in the elementary schools, are young language learners. Furthermore, in many countries, young language learners comprise the most rapidly growing segment of the elementary (primary) school population.

While in some schools there is no extra support to help young language learners acquire the language of instruction, in most countries where there are large numbers of young learners, there is a growing awareness of their special needs. There is therefore a need to identify the needs of young language learners, to determine what level, if any, of proficiency they have in the target language, to diagnose their strengths and areas in need of improvement, and to keep track of their progress in acquiring the language. Language assessment, whether this is informal, classroom-based, or large-scale, thus has a critical role to play in gathering the information needed for these purposes.

The most pressing assessment need in school programmes for young learners is for greater knowledge and expertise in language assessment among classroom teachers. Although high-stakes accountability decisions are often based largely on the results of large-scale, standardized assessments, the formative decisions that help guide student learning and inform teaching are appropriately made on the basis of classroom-based assessments that teachers make. Unfortunately, the vast majority of teachers who work with young language learners have had little or no professional training or education in language assessment. Nevertheless, teachers are involved in assessment on a daily basis, as they monitor their pupils' classroom performance, as they collect work samples or compile portfolios, and as they develop formal classroom assessments.

This book is ideally suited to meet this assessment need of practitioners who are working with young language learners. It includes discussions of the research about the characteristics and special needs of young language learners, along with discussions of the research about the conditions under which these children learn language. The volume also provides practitioners with a wealth of approaches, both informal and formal, to classroom assessment, including the assessment of oral skills, reading and writing, illustrated with numerous examples from actual classrooms and programmes for young language learners.

The author of this volume, Penny McKay, has extensive experience in teaching school-age learners and in developing programmes for these learners, and has conducted considerable research herself in this area. In addition, her long experience as an educator, mentor and teacher trainer has enabled her bring to this volume a wealth of knowledge, and to focus this and present it in a way that is readily accessible to practitioners.

In summary, this book is timely in that it addresses an important and urgent need in language assessment. There are a number of books that provide 'cookbook' examples of assessments for young learners.

However, no other volume provides both a discussion of the research to help readers better understand these children and how to assess them most appropriately, and a principled discussion of the variety of assessment approaches that are available to practitioners.

J. Charles Alderson
Lyle F. Bachman

Acknowledgments

I am grateful for the support provided by the Faculty of Education at Queensland University of Technology, and by my colleagues in the TESOL Unit and the School of Cultural and Language Studies, during the writing process. Thanks go to Professor Lynne Cameron at Leeds University, who encouraged me to write the book, and to Lynette Bowyer, who edited early drafts for no other reason than to lend me support and encouragement. Thanks also go to Julia Rothwell, Jenny Angus and Saraswathi Griffiths-Chandran for talking to me about their own assessment practices, and to all the teachers with whom I have interacted during my school teaching career, as well as during my professional development, M.Ed (TESOL) teaching and higher degree research student supervision over the years.

I am very grateful for the support given by Lyle Bachman and Charles Alderson. In particular, I am indebted to Lyle Bachman for sharing his expertise, while reading and commenting on drafts of this book.

Finally, I wish to thank my husband, Andy, for his unending patience and encouragement, and, as can be vouched for by family, friends and colleagues, his wonderful cooking.

CHAPTER ONE

A special case for young learner language assessment

Introduction

This chapter sets out to establish a special case for young learner language assessment. What are the characteristics of young learners that need to be remembered in assessment decisions? We all know that young learners are different from adults, but how do we explain the important differences in a simple, accessible way? This chapter provides some central information about young learners – who they are, where they are learning, and what requires us to give them special consideration in assessment.

Young language learners and their language programmes

Young language learners are those who are learning a foreign or second language and who are doing so during the first six or seven years of formal schooling. In the education systems of most countries, young learners are children who are in primary or elementary school. In terms of age, young learners are between the ages of approximately five and twelve. Many young language learners can be called bilingual. **Bilingual learners** are those learners who learn two (or more) languages to some level of proficiency (Bialystok, 2001, p. 5). This rather vague definition – impossible to pin down because of the variety of experiences of learners – would tend to include children who are learning a foreign language in immersion and bilingual programmes and all children in second language programmes. The term would also include many, many children who learn a foreign or

1

second language as they interact with speakers of other languages and dialects outside formal language programmes.

Young language learners may be **foreign language learners**, learning a language in a situation where the language is seldom heard outside the classroom. They may be learning languages like Vietnamese, Spanish or Chinese in Germany or the United States or they may be learning English as a foreign language (EFL) in countries like Turkey, Malaysia or Spain. Other young learners may be **second language learners**. Second language learners are usually members of a minority language group in a country where the majority of their peers have spoken the language from birth. Second language learners do not need to speak both languages fully to be bilingual, especially in a second language situation. These learners learn the majority language as their second language. For example, they may be learning Japanese as a second language in Japan, where large numbers of Japanese have returned in recent years with their non-Japanese-speaking children; or Cantonese as second language learners in Hong Kong where numbers of Mandarin-speaking children have been granted residency. They may be learning **English as a Second Language**, also referred to as English as an Additional Language (referred to in this book as ESL) in Britain, Australia, Canada or the United States. They may have been born in the country and have spoken only their home language before school or they may have immigrated because of family decisions to migrate or because of traumatic events in their home country. For young second language learners, the language they are learning is usually the main language of communication in their class-room, school and community. They are spending every moment of the week engaged in learning the language and at the same time learning through the language; for these students the language is a vital and per-vasive foundation to their life at school.

Young language learners around the world share many common char-acteristics and they learn in programmes that share many common beliefs and practices concerning the environment that young learners need in order to learn. Language programmes for young learners vary in their purposes and intended outcomes, their duration and their intensity.

Foreign language programmes

A range of different programme types exist around the world for young language learners. Some foreign language programmes are **language**

awareness programmes or **introductory programmes**, designed to raise children's interest in the language and to show that language learning can be enjoyable, but without the aim of achieving set language learning goals by the end of the course. Such language programmes for young learners often have a very small number of contact hours per week, perhaps only 20 minutes per week. However, regular **scheduled foreign language classes** are the most common type of foreign language programme in elementary schools. The contact hours for scheduled language classes for young learners are generally longer than introductory programmes, up to two hours per week or more. These classes are often taught by a foreign language teacher who moves from class to class, taking over the class from the classroom teacher for the lesson period. In some programmes classroom teachers are encouraged to work with the foreign language teacher to incorporate the language into children's content learning in other subject areas like social studies and science. **Partial immersion** and **total immersion programmes** are examples of foreign language programmes that are designed to ensure greater language learning gains. In partial immersion programmes, children study their curriculum subjects through the target language for part of a day or week and in total immersion programmes they learn through the target language for every day of the week and every week of the year. Immersion programmes are sometimes called **bilingual programmes**.

The learning outcomes expected in foreign language programmes for young learners depend on a number of factors, including the starting age, the amount of contact time and other factors, such as the appropriateness of the curriculum, the language *proficiency* and *teaching* skills of the teacher (**proficiency** is a general term denoting the degree of skill with which a person can use a language), and whether there are wider opportunities for the language to be encountered (e.g., in other subjects as part of everyday classroom learning or in communications with visitors or on the Internet). Generally, regular scheduled programmes for young learners focus on listening and speaking, especially in the first two years. Reading and simple writing may be introduced gradually, depending on the age of the children and whether the programme is an immersion programme. Children learning in immersion and bilingual programmes have opportunities to advance quickly and in more depth in their language ability because they have additional time to use the language, and expectations of what they are expected to do in the language are high.

Second language programmes

Second language learners may be learning through **intensive language programmes**, sometimes called **sheltered programmes**, in which groups of second language learners are brought together, usually for a limited period of time when they first arrive in the country, to study the language together and to be introduced to the school curriculum. Many second language learners go directly into the **mainstream classroom**, that is, the regular classroom where they begin immediately to study the established curriculum alongside their majority language-speaking peers. Their **mainstream teacher** is an important person in young second language learners' school lives, as she or he will be their main language teacher and helper. Mainstream teachers possess varying degrees of knowledge about the language needs of second language learners. Some fortunate second language learners are given additional **language and learning support** by specialist teachers; for example ESL specialists in many English-speaking countries work with the mainstream teachers in various ways to provide language-based support to help ESL learners access the mainstream curriculum. **Bilingual programmes for second language learners** are those programmes that teach children in their first language or in both the first and the second language. The philosophy behind bilingual programmes is that children need to gain access to learning through their first language, often their stronger language, until they have developed the cognitive maturity and language ability that enables them to transfer this knowledge to the second language (Cummins, 1979). Second language learners are surrounded by the target language in their work and play at school and therefore have many more opportunities than foreign language learners to learn the language. But second language learners are expected to (and need to) make huge language learning gains almost immediately in the target language; they need the language to make friends and survive socially at school and they need the language to study the curriculum. Indeed they are often unrealistically expected to use language in the classroom as efficiently as their majority language-speaking peers who have been learning the language since birth.

This brief overview of language programmes for young learners illustrates that programmes differ in their purpose, their context, in the nature of their learners and the expectations of foreign and second language learning. In all these types of programmes, whether for foreign language or second language learners, teachers and assessors have something in common; they all need to assess the language of their young learners. In this book, **teachers** are foreign language teachers, classroom teachers and second language specialists who need to assess to inform their teaching decisions, to report on progress to others (as required by their Education Department) and to monitor growth over time. **Assessors** are those personnel who have testing expertise and are commissioned by schools, Education Departments and/or governments to develop and administer tests. The differences amongst the languages, the programmes, learner characteristic and assessment or testing purposes are very real; these differences can be addressed through a common, principled, framework approach to assessment. This book describes a framework-driven approach to assessment for young learners. Every assessment decision is different; therefore teachers and assessors play a central role interpreting assessment principles and frameworks, basing their decisions on their knowledge of the particular programme and the particular characteristics of the learners to be assessed. Yet there are also many characteristics that young language learners share.

The special characteristics of young language learners

Children bring to their language learning their own personalities, likes and dislikes and interests, their own individual cognitive styles and capabilities and their own strengths and weaknesses. Multiple intelligence theory (Gardner, 1993) has suggested that children vary individually across eight types of intelligence – linguistic, musical, logical-mathematical, spatial, bodily kinesthetics, interpersonal, intrapersonal and naturalistic. Furthermore, because of differences in their socioeconomic, cultural and home background, children bring with them an experience and knowledge of the world that is individual. Thus, with regard to individuality, children are no different from older learners. Their individuality is, however, linked to the special characteristics that are discussed below. These characteristics of children set them apart from older learners. These characteristics fall into three general categories: growth, literacy and vulnerability. Since understanding of these differences is central to effective assessment, I will describe these in some detail. The descriptions are indicative only, since children develop at varying and individual rates and in ways influenced by background experiences.

Cognitive, social and emotional, and physical growth

The general assessment literature is designed for what Bialystok (2001) has called the 'stable state' of the adult mind. However, children are in a state of constant cognitive, social, emotional and physical growth. They have a limited but growing experience of the world. The following descriptions of the cognitive, social and emotional and physical characteristics of young learners are a general representation only; it is not possible to describe exactly the characteristic or the approximate age at which it occurs. Cognitive growth characteristics present clear differences between young learners and adults. The attention span of young learners in the early years of schooling is short, as little as 10 to 15 minutes; they are easily diverted and distracted by other pupils. They may drop out of a task when they find it difficult, though they are often willing to try a task in order to please the teacher. As children progress from 5 years old to 12 years old, they are developing abilities to think in new ways and are moving towards being able to reason in a systematic and logical fashion in adolescence. Children are *novices* as they learn, with help from others, to become more expert in solving problems, in reading and in many more activities.

> At first there seems to be too much to concentrate on at once and if we focus on one part, we lose control of another. But once we have mastered it, everything seems to fit together smoothly, we can perform efficiently and flexibly. The skills become more and more automatic and as this happens, progressively more of our attention becomes freed so we can begin to focus on new information, for example other aspects of the task.   (Shorrocks, 1995, p. 267)

In early elementary grades, from ages five to seven, children are continuing to learn from direct experience. They are developing their understanding of cause and effect ('I can have a pet if I take care of it.') They are continuing to expand their use of their first language to clarify thinking and learning. Their understanding of words like 'tomorrow' or 'yesterday' is developing, but they may still be unsure about length of time. They are developing the ability to count and to organize information to remember it (Puckett and Black, 2000). Before they are eight years old, children do not find it easy to use language to talk about language. The language children need to talk about and understand talk about grammar and discourse (known as **metalanguage**) does not come until this age and upwards.

As children move into upper elementary grades they move towards more objective thought, being able to recognize, for example, that three or four children can have three or four different interpretations of a single cloud formation in the sky (Slavin, 1994). They are still gaining understanding from direct experience – through objects and visual aids. At 11 to 13 years of age, they are beginning to develop the ability to 'manipulate' thoughts and ideas, but even at this age still need hands-on experiences. Their use of language has expanded to enable them to predict, hypothesize and classify. They are continuing to expand their understanding of cause and effect and are developing a sense of metaphor and puns and by around eleven to thirteen can understand double meaning in jokes. Their understanding of time has developed by 12 years of age to the point where they can talk about recent events, plans for the future and career aspirations (Puckett and Black, 2000). A small percentage of children in the upper elementary years are moving into what Piaget called the *formal operational stage*, when they begin to hypothesize, build abstract categories and handle more than two variables at a time. Their interpretation of symbols in stories and art becomes less literal and their understanding of abstract social concepts, such as democracy, becomes more sophisticated. Most children move into this stage during secondary school (Slavin, 1994).

The cognitive development of bilingual learners has been the subject of much research over many years (Bialystok and Hakuta, 1999; Bialystok, 2001; Cummins, 2001a), but, despite this, Bialystok (2001) points out that the research literature on the development of bilingual children is thin and suggests this is because of the difficulty of doing research in the area. In an early summary of research findings, Cummins wrote the following:

> Recent research findings indicate that access to two languages in early childhood can accelerate the development of both verbal and non-verbal abilities. There is also evidence of a positive association between bilingualism and both cognitive flexibility and divergent thinking. (Cummins, 2001, p. 51)

In a more recent account, Bialystok (2001) finds that there are some cognitive processes, namely attention and inhibition, that develop earlier and possibly more strongly in bilinguals, contributing to metalinguistic awareness and language learning. But Bialystok points us to advantages that go beyond those found in specific cognitive processes.

> For the most part, the cognitive and linguistic differences between bilingual and monolingual children who are otherwise similar turn out to be small. Some may even consider that the differences that have been established are arcane and trivial. But that would be to

miss the point. The development of two languages in childhood turns out to be a profound event that ripples through the life of that individual.   (Bialystok, 2001, p. 247–8)

Bilingual children not only experience and learn to master the social conventions and conversational styles of at least two languages. Their bilingual experiences 'challenge their world views and social identity' (Bialystok, 2001) and possibly give them different and broader perspectives on events and people around them. The cognitive development of bilingual learners is qualitatively different in these ways, even though they follow the generally expected steps in cognitive development outlined above.

Knowledge of children's cognitive stage of development is important for the effective assessment of young language learners. The cognitive demand of tasks should be commensurate with children's age-related abilities. Young learners are unlikely to see the 'whole' in a complex task that spans several parts. Older children, however, can see and enjoy some kind of coherence across parts in tasks if the parts are connected within a thematic or narrative approach. Assessment tasks should not extend beyond the child's experience of the world; if children have never seen or talked about the sea or sandcastles, they may not be able to respond to the instructions in the input, regardless of the general language ability. Children should not be asked to analyse a picture or an idea or to describe a language rule – this type of abstract analysis is likely to be beyond most elementary learners' cognitive ability. Assessment should take place in a quiet, calm setting that helps children to concentrate and not be distracted by noise or movement. These are just some of the kinds of actions and decisions in language assessment that teachers and assessors make when they take account of the nature of their young learners' cognitive development.

Children are also growing socially and emotionally as they are learning language in their elementary school years. They are gradually developing from a main interest in self towards greater social awareness. They are also developing a growing understanding of the self in relation to others and an ability to function in groups. Their need for love, security, recognition and belonging accompanies a gradual shift from dependence on adults to peer group support and approval. Socially, most children are gaining in confidence and reducing dependency as they progress through from 5 to 12 years of age. Children's contact with their peers expands greatly during their school years. They learn to interact with peers, to deal with hostility and dominance, to relate to a leader, to lead others, to deal with social problems and to develop a concept of self. Between five and seven, they are learning to cooperate and share and take turns with others, which means that they are developing the ability to take part in small group tasks. They are beginning to develop feelings of independence but may become anxious when separated from familiar people and places. By the time they are around 11 years of age, children have become sociable, spending time with friends of the same sex. They are continuing to develop the ability to work and play with others. They may appear relatively calm, with short-lived moments of anger, sadness or depression. They are often able to hide feelings of anxiety; their behaviour may appear over-confident because of this. At this age, they are defining themselves in terms of their physical characteristics and their likes and dislikes. They are sensitive to criticism and their feelings of success or failure are dependent on how adults and peers respond to them.

The influence of the peer group may be stronger in some cultures than others, but the increasing influence of peer groups on a child's motivations and interests from 5 to 12 is likely to influence the learner's participation in different kinds of tasks. A task that requires a 12-year-old child to stand up and perform alone, for example, would not ensure that all learners were going to participate or if they did, some would be able to do the task only with a high degree of nervousness. From around 7 years of age, right up until 12, children continue to prefer to play in same-sex groups, enjoy team games and may show a strong sense of loyalty to their group or team. Characteristics of sharing and cooperating, of being assertive and of fitting into the society they live in are social skills that vary from culture to culture and generation to generation (Phillips, 1993). Children need to be helped to learn appropriate social skills, particularly if they are in a new culture. Children in a second language context react to their new situation in many different ways. A child with an outgoing personality most likely moves into groups quickly and subsequently learns the language faster; another may be more introvert and take more time to learn the language (Wong Fillmore, 1976). Some children are traumatized by terrible events in their past or by the changes caused by migration to a new country and/or transition to a new language and culture. Again children react differently depending on their personality and the nature of their experiences. Some are withdrawn; others extremely angry; others adapt well with care and consideration from others. Bilingual children's experiences, their reactions to them and the reactions of others to their needs may influence their social development for several years.

Assessment should therefore, wherever possible, be familiar and involve familiar adults, rather than strangers. The environment should be 'psychologically safe' for the learner. Texts used in assessment tasks should deal with familiar content – with home and family and school and with familiar, simple **genres** (culturally based forms of discourse that have distinctive forms of structure and are used to achieve particular communicative goals) like children's stories and folktales. If the assessment situation permits, interlocutor support should be available to encourage the children, remind them, keep them on track as they complete the task. Immediate feedback is valuable – thus computer assessment tasks that give immediate responses (with sounds and visual effects) and teachers responding kindly to the child's efforts, are ideal for young learners. Such feedback maintains attention and confidence. As children grow they are able to work more independently and for long spans of time without ongoing feedback.

Children's physical growth is characterized by continuing and rapid development of gross and fine-motor skills. From 5 to 7 years of age, children are developing in their ability to move around (climb, balance, run and jump) and are increasing their fine-motor skills (handling writing tools, using scissors), which involve developments in hand–eye coordination. As development progresses, children can progress towards holding thinner pens, drawing finer pictures and building intricate models. At this age they are still very active, tiring easily and recovering quickly. Important for many school activities, children tire more easily from sitting than from running. They usually love physical activities, which they often participate in noisily and sometimes aggressively. Young learners around this age have a need to play and to engage in fantasy and fun. They are often enthusiastic and lively. By the time they are 9 to 12 years of age, children are still developing hand–eye coordination, but they are better coordinated than seven- or eight-year-olds. These abilities continue to develop on into secondary school. Their large muscle coordination is also continuing to develop, so that they have shown gradual increase in speed and accuracy during running, climbing, throwing and catching activities. Boys can be 12 to 18 months behind girls in physical development in the later years of elementary school. Physical development needs to be taken into account in language assessment tasks, perhaps particularly with regard to tiredness, ability to sit still and hand–eye coordination. Assessment tasks that involve physical activity to accompany the language-related response – moving, pointing, circling or colouring in a picture – are helpful to encourage young learners to complete the task, especially for children in the early grades. Children in upper elementary classes are more able to respond without this type of requirement.

Teachers and assessors therefore need deep knowledge of children's development – their cognitive, social and emotional and physical growth – in order to be able to select and construct the most appropriate assessment tasks and to give appropriate feedback. For example, assessment tasks may need careful introduction (recall of previous knowledge; reminder of vocabulary needed) before children can proceed to show what they are able to do with language. In another example, children's interests and concentration spans determine the kinds of tasks (the use of colourful pictures; a short, interesting story) that motivate them to complete the task.

Literacy

A vital dimension of difference for young learners, compared with most older learners, is that they are learning literacy skills and understandings at the same time as they are learning their target language. They may be doing this in their first language and continuing to develop literacy, in parallel, in their foreign language or they may be learning the bulk of their literacy in their second language.

The general expectations of literacy development for first language learners are summarized in Table 1.1. A defining characteristic of literacy development is that children have first to develop understandings about how reading and writing work and that these develop over several years, beginning before they start school. These understandings establish the foundation for literacy. For example, as skills of decoding and whole word recognition and knowledge of discourse organization begin to develop, children's reading is slow and deliberate at first; then they develop abilities to read aloud and silently and an ability to read for information and for pleasure. Messages are conveyed through writing in the early years with the help of drawing, the development of writing is determined by progress in fine-motor skills, in children's ability to remember words and spelling and to combine words in sentences and paragraphs. By the time children are between 7 and 9, they are beginning to self-correct and are beginning to convey meaning only through writing. Their writing skills continue to develop, until by the end of their elementary years they are able to write in ways that expand their thinking and to write in the required form or genre for the particular purpose for which they are writing. By 11 to 13, children are able to read a variety of fiction and nonfiction and importantly, to develop critical literacy skills, that is, to understand that people may

Table 1.1 *Widely Held Expectations of Literacy Development (Extract from Table 3.4, Puckett and Black, 2000, p.100)*

5–7 years	7–9 years	9–11 years	11–13 years
Are continuing to develop a sense of how writing and reading work	Begin to understand and use writing and reading for specific purposes	Can expand thinking more readily through writing and reading	Continue to expand thinking more readily through writing and reading
Combine drawing and writing to convey ideas	May combine drawing and writing, but writing can stand alone to convey meaning	Continue to increase reading vocabulary	Continue to increase silent reading rate and time spent at reading
Understand that print 'tells' the story	Develop a rapidly increasing vocabulary of sight words	Continue to self-correct errors	Continue to increase ability to adjust rate and reading to suit purpose (skim, scan, select, study)
Develop a basic vocabulary of personal words	Begin to self-correct errors	Read silently with increased speed and comprehension (Silent reading speed greater than oral speed may result in oral reading difficulties)	Continue to broaden their interests in a variety of fiction and non-fiction
Read slowly and deliberately	Develop the ability to read silently	Adjust reading rate to suit purpose (scanning)	Begin to understand that people may interpret the same material in different ways
Will substitute words that make sense when reading	Increase ability to read aloud fluently and with expression	Expand reading skills to gather information from a variety of sources. Make personal choices in reading for pleasure	

interpret material in different ways and that there may be a variety of assumptions and purposes behind material they read.

The outline of expected progress in Table 1.1 presumes that children have commenced reading and writing between five and seven with well-developed oral abilities in their first language. First language learners are able to build on their oral language to read and write. Foreign language learners bring a background of literacy development in their first language to their language learning. Their skills in literacy in the foreign language build on their developing first language literacy understanding and skills but are dominated by a lack of oral knowledge of the foreign language. Many young second language learners have not had an opportunity to develop first language literacy skills and are therefore learning literacy in their second language, compounding the challenge of second language learning. Hence, not only do these children not have literacy understanding and skills, they do not have oral knowledge of the new language.

Oral language underpins literacy development for children learning literacy skills in their first language. Throughout their elementary school years, they are increasing their ability to interact conversationally with a range of people, in different situations, with different goals and on different topics. They are able to talk about familiar topics about the home, family and school when they begin school, with topics broadening to the wider world as they grow and their experience of the world widens. They are increasingly able to talk in longer stretches of interactions and engage in different types of talk beyond narratives and descriptions, for example in instructions, arguments and opinions. They are also increasing their ability to engage in extended talk, which requires greater cognitive and linguistic abilities than conversational interaction, especially when a supportive interlocutor is usually present. For foreign language learners, literacy knowledge from their first language is available to assist them to handle reading and writing in the language, though a different script can negate this advantage. For second language learners, too, literacy knowledge from the first language can assist them to acquire high levels of reading comprehension in the second language (Bialystok, 2001).

The developing first and second language literacy of young learners ensures that young learner assessment will always require special consideration. Assessors need knowledge of the pathways of literacy development in the first language and its conflicting as well as constructing influence on literacy in the second language. They need to know about the pathways of foreign/second language literacy and its interface with oral language learning in the foreign/second language. This knowledge has importance for the appropriate choice of tasks (e.g, the texts that are used for reading; the expectations in writing) and particularly for judgments about the nature of progress over time or of performance in a task.

Vulnerability

Whilst many older learners are vulnerable to criticism or failure, young learners have a particular vulnerability that requires careful attention. For the most part young learners have confidence in their own abilities, if they have received love and support in the past. However, at this age, children have a heightened sensitivity to praise, criticism and approval and their self-esteem is strongly influenced by experiences at school. Children need experiences that help them to succeed, to feel good about themselves. These experiences can help them maintain their enthusiasm and creativity. A lack of a positive self-concept can result in loss of motivation, loss of self-esteem and can sometimes have long-term consequences. Even the smallest failure can cause a child to feel worthless. When young learners are assessed, it is important that children experience overall success and a sense of progression. Healthy adults, on the other hand, have developed a general sense of worth that can withstand failure in an assessment task and they can see the broader picture; most can see how the result fits into the present and the future (I can do something else; I can try again). This is difficult for young learners who tend to judge themselves on their accomplishments, rather than on a general sense of worth (Slavin, 1994).

Rates of development may vary markedly among children. Individual children may also vary in their own development: that is, a child may develop quite rapidly physically, but quite slowly in the social and emotional sphere. The implication of the reality of variable growth amongst children is that it is likely that assessment procedures designed for broad groups of young learners are not appropriate for all children. Some children may do badly or fail because they have not progressed at the same rate as most children in their age group, for example in their cognitive development and literacy skills development.

The fact that individual patterns of development exist should constantly ring warning bells for teachers and assessors of young learners. Observation-based assessment helps to determine the developmental phase that children are entering or consolidating and to target assessment appropriately. If this is not feasible, extreme care needs to be taken to ensure that there is some flexibility in assessment (e.g., tasks catering for all levels; passes for all at different levels) so that a degree of success can be experienced by all children.

The beliefs and practices of elementary education

Effective assessment of young learners is integrally tied to the principles of learning adopted within the curriculum in which the children are learning. If the underlying pedagogic principles of assessment and learning are not aligned, this would indicate a serious problem with the assessment procedures being used. Across different cultures, there are variations in beliefs and practices in young learner programmes (Feeney, 1992; Alexander, 2000). These differences are tied to the ideas and values, habits and customs and world views of the country or region (Alexander, 2000). This section summarizes just some central themes in elementary education in the Western tradition. These themes align with the idea of language use assessment promoted in this book. Many of these principles of elementary education also underpin the teaching of young learners in other cultures and therefore will be familiar to many readers.

Elementary school teaching, that is, early childhood and middle school teaching, is based on principles of child growth and development. Because children develop cognitively, socially and emotionally and physically at different rates and because they develop differently depending on their experiences, children are viewed as individuals, with individual needs in each of these areas. Pye (1988) refers to children's emotional needs in the following statement:

> a teacher treats a pupil as an interesting and unpredictable individual, not as an inhabitant of convenient generality. Pupils will gain from teachers with whom they make close relationships, time, patience and regard. But most important of all, they will gain from being acknowledged as not wholly known, as able to surprise.
>
> (Pye, 1988, p. 16)

In elementary education and most particularly in early childhood education, it is believed that the characteristics of each child should be known and that the child should be taught with knowledge of the combination of all of these characteristics (Jalongo, 2000; Kershner, 2000). Some children need privacy and space for reflection; others need structured group work to help them to become integrated more into the social interactions in the classroom. Children have individual learning styles. Some are mature enough to handle some types of tasks and others are not. Bilingual children have particular strengths and motivations that influence their participation and success. The extent to which teachers are able to know and to cater for each child's individual needs depends on a number of factors including the size of the class and the ability of the teacher to manage multiple goals through diverse groupings in the classroom.

It is generally believed in elementary education that each teacher should take some responsibility for the development of the whole child, that is, for the child's cognitive, social and emotional and physical development. Thus when making decisions about assessment tasks, language teachers and assessors need to know of the developmental characteristics of children, for example their curiosity and sense of wonder, their eagerness to test and practise their own powers and their fascination with words and delight in rhythm, music and movement. They need to understand the cultural backgrounds of children, their skills and abilities in their first language and the range of experiences and knowledge they bring to their foreign and second language learning. When language teachers are assessing through observation in the classroom, they need to observe children's many developing abilities, for example, in pencil-holding, in problem-solving and in group social skills as they engage in learning activities. The cognitive, social and emotional and physical characteristics of the whole child have an impact on language learning and therefore need to be monitored and, where necessary, addressed.

Theories of learning in elementary education have moved from understandings that learning centres on the individual's efforts, constructing knowledge through individual mental growth as a consequence of individual interaction with experience (Piaget, 1930) to a view of constructivist learning, in which knowledge is not constructed so much by the isolated learner but by the social group (Vygotsky, 1962). In constructivist education, children's learning skills are promoted; children are encouraged to become active learners, becoming aware of their own needs, their own strengths and weaknesses and taking some responsibility for their own learning. Children learn through a two-way communication of ideas with other people, with other children, with peers and with teachers. They try their ideas out for size through talking with others in a social mode of thinking (Mercer, 1994). In this philosophy, children are encouraged to become responsible for their own learning through the use of assessment contracts from time to time, in which they work through a list of tasks in their own time (see Chapter 5 for an example).

Learning in the elementary years is therefore seen as a reciprocal activity between students, teachers and also with parents. It is also seen as an active process, in which children interact with others and also with their environment and concrete materials within it. Language plays a central role in the learning process; thinking depends on these active, jointly constructed processes and children learn through the use of language since they are predisposed to make sense of themselves, other people and the environment around them (Urquhart, 2000). Teachers set up conditions that allow children to discover things for themselves and they plan activities that give children direct, concrete experiences requiring them to act rather than expecting them to sit and listen, read and write. They refer to children's wider experiences out of school when explaining curriculum topics and elicit ideas from children rather than telling them directly. Teachers and assessors who subscribe to a constructivist philosophy of learning expect to see active learners engaged with the assessment task in front of them and to see creative and new uses of language in their assessment responses. They set tasks that encourage active and creative response, hoping for and looking for more than a 'correct answer' in the child's work. They provide scaffolding support. Elementary teachers are very familiar with the concept of scaffolding, a means by which they can give children cognitive and language support, by talking through a task with children and thus helping them to learn.

> [Scaffolding] is not just any assistance which helps a learner accomplish a task. It is help which will enable a learner to accomplish a task which they would not have been quite able to manage on their own and it is help which is intended to bring the learner closer to a state of competence which will enable them eventually to complete such a task on their own . . . To know whether or not some help counts as 'scaffolding' we would need to have at the very least some evidence of a teacher wishing to enable a child to develop a specific skill, grasp a particular concept or achieve a particular level of understanding.
>
> (Maybin, Mercer and Stierer, 1992, p.188)

In current theories of elementary education, knowledge is not only the recall of certain (prescribed) facts, although this is important. Knowledge also involves the processes which relate to that knowledge and a growing understanding of successively higher orders in relationships (Whitebread, 2000). Gaining knowledge involves a continuous process and learning takes place when children have the opportunity to visit and revisit the knowledge in new contexts and over time. Meadows (1993) has written that children are more likely to be able to transfer understandings or processes from one task to another when:

- the skill or procedure has been thoroughly learned
- the learner encounters a range of examples with a common structure but different irrelevant characteristics
- the abstract rule is made explicit
- the new task 'appears' similar to the old task
                              (Meadows, 1993, in Whitebread, 2000, p. 149)

As learning takes place over time, concepts are refined and awareness of relationships between concepts is extended. New knowledge gained is based on the child's present understanding and on his or her previous experience. Thus children's culturally based knowledge and experience has a profound influence on their learning.

Principles and understandings about children's learning underpin approaches to language assessment in the elementary school. They are present in each move teachers and assessors make, for example, when they are engaged in assessment as part of their moment-to-moment teaching and when they are selecting assessment tasks and developing assessment criteria for more formal assessment procedures. The language assessment principles and practices that are presented in this book are built on the foundation of elementary education and interpretations of the ideas in this book into actual assessment procedures require professional knowledge of the principles and practices of elementary education.

The power of assessment on young learners' lives

Assessment has the power to change people's lives (Shohamy, 2001). The effect of assessment may be positive or negative, depending on a number of factors, ranging from the way the assessment procedure or test is constructed, to the way it is used. Effective assessment procedures (which this book aims to help teachers and assessors to produce) are assessments that have been designed to ensure, as far as possible, valid and fair information on the student's abilities and progress. The meaning of 'valid' and 'fair' is addressed in more detail in Chapter 4; briefly, **valid assessments** are those that measure what they are supposed to measure; **fair assessments** are those that provide meaningful and appropriate information about a child's language use ability and avoid bias against any child because of that child's characteristics (first language and cultural background, age, gender, etc.). Effective assessment gives educators feedback in the teaching and learning process, informing the next teaching decision and giving guidance on how students should be optimally placed, for example, in the next grade level. Effective assessment provides valuable information to administrators on the achievement of cohorts of students and on whether schools are successfully delivering the curriculum. With this knowledge they are able to make decisions about the allocation of resources (usually teachers and funding) to different schools. Parents rely on assessment to know how their children are moving ahead and how their achievement compares with the expected rate of progress of their peers. And above all, effective assessment gives students knowledge of their own progress, giving them feedback on what they have done well or perhaps misunderstood and from time to time providing some 'creative tension' to motivate them to study harder.

However, assessment is not always effective and it can play a subversive role in the lives of children. Assessment is able to establish power relationships (between teachers and students; between administrators and principals) that become established and habitual (Foucault, 1979). Assessment is able to establish and maintain social position, if it is designed in such a way that it favours the privileged in society, perpetuating the status quo. For example, the failure caused by a child's lower socioeconomic status (involving probably a lack of knowledge of school language and culture) is perpetuated through tests that do not take account of diverse backgrounds. Assessment procedures are therefore able to carry with them and maintain the culture (the language, the knowledge, the ways of being) of the established group. Second language learners in countries around the world are often caught in this position. In some countries where English is not the first language but is spoken in government service and powerful businesses, children who speak English at home (usually from elite homes) are able to succeed in English exams at school. Thus in these situations assessment perpetuates the position of those in power.

Teachers and assessors (including those developing large-scale tests) of young learners need to examine the assessment tasks and procedures they construct, to work to become aware of and if possible to redress, institutionalized power of this kind in assessment and to ensure that the impact on the child, the community, the teacher and school and the learning programme is positive.

Assessment terms and purposes

There are many reasons why young language learners might be assessed
and there are a variety of different people interested in the results of their
assessment. The decisions that need to be made determine the purpose for
the assessment procedure and this in turn determines the kind of information that is needed from the assessment procedure. Thus, for example, when
teachers need to make decisions about what to teach next, the purpose for
the assessment procedure is to assess whether students have achieved the
curriculum objectives so far and the information that is required is data on
their performance in relation to the objectives. The **stakeholders** in the
assessment procedure, that is, anyone affected by the assessment procedure itself or by the decisions made that are based on the results of the
assessment procedure – parents, students themselves, teachers, principals,
administrators – may require different kinds of information depending on
who they are and on what their interest is. Administrators, for example,
require a summarized set of data about the student cohort. Teachers require
as much detail about the performance as soon as possible, so that they can
use the information to inform their teaching decisions.

Some decisions made on the basis of assessment results are **low-stakes**
decisions. Low-stakes decisions are relatively minor and are relatively easy
to correct. There is a low cost for making a wrong decision. **High-stakes**
decisions, on the other hand, are likely to affect students' lives and decisions are difficult to correct. The costs of making a wrong decision are high
(see Bachman, 2004). Not only formal tests are high-stakes; many assessment procedures are more high-stakes for students than we think, since
many decisions that teachers and schools make have a cumulative effect on
students' futures (Rea-Dickins and Gardner, 2000). Assessment might be
informal or formal, though these terms are not concise in their meaning.
Informal assessment usually refers to classroom assessment carried out
during the course of the teaching and learning process. **Formal assessment**
usually refers to assessment that is planned and carried out following
formal procedures; for example, students are organized to do the assessment task without support or interruption and they then submit their work
to the teacher for marking at a separate time. Assessment procedures may
also be classroom-based or external. **Classroom assessment** is prepared
and conducted by teachers in classrooms, whereas **external assessment** is
prepared by those outside the classroom. Sometimes classroom assessment results are used to report to others who are interested in the children's
results. Sometimes an external test is prepared by those in a central educa-

tion office and administered by schools. The purposes of both classroom and external tests can be tied to high-stakes decisions, especially if the results are used to select students or to compare achievement across schools (in order to evaluate the quality of the school or programme).

There are many different purposes for assessment. There are sometimes tensions between **pedagogic purposes for assessment**, aimed primarily at promoting learning and **administrative purposes for assessment**, aimed primarily at furnishing information about the performance of children and schools to Education Department administrators and others, who use this information for management and accountability purposes. These two purposes overlap to some degree; however, it has been found that administrative purposes often tend to prevail over pedagogic purposes since high-stakes accountability and resource-allocation decisions inevitably impact strongly on children's and teachers' futures. For example, where teachers are held accountable for children's achievements, based on external tests often tied to standards, it can happen that teachers train children to pass the test, rather than concentrate on the wider curriculum learning needs of the children.

Recently, curriculum **standards** have been introduced to help administrators define the curriculum, monitor learner achievement and thus check accountability of teachers and schools. Standards are descriptions of curriculum outcomes, usually described in stages of progress. They may be **content standards** (describing what students should know and be able to do) or **performance standards** (describing how much or at what level students need to perform to demonstrate achievement of the content standard). Many standards combine both purposes in the one document. Achievement on standards is often measured through external tests, though data is sometimes also collected on achievement through teachers' reports based on classroom assessment.

A common distinction in assessment is between formative and summative assessment. These two types of assessment, traditionally thought of as different, may overlap, reflecting the tension between pedagogic and administrative purposes described above. Assessment is also used for placement, motivation and research purposes.

Formative assessment

Formative assessment is ongoing, usually informal, assessment during teaching and learning. Formative assessment gives teachers information about how well the student is doing. The teacher makes constant decisions about how to respond, based on the student's response or the student's work so far. The teacher is the one most interested in the results of formative assessment; the data collected helps him or her to make further decisions about teaching. Formative assessment often involves **diagnostic assessment**, when teachers analyse learners' specific strengths and weaknesses. Diagnostic assessment can also be planned and carried out through a special diagnostic procedure. Commercially prepared diagnostic procedures are often used, for example, with young learners to assess their reading strengths and weaknesses. Formative assessment is predominately used for pedagogic purposes, though increasingly, teachers are asked to observe children's performance over time and from these observations devise a summative report. Thus the purpose behind formative assessment can possibly shift from involving low-stakes decisions to more high-stakes decisions. **On-the-run assessment** (a term adapted from Breen (1997)) refers to informal, instruction-embedded assessment that is formative in purpose and carried out by teachers in classrooms. On-the-run assessment involves teachers in observation and immediate feedback, usually of individual learners, as they teach. **Planned assessment** may be formative, helping the teacher to target specific observations or plan language use tasks to check if children have achieved the objectives along the way.

Summative assessment

At the end of a course of study, a teacher and others too, want to know how a student has progressed during a period of study. This information is needed not only to measure what has been learned during the course, but also to report to others about achievement. This is summative assessment, which usually takes place at the end of a school term or school year. Summative assessment may be based on results of internal or external tests or on a teacher's summative decisions after observations of the child's performance made during the year. Stakeholders become more involved at this point. Parents want to know how the child has progressed and perhaps how he or she compares with others. School administrators want to know how individuals and classes have progressed. Education departments want to know how schools and districts have progressed and may be required to report this information to a central government authority. Summative results may be made public and may be used for comparisons with past and future results. A child's acceptance into the next level of schooling may rest on their summative results. Therefore the stakes can be raised high in summative assessment and careful consideration is needed of the validity and reliability of the assessment procedures used to come to decisions.

Assessment for placement purposes

When children enter a new school or classroom, assessment procedures are used for placement, that is, to place them in the most appropriate class or group. Assessment for placement of young learners may involve an interview, a short reading session and a writing task. Since teachers are able to continue to check children's abilities further as they teach, the initial decision can be confirmed (or otherwise) as time goes on. In most elementary school situations, teachers teach to meet a range of different learning abilities and therefore placement in one class or another is not critical. However, placement assessment might involve high stakes; when the placement decision is fixed and children are wrongly placed (perhaps in the wrong year level), then this can have a major impact on children's lives.

Assessment to encourage and motivate

Assessment can also encourage and motivate learners. Teachers and assessors of young learners have found ways to structure assessment procedures to encourage children by showing them what they have learned and to give positive feedback, motivating them to succeed. They 'bias for best' (Swain, 1985), making sure that the tasks are appropriate and motivating and give some indication of success, however small. Large-scale external tests for young learners can motivate by using, for example, two or three shield rewards rather than pass–fail results (see details of the Cambridge Young Learner English Test in Chapter 9). However, internal and external assessment can also discourage and demotivate. It requires knowledge of child development, child language learning and (in the classroom) knowledge of the individual child to incorporate and maintain a purpose of encouragement and motivation into assessment.

Assessment for research

Assessment is also carried out for the purposes of research. Children's performance is measured to inform researchers about the nature of second language ability and acquisition and the rate and order of acquisition of particular areas of language knowledge (Bachman and Palmer, 1996). Research into the role of assessment in the classroom learning process also relies on information about the assessment decisions of teachers to advance knowledge in the area.

Summary

Young language learners are learning a foreign language or a second language and are doing so in a number of different kinds of language programmes around the world. A special approach to the assessment of young language learners is needed because of the special characteristics of growth, literacy and vulnerability that children bring to language learning and assessment. Children are growing cognitively, socially, emotionally and physically. They are developing literacy knowledge, skills and understandings that may or may not be transferred from their first language; young children take some time to develop in this way and most are still doing so as they begin to learn the new language at school. In addition, children are vulnerable to criticism or failure, more than older learners who in general are able to draw on a sense of worth that can withstand failure in an assessment task. Older learners are in a more stable state in this regard and therefore assessors do not need to take into account the age-related and individual features of growth in the same way as assessors of young learners. Most adults have mature literacy knowledge and skills when they learn their new language. Differences such as these warrant a special approach to the language assessment of young learners.

The beliefs and practices of elementary education underpin any educational endeavour with young children, including assessment. Elementary education is based on principles of child growth and development, recognizing that children develop at different rates and bring different experiences, learning styles and emotions to their learning. In constructivist theories, children learn through active engagement with their environment and with others and are encouraged to become creative and reflective learners. Language plays a central role in the learning process. Current theories in elementary education also suggest that knowledge entails not only the recall of certain facts, but also the processes that relate to that knowledge. New knowledge is gained through a refined awareness of relationships between concepts and is based on a child's present understanding and on past experiences. Theories of elementary education necessarily underpin teachers' and assessors' decision-making in language assessment.

Assessment has the power to change children's lives; the effect of assessment may be positive or negative. Effective assessment provides valuable information to educators, parents, administrators and students themselves. The power of assessment is wielded both explicitly and implicitly within society. Young learners are particularly vulnerable in their formative years to assessment that sends messages of worth and status and that thus perpetuates power relationships in society. Teachers and assessors are obliged to examine the impact of their assessment on young learners and to work towards a positive impact for the present and future.

The next chapter describes how children learn a foreign or second language and presents a framework of the components of language use ability needed to make informed decisions about young learner language assessment.

CHAPTER TWO

Young learners and language learning

Introduction

Assessing the language learning of young learners requires knowledge of both the general characteristics of young learners, as were outlined in Chapter 1, and tied to this, knowledge of the characteristics of their language learning. Knowledge of children's approach to, and needs in, second language learning is critical for fair and valid language assessment. Without an understanding of children's language learning, teachers and assessors might make choices about assessment that result in some or all children being disadvantaged. This might happen in the assessment process itself, or in the teaching that follows as a result of the assessment.

This chapter first defines what is meant by language use ability and makes a case for the assessment of language use. It provides a brief overview of current thinking about the processes of foreign and second language learning in young learners. There are both sociolinguistic and cognitive perspectives on children's foreign/second language learning that give insights into the complex nature of language learning. Knowledge of these processes helps teachers and assessors to select and sequence assessment tasks, and to formulate and apply assessment criteria appropriately. The chapter then draws on a framework from the general assessment field to provide an outline of the components of language knowledge of young learners. These components make up a theoretical framework of communicative language ability which provide a basis for assessment of language use.

What is meant by language use ability?

The definition of language use ability that underpins the ideas in this book can be summarized in the following way: the ability to use the language for the purpose of achieving a particular goal or objective in a particular situation (adapted from Bachman and Palmer 1996, p. 44). Language use ability is also known as the ability to use language communicatively. The meanings that children exchange involve children creatively using the language they have learned to fit the purpose of the interaction (e.g., to answer questions about a task) and to suit the context (e.g., when they are talking to the teacher at school). It is possible and desirable that all young learners learn to use language, that is, to communicate in their target language in some way, depending on the needs of their context and the requirements of the curriculum. Indeed young learners' close relationship with, and dependence on, the immediate physical environment means that their language learning is, by its very nature, closely integrated with real, meaningful communication (Brumfit, Moon and Tongue, 1995).

We can see evidence of language use ability when children in the early stages of language learning:

- understand new language uttered by the teacher, spoken by another student or written in a story (using strategies to guess what is being said from the context);
- respond appropriately to directives (perhaps with physical movement);
- create their own utterances, substituting their own word in a practised sentence; or form their own sentence(s) based on vocabulary and structures they have learned or heard;
- use language appropriately in non-rehearsed interactions, that is, in situations where they are not practising language in rote-learned routines.

We see children in more advanced foreign language classes and in second language classrooms extending their language use ability into situations where they can, for example,

- understand extended teacher input and interaction on classroom content;
- interact with peers, teachers and others for both social and academic purposes;
- read and write in the language on social and academic topics;

- use the language appropriately, according to purpose and context, and according to the expectations of their age level;
- employ language learning strategies that enable them to take responsibility for their own language learning.

There are different ways of describing language use ability, depending on the theoretical framework employed. A theoretical model of language use ability, such as the one presented later in this chapter, gives teachers and assessors a reference point to check that children are developing knowledge and skills that will enable them to use language in a range of situations, according to the curriculum and according to their needs. The developing language abilities of foreign language and second language learners, over time, have been described by educators in a number of foreign and second language standards (McKay, Hudson and Sapuppo, 1994; The National Standards in Foreign Language Education Project, 1996). These language performance standards, examples of which are given in Chapter 8, describe the development of language use ability; they are usually based on teacher observations of growth rather than on second language acquisition research, but it is possible to see that even in the very early stages of language learning, despite having a limited language ability, children are able to make an initial move towards language use, both in the receptive and productive modes. Children are also able to make rapid and sure advances in their ability to use language if they have the right language environment in which to grow, as I will discuss below.

There are different theoretical perspectives in the field of **second language acquisition** ('second language acquisition' is the overall term for the study of both foreign and second language acquisition, and from now on will be referred to as SLA) on how children learn a foreign or a second language. The two main perspectives come from a sociocultural perspective and from a cognitive perspective. Almost all theorists accept that each perspective incorporates ideas from the other; that is, that children successfully learn a foreign or second language when both sociocultural and cognitive influences are activated and interact as they learn.

Sociocultural perspectives in language learning

When children are learning how to use a new language, they are developing a complex array of knowledge and skills. They are developing much more than knowledge of the grammar and vocabulary of the new language. Sociologically oriented modes of language and literacy learning stress the significance of the socialization process in the language learning process. Language learning is seen as a primarily social process rather than an individual process (Gee, 1996). Sociocultural perspectives are widely discussed in the literature, and readers are encouraged to read further in the area. The main ideas in sociocultural theory in relation to school language learning are covered here under four main headings:

'Learning how to mean'

Developing new identities

Learning the discourses of the classroom

Learning the specific discourses of curriculum content areas

'Learning how to mean'

'Learning how to mean' is a term coined by Halliday (1975), and used by sociolinguists subsequently (Luke & Freebody, 1990; Gee, 1996; Carr, 2003) to emphasize the idea that when we learn to use language, we are learning how to communicate meaningfully, and that meaning is tied inextricably to our social and cultural context. The ideas behind the term 'learning how to mean' underpin what is meant when I talk about 'learning how to use language' in this book. Language use is engagement in discourses into which members of a community are socialized. Children need to learn the 'social text' (the way people are expected to interact) of the language use situation when they are learning language. They have to learn what is expected when they engage in language use – who can talk, when, where, in what ways, with whom and for what purposes. It is not possible to use a new language in culturally appropriate ways without learning the **cultural codes** (the rules of interaction) of the language. It is not easy to identify these cultural codes, even for the native speaker, because they operate largely at the unconscious level. 'When two people use the same language to communicate but come from different ethnic backgrounds, the cause of at least some of their misunderstandings is likely to come from the different cultural codes they use in communication.'(Crozet, 2001, p. 3).

Language carries these and other cultural codes, and learning a language involves learning these codes, gradually, and over time. Crozet

(2001) suggests that the following four areas help to identify the cultural codes in a language:

• The role of speaking and silence: e.g., the ways that silence in a conversation is accepted or filled; rules about who speaks when.

• Approaches to interpersonal relationships: e.g., differences in naming systems; different ways that children, women and men are expected to interact.

• Rules of politeness: the ways that eye contact is used; the ways to respect elders; the way to ask for information (directly or indirectly).

• Non-verbal behaviour: the expected ways of using body language (gesture, posture, stance, facial expression, etc.) and of using accent, intonation and rhythm in speech; the ways that hand signs are used to accompany speech.

As children go through the process of participating in social interaction and becoming familiar with the cultural codes, they also acquire vocabulary and structures that allow them to express more and more complex meaning. In sociolinguistic terms the process of language learning is primarily one of entering into a new discourse community or communities, of a 'struggle to participate' (Pavlenko and Lantolf, 2000).

Developing new identities

As children learn a language, they are in the process of developing new identities. They are venturing beyond their experiences in their first language and culture, to a point where their identity and subjectivity are being opened up to new possibilities (Carr, 2003). Language is 'the most salient way we have of establishing and advertising our social identities' (Lippi-Green, 1997). Young language learners, particularly second language learners, are developing new identities in the community and at school. In formal learning settings, the nature of the classroom – the way that teachers acknowledge and build on first language experiences, knowledge and skills – determines how well children develop their new identities in the second language. Is the second language a replacement for the first language, or is it a new tool with which to communicate about new things, to add to existing knowledge and identity? If it is a replacement, the denial of children's first language identities is likely to be detrimental to their learning of the second language and the development of their new identities in this language. Looking at children's progress in language learning through the window of identity has provided powerful messages that language learning is more than the development of language knowledge (see, e.g., Toohey, 2000; Miller, 2003).

Learning the discourses of the classroom

All children entering a new school need to learn the discourses of the new classroom and school; how people interact (teachers, students, principals, parents) and how the language of school is used for different purposes and in different contexts. The discourse of the classroom can be said to be made up of the social interaction amongst participants (peers, teacher, visitors), the everyday business or busy-ness of the classroom when teachers manage learning, giving instructions and setting class tasks, and the actual academic work of the classroom. Teachers and others construct meaning in the classroom in ways that reflect the culture of that classroom, the school system and the society beyond. For some children, it is easier to learn the discourse of the classroom because it reflects the language practices of their home. For others, there may be a wide gap between the way language is used at home and at school. If children's linguistic and cultural experiences at home do not match the communicative and cultural environment of the classroom and of school there can be *discordance*, and this can result in learning difficulty. This discordance may be experienced by native speakers of the language (Heath, 1983; Wells, 1989) as well as by children learning a foreign or second language who have come to school from a minority linguistic or cultural background. Children from a particular cultural group may, for example, tell stories in different ways from the majority of the children in the class. They are likely to find the new ways of telling stories strange; they need acknowledgment of this, and help with understanding the new culture's narrative genre. They may understand instructions differently, perhaps not being accustomed to the indirectness often used in middle-class communications ('Sam, it's time for you to settle down!'). The extent to which children are able to learn to use the target language successfully in the classroom will depend to a large extent on the nature of that classroom and, in particular, whether there are opportunities (clear explanations, modelling, references to first language experiences, etc.) to help children to enter into the discourse of that classroom. Evidence of discordance will be seen in children's performance in assessment tasks.

Language learners in school have to learn not only how to interact socially in (and outside) the classroom, but also how to participate in the discourse of academic study. Cummins (1980; 1983) has described social language (Basic Interpersonal Communication Skills or BICS) and academic language (Cognitive Academic Language Proficiency or CALP) as different on two dimensions: the degree of active cognitive engagement and the degree of contextual support that is available. He thus recognizes the role of both cognition and context in language learning and language use, that is, that children's cognitive skills are engaged in, and also influenced by, opportunities for language development in these two types of language use. Cummins represented BICS and CALP through two continua as illustrated in Figure 2.1. The horizontal continuum refers to the degree of contextual support that is available (intonation, gestures, pictures, etc.). The vertical continuum refers to the degree of active cognitive involvement in the task or activity 'in other words, to the amount of information that must be processed simultaneously or in close succession by the individual in order to carry out the communicative activity' (Cummins, 2001b). Thus tasks in quadrant A (e.g., a face-to-face group discussion, playing with others in the playground) are more characteristic of BICS, while tasks in quadrant D (e.g., writing a report, giving an oral presentation on crocodiles) are more characteristic of academic tasks.

Research has shown that it takes considerably longer for second language learners to develop the abilities they need for academic language use than it does for them to be conversationally fluent (Cummins, 2000). When young bilingual learners learn language in the classroom they need to learn how to perform in the range of different discourses relevant to the school context. Thus, what Cummins is saying is that if young children are not

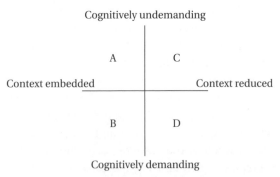

Figure 2.1 Range of contextual support and degree of cognitive involvement in communicative activities (Cummins, 2001b, p. 144)

given the instruction they need to become proficient in the kind of academic language they need in the classroom, then they are unlikely to succeed at school. Our assessment procedures need to reflect this imperative; we need to devise and include academic tasks that tap into and monitor children's ability for academic language use as well as for social language use.

Learning the specific discourses of curriculum content areas

Cummins talked generally about the type of language use ability that children need to enter the discourse of the classroom. We can also look more closely at children's need to learn the specific discourses of subject **content areas** such as science, social studies, physical education and mathematics. Young learners are already engaging at an early age with beginning versions of the discourse of specific curriculum content areas (for example, 'Pour the sand into the scales. Is it heavier or lighter than the stone on the other side?'). As they progress through the elementary years, the content areas become more specialized, and the language used to talk about and learn the content becomes more linguistically complex and academically demanding. In many ways, there are commonalities across different content areas. Mohan (1986), for example, has devised a 'knowledge framework' that picks out the knowledge structures common to activities across the curriculum. For action situations these are description, sequence and choice, and for organizing information these are classification, principles and evaluation. Mohan identifies the language of the different knowledge structures, for example the language of classification is set out in Table 2.1.

By following Mohan's knowledge framework as a guide to understanding the commonalities of knowledge structures and related language across different curriculum content areas, teachers can help with the transfer of thinking skills from one content area to another.

Different academic content areas also have, to some degree, their own special way of constructing meaning, their own discourse. For example, analysis of student talk in elementary school science lessons has revealed that students mainly explain, describe and compare scientific concepts (Bailey and Butler, 2003). Across content area, genres and functions differ somewhat, but in general, vocabulary is more specific and specialized than anything else. Children, particularly those who are learning through a foreign or second language need to be taught explicitly and not 'invisibly' (Fairclough, 1989) in a way that ensures that they learn both the new

Table 2.1 *Classification: thinking processes and language (Mohan, 1986, p. 79)*

Thinking processes	Related language
Observing/Measuring/ Describing	*This is an apple. Mary has three slices of bread.* POINTER WORDS: this/that VERBS OF CLASS MEMBERSHIP: be VERBS OF POSSESSION: have POSSESSIVES: his GENITIVES: Mary's REFERRING TO OBJECTS: Singular/plural, count/mass, part/whole. Articles AMOUNT OR QUANTITY: some/two/half UNIT NOUNS: piece/lump NOUNS OF MEASURE: a pound of / a pint of
Comparison	*Mary has more bread than Sarbjit.* COMPARISON: more than/taller
Classification	*Apples are a kind of fruit.* GENERIC FORMS: apples/music SPECIAL NOUNS: kind/sort/species/class CLASSIFICATION: be/include/place under

culturally based understandings in the curriculum area (for example, the shared background knowledge, the expectations of teachers) and the language (vocabulary, structures, genres) of the new discourse. Assessment practices can help to make the language of content areas more visible to children and also give teachers the chance to ensure progress in academic language.

Young learners are therefore developing new identities, learning to become members of a range of different discourse communities. And they are learning to participate in the language of the classroom and of content areas. For foreign language learners, opportunities to participate in the discourse communities of the language they are learning may come later rather than earlier, though opportunities to interact with pen pals on the Internet or to read children's literature from the target culture bring them closer to the new discourse community. Young learners in immersion and bilingual programmes meet these challenges earlier than those in regular foreign language programmes, as they interact with native speakers and study content areas through the language. Children's success in language learning is therefore not simply a matter of their ability to study successfully or to have the right attitude; it is much more complicated than that: 'what we perceive as language learning ability is not a fixed characteristic of a person but rather a complex reflection of the whole learning situation'(Bialystok, 2001, p. 89).

Cognitive processes in language learning

Most cognitive theorists acknowledge the importance of sociolinguistic processes in language learning; however, they stress the importance of cognitive processes in SLA. To understand and respond appropriately to a child's performance, it is important to understand the cognitive processes of language learning. Why is a child using 'me' instead of 'I'? (*me go too*). How is it that a child might be able to produce seemingly complex language early (e.g., *I don't want to*), but appears not to be able to do other seemingly simple things (for example, correctly using, for third person singular, *he goes*). How is it that young foreign and second language learners continue to make errors despite the fact that they are able to communicate successfully with words, phrases and gestures? Cognitive theorists believe that an understanding of cognitively based language learning processes helps teachers and assessors to make judgments about children's performance and to act accordingly with ongoing teaching and assessment strategies.

In order to illustrate some current thinking about cognitive process in language learning, this section refers to the theories of three applied linguists concerned with cognition, Schumann (1997), Skehan (1998) and Cummins (Baker and Hornberger, 2001). Readers are encouraged to refer to the original publications for a full understanding of these theories. Skehan is concerned with explaining how second language acquisition happens through the cognitive abilities of the learner, and how cognitive-processing problems are overcome. Schumann believes that emotion underlies most, if not all, cognition and attributes variation in success in second language acquisition to the role of emotion. Cummins deals with the influence of children's first language on their second, and on their opportunities to become a proficient bilingual at school.

A dual-mode system in language use and language learning

Skehan's model is motivated by the fact that human memory is a limited capacity processor, and that it would not be possible to use language fluently, if we were limited to the processing of rules alone. He hypothesizes that all language users employ a dual-mode system to process and use language. The two systems that contribute to the dual-mode system are the formulaic system and the rule-based system.

New computer-driven research suggests that language use is based much more on lexical elements or chunks than we have realized in the past. When learners apply their **formulaic system** (Skehan also uses the term 'examplar-based system') they are relying on the use of chunks of language and idioms. Chunks might be words or groups of words and in some cases formulaic units that may contain structure but are unanalysed (the learner is not able to recognise its grammatical rules or perhaps even its individual words). Thus 'Open your books and turn to page twenty-five' may be an unanalysed chunk for beginning school learners, who may follow the action response of others, understand what the sentence means as a whole, without understanding its parts, except for the page number at the end. The formulaic system has only a limited potential for expressing new and precise meanings – language users can only (in this system) use the formulaic expressions they have learned, and in the context in which they are relevant. The value of the system is that learners can draw on the resource of formulaic expressions more quickly than their knowledge of grammatical structures, and they will tend to do so in moments of communicative pressure (p. 63). Learners can also use their formulaic system as a learning strategy, to reach for something they don't yet understand properly, and to push themselves on towards increased proficiency. According to Skehan, the formulaic system is likely to be 'context-bound', with language learned well for a particular context, but not easily transferred to another context (p. 89).

We know that when young learners are learning language, they rely heavily on the formulaic system, accumulating chunks, or formulaic items, and using these to understand and get their meaning across. This is so in first and second language learning. A newly arrived learner in a second language classroom learns many chunks of language very early, especially receptively, but is not able to analyse its rules until later. Cameron (2001, p. 50) describes how language learners also employ 'slots' (*it's. . .*) that can be filled by different nouns and adjectives. For all learners, chunks continue to be learned throughout language learning, for example in idioms and phrases (*the big bad wolf; white as chalk*). As the next section shows, chunks play an essential role as building blocks for further language learning for both young and some older learners (depending on their learning style and exposure to the language), but particularly for young learners.

According to Skehan, learners also use their **rule-based system**, when they draw on underlying rules of the language to construct sentences and discourse. Language learners develop their language by:

- accumulating memory-based chunks of language which they then combine to build language.

- inducing underlying rules from the language they see and hear (gaining implicit knowledge of the language rules), or become consciously aware of rules by studying the language (gaining explicit knowledge of the language rules).

In a well-developed system (e.g., in a first language speaker's system) all of this is done without conscious thought. The demands on the proficient user's memory storage are not great in a well-developed system, since users can generate an infinite number of possible meanings from a limited set of language rules by drawing on a large pool of memory-based chunks of language. There is maximum creativity and flexibility in what the learner is able to process or comprehend, and what he can produce, and there is no constraint on the production of new combinations of meanings (p. 30). However, in a system that is not well developed, reliance on the rule-based system during language use, which can happen especially with learners (young and older) who are learning by focusing on grammar and vocabulary only, creates a heavy processing burden. Thus, foreign and second language learners who have had little opportunity to draw on a formulaic system developed through language use opportunities, quickly become tongue-tied and anxious as they try to construct a sentence in their head based on the rules they have learned. The processing constraints are very high. These learners have more chance of success if they have a supportive environment, for example a listener who is willing to wait, and who signals encouragement, a speaker who is willing to repeat, or enough time to write and revise without pressure. This kind of situation can be exacerbated for young learners who are limited to grammar study because young learners' rule-based system is limited by their still-developing metalinguistic ability (their capacity to use knowledge about language). Skehan suggests that neither system works entirely alone: 'Clearly, neither the rule-based nor the exemplar system is ideal separately' (Skehan, 1998, p. 86)

Language learning takes place when learners engage in meaningful communicative activities, that is, language use tasks, on the one hand (activating the formulaic system), and through focus on form in the context of language use within communicative tasks (activating the rule-governed system) on the other. Through focus on form learners are given an opportunity to 'notice' (Schmidt, 1990), that is, to be consciously aware of the form of language (such as vocabulary and structures) so that this can assist knowledge to move from the short-term memory to the long-term memory. Information that is not encoded into long-term memory will be lost. Thus, a dual mode system is involved in language learning. It is through communicating meaning through language use that the two systems, the formulaic system and the rule-governed system, are activated. Skehan suggests that adult language learners' attention needs to be channelled in a balanced way towards both communication on the one hand, and form on the other hand, so that neither dominates at the expense of the other (1998, p. 126). Since children have less developed metalinguistic ability the need to channel the bulk of children's attention towards meaning communication is vital if fluency is to be achieved.

Young learners tend to rely on the formulaic system as they hear and see language in use; and through this they gain implicit knowledge of the language rules, and thus they are able to create their own structures and discourse. It is likely there will be some differences in learning style amongst younger learners that may need to be accommodated by teachers. Older learners in the later elementary school years develop greater metalinguistic awareness and become more able to gain knowledge of language rules from explicit language study. However, depending on the learning context, older elementary age learners still tend to rely strongly on a formulaic system.

Skehan's theory helps to highlight the differences between adult and child SLA, in particular children's greater reliance on the formulaic system, and their subsequent need for a rich language use environment.

Emotion and language learning

Schumann's (1997) theories are concerned with the role of emotion or affect in second language learning. As children experience the world they develop appraisal systems. **Appraisal systems** are the value systems that individuals develop and bring to their language learning. Gradually, through interaction with their mother, and with their environment and others, children develop a value system which is uniquely their own. The inherited culture of the society is transmitted through these types of interactions. Some learning, such as learning to walk and learning one's first language, is generated by innate mechanisms. This type of learning is less influenced by a learner's appraisal system. However, foreign or second language learning is strongly influenced by a learner's appraisal system. Because people have different experiences, the way they react emotionally (through their appraisal systems) are different, this is why different learners achieve different results when they have opportunities to learn a foreign or a second language. Each person and child differs in their motivation, interest and attention in second language learning. 'These value mechanisms influence the cognition (perception, attention, memory and action) that is devoted to learning' (Schumann, 1997, p. 2).

In addition, Schumann suggests that foreign and second language learning is a form of **sustained deep learning**. That is, it takes place over an extended period of time (often several years), and when it is complete (or, in the case of language learning, we would say, highly proficient) the learner is seen as expert (p. 32). Sustained deep learning is never inevitable and is highly dependent on cognitive factors, such as emotion, attention and motivation. Some sustained deep learning occurs because the learner is forced to acquire the material (as in some school learning) and doesn't resist. More often, deep learning happens because the learner is attracted to the field and likes it (p. 35). This type of learning has a strong emotional and motivational component (p. 35). Learners evaluate their own performance and listen to and observe the evaluations of their performance passed on to them by others. All these factors lead to variable success in second language acquisition amongst learners. Successful foreign and second language learning is therefore strongly reliant on positive emotion and attitudes on the part of the learner, and on positive feedback on the part of others and on self-evaluation. To assume that exposure to language use and constant study of language forms is sufficient for language learning is erroneous. Since it is not inevitable that young learners will succeed in foreign or second language learning (I include here the higher levels of learning required to succeed in academic discourse), it is clear that young language learners at school are influenced by these factors as much as older learners.

Linguistic interdependence

Cummins has been especially concerned with bilingualism and with the influence of children's first language on their second language learning and cognitive development. A collection of Cummins' work is now available (Baker and Hornberger, 2001). Cummins' influential theories have suggested that successful SLA is dependent on a well-developed first language. That is, that there is interdependence between the first language and the second language. The cognitive skills tied up with children's linguistics skills can transfer from one language to the other, and when this happens children have the best opportunities for success at school. For children to achieve some success at school, they need to at least reach a **lower threshold level** defined as the point where they achieve the language use ability they need 'to avoid cognitive deficits and to allow the potentially beneficial aspects of becoming bilingual to influence their cognitive growth' (Cummins, 1979, p. 229). This point will vary according to the children's stage of cognitive development and the academic demands at different stages of schooling (Cummins, 1979, p. 229). Once they have reached this lower threshold, then they are able to access, through language, the abstract concepts they need to be successful in school. For the best opportunities for success, children need to achieve a **higher threshold level**, when the first language is sufficiently developed to support academic proficiency in SLA. At this point they are adding another language to an already well-developed first language, and positive cognitive effects result. These are the children who gain the most positive cognitive effects from their bilingualism, and who therefore have the best opportunity to be successful at school. 'It is clear that in minority language situations a prerequisite for attaining a higher threshold level of bilingual competence is maintenance of L1 [first language] skills' (Cummins, 1979, p. 232).

Cummins suggests that a range of factors influence the child's opportunity to become a proficient bilingual, in particular first language maintenance, but also background variables (community and parental attitudes towards participation in the second language culture and maintenance of the first language) and input and process variables (e.g., exposure to the second language, teacher attitudes and expectations, and motivational factors).

Cummins' theories remind us that cognitive processes in language learning do not happen in isolation but are tied to the child's first language abilities, and to the child's cognitive abilities developed within the first language. The foreign and second language learner is not a *tabula rasa*, or a blank slate, but comes with linguistic and cognitive abilities that have a strong influence on subsequent language learning and cognitive development. Cummins' later writing (e.g., 2000), addresses the socio-political contexts in which bilingual children learn, and the effect of power relationships in the society on the possible marginalization and disempowerment of second language learners. His later theories turn our attention back to the sociocultural contexts in which children learn and remind us that both sociocultural and cognitive perspectives are insep-arably relevant to SLA.

Optimal conditions for language learning

Optimal conditions for language learning are those which include, at least, the following four features: a focus on meaning, interesting and engaging input and interacting, selected opportunities to focus on form, and a safe and supportive learning environment. The current consensus in SLA, reflecting the theories outlined above, is that in foreign and second language classrooms, children's language learning flourishes when there is a focus on meaning, and when their teachers and other vis-itors give them opportunities to interact in ways that reflect the wider discourse communities relevant to the language they are learning. Children learn to use language because the interesting activities in which they are engaged absolutely necessitate (from the child's point of view) cooperation and interaction. Teacher-talk around an irresistible focus of interest in the classroom can encourage children to become involved, provide meaningful input about something they can see in front of them (enabling them to confirm their predictions about what the teacher is saying) and encourage them to respond to questions, as in the following example:

> Now come and look at the rabbit in the cage. (*Everyone comes to the cage and looks in.*) Can you see his long back legs? They're very strong. That's how he can run fast and jump very high. Peter, point to the rabbit's back legs. Can everyone tell me how many back legs the rabbit has got? Everyone – jump up high. The rabbit can do that too. Let's look at some pictures of a rabbit running and jumping.

Language-rich activities give children opportunities to listen and guess from the context, to take risks to use the second language (which they are more likely to do if the environment is safe) and to engage in inter-actions, when they are ready, with the teacher and each other. Children are more likely to learn through language use activities that engage them in doing, thinking and moving. Talk around physical activity, pictures and objects, and problem-solving activities brings optimal opportunities for language learning. Right from the beginning of language learning, in both foreign and second language classrooms, the use of literature can provide a strong basis for the promotion of language learning through language use (Falvey and Kennedy, 1997). Reading and writing skills grow as children use language in print; literature and content-based activities (e.g., maths, science and social studies) play an important role as input, and as the basis for problem-solving and stimu-lating interaction (see Chapters 6 and 7). Through these experiences children learn the social rules of interaction and belonging, that is, the discourses with which they are engaging, and their language knowledge (e.g., knowledge of vocabulary, grammar and pronunciation) expands and strengthens.

Young learners also benefit from opportunities to **focus on form**, that is, to focus on the 'stuff' of language – the grammar, vocabulary, pronun-ciation, stress and other features, within the context of tasks in which they are engaged. Children do not need to be told explicitly about lan-guage rules in order to learn how to use language, nor do they necessar-ily gain any advantage from being told about language, since they may not be cognitively ready for this kind of analysis. Their natural tendency is to attend to meaning rather than form (Bialystok, 2001) and therefore their attention will quickly swing back to meaning or away on to some-thing else in the environment that is more interesting. Well-chosen litera-ture can supply many opportunities for this type of incidental focus on form. The following extract from *The Very Hungry Caterpillar* provides valuable input for second language acquisition because it is supported by colourful illustrations that allow children to predict the meaning, and it repeats, through the days of the week, many of the same words and phrases, giving children a chance to understand and internalize these items of language.

> On Monday, he ate through one apple. But he was still hungry. On Tuesday he ate through two pears, but he was still hungry. On Wednesday he ate through three plums, but he was still hungry.
>
> *The Very Hungry Caterpillar* (Carle, 1974)

Young learners benefit from this kind of focus on form in carefully chosen tasks. Focus on form may involve, for example, labelling pictures and diagrams, filling in gaps in sentences whose meaning is illustrated through accompanying pictures, and playing games that involve some kind of focus. As teachers draw children's attention to certain aspects of language in one-to-one and whole-class activities, they are also involving children in focus on form. As children grow older, their ability to think about language grows as part of their maturational development until they are able to handle more explicit focus on form. Older learners are likely to benefit from working together on focusing tasks, when they have an opportunity to talk about and think through the language together (Swain and Lapkin, 1998). It helps learners when focusing tasks are contextualized, that is, when a connection is made explicitly to purposeful language use in tasks. When a language worksheet is handed out, for example, it is helpful to tell children why they are doing it:

> We're going to do this worksheet on science language to help you to write about the science experiment we did together this morning.

Like first language learners, young foreign and second language learners need a safe environment, where they can take their time before they start to talk, but where they are encouraged to take risks. That safe environment also gives them opportunities to learn the different discourses of the classroom, to become full members of the classroom community, and to develop, without fear, new identities within it. While children are interacting, they benefit from positive experiences and positive feedback. Children are encouraged to use language when their teachers and others use facial expressions and tone of voice to enhance meaning, when they display real pleasure when children attempt to interact, and when they show real interest in what children have to say. Classrooms that promote value and draw on children's first language help the language learning process. Teachers' positive attitudes to children's first language, and the inclusion of children's first language and culture in tasks in the classroom are optimally important for language learners. This applies to all minority language learners, whether they are learning a foreign language (such as Hmong children in Vietnam learning English) or a second language (such as Sudanese children learning Dutch in Holland).

Children need to work hard to learn a language

The implication of what is known about cognitive processes in language learning is that language learners, including children, need to work hard to learn a new language. Children do not simply absorb the language around them. They need to engage with their language environment in strategic ways in order to learn the language. Indeed, Bialystok (2001) tells us that children, as much as adults, need to use 'brute learning strategies' in order to learn a new language.

Pinter (1999) has observed children's language learning strategies in a foreign language situation, and has seen that children:

- 'use L1' in order to double-check words or expressions not available in L2, and to engage in task-related discourse to establish common grounds about the task before carrying it out.
- 'appeal for assistance' from the adult.
- 'build patterns' whereby they repeat what they are comfortable with over and over again. In this, they play safe and try to exploit a given phrase as much as possible.

(adapted from Pinter, 1999, p. 16)

Children's language learning strategies differ depending, for example, on personality, or on the nature of their language environment. Some children need to go through a 'silent period' when they watch and listen and interact, but do not speak. Some children have a strong need for social interaction and learn quickly because they want to engage with others. Some children have been seen to pick up language by observing their teachers and peers, with little direct interaction with them (Wong Fillmore, 1991), though this will occur only if there is access to the right conditions for language learning.

As young learners progress in their language learning, they continue to use language learning strategies. As they learn to write, for example, they are learning how to process text, to plan, to organize and goal set, how to engage their long-term and working memory effectively. They are learning how to revise their work, to edit for content and organization and to take account of their audience (Weigle, 2002). In reading they are learning to recognize the important information in text, to adjust their reading rate, to skim, to preview, to use content to resolve a misunderstanding, to formulate questions about information (Alderson, 2000).

The following list of descriptors from the TESOL Standards for Grades 4–8 outlines the strategies children are expected to learn in order to be able to begin to achieve academically in curriculum content areas:

- following oral and written directions, implicit and explicit
- requesting and providing clarification
- participating in full-class, group, and pair discussions
- asking and answering questions
- requesting information and assistance
- negotiating and managing interaction to accomplish tasks
- explaining actions
- elaborating and extending other people's ideas and words
- expressing likes, dislikes and needs   (TESOL, 1997, p. 83)

The recognition of the role of learning strategies is important, both in teaching and learning, and in assessment. As a point of interest, children who have learned a foreign or second language do have an advantage over monolingual children in being able 'to treat language as a formal system and examine its properties' because as they have learned their language(s) they have had to focus on and become more aware of language; for example, they have had to be aware of which of their two (or more) languages is being spoken and in which language they should respond (Bialystok, 2001).

There are many publications concerned exclusively with the teaching of languages to young learners (see, e.g., Halliwell, 1992; Brumfit, Moon and Tongue, 1995; Cameron, 2001). In this section I have summarized some key points and will now turn to the implications for assessment of what we know about optimal learning conditions for young learners.

Implications for assessment

What we know about language learning holds many implications for foreign and second language assessment. Assessment of language learning by teachers and assessors requires knowledge of the social and cognitive processes at play as children respond to the assessment requirements placed before them. Effective language assessment builds up children's abilities to use language in the full meaning of the term; assessment should both promote and monitor children's ability to enter into the new discourses relevant to the language they are studying, whether they are predominantly the discourses of social communication for present and future encounters with native speakers, and/or the discourses of the classroom and of the content areas they are learning.

Effective assessment is done in a climate where the first language and the first language identities that children bring to their learning are acknowledged and built upon.

Children's greater ability to understand and use formulae in the early stages of learning requires selection of particular types of tasks in those early stages, where children are able to draw on their known formulae and vocabulary to participate. Such a task would be familiar, routine and probably contain a repetitive element. Early morning whole-class routines when children check on the day, the date and the weather are one such example. Simple games are another. More rule-based assessment tasks should then be used when children are more advanced in the language and mature enough to handle explicit language-focused assessment work. As they progress, children can handle language use in which they are asked to go beyond the predictable and the routine; they can be asked to tell others what they did at the weekend, or describe a shared event, or write a report about a chosen animal. As rules emerge, assessment needs to be targeted to the range of language rules, vocabulary and meaning that children can handle; however, there will still be a need for teachers and assessors to monitor the continuing development of formulae, since these continue to play an important role in successful language use.

Assessment and feedback need to evoke positive emotions in children about language learning, about themselves and about others. Since children bring different experiences and motivations to their learning, individualized needs assessment and subsequent targeted feedback during teaching helps to enhance success and therefore motivation. Teaching of self-assessment strategies and promotion of self- and peer-assessment in the classroom gives children a chance to become engaged in the sustained deep learning that is required in successful foreign and second language learning and to build up their language learning strategies.

Effective assessment requires an acknowledgment of the role that children's first language plays in their foreign and second language learning. This is mostly done through the teacher's and assessor's acknowledgment of the first language in the assessment process (e.g., their acceptance of the use of the first language, in certain instances, to help children understand what is expected in the assessment procedure), and of their acceptance of children's use of the first language when their second language 'falls down'. Such acknowledgments in classroom and external assessments can be done, with planning, without loss of trustworthy assessment data. In addition, decisions about children's foreign or second language learning with no regard for the nature of their progress in their first language are likely to be ill-informed, and resulting actions, for example about placement and intervention, may be inappropriate and even harmful. Assessment tasks that are concerned with ascertaining young learners' ability to use the language need to reflect the language use activities in which children engage within a successful language learning environment. Since a large part of assessment in elementary schools is carried out in the classroom and during the day-to-day business of learning that makes up the curriculum, it follows that much of assessment takes place through the kinds of tasks children are regularly engaged in in the classroom. Children show their language ability through the kinds of tasks with which they are familiar, and through tasks that are most likely to promote their interest and motivation to use the language. Even in more formal assessment tasks involving language use, such as a one-to-one interview with the teacher, or a short picture description, it makes sense to structure the assessment task in a way that reflects the kinds of learning tasks that optimize their motivation and interest in language use. The kinds of tasks that do this are those that reflect the ways they learn language most effectively.

It is axiomatic that the way that children learn best be reflected in the way that they are assessed, and the knowledge of how young learners learn language is therefore fundamental for those involved in the language assessment of young learners.

It is at all points of the assessment process, when teachers and assessors select or construct assessment tasks, make decisions about the nature of children's performance, and give feedback and provide reports about that performance, that they require knowledge of language learning. At any of these points there can be a positive or negative impact on the children's progress and long-term success.

The influence of the language curriculum and external tests on language learning and assessment

Language learning in schools is generally embedded in a curriculum set out by the state, the district, the school or the classroom teacher, and this will have a major impact on the nature of language learning. The curriculum may also be established through a set textbook. The way that a curriculum or textbook is set out and sequenced reflects the understanding of language learning held by the curriculum writer, teacher or textbook developer. Assessment should reflect the goals and objectives of the curriculum, and will also be influenced by understandings of language learning embedded in the curriculum. If the established curriculum emphasizes the learning of grammar and vocabulary in isolation, then it will be difficult if not impossible for teachers and assessors to assess children's language use ability. When, however, the curriculum is designed to promote language use, children will have opportunities to use language meaningfully, and hence assessing language ability through language use tasks is the most appropriate and accepted way to assess language learning.

In many curricula, knowledge and skills that are integral to language learning are also explicitly stated as goals or outcomes. Table 2.2 shows extracts from the Queensland Schools Curriculum Council (2000) Guidelines, outlining curriculum goals for language learning. These goals stretch beyond the immediate knowledge, understanding and skills of language learning to include important, related areas such as the development of understanding of the ways children approach life (intercultural understanding), the development of language awareness and learning-how-to-learn skills.

These goals establish what children need according to this curriculum, in order to learn language and to learn beyond language successfully, and they set the scope for assessment in the language learning programme. Goals and learning outcomes are also established by education departments in standards documents. Some curricula for young learners (although this is rare) may be narrower in their scope, defining mainly the structures and vocabulary to be learned. Thus the curriculum within which teachers and assessors work, and the textbooks that accompany that curriculum, define the scope and nature of language learning, and therefore have a key influence on what is learned and assessed.

External tests also have a strong influence on what and how children learn, and on how teachers are inclined to teach and assess in the classroom. If an external test assesses children's language use, as defined in the curriculum, then there is alignment, and "teaching to the test" may be a productive part of the teaching. If, however, the external tests focus on areas of language ability that are only part of the curriculum, then there is a lack of alignment. For example, if the external test focuses on children's knowledge of vocabulary and grammar above all else, then the external test has imposed this construct for learning and assessment (even if a language use curriculum exists). If the curriculum and the teacher's learning activities do not focus on vocabulary and grammar, then teachers are caught in a trap; they are required to teach with a focus

Table 2.2 *Curriculum goals for language learning for years 1 to 3 (adapted from Queensland Schools Curriculum Council, 2000)*

Intercultural communication

As children participate in tasks using another language, they become aware of cultural practices and develop skills in communication in many contexts. . . Learning to communicate interculturally involves children in developing

- socioculturally appropriate ways of communicating in a particular language (intercultural understandings);
- familiarity with the functions of language (language awareness);
- the skills and strategies used to internalize the new language together with self-management of their learning (learning-how-to-learn skills);
- general knowledge according to their needs, interests and prior learning (topical knowledge).

Intercultural

In learning another language, children develop an awareness and appreciation of the culture of the people who use it. They can use this knowledge as a basis for comparing their culture with others and take their first steps in negotiating another cultural system. . . . Through an awareness of culture and how to communicate in appropriate ways, young children tend to move towards a greater acceptance of their own personal identity in a global society.

In the early childhood years sociocultural language learning promotes and fosters an awareness of aspects of the target language community. These could include:

- how young children in the target language community live;
- contemporary society in the target language community;
- relationships to the children's own communities;
- cultural practices – dress, festivals, songs, games and family life.

Language awareness

Children will begin to develop an awareness of the role of language as well as culture within their world as they learn about language. An understanding of these roles helps children to become more conscious of the diversity of the world that surrounds them and to learn how to respond appropriately. Children will begin to develop an awareness of

- the features of their own language and the language of others;
- the function of language in their everyday life;
- language as a system and how it works;
- appropriate language for varying contexts;
- how language is learnt;
- how diversity is enriched through cultural variation.

(Scarino, Vale, McKay and Clark, 1988).

Table 2.2 *(continued)*

Learning-how-to-learn

. . . By participating in learning experiences in the target language, children begin to develop an awareness of the skills and strategies required to take responsibility for their own learning. These include:

- identifying and discussing a problem;
- taking initiative and being persistent in completing tasks;
- sharing with the teacher and other class members the ways in which they have solved problems;
- exploring new ideas and applying prior learning;
- accessing and locating information.

===

on vocabulary and grammar to ensure that children pass the test. Thus the nature of the curriculum and external tests are central influences on the nature of language learning and assessment of young learners, even when teachers and assessors have knowledge of current theories of child language learning as they have been outlined in the previous section. This is a reality which, it is hoped, would be changed by those in authority, to a situation where curriculum and assessment are aligned with each other, and with what we know about children's SLA (that is, that children need to and can learn to use language in communicative ways).

Describing the components of children's language use ability

We now move on from examining language learning processes to examining the nature of language ability. How can we describe language ability in order to 'capture' it in assessment? How can we examine a child's language use in an assessment task, and know whether it is appropriate to the situation, whether it will achieve what it intends to achieve, and what its strengths and weaknesses are? The framework in this section is complex; but children's language ability is no less complex than adults' language ability, and I would argue that it is important that teachers and assessors of young learners have a deep knowledge of the nature of language ability. This section can be referred to at any time by readers. It is not necessary to understand this section to access the remainder of the book. Rather, this section is for those readers who are ready to make sense of the complex nature of children's language knowledge in assessment tasks.

I have chosen to use Bachman and Palmer's (1996) framework of language ability to describe children's language use ability. It provides a comprehensive and well-respected tool with which to make sense of its nature. Note that the components in a framework of language ability are different from language learning systems such as Skehan's formulaic and rule-based system discussed earlier in this chapter. Skehan's systems are processes for *learning*. The following components describe the actual knowledge and processes that learners need when they are *using* language. In a language assessment task, according to Bachman and Palmer (1996), a number of components of language ability interact to engage test takers in language use. One of the components of language ability is language knowledge. We will focus on the characteristics of language knowledge first because they reflect and link the model to the sociolinguistic and cognitive perspectives we have already described in language learning above.

Language knowledge

Language knowledge is made up of the elements listed in Table 2.3. It can be thought of as 'a domain of information in memory that is available for use by the metacognitive strategies in creating and interpreting discourse in language use. There are two broad categories of language knowledge: organizational knowledge and pragmatic knowledge.

Language learners need **organizational knowledge** if they are to organize and produce their own spoken and written texts, and to understand the texts produced by others. They need **grammatical knowledge** which, according to Bachman and Palmer (1996), involves knowledge of vocabulary, syntax and phonology/graphology to organize individual utterances or sentences. (See Purpura (2004) for more recent, additional thoughts on the nature of grammatical knowledge and its relationship with performance.) They need **textual knowledge** made up of knowledge of cohesion, and knowledge of rhetorical or conversational organization, to be able to form texts by combining utterances or sentences. Knowledge of cohesion is involved in producing or comprehending the relationship among sentences in written texts or among utterances in conversations. For example, the pronoun 'she' provides a cohesive reference to 'Jenny' in the following sentences:

A: Is Jenny coming to the party?
B: Yes she is.

Table 2.3 *Areas of language knowledge (Bachman and Palmer, 1996, p. 68)*

Organizational knowledge
(how utterances or sentences and texts are organized)

> **Grammatical knowledge**
> (how individual utterances or sentences are organized)
>
> Knowledge of vocabulary
> Knowledge of syntax
> Knowledge of phonology/graphology
>
> **Textual knowledge**
> (how utterances or sentences are organized to form texts)
>
> Knowledge of cohesion
> Knowledge of rhetorical or conversational organization

Pragmatic knowledge
(how utterances or sentences and texts are related to the communicative goals of the language user and to the features of the language use setting)

> **Functional knowledge**
> (how utterances or sentences and texts are related to the communicative goals of language users)
>
> Knowledge of ideational functions (enabling learners to express or interpret meaning in terms of our experience of the world)
>
> Knowledge of manipulative functions (enabling learners to use language to affect the world around us)
>
> Knowledge of heuristic functions (enabling learners to use language to extend their knowledge of the world around us)
>
> Knowledge of imaginative functions (enabling learners to use language to create an imaginary world, or extend the world around them for humorous or aesthetic purposes. Examples include jokes and the use of figurative language and poetry)
>
> **Sociolinguistic knowledge**
> (how utterances or sentences and texts are related to features of the language use setting)
>
> Knowledge of dialects/varieties
> Knowledge of registers
> Knowledge of natural or idiomatic expressions
> Knowledge of cultural references and figures of speech

Knowledge of rhetorical or conversational organization is involved in producing or comprehending organizational development in written texts or in conversation. For example, we know that English written narratives, in their ideal form, have a beginning, a climax and a resolution.

In language use situations, children also need **pragmatic knowledge** if they are to achieve their communicative goals. They learn, for example, that if they want to get someone else to do something, or tell them something, they have to ask them in polite and appropriate ways, using forms of the language (structures, vocabulary) that are required to achieve the goal. Pragmatic knowledge is what language users need in order to be able to *use* the organizational knowledge that they have. Pragmatic knowledge enables us to create or interpret discourse by relating utterances or sentences and texts to their meaning, to the intentions of language users, and to relevant characteristics of the language use setting. That is, pragmatic knowledge is what activates the organizational knowledge that a language user has.

There are two areas of pragmatic knowledge: functional knowledge and sociolinguistic knowledge. **Functional knowledge** enables us to interpret relationships between utterances or sentences and texts and the intentions of language users. Bachman and Palmer (p. 69) give the following example to explain this:

> For example, the utterance 'Could you tell me how to get to the post office?' most likely functions as a request for directions rather than as a request for a 'yes' or 'no' answer. The most appropriate responses are likely to be either a set of directions or, if the speaker does not know how to get to the post office, a statement to this effect. A verbal response such as 'Yes, I could', while accurate in terms of the literal meaning of the question, is inappropriate, since it misinterprets the function of the question as a request for information.

To answer appropriately, language users often need prior knowledge of the language use setting, including the characteristics of the participants.

Sociolinguistic knowledge enables us to use language to create or interpret language that is appropriate to a particular language setting. This includes knowledge of the conventions that determine the appropriate use of dialects or varieties, registers, natural or idiomatic expressions, cultural references and figures of speech. **Dialects or varieties** are versions of a language that are used in different regions or social classes, and to different versions of a language used in different countries (for example, American English; Indian English; Singaporean English). **Registers** are variations in language used by people usually sharing the same occupation (e.g., doctors, lawyers) or the same interests (e.g., stamp collectors, baseball fans) (Richards, Platt and Weber, 1985). **Idiomatic expressions** and **figures of speech** are words or phrases that may not have their usual or literal

Individual characteristics

Language knowledge
Personal characteristics
Topical (or background) knowledge
Affective schemata/emotional state

Strategic competence

Language use task context or situation

Figure 2.2 How components of language use work together in a language use task (adapted from Bachman and Palmer, 1996, p. 63)

meaning but have been passed down through the culture ('Try and get your head around this'; 'Be as quite as a mouse') and **cultural references** are references to ideas or events or things that people in the culture know about (the Taj Mahal; Christmas Day; ceremonies and literature and so on).

Language knowledge is central to language use; if learners do not have, or are weak in certain components of language knowledge, then they will have greater difficulty engaging in language use than others who are stronger.

In order to engage in language use, language knowledge is not enough. Learners need to 'activate' their language knowledge in ways that are appropriate to the language use context. As depicted in Figure 2.2, they will activate their language knowledge according to their own individual characteristics (e.g., their outgoingness, their background knowledge, and their emotions on the day) and they will do this using their strategic competence which helps them to weigh up the situation and make decisions about their participation in the language use.

Language knowledge interacts with (1) individual characteristics

When children use their language knowledge in language use tasks, they also bring to the task a range of individual characteristics that inevitably influence their performance on the task. The individual characteristics of language learners can be described under four headings (Bachman and Palmer, 1996):

- language knowledge
- personal characteristics
- topical (or background) knowledge
- affective schemata or emotional state

The components of language knowledge have been described above. The other three areas are described below.

Personal characteristics

For young learners, the most obvious personal characteristic (and therefore the most defining) is their age and developmental maturity. As discussed in Chapter 2, children's language ability is characterized by the fact that they are in the process of developing in their cognitive, social, emotional, and physical maturity. Their approach to language assessment tasks, and their ability to perform in tasks, is determined by their maturity in the ways I described in Chapter 1. Maturational development varies across different age groups and across individual children. Their personalities may, for example, bring differences in tenacity and concentration span.

In addition, each child is influenced strongly by their cultural background, first language, educational background, and type and amount of preparation or prior experience. The nature of their bilingual and home experiences will influence their performance. What is the nature of their educational background? Has their education been disrupted because of migration or refugee experiences? Does the home provide opportunities to experience literacy? Children's personal characteristics will influence their ability to take part successfully in a task, and thus will necessarily influence the nature of the tasks in which children are asked to participate.

Topical (or background) knowledge

Young learners bring their topical or background knowledge to oral communication, and to their reading and writing. When children use language they communicate about something, and this 'something' will be related to the world in which they live. All language users need topical knowledge in order to be able to communicate at all. Topical knowledge usually contains cultural knowledge. Native speakers of a language may not be aware of the load of cultural content in a task; most foreign and second language learners are dealing with degrees of new cultural knowledge in every task.

Young learners' topical knowledge relies on their *developing knowledge of the world*. The growth of learners' topical knowledge can be seen as four conceptual spheres.

> Sphere 1: The first and innermost sphere represents what learners can see, hear, and touch directly. In practice, this is the classroom situation. Here, words are merely an accompaniment of action.
>
> Sphere 2: The second sphere represents what the learners know from their own experience, their daily life, what they have seen and heard directly but cannot see or hear at the moment. This can be brought to mind by the use of words together with the classroom situation. Examples of themes and topics within this sphere include self, family and friends, home, school, free time, holidays and pets.
>
> Sphere 3: The third sphere represents what the learners have not experienced directly, but what they can call to mind with an effort of the imagination, with the help of pictures, dramatization, charts, and plans. Examples of themes and topics within this sphere include literature, events of general interest, and topics related to other subject areas.
>
> Sphere 4: The fourth sphere represents what is brought into learners' minds through the spoken, written, or printed word alone. Examples of themes and topics within the sphere include social issues, environmental issues, jobs and careers, comparisons between their own country and the target country, relationships with others, and current events.   (Billows 1961, cited in Scarino et al., 1988, Book 2, p. 8)

Thus, young learners' topical knowledge grows as their experience of the world grows and as they develop cognitive and social maturity. Children's language use will be influenced strongly by the topical knowledge they bring to the task or language use situation. This includes the general academic knowledge and content area specific knowledge that children are learning at school.

Affective schemata or emotional state

The characteristics of a task may evoke an emotional response from test takers, based on their previous experiences, or also in the case of young learners, on their emotional maturity. Emotional responses can either help or hinder a test taker's performance on a task. Bachman and Palmer suggest that it is important to promote feelings of comfort or safety in test takers, but at the same time we should balance the need for comfort for the test taker and the performance to be measured (p. 66).

In Chapter 1, I outlined the social and emotional development of young language learners, from 5 to 12 years of age. The growing confidence and independence, and developing ability to cooperate and share over the years means that the affective schemata of young learners changes dramatically over the space of time from 5 to 12, and that teachers and assessors need to design assessment tasks to cater for these differences. Cultural differences in experience and attitude will also influence what a child brings to an assessment task. A young girl may find it difficult to be interviewed by an adult male – perhaps the power relationship (in the child's eyes) is too great. The girl may believe that she should stay quiet and respectful rather than speak to show what she knows.

Topics in assessment tasks may be emotionally charged for children. This may be negative or positive. Talking about their weekend may bring unhappy memories for children in dysfunctional families, whereas remembering how they were able to touch and talk to a koala on a school excursion would bring an enthusiastic response. Assessment materials (colourful, shiny paper; music; friendly-looking puppets) can also influence emotional response in young learners. The stakes involved – what happens if I fail – influence all test takers, including children. Many aspects of the task need careful analysis by teachers and assessors who know the children, or in the case of large-scale testing, by test developers who know the age-group and the broad characteristics of the test takers.

Teachers and assessors who know children individually have the best advantage in assessment. Young learners, especially those in the junior elementary years, develop emotionally at different paces because of maturational and experiential factors. This is an important reason why classroom assessment undertaken by the child's teacher is best for young learners. Testers who prepare tests for young learners require special skills to be able to cater for the affective needs of young learners in tests, and to avoid inhibiting each child's best efforts.

Language knowledge interacts with (2) the characteristics of the language use setting

The characteristics of the language use setting interact with language knowledge and influence the nature of the child's language performance.

Children who have more advanced levels of language knowledge make different choices when speaking to a teacher than to a friend. The teacher uses language in one way when giving them classroom directives and in another when telling them a funny story. The setting influences the performance of children in an assessment task. A task to be performed in front of the whole class will possibly negatively influence the performance of a shy child. The use of colourful and interactive computer-based material will probably stimulate interest and elicit a possibly different performance from black and white pictures.

The importance of the language use setting is hard to overestimate. As I will show in Chapter 4, the selection of a task is central to valid and reliable assessment.

All components work together through (3) strategic competence

Strategic competence

The strategic competence component of language ability involves the language user being engaged, bringing all the components together in relation to the communicative purposes and the context. The result is *fluent, accurate* language use *appropriate* to the task or the language use context. Bachman and Palmer hypothesize that strategic competence is required by all language learners as a 'cognitive management function in language use' (1996). Strategic competence is a **metacognitive function** (a function concerned with learning strategies that involve planning and directing learning at a general level) that integrates all the components of language use, enabling language users to create and interpret discourse.

Strategic competence is hypothesized to be made up of cognitive strategies that involve *goal setting* (deciding what one is going to do), *assessment* (taking stock of what is needed, what one has to work with, and how well one has done) and *planning* (deciding how to use what one has). When language learners are taking a test, for example, they would first *set their goal* – identifying the test tasks, choosing a task, and deciding whether to attempt the tasks selected; *assess* – determine the desirability and feasibility of successfully completing it, assessing their knowledge and relevance of their knowledge for the task, and assessing the correctness of the response; and *plan* – select elements of their topical and language knowledge to complete the task, formulate a plan to complete the task, and select one plan for implementation as a response to the test task. Language learners go through the same strategic processes when they are involved in any language use, for example a conversation or a writing task.

Young learners have a limited but growing ability to think about what needs to be said in different situations to different people, and to plan what they are going to write in ways that are appropriate to the purpose and audience. They have been developing strategic competence in their first language from birth (Halliday, 1975). They are still developing skills to handle discourse in their first language for most of their elementary years, and beyond. The development of their strategic competence in their foreign or second language will depend on their experience with real language use in communicative situations. The metacognitive skills required in strategic competence are part of this development. The metacognitive skills required in strategy use are reliant on a degree of cognitive maturity. The cognitive maturity, metacognition and communication strategies of young learners cannot be assumed. Using their strategic competence, children therefore bring their individual characteristics to their language use, drawing on their topical knowledge and their affective schemata.

For language teachers in Europe, the Common European Framework of Reference for Languages (Council of Europe, 2001) is a framework that also sets out components of language use ability. The European framework serves the same purpose as the Bachman and Palmer framework; it describes what is involved in language use. With knowledge of what makes up language use, it is possible to monitor the development of the components, and to decide what should be focused upon in assessment.

Summary

Even from the beginning learners can use language in simple ways, for example by using learned formulae and new vocabulary slotted into learned sentences in spontaneous and flexible ways, and by using gestures and facial expressions to supplement what they are saying. As children become more proficient, they will become more able to use language for social and academic purposes, in both spoken and written form.

There are both sociocultural and cognitive perspectives on language learning, both of which complement each other (Bialystok, 2001). As children learn to use language, they are 'learning how to mean', that is, learning how to interact within new discourses. Language learners take on new identities as they do so. Young learners, especially those in second language and immersion programmes, are under pressure to learn the new discourses of the classroom and of content areas learned in the new language. Cognitive perspectives on language learning include Skehan's (1998) dual-mode system, in which both formulaic and rule-governed systems work together (in children with more emphasis on formulaic systems), Schumann's theories concerned with emotion in second language learning, and Cummins' (1979) theory of linguistic interdependence. Optimal conditions for language learning are those in which favourable sociocultural conditions (opportunities to use language, to engage with relevant discourses and to bring their language and first language identity to their learning) are present, and cognitive processes suitable for children's age level (opportunities to activate the dual-mode system; opportunities to have positive experiences with the language and with each other) are activated. The implications for assessment of these perspectives are that assessment procedures should promote and monitor the development of relevant discourses and new identities, engage and monitor cognitive processes, and include knowledge of first language progress. These implications are relevant through each step in the assessment process. Language curricula and external tests are able to influence the conditions under which young learners learn language; good curricula and tests reflect what is known about language learning.

A theoretical framework of language ability (in this case Bachman and Palmer (1996) is used) assists teachers and assessors to plan for language assessment by laying out the components of language ability. Other frameworks, such as the Common European Framework for Languages might be used in the same way. Effective assessment of young learners combines knowledge of children's growth (their physical, cognitive, social and personal growth), and their language learning processes with such a framework to ensure best assessment practice. Curricula designed for young learners do this to some degree. However, often curricula are not detailed to the point of defining what they mean by language ability.

The next chapter looks at research into the assessment of young language learners.

CHAPTER THREE

Research into the assessment of young language learners

The aim of this chapter is to outline the scope of recent research into the assessment of young language learners. The chapter is also designed to help teachers and assessors to identify the directions in which research is currently going, and those that are waiting to be pursued. It is very clear that there are many questions still to be answered, but that there are some pockets of strong research activity in relation to selected areas of young learner assessment, in particular, teacher-based assessment.

Research into the assessment of young learners is a new field of endeavour, and whilst there has been relatively little published research to date, a growing amount of work is being undertaken by researchers and teachers around the world. The main source of information about research is professional journals, where researchers, often academics in tertiary institutions around the world, publish their work. Sometimes the findings of research are available within reports from government agencies such as the Council of Europe, Language Australia, and the National Centre for Research on Evaluation, Standards and Student Testing (CRESST) in the United States. Teachers' work is sometimes published in government-sponsored educational publications, or included in academic research articles in journals. Recently research into young learner assessment has been more evident because of the following: firstly, increased numbers of researchers, particularly in Europe, sharing their findings in commercial publications; secondly, the impetus of the **standards movement** (the introduction by governments of external criteria of learning known as standards, as both curriculum guides and accountability measures) which has provided a focus for reflection and empirical research into language proficiency pathways, and thirdly, arising out of the latter, increased research activity into teacher-based formative assessment in the classroom.

Why is assessment research important?

Why is it important to know about research into the assessment of young language learners? Ideas are raised by researchers that may not be thought about in the classroom as teachers work to meet the teaching and reporting requirements of language teaching. Questions are raised by researchers who work beyond the classroom and who see areas of weakness or concern in assessment practices, perhaps in external or large-scale testing. Teachers themselves stand back and examine what they are doing and tell others about it, for example in action research projects supported by teacher educators.

The work of researchers reminds practitioners, teacher-trainers and other researchers, that it is unwise to accept current assessment practices without question. What are researchers looking at? What are they finding out? How should their findings change what teachers are doing in the classroom or how an external test is designed? How does this affect how teachers should be trained? The relatively small amount of current research points to some initial answers to these questions. As the research grows, more questions will be answered. Research will both confirm current good practice and point to new directions for further work and thinking.

Finally, the value of research for the validation of the field of language education of young learners, and more specifically young learner language assessment, cannot be underestimated. Research indicates that this section of the profession is taking its work seriously, and that it has the expertise to nominate key issues and to investigate and report them.

This chapter therefore underpins the rest of this book, signalling to readers the questions that researchers are asking about the practices which are discussed and described in each of the other chapters. Readers are likely to think of their own questions as they read; these questions may lead to further, much needed research in young learner language assessment.

Challenges for researchers

There have been, and continue to be, some major barriers to research into the assessment of young language learners. These are programme variability, understandings about expected language proficiency, and teacher expertise (Johnstone, 2000).

Variability across programmes and lack of consensus about proficiency

Researching foreign language programme assessment practices within and across systems is often hampered by the variability that exists in programme delivery. Researchers have written of major differences in foreign language programmes across member states of Europe in terms of starting age, amount of time available each week, numbers of teachers available, teachers' foreign language proficiency, teachers' knowledge of how to teach another language, and the degree of support available to teachers. Johnstone (2000, p. 128) refers to differences in relation to:

- the extent to which foreign languages are taught as a separate elementary school subject or are embedded in the wider curriculum that children experience;
- the extent to which school ethos supports foreign language learning, or, in fact, perceives it as an imposition from the outside; and
- the extent to which staff in secondary schools are supportive and seek to build on what children bring with them from their elementary school foreign language experience.

Second language programmes also vary. In some situations children begin their language study in a new country in intensive language reception centres; in many other situations they enter directly into mainstream classrooms. Some children receive specialist language support while they study in the mainstream; others do not. The nature of children's language proficiency will depend on their background: they may be born in the country but speak a minority language, entering school with some little knowledge of the majority language; they may be migrants who begin learning the second language when they arrive, in the early or later years of elementary school. Children's educational background in their country of origin may be disrupted and this can result in some unexpected influences on their progress in learning their second language.

Differences in programmes and experiences result in a lack of consensus about the nature of proficiency, and the levels of proficiency expected as children progress. Some frameworks, designed to remedy this problem and help give a common view of language proficiency, are being developed and used across districts and countries, bringing a greater opportunity for consensus.

Variable teacher expertise

For a number of reasons, particularly lack of professional development opportunities, language teachers of young learners are not highly skilled in assessment (Edelenbos and Johnstone, 1996; Nikolov, 2000). Nor is assessment a top priority for language teachers, as indicated by responses to surveys of teacher concerns conducted in Italy (Hill, 2000), in Scotland (Low, Brown, Johnstone and Pirrie, 1995) and in Austria (Jantscher and Landsiedler, 2000).

ESL teachers in England and Wales have been found not to hold assessment as a priority in their professional cultures and values. In a survey in which teachers were asked about ways in which teaching English could be improved in elementary schools, teachers' responses did not mention assessment (Teasdale and Leung, 2000), although they have a heavy assessment requirement through set assessment tasks in which the children are assessed alongside their English mother-tongue peers.

The issue of teacher expertise in some situations extends to tertiary institutions, where there may have been little training in assessment in the past. In Hong Kong, teacher-trainers' understanding of and practice in, formative and criterion-referenced assessment has been found to be somewhat 'impoverished' (Klenowski 1999 cited in Morris, Lo, Chik and Chan, 2000, p. 215). There are, too, many highly experienced and expert teachers and teacher educators who have knowledge of, and skills in, assessment, and knowledge is growing in areas where accountability-based teacher assessment is now required (Breen et al., 1997). Nevertheless, a lack of expertise in and prioritizing of assessment, particularly in situations where external assessment prevails, provides a real challenge to researchers.

The purposes for assessment research in young learner language education

This section is organized around four main purposes for assessment research in young learner language education. Research in language assessment is carried out for the following purposes:

- **To investigate and share information about current assessment practices.** Researchers, teachers and assessors need to know what others are doing, to find out what is successful and to share what others have learned. Researchers act as distributors of information by observing, analysing, and distributing information about current assessment practices.
- **To find ways to ensure valid and fair assessment tasks and procedures.** Researchers examine the factors that render assessment tasks and procedures valid and fair, referring to or developing theoretical frameworks to analyse the characteristics of learners and tasks, and observing, analysing and recording the strengths and weaknesses of assessment tasks and procedures they have designed.
- **To find out more about the nature of young learner language proficiency and language growth.** Assessment procedures are devised and used in research to find out more about the nature of learner pathways and progress in foreign and second language learning. Children's progress may also be mapped in related skills, such as metalinguistic awareness and attitude.
- **To investigate and improve the impact of assessment on young language learners, their families, their teachers and their school.** Researchers are concerned to find out whether assessment practices and materials will have a positive impact on young learners' lives. Assessment may have a positive or negative impact, or effect, on a young learner, on their families and community, their teachers, their school and education department. The impact may occur because of classroom assessment practices, or through large-scale tests, and may influence individual children or the whole education system. Researchers have investigated widely the impact of large-scale tests on young learners. Their efforts have been directed in particular towards the investigation of test-bias. The impact of classroom assessment is only recently being investigated. Under this purpose I have examined research that raises teachers' understandings and expertise, since this is likely to improve the impact of assessment in the classroom.

These purposes are not mutually exclusive, as it is clear some research will cover more than one purpose; for example, Gatullo (2000) conducted research that both investigated practice in assessment (the first purpose) but also raised teachers' professional understandings (the fourth purpose).

Investigating and sharing information about current assessment practices

Relatively little has been published about current assessment practices in young learner language education. More is shared about teaching and learning, though often teaching publications do not dwell on assessment, and in many there is little mention of assessment. The reality is that many teachers are concerned first with ways to teach.

Sharing information about assessment procedures and contexts

Guidelines on how to assess language give an opportunity for the profession to share experience and think about assessment. We need to learn as much as possible from the experience and knowledge of others about assessment. We also need to know as much as possible about what others are doing with regard to assessment. What do experienced teachers say about the language assessment of young learners? What tests are available? What kinds of tests are being devised for system-wide assessment? What kinds of assessment procedures are teachers using in their classrooms? Which procedures are best for special needs students? Sharing this kind of information is, in my view, a form of research requiring systematic presentation and dissemination.

Guidelines for assessment are probably more widely available in young learner ESL than in foreign language teaching. For example, Law and Eckes (1995) give teachers of school-age ESL students in Canada a useful handbook of ideas on assessment. Hall's (1995) booklet on assessing bilingual children gives advice on assessment in the classroom, with particular reference to children with special needs. Genesee and Upshur (1996) and Genesee and Hamayan (1994) are valuable references for assessment of school-age second language learners, and for classroom-based assessment. O'Malley and Valdez Pierce (1996) gives useful assessment guides for teachers of school-age children. These books are not specifically targeted at teachers who are assessing elementary-age learners experience.

A number of books written for elementary-age learners dedicate a section to assessment, including Cameron (2001), Rixon (1999) and Brumfit, Moon and Tongue (1995). Professional associations make available assessment guidelines for teachers. For example, the TESOL Association has produced a number of volumes dedicated to assisting teachers to assess using the TESOL standards (Smallwood, 2001). Local curriculum documents often provide guidelines for assessment, usually attached to the syllabus. Thompson (1997) has produced an annotated bibliography of assessment instruments for foreign language assessment in Grades K-8 in the United States. These are some examples of guidelines and information that is made available to the profession. These publications are contributing towards a growing critical mass of knowledge about the assessment of young language learners.

In Europe, the Common European Framework for Languages (Council of Europe, 2001) has provided a conceptual framework and guidelines for assessment for all language learners, though there is not direct reference to young learners. Work is being carried out in Europe translating these frameworks into syllabuses and specific assessment frameworks for young learners. Dissemination of this work is important to help curriculum writers and teachers across member states to proceed towards shared assessment frameworks for young learners.

The University of Cambridge ESOL Examinations has made descriptions of its Cambridge Young Learner English Tests easily available, together with research information through Research Notes (e.g., Ball and Wilson (2002). Their research investigates various aspects of the Young Learner English Tests' design, validity and reliability.

Researchers also share information about the assessment procedures they have devised and trialled. A special issue of the journal *Language Testing* (volume 17, no. 2, 2000), edited by Rea-Dickins, was devoted to the issues of assessing young language learners. This issue contained several descriptions of assessment that has been carried out or was in progress. Earlier in *Language Testing*, Carpenter, Fujii and Kataoka (1995) had described and critiqued in detail a procedure they had devised and carried out assessing young learners learning Japanese in the United States. This procedure is described in detail later in this chapter as an example of assessment research. Researchers also report on the nature of assessment practice that they have observed. In some programmes researchers have reported that they have observed poor teaching, lack of teacher continuity, and little opportunity for making connections with other subjects (Nikolov, 2000; Warwick, 2000). This, they say, has influenced learner motivation. These 'quality of experience' issues are reported by many researchers as problems in teaching and assessment, particularly in young learner programmes that are struggling to become established.

Sharing experience and information about assessment procedures and contexts is clearly a vital component of research, leading to increased knowledge about assessment.

Investigating teacher classroom assessment

Teacher classroom assessment ranges on several dimensions from formative assessment to summative assessment in the classroom. Formative assessment, sometimes called the 'developmental role' of assessment (Masters and Forster, 1997) or 'assessment for learning' (see Chapter 5), is carried out by the teacher as part of the teaching process and is central to effective teaching. Summative assessment may be constructed and carried out by the classroom teacher as a set of assessment tasks during or at the end of the course of study. In recent years, the distinction between formative and summative classroom assessment has blurred for some teachers. The requirement that they report on children's progress over time using externally developed criteria has meant that the summative purposes of reporting to others outside the classroom have intruded into formative assessment (Breen et al., 1997; Rea-Dickins, 2001).

Research into teachers' formative assessment in second and foreign language classrooms has only recently been undertaken. Rea-Dickins and Gardner (Rea-Dickins and Gardner, 2000; Gardner and Rea-Dickins, 2001; Rea-Dickins, 2001) have explored the nature of formative assessment in elementary classrooms, examining the range and quality of teacher assessment, the issues and the assessment processes. Their detailed analyses of teachers' assessment procedures, of classroom interaction and teacher talk are seminal in promoting our understandings of teacher assessment and provide new insights into classroom assessment. The iterative characteristic of formative assessment is, for example, captured in comments from teachers and in classroom interaction analysis. These authors' findings lead them to warn us that it is not always appropriate to characterize classroom assessment as a low-stakes assessment situation. Crucial decisions can be made on the basis of children's performance in class, in particular when teachers pass on their evaluations of performance, through their reports, to others who make high-stakes decisions. The researchers found some sources of inconsistency, and therefore of lack of validity and reliability in teacher assessments. This is of concern when high-stakes decisions are made.

Rea-Dickins (2001) traces different stages in the teacher assessment process and presents a working model for the analysis of teacher decision-making in formative assessment. She concludes with further questions:

- What constitutes 'quality' in formative assessment?
- Are these assessments creating opportunities for language learning? and if so
- What constitutes evidence of language learning?
- Are teachers in the EAL context able to distinguish between a language learning need, a special education need, a curriculum content need?   (Rea-Dickins, 2001, pp. 457–8)

These investigations reveal the intricacies and complexities of teacher assessment in elementary language classrooms. Whilst most of this work has been conducted in situations where second language learners are learning in mainstream classrooms, there is no doubt that the assessment processes being investigated are also important to foreign language classrooms where teachers carry out formative assessment in the classroom.

A study of formative assessment carried out in Italy has shown areas of weaknesses in teacher assessment, and areas of teacher concern about their own assessment. Gatullo (2000) reported on a two-year pilot study in Italy in which she found that teachers tended not to make productive use of information they collect for formative purposes, and they make little or no use of some types of questioning and negotiations that could be fed into formative assessment and enhance the learning processes. Gatullo also found that teachers tended not to ask pupils about the way they are thinking (metacognitive questioning) in language classes even though they believed it is important to do this in other subjects. She believes that discussion with teachers, and deeper data analysis could cast further light on this 'looseness' of formative assessment that she has observed. Gatullo found that teachers were extremely positive about being involved in the research project which involved classroom observation and audio taping, transcribing and analysis of selected assessment events, peer-teacher observations and collegial discussions about the research and assessment.

Leung (2005) raises questions about the validity and reliability of teacher assessment when teachers are required to monitor lists of pre-specified criteria set out in national curriculum statements or standards.

> It is not clear how possible it is for the teacher, any teacher, to operate the full range of pre-specified criteria which would cover all possible aspects of student learning, modes of participation and learning strategies, to name a few possible issues that can emerge in the teaching and learning process that might impact on teacher assessment; the fluid, socially dynamic and sometimes unpredictable nature of classroom activities would preclude this possibility . . .. The point is that one cannot assume that non-contrived classroom events would always provide the necessary opportunities to sample the language use (or any other kind of 'evidence' required for the intended criterion-reference assessment.   (Leung, 2005, pp. 874–5)

He questions whether teacher judgments of student performance and progress may be qualitatively different from the judgments that are made in formal testing situations. He suggests we need to explore the kinds of information teachers seek and the basis of their decision-making in formative assessment. Specifically, he argues that three kinds of questions require some immediate attention:

- what do teachers do when they carry out formative assessment?
- what do teachers look for when they are assessing?
- what theory or 'standards' do teachers use when they make judgments and decisions?   (Leung, 2005, p. 880)

The research discussed in the next section incorporates teachers' formative assessment practices but looks further to teachers' use of externally developed criteria to inform their formative and summative assessment.

Investigating teachers' use of externally developed criteria for formative assessment

Externally developed criteria are usually presented in the form of standards, or staged descriptions of curriculum outcomes. They may be accompanied by expectations of progress, that is, by the end of Year 3 most children will be expected to reach Level 2. The descriptions of progress may come from standards or outcomes-based curriculum documents. They may also be proficiency scale-type documents describing progress in language development outside a specific curriculum context (e.g., bandscales or scales). Teachers are expected to observe children's progress over time, and then report, usually at the end of the school year, at what level each child is performing. The accompanying expectation is that teachers will aim for children to achieve these levels; therefore the externally developed criteria are often used to inform teaching and ongoing, formative assessment. (For a fuller discussion of these types of documents, see Chapter 8.)

What we need to know here is firstly, whether the external criteria are valid; this is discussed later in the chapter. We also need to know how teachers are assessing with respect to the externally developed criteria. How are they interpreting the criteria? For example, do the criteria mean the same thing to all teachers? What do teachers think about the processes they are expected to follow and about the descriptors? Is the fact that teachers have to report on children's progress against a set of criteria actually narrowing the curriculum? Are teachers still able to meet the individual needs of children if they are aiming towards a tightly defined set of outcomes to be met by the end of the year?

Breen and colleagues (1997, p. 92) have investigated the nature of teachers' adoption of the various ESL assessment frameworks available in Australia. This research team conducted a wide-reaching research project in Australia, where they conducted case studies of Australian ESL teachers using ESL standards, or assessment frameworks, in their classrooms. Breen and his colleagues observed that genuine 'accommodation' or take-up by teachers of external curriculum frameworks entails three phases: firstly, teachers need to recognize both conceptually and affectively the ultimate benefit to their own pedagogic priorities; secondly they need to trial and adapt the framework to their established assessment procedures; thirdly, they need to fully integrate the procedures into their practice. The ESL teachers in the Australian case studies were generally found to accept one or other of the assessment frameworks introduced in Australia as, at least, potentially beneficial to their pedagogy, though there was an initial wish to reduce their impact so that they did not intrude upon strongly held teaching priorities (p. 92). Almost all of the teachers entered the second phase of selective adaptation, whilst, as Breen and colleagues observed, only *some* of the teachers had fully integrated them. The case studies reveal a range of differences in approach to the application of the standards and to assessment in the classroom. The majority of teachers in the Australian case studies were teachers of young learners. Teachers were interviewed as part of these case studies and the researchers' analysis of their comments revealed that, in general, teachers' ideal assessment framework was one that:

- provides a strong link between teaching (including goals and planning) and assessment
- has a strong professional development focus, particularly for mainstream teachers, by providing an understanding of the varying backgrounds of ESL learners and by proposing strategies for teaching to the various levels of development in the framework
- Includes a framework to assess or, at least, understand the major characteristics of the first language of ESL learners, particularly those in bilingual programmes. This would include provision for assessing literacy in the first language of ESL learners
- details the development of oracy in English as a second language and which accounts for the role of oracy in the development of reading and writing at particular stages
- is sensitive to different teaching contexts. For example, the contextual differences between pre-elementary, mainstream elementary, and Intensive Language Centre teaching in terms of environments, priorities and procedures
- is inclusive of the range of ESL learners and does not characterize such learners as if they were a homogeneous group

(Breen, 1997, p. 212)

This list supports the generally held view that these teachers see a close relationship between teaching and assessment and wish the criteria to inform their teaching. This has important implications for developers of standards for young language learners.

In England, Leung and Teasdale (1997) have investigated teacher assessment of speaking and listening of ESL learners at Key Stage 1 of the National Curriculum. They researched the criteria teachers used to make their assessments – to what extent they were common and to what extent they were different from the National Curriculum descriptors. In summary, they video-recorded classroom interaction, interviewed teachers who observed the videos to elicit the constructs used by the informants and asked panels of teachers to rate children's performance. They found that teachers did have some shared understanding about the general criteria for Speaking and Listening. There were also criteria that were used that were not specified in the National Curriculum. They suggest that some criteria were based on an understanding of an idealized native-speaker norm rather than a model that reflects the language of ESL children.

Researchers have found that primary school teachers also adapt systems of mandated classroom-based assessment to suit the exigencies of their classroom situation. In Hong Kong elementary schools (and in many EFL contexts in Asia) high-stakes assessment is a stark reality (Morris et al., 2000), and assessment is seen as a preparation for survival in a highly competitive society and a source of motivation for pupils (Morris et al., 2000). Teachers are not keen to take on the responsibility of assessment because of parents' and principals' concern that children's grades are fairly and transparently calculated. As part of the implementation of a new system of formative assessment against Bands of Performance for the Target Oriented Curriculum, teachers were instructed to assess formally each outcome in the Bands and to note each assessment result in detailed records. However, teachers reported that they had little time to do follow-up work, and that their workload was greatly increased. The lesson to be learned from this, according to the researchers, is that governments need to consider long-term and coherent strategies that address both the structural features of schooling and the prevailing beliefs about assessment. They suggest that, in educational environments such as Hong Kong, the following are needed if teacher-based criterion-referenced assessment is to succeed:

- a clear linkage between external and school-based assessments
- the development of a system of recording and reporting assessment which stresses the role of teacher collaboration, the exercise of professional judgment and the provision of feedback designed to support learning
- ongoing support for teachers' professional development designed to promote their understanding of the roles and processes of assessment. (Morris et al., 2000, p. 215)

Morris and his colleagues did observe, however, that some elementary teachers engaged in ongoing formative assessment and provided feedback to pupils during teaching. They observed many examples of classroom interaction in which the teachers provided extensive comments and feedback on pupils' progress.

Some were also able to skillfully encourage pupils to assess their own work, and to encourage peer-assessment in ways which required the identification of strengths, weaknesses and areas of improvement. Generally, the teachers were also able and willing to identify from their experience pupils' competencies, strengths and weaknesses.
(Morris et al., 2000, p. 207)

These observations by researchers highlight the recurring theme in the language assessment literature, that is, the tension between assessment for pedagogic purposes and assessment for administrative purposes. When governments mandate the criteria for assessment and collect data from teachers about learner progress, there will be an inevitable influence on teachers' assessment practices. Accountability will push teachers to teach to the criteria, the curriculum is likely to be narrowed and children's individual needs may not be addressed. Unfortunately, as Brindley (2001) warns, when pedagogic purposes and administrative accountability purposes meet, it is usually the administrative purposes that win out.

Investigating the assessment of language and content

Content refers to the topics about which children are communicating, and for which they are using the language. **Content-based assessment** is a term covering assessment in which language and content are assessed together. The content in foreign language programmes for young learners might relate to children's personal and community life, their leisure and recreation, the natural world, or the imaginative world. In second language learning contexts, and in some foreign language contexts, the school curriculum provides the content. Language use is tied to communicating about, and studying, the topics in question. How do teachers assess language in content-based programmes? Should the two components be separated, or are there ways in which that the two can be combined and a valid assessment made? In some situations, language learners' knowledge of the content is assessed alongside that of native-speaking children. But is this fair? How do we make tests like this as fair as possible for language learners who may know the content but are not able to express what they know? These are some of the many questions in content-based assessment that need to be investigated.

Embeddedness in content and in 'a flow of events'

Johnstone (2000) has introduced the concept of embeddedness to address the question of whether content can be successfully integrated into the language teaching and assessment of young learners. In embedded language learning, curriculum subjects like history, drama and art are integrated into the process of learning. Language learning is not separated out from other curriculum areas but becomes part of and is integrated into the wider curriculum. This can be done either by the mainstream teacher, or by the foreign language teacher.

> This natural flow of events in which the foreign language pops in and out of relevant classroom activity reflects a view of the elementary school curriculum in which the universe of children's knowledge is not divided into discrete areas called 'subjects' but is organized more holistically into broader areas that allow children to integrate a variety of different experiences. (Johnstone, 2000, p. 129)

Foreign language curricula can be written in which nominated content knowledge will be embedded by teachers (Queensland Schools Curriculum Council, 2000). In second language contexts, especially where children are learning in mainstream content classrooms, embeddedness is natural; children learn language and content through the same activities. Johnstone (2000, p. 130) sees embeddedness as a challenge for assessment. He sees that young learners naturally learn in activities that happen 'in a flow of events'.

> this very embeddedness constitutes a problem to testing, since in a test there may not be time in which to embed the assessment activity in a series of prior activities. In the case of elementary school children an assessment task is unlikely to be valid unless it represents a type of activity with which they have some familiarity; however, in addition, if they are asked to make a 'cold start' in an assessment task, when they are accustomed each day to being 'warmed up' for it cognitively as well as linguistically, then questions must arise about the validity of the process. (Johnstone, 2000, p. 130)

In content-based assessment of young learners and indeed in most young learner assessments, children need to be 'warmed up' in terms of the topic as well the language they need. We need investigations into how teachers and external assessors are dealing with these requirements in assessment. As children progress to their upper elementary years, assessment can be done with less embeddedness, as children are able to retain more knowledge about the topic, and to apply it to a 'cold start' assessment. However, most upper elementary children still require reminders and modelling to give them the best opportunity to perform well. The difference between approaches to assessment of language and content in young and older learners requires further examination.

Assessing the quality of performance with reference to systemic functional linguistics

Some researchers have turned their attention to how to assess the quality of a child's performance in a task involving language and content. Mohan and Slater (2004) describe how content assessment and language assessment can work together, using systemic functional linguistics (SFL) as a theoretical base and analysing tool. They suggest that the teacher's perspectives on language (whether they are focused on the sentence level or the discourse level, for example) and subsequent approach to feedback and assessment will necessarily influence the learning that takes place, and the grade the student is granted for the piece of work. They have investigated how a SFL approach can be used to assess language and content together. In this framework language and content cannot be separated because they are one and the same thing. The language carries the content, and the content carries the language.

In traditional grammar, teachers look for correctness of form to see whether language rules are violated or not. However, using an SFL approach, teachers check whether the discourse as a whole (and its elements) works appropriately to convey the intended meaning required by the content. The emphasis shifts from what the learner *cannot* do to what the learner *can* do. The use of SFL has also been applied in the assessment of ESL learners in several ESL contexts. (There have not been reports, of which I am aware, about SFL assessment in foreign language teaching.) Teachers identify the genres that children are expected to use or understand (reports, narratives, oral presentation, etc.) and then explicitly teach children what the features of that genre are, providing models. Assessment is guided by criteria for the genre in question. Table 3.1 shows a set of assessment criteria developed from a systemic functional perspective for an elementary written language assessment task. Systemic functional linguistics provides the basis for a deep analysis of elementary learners' ability to write persuasive arguments, for both formative and summative purposes. Sets of criteria such as these for a range of genres, both spoken and oral, have been prepared in projects and made available to teachers (e.g., Mincham, 1985).

Research involving the development of frameworks to assess language and content tasks is important, both to enhance teachers' understanding of the discourse features of different tasks, but also to improve the validity and reliability of content-based assessment.

Table 3.1 *Extract from Elementary Written Language Assessment Criteria for a Persuasive Argument (Mincham, 1985, p. 85)**

Schematic structure. Did the student

- make an opening statement previewing the issue?
- make a position statement?
- present relevant arguments to support the position statement?
- support the arguments with appropriate evidence?
- anticipate and refute an opposing viewpoint (optional)?
- summarise evidence and (optional) make an appeal for action?

Language features. Did the student

- focus on specific and generalized participants e.g. the ban, nets?
- use expanded nominal groups e.g. the pollution of our rivers?
- use topic-specific/technical vocabulary e.g. habitat?
- use a range of verbs/processes e.g. is, kill, say, feel, believe?
- use a range of circumstances e.g. how, when, where, why?
- vary use of person e.g. I, we, he, she, they, you?
- use language in a personal and interactive way? For example,

   writer as 'equal', making suggestions/inviting responses
   attitudinal words to evoke emotions e.g. slaughter, horrific
   literary devices e.g. alliteration, repetition, etc. (optional)
   use modality to express obligation e.g. 'we must . . .'
   use mainly human participants and/or conjunctions in Theme position, e.g. 'But we are worried that . . .' 'Ms Cox claims . . .'

- use nominalizations, e.g. 'The production of wood chips'?
- use appropriate tense, e.g. is, used, has, led, will show?
- use a range of conjunctions, e.g. and, but, so, yet, although?
- * use complex clauses, e.g. 'Rabbit numbers which are now estimated to be x will reach . . .', 'To address this issue we . . .' ?
- use reference items, substitution, ellipsis, e.g. this, its?

*Other criteria, not shown here, relate to accuracy and the degree of support required.

Investigating ways to ensure valid and fair assessment tasks and procedures for young learners

A central aim of assessment research is to find ways to ensure that assessment tasks and procedures are valid and fair. The terms 'valid' and 'fair' refer to a set of complex ideas that are treated in more detail in the next chapter and through the rest of the book (see Chapter 4). Valid and fair assessment procedures provide meaningful and appropriate information about children's ability and generate information that is without bias.

Investigating characteristics of assessment tasks that affect young learner performance

There are some characteristics of assessment tasks that we know affect the performance of young learners and that thus may have an impact on the validity of score interpretations and the fairness of decisions made. Frameworks for analysing the characteristics of assessment tasks have been developed by researchers in the general assessment field. Bachman and Palmer's (1996) framework of task characteristics analyses the following components of tasks:

The characteristics of the setting

The characteristics of the input

The characteristics of the expected response

The relationship between input and response

This framework is used in the following section to categorize what researchers know in these areas about young learner assessment.

The characteristics of the setting

The characteristics of the setting include the physical setting, the participants and the time of the task (Bachman and Palmer, 1996). The physical setting of the assessment activity can be distracting for young learners. The arrangement of physical space can increase the frequency of certain behaviour and minimize distractions. Carrying out the assessment task in a room away from other physical activity will, for example, give children a chance to give the task their full attention and show their best ability.

Settings suitable for young learners have been seen, rather than discovered, in researchers' work. Zangl (2000), for example, recognized that playful, non-threatening situations elicit valuable information about learners' language development. Researchers make sure they use visual and tactile stimuli to arouse children's interest and keep activities short to avoid tiredness or loss of concentration (Carpenter, Fujii and Kataoka, 1995; Zangl, 2000). These researchers make sure that children have time to warm up, because without this they take longer to respond than older learners, even when they know the necessary vocabulary and grammar well. The characteristics of the setting are often evaluated by intuition, but systematic examination of the influence of the assessment environment on young learners is an important element of young learner research.

The characteristics of the input

How can the input influence a child's performance on a task? What kind of teacher talk, as input in an assessment task, influences a child's performance? What kind of pictorial information is helpful? Is hypertext on the computer more stimulating than text written on paper? Is hypertext confusing for young learners?

Alderson (2000) reports on several findings concerning choice of texts for young learners. Texts need illustrations, since texts that contain only verbal information will be not only intimidating but denser and therefore difficult to process. The print should be laid out with judicious use of size and space. When complex sentences are presented to children graphically laid out in segments that conform to the phrase structure, they are easier to read than text graphically presented in segments that violate phrase structure (Wood, 1974, cited in Alderson, 2000). Information presented in tabular and other forms provides support for the processing of the verbal information; children need to understand the relationship between the verbal and the non-verbal in text. In addition, comprehension of expository or informational material is believed to be more difficult than comprehension of narratives, and may be more dependent on background knowledge (de la Luz Reyes, 1987).

There has been debate for many years about the practice of modifying texts for second language learners. It has been found that a modified text can be more difficult, even for native speakers, because the redundancy of the text, or degree to which the text contains more information than is needed, is reduced. Researchers have also found that providing supplementary background information can improve reading comprehension more effectively than simplifying syntactic structure (Butler and Stevens, 1997).

The questions and prompts used in an assessment procedure are components of input. In Norway, foreign language assessors have devised and then researched and reported on a procedure that has been successful with 11- to 12-year-old children. Prompts were used that stimulated children's interest. A four-episode, cartoon-picture-packed mystery story booklet, with CD-Rom, is used to assess children from year to year. The stimuli texts are broadly based on comic-strip-type illustrations, with 'natural' recorded material. The main action involves a hunt for a stolen elephant, and within this theme, a variety of familiar adventures arise. Each episode is short, about 25 minutes. Each episode is primarily testing a different macro-skill and is administered over a two-week period.

The test culminates in a writing activity in which children write about what happened through the eyes of the two main characters.

> The reading test presents a series of texts introducing the characters and the situation. Tasks largely involve matching (with widespread use of pictures), true–false choices or gap filling. The listening test carries the action further in radio-drama, on CD. Tasks here generally involve identifying specific things referred to on the CD by crossing or numbering pictures or maps. In addition, a series of open questions on the action as a whole is presented at the end of this test, and pupils are invited to give their solution to the mystery. The general language test takes the story to its conclusion and is designed to assess a number of specific skills, such as word recognition, spelling of common words, and everyday colloquial expressions. The writing test places the pupils in the situation of the two main characters, and invites them to write a diary entry and letter in response to the events in the story. Pupils are encouraged to use the materials in the booklet as a resource in this test.   (Hasselgren, 2000, pp. 264–5)

The trials of these materials have involved over a thousand children aged 11 and 12, and have indicated that children became genuinely involved in the tasks, hoping to solve the mystery. Input characteristics such as these are innovative and child-centred; they are likely to motivate language learning and maximize opportunities for children to show their language knowledge and skills.

The characteristics of the expected response

Different tasks require responses at different levels of difficulty. Various researchers and writers have considered the difficulty level of tasks for older learners (Candlin, 1987), but little systematic research has been done into this in the assessment of young language learners. Scarino, Vale, McKay and Clark (1988) summarized research pertinent to expected response difficulty in tasks as set out in Table 3.2.

What level of proficiency should teachers and assessors be expecting in responses from young learners at different ages, and with different levels of experience? Hasselgren (2000) argues that, since we are not always clear on what children *should* be able to do at different stages of their learning, we should begin with documentation about what children *can* do at each stage of their schooling. This would need to be categorized according to the programme of learning in which they have participated (foreign language,

Table 3.2 *Factors influencing response difficulty in tasks (adapted from Scarino et al., 1988, Book 2, p. 27)*

An expected response is more difficult for young learners under the following conditions:

Unpredictability:	the language has fewer contextual clues; the activity is open-ended and more abstract; the activity demands a level of abstraction (e.g., decontextualized verbal description)
Dynamic descriptions:	the speaker has to describe changing events and activities
Experientially new:	the language, or activities are outside the learner's experience; the information contained in the activity is unknown to the learner
Socioculturally specific:	the activity is socioculturally specific
Level of support:	little or no help is available from others
Level of linguistic processing:	much cognitive and/or psycholinguistic processing is required (i.e., the language is conceptually difficult: e.g., complex sentences)
Level of cognitive demand:	a high level of thought has to be applied to complete the activity
Other characteristics:	more participants are involved; more steps are needed to complete the activity; more motor skills are needed

second language, immersion), contact hours per week, and age on entry. Some documentation has taken place as standards and outcomes map out pathways and expected achievement (see later in this chapter), but many of these maps have not been empirically validated (Brindley, 1998).

Further research into the identification of factors that present difficulty to children and to particular groups of children is of interest to the field.

The relationship between input and response

The relationship between input and response in the Bachman and Palmer framework refers to the degree of reciprocity between the input and the response or, for example, the interviewer and the child. **Reciprocity** happens when a child's response affects the subsequent input, and when the child receives feedback about the relevance and correctness of his answers from the assessor. How, for example, should an interviewer ask questions and respond to a child in an oral interview task? Are there differences in interviewer–child interactions compared to interviewer – adult interactions? There may be intuitive answers to these types of questions; it would be valuable to have some research-based answers (through, for example, observation, and trialling of different interaction types) that can be shared and further researched.

Support in the young learner classroom often involves reciprocity, with the teacher and child responding to each other with spoken input and response (e.g., questions from the teacher or the student, with responses), or material input (e.g., a model given) and response. The nature of the response influences the further support given. Support may be given through teacher talk, in written form on the board or on the child's paper; it may also be given by changing the nature of the expected response. We need to know more about support, about its nature and its value.

Liddicoat (1997), in a study of the types of tasks teachers use to report on school foreign language learners' progress against national language foreign standards in Australia, found that teachers were not as aware of the support they were affording learners as they should be. He found that tasks can be *over-supported* and thus judgments can be constrained. Table 3.3 shows the types of support-originated constraints on judgments he observed in speaking tasks.

Table 3.3 *Constraints on judgments of speakers' language use in tasks from support provided within the task (adapted from Liddicoat, 1997, p. 25)*

Constraints on judgment	Types of support
1 Judgement is constrained in a task *by the teacher*	Material has been provided by the teacher, either as a set piece of work or as a model for reproduction.
2 Judgement is constrained in a task *by prior work*	The language has been prepared in advance or rehearsed and therefore does not represent spontaneous language use.
3 Judgement is constrained in a task *by the situation*	The situation in which the task is performed is a routine situation in which language use is formulaic and predictable. There is no inherent need to go beyond the predictable.
4 Judgement is constrained in a task by *the requirements for interaction*	The task requires original, developed or spontaneous language from one participant only. There is no inherent need for the other participant to contribute language that is neither formulaic nor predictable.

Liddicoat recommends that teachers ensure that they are aware of the features of support that they are using and that they are making appropriate decisions to ensure best performance is observed.

Nicholas too (1999), observed the phenomenon of support in elementary classrooms and was frustrated by it, finding that its constant presence made it difficult for researchers to determine, through observation, the language proficiency of children in foreign language classes. He saw many advantages of this use of support in relation to the teaching and learning process, in particular in the opportunities for scaffolding and in the relationships and understandings created through the familiar routines and expectations. However, he found that the supportive context, familiar audience (the teacher and other children), and the use of familiar tasks already rehearsed several times tended to reduce the ability of the observer to see what the children could do individually. This has implications for teacher assessment through observation of children in classroom tasks.

There are therefore a number of characteristics of assessment tasks that can influence the performance of young learners and hence may impact the validity of score interpretations and the fairness of decisions made on the basis of assessment. Tasks for young learners, as for older learners, can be influenced by four main factors: the characteristic of the setting, the nature of the input, the nature of the expected response, and the relationship between the input and the response. Researchers into young language learner assessment have found some characteristics of tasks that influence validity and fairness; more systematic, published research is needed in this area.

An example of a research project investigating an assessment procedure for young learners

Carpenter and her colleagues (1995) have provided the field with a rare example of in-depth research into an assessment procedure for young learners and this research is therefore summarized here to illustrate how research into young learner assessment tasks can be conducted. The research team was interested in developing an assessment instrument to evaluate their Japanese language immersion programme for young learners in the United States. The assessment instrument they devised and investigated was conducted through an adult–child interview that consisted of several tasks, summarized in Table 3.4.

Table 3.4 *Summary of assessment items in an Oral Interview Procedure for young learners (Carpenter, Fujii and Kataoka, 1995)*

1 **Toybox** (3–4 minutes)
   A warm-up activity ('children require a much longer warm-up period than adults'), with attractive concrete physical objects to motivate children to talk more readily. Questions and commands requiring only comprehension ('Is there a truck?' 'Put the rabbit in the truck') move on to questions requiring language production responses ('Which is bigger, the boat or the airplane?').
2 **Conversation** (2–3 minutes)
   A naturalistic conversation, exchanging information unknown to the tester, such as favourite food, pets, family and chores at home.
3 **Information gap** (5–7 minutes)
   The child and the adult exchange information about the differences in their 'peel and press' picture.
4 **Categorization** (2–4 minutes)
   The child chooses one picture that doesn't belong out of four pictures.
5 **Story telling** (0–4 minutes)
   More advanced children were asked to tell a story, given a sequence of pictures (Goldilocks and the three bears).
6 **Classroom role play** (2–4 minutes)
   The child participates in two role plays with the tester. In the first the tester is a new student at the school and the child tells the new student about their school. In the second, the child acts out the role of the teacher, and the tester speaks through two puppets, who are students. The tester asks questions about school (e.g., 'Where do you eat lunch in this school?').

The test was designed to overcome a common limitation in interview procedures for young learners, that is, that adult–child interviews often only elicit a limited repertoire of functions. The researchers took careful note of the social pragmatics of the assessment procedure, in this case the adult–child interview, where often the children are penalized because they tend to make minimal responses in this social situation. They recognized that the cognitive and social elements in children's use of language are integrally related, catering for children's short attention spans by changing activities within the interview situation, giving children six short activities in all, no activity being more than seven minutes long, and the shortest being two to four minutes. The activities employed referential questions (e.g., referring to stuffed toys, and 'peel and press' pictures) and dealt with relevant and personalized topics (children's favourite food, pets, family and chores).

In order to avoid disadvantage for children in the interviews, Carpenter and her colleagues introduced warm-up activities in which the adults spoke with the children in their first language.

In the first portion, the tester asked the questions and issued the commands, and the child simply responded and moved the objects and people around as directed. This was really a warm-up and hands-on preparation for the second part, in which the child was to ask the questions and issue the commands. In both portions, the children's performance anxiety was lowered by being told that they could compare pictures to find out how well the tester issued commands and how well the tester followed directions.

(Carpenter, Fujii and Kataoka, 1995, p. 166)

They were aware of the demands on children in discourse with adults to remain passive and wait for the next question rather than to volunteer information. They found in their trials that assessing young learners in pairs was 'extremely problematic'. This was because the children tended to use more English (their first language); the children appeared to be reluctant to use Japanese together. They also found that after a brief period of negotiation in the pairwork, one member of the pair usually assumed a dominant role, and talked more, while the other child became increasingly passive and talked less (p. 168). They therefore used adult–child interviews, finding ways to minimize problems of shyness and avoidance in the discourse.

Carpenter and her colleagues catered to children's developmental needs in their test. They observed that children are less likely than adults even to attempt an utterance that they feel they might get stuck in, even if they possess the competence to begin it.

Failure to respond on the part of the child could be due to uncertainty over one vocabulary item, or it could be due to lack of one vocabulary item, or it could be due to lack of any knowledge of the relevant grammatical structures, or it could be due to a conservative or reticent personality on the part of the child.

(Carpenter, Fujii and Kataoka, 1995, p. 160)

The researchers realized that children responded to some items by moving items randomly rather than saying 'I don't understand', 'Could you repeat that?' 'What's sushi?'. The socially determined discourse strategies of young children with adults could clearly, then, intervene in our judgments of children's proficiency. The young child, in these situations, may simply be waiting for confirmation, not being aware of the importance of 'getting it right the first time'. In another strategy the researchers used two interviewers in the adult–child interviews rather than one. The first interviewer used the child's first language, English, and talked to the child, putting him or her at ease. The second interviewer used only the target language, Japanese. This strategy was designed both to put the child at ease by using his first language, but also to help minimize the child's temptation to resort to English in the main part of the interview with the Japanese-only speaking adult. Illustrations shown one by one to children tended to be treated by children as separate units. This did not elicit paragraphs or a connected story in the children's talk about the pictures (Carpenter, Fujii and Kataoka, 2000). Carpenter therefore revised the presentation of the text by showing the children the entire sequence of pictures first, and then asking for the story, with better results.

Carpenter's team compared the results of their test with the results of a test they had been using, adapted from the SOPA (Spanish Oral Proficiency Assessment) test, administered to 40 children, and analysed all utterances of two children representing opposite ends of the proficiency spectrum. The SOPA is based on an oral proficiency test for older children known as the CAL Oral Proficiency Exam or COPE (Rhodes and Thomas, 1990) and is appropriate for first- to fourth-grade immersion students. They found that their test elicited a greater percentage of complete sentences and more sophisticated grammatical productions in students, more attempted verb uses, a greater variety of verb types, and a wider variety of noun types. They concluded that their test 'elicits a more representative sample of children's abilities, independently of their shyness or talkativeness' (p. 169). This might have been due, in large part, to their ability to target their test characteristics to the characteristics of their young learners.

Carpenter's research is one of the few examples of research into assessment of young learners that treats the design, implementation and evaluation of the assessment procedure in such depth. This is an example of research that can be of great value to other researchers and to teachers in young learner assessment.

Finding out about the nature of young learner language use ability and language growth

The third purpose of assessment in young learner assessment is to find out more about the nature of growth in language use ability.

Investigating the nature of language ability

We need to know more about the nature of the language that language learners need to be able to use and understand. In foreign language situations and in second language situations this is usually done through a needs analysis of the real-life situation, indicating the kinds of language children will need when they use the language in the real world.

For second language learners, the real world is in the here and now of the classroom. Bailey and Butler (2002) have been carrying out needs analyses of the world of science classrooms, in order to find out more about how to assess ESL children's science abilities. They examined the language functions used by science teachers and the instructional contexts in which these appear in fourth- and fifth-grade science classes. They also examined the language used in print materials selected by teachers, and evidence of academic language in student talk and written products. From this, they have been able to construct meaningful measures of the readiness of second language learners to enter mainstream content instruction.

> As with teacher talk, students were mainly explaining, describing, and comparing scientific concepts. They also asked the teacher questions of scientific substance and added commentary in isolated cases. In terms of repair strategies, students both requested and provided clarification, and showed understanding of classroom management by their appropriate responses to teacher questioning.
>
> (Bailey and Butler, 2002, p. 9)

These researchers continue to build on this and previous work into academic proficiency in the school context (e.g., Stevens, Butler and Castellon-Wellington, 2000; Butler, Lord, Stevens, Borrego and Bailey, 2004). Other work helps to define learner language need and proficiency growth using a framework approach. Bachman and Palmer (1996) provide their framework of language ability as described in this book. The Common European Framework of Reference for Languages outlines a descriptive scheme of language, detailing categories of language use, the domains and situations providing the contexts for language use, the themes, tasks and purposes of communication, communicative activities, strategies and processes, and text. Curriculum writers, teachers and assessors are able to refer to these frameworks to conceptualize language ability and to designate the language needs of their learners.

Investigating language growth

No assessment scales describing progress of young learners' language ability were available until the early 1990s, when work began in various parts of the world on the development of ability scales and standards for school-age second language learners. The first scale was developed in the United Kingdom by Hester (1996); this was a short five-level scale that mapped young learners' developing language proficiency in the school context. The Australian (NLLIA) ESL Bandscales (McKay, Hudson and Sapuppo, 1994) were developed soon after, providing a more detailed set of descriptors for school-age second language learners, with two separate scales for young learners (junior and middle/upper elementary). Soon after, a number of standards documents began to document progress in language learning. For example, expected or hoped-for outcomes at each grade level were documented in the California Department of Education (2003) Standards for Grades K-4, illustrated in Table 3.5. The California Draft Interim Standards were organized around five goals: (1) To communicate in languages other than English; (2) To gain knowledge and understanding of their cultures; (3) To connect with other disciplines and acquire information; (4) To develop insight into our own language and culture; and (5) To participate in multilingual communities at home and around the world.

The purpose of the California standards was to provide a basis for the monitoring of progress of cohorts of students over time, and therefore to enable accountability checks across the sytem. The California Department of Education now has a new curriculum framework for foreign languages on its website. Around the same time in the United States the ESL

Table 3.5 *Targeted standards for foreign language: Draft Interim Standards (California Department of Education)*

Grade 1:
2 Students engage in conversations, provide and obtain information, express feelings and emotions and exchange opinions.
3 Students demonstrate an understanding of the relationship between the products and perspectives of the cultures studied.

Grade 2
1 Students engage in conversations, provide and obtain information, express feelings and emotions and exchange opinions.
2 Students understand, and interpret written and spoken language on a variety of topics.
3 Students demonstrate an understanding of the relationship between the products and perspectives of the cultures studied.
4 Students demonstrate an understanding of the concept of culture through comparisons of the cultures studied and their own.

Standards for Pre-K-12 Students (TESOL, 1997) were being developed by the TESOL Association. These were designed to establish a common framework of understanding in the ESL profession about the goals and processes of teaching and learning for ESL learners in schools across the United States. A more recent example of standards are the English Language Proficiency Standards for English Language Learners in Kindergarten through Grade 12 (WIDA Consortium, 2004). These standards have been developed by a consortium of states in the USA as the basis for research and development related to the assessment of ESL learners for accountability purposes. They provide a new dimension to ESL standards because they describe language development within subject content areas (language arts, social studies, mathematics and science). These are just some examples of standards designed to establish outcomes and monitor progress in language learning. Now many countries around the world (e.g., Hong Kong, South Africa and Malaysia) include standards in their curriculum documents. Because writers of standards tend to refer to already published standards, there is a sense that there may have been a circular development of descriptions around the world. We need empirical research to check that we have valid descriptors of young learners' language learning progress (see below). In Chapter 8, I give three more examples of standards documents and discuss issues around their construction and use.

Johnstone (2000) is one researcher amongst many who has pointed out that these descriptions of progress, generally prepared by teachers who are recalling their own experience of what can be expected, may have questionable validity. How do we know that these standards and outcomes provide us with valid descriptions of growth? Are the descriptors organized validly into each level? McKay (2000), drawing on the experience of developing a set of bandscales for ESL school learners from K-12 (McKay, Hudson and Sapuppo, 1994) has provided a series of questions to evaluate standards.

- Are the purposes for the standards clear?
- Do the standards provide separate descriptions for young learners?
- Have principled decisions informed the construction of the standards?
- Is the choice of descriptor-type appropriate to the purpose and appropriate for ESL description?
- Do the descriptors convey a sense of what we know about second language learning of school ESL learners learning in mainstream contexts?
- Are accompanying assessment procedures valid?

Other developers of standards have written about the principles underpinning their descriptions of language development. Hester (1996) was a pioneer in this area of elementary second language education and writes of the need to consider attitudes and feelings, and to take into account the social context in which the children are learning (p.184). She believes that descriptions of learner progress should recognize the importance of the continuing use and development of the first language and also recognize that children will take on language in individual ways. Children might broadly follow the pathways outlined in the descriptions, but teachers and assessors should recognize individual characteristics of development, and record and report on these individual differences qualitatively.

Levels of progress have also been derived from the Common European Framework of Reference (Council of Europe, 2001). Johnstone (2000) suggests that even this 'distinguished' scheme must be treated with caution when applied to young learners, since statements such as

> 'I can use simple phrases and sentences to describe where I live and people I know'
> [do] not reflect the songs, poems, games and aspects of mathematics, science, history, geography and drama that young language learners soon experience through their foreign language, and which enables them to pull chunks of language from their long-term memory store that can go well beyond 'simple phrases and sentences.'
>
> (Johnstone, 2000, p. 132)

To summarize concerns over standards, critics of standards comment on the following issues, calling for empirical research to examine these issues further:

- the actual levels of achievement possible in different foreign language learning contexts at elementary level and thus the appropriateness of current standards
- the validity of current standards documents (the degree to which the description is a true representation of second language acquisition; the degree to which the descriptions include the components of learning that represent progress in language learning; the degree to which the standards represent the growth patterns of the learners being assessed)
- the validity of teachers' assessments using standards (including the variability of tasks used to assess the same descriptors)

- the nature of the impact of different types of descriptions on teaching and learning
- the nature of the impact of the use of the standards on children and their families.

Empirical approaches to validation

Butler and Stevens (1998) are amongst the few researchers known to the writer who have approached the question of validity of standards through an empirical process. This research is described in Chapter 9. In Australia a research project is also underway (Mckay, Queensland University of Technology) to validate the Australian (NLLIA) ESL Bandscales (McKay, Hudson and Sapuppo, 1994) through focus groups, teacher interviews around children's progress and analyses of children's samples of work. A statistical procedure, Rasch analysis, may also be used. The use of Rasch analysis in language assessment and in the validation of language scales is addressed in detail by McNamara (1996) and North (1995) who have used this statistical procedure in the validation of scales for adults. This research gives researchers a closer look at language proficiency growth of second language learners, which, backed up by empirical methods, may bring more trustworthiness in descriptions of language progress.

Investigating and improving the impact of assessment on young language learners

One quality of tests or assessment procedures is their impact on society and educational systems and upon the individuals within those systems (Bachman and Palmer, 1996, p. 29). Most educators and parents would accept that assessment practices could potentially have a negative impact on young learners unless they are carried out with extreme care. We thus need to know, and have clear evidence about, the effect of class-room-based assessment and large-scale tests, and the ways that test bias can influence children. We also need to find ways that we can apply assessment research to improving teachers' understandings about assessment, therefore promoting positive impact. In addition, we need to know more about the influence of teachers' professional understandings about assessment on the quality of learning.

The impact of classroom assessment

How much do we know about the impact of classroom assessment on young learners? Most classroom research is concerned with the processes of assessment (e.g., Rea-Dickins and Rixon, 1997; Rea-Dickins and Gardner, 2000). Some research is now underway into the impact of classroom assessment on teachers who are now required to report against standards and to prepare children for large-scale tests tied to standards (e.g., McKay, 2004). Teachers become stressed and resentful of the time taken in assessment and paperwork, and there is clear evidence of stress on young second language learners as they are prepared for large-scale tests through mini practice paper-based tests in the classroom. More research of this nature is needed.

In Hong Kong where pressure from tests and examinations is high, Carless and Wong (2000) have found that less successful pupils in English language classrooms become easily discouraged. At elementary school in Hong Kong, children learning English as a foreign language have at least two tests for each subject every school term and a 'surfeit of homework'. It is possible that the children may already be discouraged by previous assessment procedures or negative learning experiences when they face the assessment procedures.

Looking for positive impact in large-scale tests

Large-scale, standardized tests, prepared centrally may lead to negative impact on young learners, both at the micro and the macro level (see next section). However, some researchers have found that there are opportunities to avoid negative impact in large-scale external assessment. Norway's innovative large-scale assessment described above was possible because there was no requirement for formal reporting of results. Formal assessment would mean that a new test would be needed each year to ensure security. Hasselgren (2000, p. 267) has reported that because the testing was entirely up to teachers, and supported by professional development activities, a positive washback resulted as teachers participated in the research and brought these opportunities for flexibility and creativity.

Some assessments are designed primarily to motivate rather than to discriminate amongst student performances, and this approach is likely to result in a more positive impact on teachers and students.

A large-scale test of foreign language for school learners, the Australian Language Certificates (Australian Council of Educational Research) is one such battery of tests. These tests, designed for both elementary and secondary language learners, has no "fail" result; all children pass, and do so at different levels. Teachers volunteer their classes to participate. The test is administered by an independent research agency, separate from educational authorities who nowadays carry with them real or imagined undertones of accountability. Research around the use of the certificates by teachers and schools found that the majority of survey respondents do use the tests for their motivational value, but that they are also used for a range of other purposes including monitoring progress from year to year, as a model to develop teachers' own tests, to practise and extend skills, as a teaching resource, and to expose students to testing in a language. Most of the extended purposes show that the certificates are likely to be having a positive impact on teaching and learning. The Cambridge Young Learner English Tests (University of Cambridge ESOL Examinations, 2003), described in detail in Chapter 9, are also tests designed to motivate, through the achievement of certificates. All children who participate take the test at three different levels (Starters, Movers and Flyers) and each student 'receives an award which focuses on what they can do (rather than what they can't do) and gives the children credit for having taken part in the test' (University of Cambridge ESOL Examinations, 2003, p. 7). While the aim is to motivate, it is inevitable that sometimes these tests are also used to discriminate (e.g., at the local level, the test may be used as an entrance test). This kind of use is beyond the jurisdiction of the test developers, who make it clear that the test is not designed for this purpose. Another assessment tool, the European Language Portfolio (Ingeborg, 1998), is also designed to motivate children through awareness of their progress through self-assessment. Research into assessment strategies such as these that may achieve positive impact can alert educators to large-scale assessment possibilities appropriate for young language learners.

Research into test bias

Researchers have been concerned with test bias, and the negative impact of standardized tests on second language learners in the USA, as well as everywhere, for a number of years (for overviews, see, for example, Valdes and Figueroa, 1994; August and Hakuta, 1997). **Standardized tests** are those that have been prepared with careful attention to validity and reliability, the establishment of norms, and the use of uniform and standard procedures (Richard, Platt and Weber, 1985). It has been reported in this research that major injustices have resulted from content-based achievement tests that have been culturally biased, have failed to control for socioeconomic factors and have not assessed content knowledge in the children's first language. Researchers in the UK and Australia too, where the National Curriculum and common Literacy Benchmarks are used to monitor and report on progress of the whole population regardless of ESL background, have observed negative impact on ESL children. Negative impact has been evident in children's and parents' sense of failure (despite often strong progress in second language terms), in the resulting 'invisibility' of the specific learning needs of ESL learners in teaching and in professional development, and in strategies some schools use to exclude or at least hide ESL learners with lower marks in the test results.(e.g., Leung, 1996; McKay, 2001).

Butler and Stevens' (1997) research into accommodations is targeted directly at avoiding the negative consequences of large-scale content-based assessment on second language learners in the USA. **Accommodations** are strategies used in tests to give test takers an opportunity to perform to their best ability. They are designed to redress disadvantage. Thus accommodations for second language learners in a large-scale content test might be that the test takers are allowed to use a dictionary, or are given more time. Butler and Stevens have found that different learners may benefit from different types of accommodations. They recommend specifications for the development and use of accommodations, and training for test administrators in their use. (See Chapter 9 for more details.)

Research is regularly and systematically carried out into the Cambridge Young Learner English tests in order to check for test bias (Ball and Wilson, 2002; Marshall and Gutteridge, 2002). A corpus of Young Learner Speaking Test performances has been collected to provide data about what happens in speaking tests, and to make decisions about further tests (Ball and Wilson, 2002, p. 8). Data is analysed about children's performance at each level; this reveals, for example, whether appropriate patterns of performance occur at the different levels (Marshall and Gutteridge, 2002). The test is also reviewed from time to time and minor adjustments made where necessary. Research accompanies large-scale tests to ensure that children are given the fairest test, devoid of test bias.

Research leading to improved teachers' understandings about assessment

Researchers have found that many teachers of young language learners are not skilled in language assessment. We need research that has a positive impact on teachers' understandings about the why, what and how of assessment for young learners.

Gatullo (2000) gives us an example of research where teachers gained skills and confidence as a result of the research project in which they worked collaboratively on classroom-based assessment. Hasselgren (2000) also reports on teachers' increased understandings after an innovative state-wide, teacher-based assessment. Liddicoat (1997) worked with groups of teachers to provide samples of work to underpin descriptions of progress in foreign language standards. These activities followed a planned research design which elicited data for the researcher, but at the same time gave teachers hands-on experience with materials and procedures, and opportunities to learn. The impact on learners in these kinds of research projects is very likely to be positive.

Summary

An overview of research into young learner assessment helps language teachers and tertiary educators to understand the scope of issues that are currently relevant and probably need improving, and where further knowledge is needed. Research, too, indicates that the profession is taking itself seriously, and sharing its expertise and research findings. There are challenges for researchers of young learner assessment, with variability of programmes, lack of consensus about proficiency and variable teacher expertise the most evident. These challenges make it difficult for researchers in both foreign language and second language research to carry out research.

Four main purposes for research provide a useful way to organize a discussion of the scope of research in young learner assessment. The first purpose is to investigate and share information about current practices. Ideas about assessment of young language learners are available in a number of teaching publications. Some research on tasks and procedures is produced in language testing journals, but to date this is not extensive.

The second purpose is to find ways to ensure valid and fair assessment practices. Factors that affect performance of young language learners are multidimensional, involving complex interrelationships amongst the characteristics of the children, their learning context and the task. Examples of research into fair assessment practice for young learners show that more research is needed in this area. Assessment carried out by the teacher in the classroom is a rapidly growing area of interest in research. The role of teachers as mediators in classroom assessment is important and requires further investigation. Teachers interpret criteria and report on learner performance through the filter of their knowledge of individual pupils, and their awareness of the requirements of stake-holders. Research interest in this area has developed as standards documents require teacher-based assessment and reporting.

The third purpose of research that I have identified is to find out more about the nature of young learner language proficiency and language growth. Researchers develop instruments to describe the nature of language proficiency in order to be able to assess it; they also map learner progress over time in order to monitor progress over time. Tests of children's academic language in content-based assessment and language standards have been a recent impetus for this type of research. There are issues in the construction of standards that require further investigation.

The fourth purpose is to investigate and improve the impact of assessment on young language learners. Ultimately the impact of young learner assessment is a matter of great concern to educators and parents. Negative impact is possible if assessments are inappropriately constructed or used and if the results are used in ways that influence children's sense of self and parents' attitudes. Research has examined the impact of school and system-wide assessment, and large-scale tests on children. Research into test bias for second language learners in the United States has been reported for a number of years. Research has also been conducted by developers of large tests. Under this purpose is also research that has led to improved teachers' understandings about assessment, which will often, in turn, have a positive impact of assessment on children, parents and learning.

These purposes are not mutually exclusive; however, they help to present the scope of research and to show examples of the kind of research that is, or needs to be, conducted. In the next chapter we focus on the task as the 'unit of analysis', or focus point, for assessment. The concept of task ties assessment closely into language use as the target for teaching and learning.

CHAPTER FOUR

Assessing language use through tasks

The primary aspiration in language teaching programmes, for most parents and teachers, is that their children will become effective language users, that is, they will be able to communicate in the target language. When children are language users they are able to use the target language to exchange meaning in ways appropriate for the purpose and context. This may happen when they are interacting orally with their teachers, their peers in the classroom or others outside school, or when they are listening to and understanding their teacher talk, and when they are listening to stories or viewing videos. Language use takes place when children are reading stories and information texts and understanding the events, ideas and information in what they read. When children are producing their own writing in the target language, however simple the writing may be, they are using language.

In some teaching situations where external testing exists, parents and teachers also hope that their children will pass the required tests. Most parents and teachers would expect that tests promote their children's ability to use the language, though this is not always the case. Since external language tests can influence strongly the nature of language teaching and learning in the classroom, the alignment of formal tests with language use is highly desirable, as I discuss further in Chapter 9. Language educators can ensure that children learn to become language users by giving them the kinds of learning opportunities and conditions I described in Chapter 2. Alongside this, assessment can be structured so that it supports the development of language use; this is done by assessing primarily through language use tasks. Language use tasks give teachers and assessors information about the child's ability to use language in communicative ways.

Recent developments in performance assessment have provided new directions in assessment that inform the approach to assessment through language use tasks. Therefore the first section of this chapter looks at the assumptions and characteristics of performance assessment. Further principles of effective task-based assessment of young learners follow. These assumptions underpin the approach to assessment adopted in this book. Through language use tasks children have the opportunity to show their ability to use language, exchanging meaning according to their own purposes, and in spontaneous ways according to the context.

Principles and frameworks for the selection of language use assessment tasks are needed, whether for the classroom or for external tests. How do teachers and assessors select the best assessment tasks for young learners? What kinds of assessment tasks give children the best learning opportunities, as well as the best opportunity to show what they can do? Wrongly selected assessment tasks may disadvantage some children. Some children may require support during tasks – are there ways that assessment tasks can be analysed beforehand to ensure that adjustments can be made to ensure the child's best performance? Principles and frameworks for the selection of assessment tasks are provided in this chapter before we move on to ways of assessing in the classroom in the next chapter.

Performance assessment

I use 'performance assessment' here as an overall term to refer to a family of like-minded assessment approaches including 'alternative' and 'authentic' assessment (see, for example, Herman, Aschbacher and Winters, 1992; O'Malley and Valdez Pierce, 1996). Performance assessment refers to assessment that 'involves either the observation of behavior in the real world or a simulation of a real-life activity' (Weigle, 2002). In these approaches, assessment through **selected-response items** is avoided. The item in Figure 4.1 in which children are asked to select the right word is a selected-response item. It is also called a **discrete-point** assessment item because it is intended to measure one point of language knowledge only (in this case knowledge of accurate use of personal possessive pronouns).

Fill in the blanks with the correct words from the box. You may use the words more than once

my	her	his	our	their	she	your

She has a dog. She likes to play with _____ dog.
I have a storybook. Would you like to borrow _____ book?
He has a canary. He takes good care of _____ bird.

Figure 4.1 Example of discrete-point assessment: a fill-in-the-blank task. *only assess 1 point of lang. knowledge*

In **performance assessment** teachers tend to avoid using assessment items like the one above that specifically target language for its own sake. Rather, performance assessments give children opportunities to use the language for real purposes, and in real or realistic situations, and assess their attempts to do so successfully. Children's grammar and vocabulary knowledge is assessed as part of their performance in real-world or realistic tasks rather than separately in discrete-point assessment items. Teachers can observe and evaluate the performance as a whole (did they achieve the purpose of the task?) and also the elements of language use, such as vocabulary and grammar, within the performance in the task (to what extent did they use a range of vocabulary? To what extent was the performance accurate?). Performance assessment involves teachers and assessors making decisions on performance by checking performance against criteria, rather than by comparing students' performance against the average performance of all learners. Ways to do this in language assessment are described in Chapter 8.

The principles of performance assessment also stretch beyond assessment into the teaching and learning process. The assumptions and characteristics of performance assessment have been summarized by one writer as follows:

- Students are active participants rather than passive subjects
- Evaluation and guidance occur simultaneously and continuously
- Processes as well as products are evaluated
- Development and learning need to be recognized and celebrated
- Multiple indicators and sources of evidence are collected over time
- Results of the assessment are used to plan instruction, improve classroom practice, and optimize children's learning
- The assessment process is collaborative among parents, teachers, children, and other professionals as needed

(Jalongo, 2000, p. 287)

Thus, performance assessment brings with it both a focus on children's abilities in real-world tasks, but also attention to broader characteristics of assessment that encourage amongst other things active participation, attention to the processes of learning, and involvement of parents and children in the assessment process. The various assumptions and characteristics of performance assessment underpin the approach to assessment outlined in this book. Young learners learn best through activities that are concrete and meaningful, and evidence of their language learning is most likely to be present in language use assessment tasks that have similar characteristics to those in the child's real world. Performance assessment has had a major influence on thinking in assessment in recent years; this influence has been particularly strong in classroom-based assessment where there have been more opportunities to implement some of the ideas, than, for example, in external testing. However, there continues to be a push to incorporate characteristics of performance-based assessment into more formal assessment situations, including large-scale testing. → would not be practical

Language use tasks

We will now look more closely at a definition and examples of language use tasks. Tasks, traditionally discussed as teaching activities with an intended pedagogical purpose (Purpura, 2004) have more recently been characterized by their ability to elicit interaction and negotiation of meaning and to engage learners in complex meaning-focused activities (Nunan, 1989, 1993; Berwick, 1993; Skehan, 1998). This emphasis on the communicative goals of tasks is taken up in the definition of a language use task used in this book. A language use task is 'an activity that involves individuals in using language for the purpose of achieving a particular goal or objective in a particular situation' (Bachman and Palmer, 1996, p. 44). Language use tasks are goal-oriented, meaning that the learner knows what is to be achieved in the task, and they are specific to a particular situation. Each instance of language use is virtually unique (Bachman and Palmer, 1996, p. 44). Language use tasks can involve listening, speaking, reading or writing and may entail a combination of these activities.

I interpret and expand this definition for young learners. In language use tasks, children's language participation involves a degree of spontaneity and creativity; they make their own meaning, producing meaning or comprehending meaning, according to the purpose and the requirements of the situation. The creativity and spontaneity rests in children drawing from their 'language resource', that is, from the language and language rules they have internalized. These may be chunks of unanalysed language or new rule-based constructions (see Chapter 2). Children use this language to fulfil a communicative purpose and do so in an appropriate way for the language use context. Language use tasks can take place in a very simple and supported way, or in a more extended, complex and independent way. We do not necessarily expect creative language use in language use tasks to be accurate, wide in vocabulary use or appropriate, but we expect to see growth in these features as experience grows. Language use tasks do not necessarily need to be noisy or time-consuming (characteristics that are avoided in some teaching situations).

The example of a language assessment task for beginning young language learners in Figure 4.2 involves children filling in blanks in sentences helping them to write about a story they have heard. They are asked to use their own words to fill in the gaps. The task is different from the discrete-point item in Figure 4.1 above because it has gaps for children's own language. Children can write the story they have heard in their own words, with support from the part-sentences supplied, and the teacher can expect to find some spontaneous language use in the gaps. This simple task requires children to write a story (the purpose) in language appropriate to a narrative (the situation). The task could be left more open, with children being able to choose what happened in the story.

The example of a language assessment task shown in Figure 4.3 is for more advanced language learners. Children are asked to write what happened in a science experiment they have observed. The questions give them guides for the task and, at the same time, provide a learning structure for a procedural genre.

Children are given a stapled booklet with eight pages, with a simple story written by the teacher through the pages. There are blanks in the sentences on some pages. Children are asked to fill in the blanks, and to draw a picture for each page, illustrating what is happening in the story. The children have already heard the story: it has been read to them several times, and talked about in classroom activities.

Page 1:   The little girl's name was Jane.

Page 2:   One day she found a ....

Page 3:   She felt very .... about this.

Page 4:   Then she ....

Figure 4.2 Example of a language use task for beginning young language learners.

Children have observed a simple science experiment. They take notes. They are then asked to write what happened in the science experiment. They have been given a paper with headings to guide them.

Name: _____

> What were we trying to find out?
>
> Describe the equipment that was used.
>
> What did we do?
>
> What happened?
>
> What did we find out?

Figure 4.3 Example of a language use task for more advanced young language learners.

Language use tasks in the classroom

There is virtually an infinite number of language use tasks that can be used in assessing young language learners. Many classroom language teaching tasks can be used for assessment. Teachers might observe children's performance through the task, carry out on-the-run assessment as they teach, or set up the task for formal assessment with criteria made known to the children at the beginning of the task. On-the-run assessment is that which is integrated into the busy-ness of teaching (see Chapter 5). The following list of classroom language use tasks (Table 4.1) from Williams (1994) evokes the young learner language classroom and illustrates the characteristics of tasks that are suitable for young language learner assessment. Many, if not all, of the teaching and learning tasks used in the classroom, or parts of them, may be suitable for assessment. While these tasks are aimed at children at the lower end of elementary school, adaptations of these, moving into more content-based instruction, would be suitable for learners in upper elementary school.

Teachers are able to select from a range of different language use tasks, depending on the proficiency level of the children and their interests and the demands of the curriculum. Tasks can involve problem-solving, they can be information gap tasks (where children need to find out information to complete the task), opinion gap tasks (where children have to find out someone else's opinion in order to complete the task), affective gap tasks (where children have to find out what others are feeling to complete the task), games, drama tasks, tasks using pictures, literature-based tasks,

Table 4.1 *Examples of classroom language use tasks for young learners (Williams, 1994, p. 209)*

Doing puzzles and solving problems	Writing and solving riddles	Using maps
Measuring and weighing things	Conducting surveys (e.g., food, birthdays, traffic surveys)	Growing plants
Following and writing recipes	Interviewing people (e.g., parents, people in the neighbourhood, different occupations)	Making things (e.g., witches, spacemen, stranded on an island)
Inventing and designing things (my ideal . . . A machine to . . . fashions)	Planning things (e.g., an outing, a party)	Inventing games (e.g., board games, writing the instructions)
Choosing (e.g., films, clothes)	Writing letters (for real purposes)	Reading and designing brochures
Designing and recording a TV programme	Finding out (e.g., what things are made of, what materials are used for, how things grow, whether objects float or sink)	Filling in forms
Studying the local environment (e.g., plants, birds, buildings)	Making charts and graphs	Using songs and rhymes
Listening to stories (a particularly motivating form of language input, and recommended as a daily activity)	Painting, drawing and talking about what we are doing	

and writing tasks to name a few (Scarino, Vale, McKay and Clark, 1988, Book 4, p. 29). Many games and drama tasks are suited for classroom assessment where the teacher observes and notes children's performance as the rhythm of the task proceeds. Personalized assessment tasks are suitable for young learners – that is, tasks where the topic is related to their own interests and lives. Expressive writing about oneself and one's family and friends, questionnaires and surveys, individual interviews about feelings and ideas are examples of personalized tasks. Literature-based tasks are very suitable for all learners (Falvey and Kennedy, 1997). Literature-based tasks generally use stories that children have been reading. Children may, for example, read stories aloud (assessing their ability to read this level of text aloud), draw pictures based on a part of the story (assessing various constructs including comprehension of the sequence of events in the story, comprehension of description), write questions about a story or a poem (assessing comprehension as well as ability to write questions), complete an unfinished story or play (assessing comprehension of the story so far, as well as ability to write and to write creatively), or answer questions about the story (assessing different levels of comprehension depending on whether the questions are literal or interpretive). The following task is a simple writing task asking children to read a poem and answer a question.

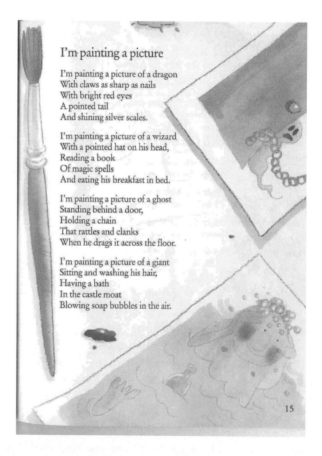

I'm painting a picture

I'm painting a picture of a dragon
With claws as sharp as nails
With bright red eyes
A pointed tail
And shining silver scales.

I'm painting a picture of a wizard
With a pointed hat on his head,
Reading a book
Of magic spells
And eating his breakfast in bed.

I'm painting a picture of a ghost
Standing behind a door,
Holding a chain
That rattles and clanks
When he drags it across the floor.

I'm painting a picture of a giant
Sitting and washing his hair,
Having a bath
In the castle moat
Blowing soap bubbles in the air.

15

What is the wizard doing in bed? Write down what you think.

Figure 4.4 An example of a literature-based response (Poem from Foster and Lewis, 1996)

Classroom teaching affords many opportunities for language use assessment to be embedded in teaching tasks. In Cameron's (2001) teaching task framework in Figure 4.5 there is at least one language use assessment task (see teaching activity in bold) that gives the teacher opportunities to assess children's language use. In this assessment task, early language learners are asked to write their own sentences about Hani's weekend. Children will be putting into action the language they have recalled and practised in the teaching task. There are also on-the-run assessment opportunities to observe children's developing vocabulary and grammar, and their ability to construct the sentences that are being practised.

TASK Say sentences about Hani's weekend			
	Preparation	CORE	*Follow up*
Language learning goals	Activate previously learnt lexis. Practise past forms of verbs.	Oral production of sentences from grid.	Written production of Hani's sentences. Composition of own sentences.
Teaching activities	Teacher-led: (1) Use of single pictures to prompt recall of lexis. (2) Divide board into two and recall/practise past forms. (3) Pairs practise with single pictures.	(1) Whole class introduction of grid and teacher modelling of sentences (2) Pair production of own sentences about Hani's weekend e.g. P1 points to a box and P2 says sentence.	(1) Teacher writes key words on board, next to pictures. (2) Teacher models writing sentence from grid. (3) **Pupils write own sentences about Hani's weekend.** (4) Pair checking of accuracy.

Figure 4.5 An example of an embedded language use assessment task in a classroom teaching task (Cameron, 2001, p. 34)

Language use tasks therefore give teachers opportunities in the classroom to assess children's ability to use language. Chapter 5 deals in more detail with language assessment in the classroom.

The place of selected-response and limited-response tasks in young learner language assessment

In **selected-response tasks**, children are expected to select a response from input which may be language (spoken or written) or non-language (e.g., pictures). Selected-response tasks include multiple-choice items, picture cloze and picture-matching vocabulary items, where children are given input (lists of words, pictures) from which to select. **Limited-production tasks** are those in which only a limited response is required, usually a word or a sentence. Limited-production items include gap-fill (where children fill in a gap in a sentence), fill-in-the-blank items and short-answer tasks. Selected-response and limited-production tasks are often used with young learners because of their limited language proficiency, and because they need support within the task to understand what is required and to be able to complete the requirements of the task.

Selected-response items and limited-production items may be **language-use oriented** or they may be **language-item oriented**. This distinction is important for those involved in the assessment of young learners. In the example of a language-use oriented selected-response task used in the Cambridge Young Learner Test in Figure 4.6, children are required to listen to a tape-recording of a description of a scene at the beach. They have a picture in front of them showing children and adults playing, doing different things (playing with a ball, rowing, eating an ice cream and sitting under an umbrella). A list of names accompanies the picture. The children are asked to draw a line from the name to the action. This item involves the specific ability to listen for detail. The item has been checked with children for its age-appropriateness. Children are using language when they listen to the input, look at the picture and make a decision about who is doing what.

Language-item oriented selected-response and limited-production tasks need to be used with more care with young learners. Examples of these are gap-fill items (*She is _____ some water to make a cup of tea. (1) baking (2) steaming (3) boiling (4) roasting)* and change-the-structure items (*Kelly wants to be a singer. She wants to sing*) where children are asked to repeat the same change in other similar sentences. These items are generally concerned with vocabulary or grammar. Although these tasks can be said to involve some use of language, they do not involve children in language use as we have defined it above, that is, in purposeful, creative and spontaneous language use in a particular situation.

Taped input:
After giving an example of what is required, the instructions are 'Now you listen and draw lines'

One

Male	Who's the baby playing on the beach?
Female	That's Sally.
M	Oh Right! Her Dad's with her.
F	Yes. He's putting the lunch out.

Two

M	Look at the old man.
F	That's Fred. He's sleeping in the chair.
M	He read his book and then went to sleep, I think.
F	Yes.

Answer sheet:

Figure 4.6 Example of a listening assessment task (University of Cambridge ESOL Examinations, 2002, p. 23).

They are low in if not devoid of contextual support, and lack authenticity. Purpura (2004) discusses the place of these kinds of items in the assessment of grammar and vocabulary; he recognizes some value for them in certain assessment purposes (e.g., where the aim is to emphasize individual grammatical forms, such as in form-focused instruction) but repeats an earlier comment:

> context-independent, discrete-point tasks, or those that lack authenticity of topic, are perceived by current and past students, teachers, administrators and content teachers as being 'old-fashioned' and 'out-of-touch' with their language learning goals.
>
> (Purpura, 2004, p. 253)

Language-item oriented selected-response and limited-response items can be used with care by teachers and assessors:

- in the classroom, to diagnose specific underlying skills and abilities (e.g., ability to discriminate different sounds; knowledge of selected vocabulary and grammar items; ability to read or hear specific information in a text and select the most appropriate response from a given list);
- in external tests, to test specific contributing knowledge and skills. They are combined with language use tasks (extended-response tasks) to gain an understanding of children's language use ability in the domains of language use being tested.

The use of selected-response and limited-response items therefore requires some careful decision-making; about their purpose (is it quite clear whether they are being used to assess language use, or to assess a language item?); about their role in the total assessment procedure (are there accompanying language use tasks in the procedure that assess language use ability?); and about their appropriateness for the learner group (are they cognitively appropriate for the young learners in question?). The use of the framework for the selection of tasks presented later in this chapter will help teachers and assessors to make decisions about the use of these types of tasks.

Selecting appropriate assessment tasks and procedures for young learners

What principles lie behind the selection of assessment tasks? Are some assessment tasks better than others?

Language assessment tasks may be selected by the classroom language teacher, by the textbook writer or by others, for example other teachers in the school, test developers in the education department and in commercial testing companies. These language assessment tasks may stand alone, or may be part of an assessment procedure consisting of assessment across a number of tasks. For example, teacher observation, portfolios and self-assessment (described in the next chapter) are assessment procedures.

The following are considerations in the selection of language assessment tasks and procedures.

Some first-base principles to guide the selection of assessment tasks and procedures

The following are some first-base guiding principles on selecting tasks and procedures for the assessment of young learners. These first principles come primarily from young learner education and assessment. They are followed by more specific principles and analytic frameworks taken from the field of assessment.

- *Select tasks and procedures to suit the characteristics of young learners:*   The characteristics of the learners being assessed – their age, their interests and motivations, their social and personal characteristics will be known by the teacher and assessors, who will then be able to select tasks and procedures to suit these characteristics. We have looked in depth at the characteristics of children at different ages in Chapter 1, at their approach to language learning in Chapter 2, and of the implications for assessment of each. Teachers and assessors need to take account of many factors based on their knowledge of the purpose for the task and the characteristics of the learning situation.

- *Assess the learners' most relevant abilities for language use:* Teachers need to make sure that they assess those abilities that children need in order to be successful in their language learning. The curriculum usually establishes the range of knowledge, skills and abilities that need to be taught, and therefore need to be assessed. A communicative curriculum would establish the ability to use the target language as a central goal, with other related goals, for example socio-cultural knowledge, learning-how-to-learn skills and language awareness included.

If no curriculum exists then teachers need to make their own judgment about the relevant abilities to assess. Teachers can carry out a **needs analysis**, a survey of the kind of language abilities children need, at school, in the community, in near-future language use activities (such as a class excursion to a target language speaking environment). Theoretical frameworks of language ability like the Bachman and Palmer (1996) framework of communicative language ability and the Common European Framework (Council of Europe, 2001) can inform teachers about the elements of language proficiency that need to be assessed.

- *Make assessment choices that ensure that assessment is valid and reliable and has a positive impact:* Many questions need to be asked about assessment tasks that are used, both in the classroom and in external tests. Is the task suitable for all children? Is it assessing what it sets out to assess? Is the scoring of the task appropriate? Will the task have a positive impact, for example on learning, and on the children's future progress? Ways to analyse tasks and procedures in relation to these important questions are outlined in the next section.

- *'Bias for best' but maintain high expectations:* The best assessment tasks and procedures are those that give children the chance to show their best performance. Swain (1985) coined the term 'bias for best' to convey this idea. We need to do everything possible to give children the chance to do their best. If a child's performance is not strong, is that because there were factors in the task or the procedure preventing the child from showing what he or she could really do? Did the child have adequate time? Were the instructions given in a way that could be understood? Were there background noises – children playing outside – causing him or her to lose concentration? Were there culturally based references in the task that the child had no experience of? Was the task or procedure sufficiently motivating for this particular child? The analytical tool in the following section provides many more questions that can help teachers and assessors to give children their best chance.

If teachers 'bias for best' there is no implication that the task should then hold low expectations of children. Children will often rise to expectations, if they are given the right conditions and support, and benefit from experiencing success in challenging tasks. Sometimes additional support can be given within an assessment task to assist those who, with just that little extra help, can achieve the task and experience success.

- *Engage learners intellectually:*   Assessment tasks can be appropriate in terms of hitting the right developmental and proficiency level for the children concerned, but at the same time they may be relatively lacking in intellectual challenge for the children. Sometimes a simple task is required and can be balanced with more intellectually challenging tasks. The issue here is asking teachers to question their choice of tasks overall – is there a degree of intellectual challenge for the children within at least some of the tasks?

Children might like the following task because they can do it – it is easy to colour in, and easy to hear the same sentence patterns repeated with substituted words.

> **Instructions: Colour in the picture of the house and garden with the right colour when you hear the sentences.**
>
> Spoken sentences: The house is yellow.
> The trees are green.
> The car is red.
> Etc.

This task gives the teacher information about whether children know their colours, but little else. Making it more intellectually challenging might mean bringing in a story or a problem. The following is a very simple example of how to make a listening task more interesting for young learners. Children need to know a small amount of additional vocabulary, but it would be possible to encourage them to listen for the meaning in the stream of language they hear (that is, they don't have to understand every word to be able to carry out the task).

> Instructions: Mimi is looking for some things in her house. Can you help her find them? If you find what she is looking for, colour it in in the right colour!
> Her book is red. Can you help her find it?
> She has lost her blue toy elephant. Is it there?

Engaging learners intellectually is easier as they get older and as their proficiency grows. General knowledge and curriculum-related topics (from science, social studies, etc.) can be included to enhance interest and motivation.

- *Draw from multiple sources of information:*   It is important to draw from many sources of information when decisions are to be made about children's abilities, especially in high-stakes situations. Teachers should, whenever possible, collect data from a number of different tasks, selected to observe the desired range of behaviour. They should use different procedures if they can – observation, portfolios, self-assessment, quizzes and tests to make sure they gain the most accurate and composite picture of the child's abilities. Making a decision about a child's performance based on one source of information is 'dangerous and maybe even foolish' (Brown and Hudson, 1998). External testers are limited to collecting information from one test – perhaps with around six tasks in it. Because of this the tests are carefully designed and thoroughly trialled. Despite this, external tests are not able to capture the breadth and depth of the child's knowledge and ability. They are used for particular purposes (providing information about progress in comparison with others; giving information about progress on specified areas of the curriculum for motivational purposes) and simply cannot collect information about the full scope of the child's abilities in the same way as the classroom teacher, who has multiple sources of information available to her during the course of her teaching and classroom-based assessment.

These principles are first-base considerations for the selection of assessment tasks and procedures. We will now turn to further ways of analysing tasks and procedures to ensure that they are the best for the children in question, for the assessment purpose and the assessment situation.

Frameworks to analyse assessment tasks and procedures systematically for selection

The assessment field provides us with frameworks and tools to look more closely at the tasks and procedures we use in assessment to make sure they are valid and fair, or 'useful'. The rest of this chapter describes components of an assessment framework that can be used as an additional tool by teachers and assessors to check their selection and design of assessment tasks and procedures. The framework might be understood best through discussions in professional development groups, or in higher degree courses. The framework can be used to enhance teachers' professional understanding, to raise awareness of issues in task selection and design, and to guide opportunities for close planning and analysis of assessment tasks and procedures.

The concept of 'usefulness': ensuring that assessment tasks and procedures provide 'useful' evidence

The concept of 'usefulness' (Bachman and Palmer, 1996) incorporates the idea of fairness, that is, the idea of ensuring that each child receives a score that most closely represents his or her abilities. 'Usefulness' includes important ideas that help us to ensure that assessment procedures will give assessors the best evidence for assessment decisions about children's language use ability. The framework of 'usefulness' is a first-base approach to assessment used in formal assessment situations. There is some debate in the literature about the nature and role of validity and reliability in formative classroom assessment. This issue will be addressed below, and in Chapter 5. Bachman and Palmer suggest that the following questions should be asked about assessment tasks and procedures:

- To what extent are results *reliable?* (To what extent would the child get the same results if another teacher or assessor were to assess their work, or if they were to assess it in the same way again the next day?)
- To what extent is there *construct validity?* (To what extent are the interpretations that teachers and assessors make on the basis of an assessment meaningful and appropriate?)
- To what extent is the assessment task *authentic?* (To what extent does the assessment task reflect the kind of language children use in the classroom, or need in situations outside the classroom?)
- To what extent is the assessment task *interactive?* (To what extent is the child's language ability involved in accomplishing the task?)
- To what extent is the assessment *practical?* (Are there sufficient resources for the task to work in the assessment situation, and with young learners?)
- To what extent is *the impact* of the assessment *positive?* On the learners? On ourselves as teachers? On parents? On society?

Each question is dealing with a particular quality of 'usefulness', summarized below. It is not possible to say that a procedure is absolute, that is, that it is 'reliable' or 'authentic' but rather the quality is described in terms of degree. *This assessment procedure has high degrees of reliability; this procedure is highly interactive.*

To what extent are results reliable?   Reliability refers to the consistency of the scores that teachers and assessors give learners – it is a measure of the degree to which an assessment procedure gives consistent results. We want to know that the results students are given are the same results that we, or another assessor, would give them for the same activity or group of activities on another occasion. If a teacher assesses a child's work at a higher level of ability than another teacher, then there is a low degree of reliability in the scoring of this assessment task. If we give a student different assessment tasks to assess the same ability, but have different results, this is also cause for concern about the reliability of the score.

To what extent is there construct validity?   Construct validity pertains to the meaningfulness and appropriateness of the inferences about students' ability and the decisions teachers and assessors make about students on the basis of the assessment procedures used. If, in the assessment of children's language ability, it is decided that we are aiming for their ability to use language, for example to tell the class something about their weekend, or to read and comprehend a short paragraph, that is our 'construct' or the theoretical definition of the ability we are looking for. Teachers and assessors therefore need to be sure that the interpretations of the scores on an assessment task are a reflection of the nominated construct and very little else (Bachman and Palmer, 1996). If the aim is to assess the ability to 'engage in a simple conversation' it is important to make sure that the conversation is not concerned with concepts that are too difficult for the child (for example, concerned with things in the future that the child is unable to imagine yet). The child may be able to talk about home and school, or about objects and pictures placed in front of him or her, but being asked to talk about abstract concepts hampers the child's ability to engage in the conversation successfully. The inferences that would be made about the child's ability to engage in a simple conversation about such a topic would not be valid.

To what extent is the assessment task authentic?   Teachers would generally want assessment tasks to be as authentic as possible, that is, they want children to be using language in tasks that are relevant and natural to the child's world. Paper-and-pencil tests have little if any authenticity to the child's world; writing e-mails to pen-pals has some authenticity for upper elementary foreign language learners keen to find out about children their own age in the target country; playing a fun game in the foreign language has high authenticity for young learners; and listening to a teacher's talk on social studies has very high authenticity for a second language learner who is studying in a mainstream classroom. Because young learners are growing, and changing in their use of language as they develop cognitively and socially, there is a question concerning the language they should be learning (and being assessed for). Should we be looking beyond the current world of the child to the future world? Cameron (2001) suggests children can be helped to grow into the language they will need as they grow older. ✴ assess children for both

> What 'real language use' (Skehan 1995: 23) is for these children is not obvious; it might be seen as the language used by native speaker 7 and 9 year olds, but by the time they have learnt it, they will be 9 and 10 years old, and will no longer need to talk about, say, teddy bears or dolls. The best we can do is aim for *dynamic congruence*: choosing activities and content that are *appropriate* for the children's age and sociocultural experience, and language that will *grow with* the children, in that, although some vocabulary will no longer be needed, most of the language will provide a useful base for more grown-up purposes.
> (Cameron, 2001, p. 30)

To what extent is the assessment task interactive? An interactive task engages children in using the language knowledge and skills that are being assessed. Without interactiveness there is no evidence of language use on which inferences can be made about the child's proficiency in the language. To give a straightforward example, if teachers give children a task that asks them to sort objects into different colours without having to listen to any instructions, or without having to say anything (that is, without having to use language in any way) the task is not interactive.

To what extent is the assessment task practical? An assessment procedure is practical if the necessary resources are available for it to be implemented. If too many resources (time, space, energy, materials) are needed, then the procedure will be impractical. A teacher might decide to assess all of his 45 foreign language students in a ten-minute individual oral interview. But this will take over seven hours. The ten-minute interviews are impractical in his teaching situation, with the present resources he has available. It might be practical for someone else's teaching situation. Practicality is as important as the other qualities of usefulness: practicality is needed if assessment procedures are to be 'useful'.

To what extent is the impact of the assessment positive? Impact is the effect of the test on teaching and learning, and on the many people involved in the assessment process – the children, their parents, their teachers, their school community and the community at large. Impact may be positive or negative. Teachers and assessors would, clearly, seek positive impact for their assessment procedure. Impact on teaching and learning is also known as *washback*. Assessment will not automatically have a washback effect on teaching and learning (Alderson and Wall, 1993), though many teachers are aware of signs of what appears to be positive washback (e.g., motivation to learn) and negative washback (discouragement of students, narrowing of the curriculum) in their classrooms. Positive and negative impact on teachers and on the community can be seen from high-stakes external tests, as I discuss in Chapter 9. Teachers should aim for high degrees of positive impact to help to ensure that the procedure is 'useful'.

A 'useful' assessment procedure is therefore one that (to varying degrees) is characterized by the presence of all of these qualities, each prioritized to be as high as possible but in balance with the whole. Teachers and assessors can use the checklist provided to evaluate their assessment procedures. Evaluation can be done most effectively in group discussions in which teachers come together to talk about each of the qualities. Together teachers and assessors can consider each quality, and ensure that each is prioritized as much as possible according to the purpose of the assessment procedure, and the teaching situation (the nature of the children, the resources available and so on).

Recent thinking about validity, reliability and impact in classroom assessment

In recent years researchers in generalist education (e.g., Black and Wiliam, 1998; McMillan, 2003; Smith, 2003) have considered the nature of formative classroom assessment (for a definition of formative assessment, see Chapter 5), and whether and how the concepts of validity and reliability apply to this type of assessment. Formative classroom assessment is carried out for the purpose of improving learning and can be embedded in instruction in an iterative and complex way, especially in what we have called on-the-run assessment. It has been suggested that there should be different ways of looking at validity, reliability and impact in formative assessment. Writers suggest, for example, that there is validity in formative classroom assessment when an assessment decision has resulted in more student engagement, and when progress can be identified: 'Validity is a characteristic that refers to the soundness, trustworthiness, or legitimacy of [teachers'] assessment decisions' (McMillan, 2003, p. 9). They suggest that reliability should be de-emphasised in formative assessment, since teachers are typically interested in how well the student does in the task, rather than finding out how well the student has performed in relation to other students (Smith, 2003, p. 5). They suggest that reliability can be checked in classroom formative assessment, through the collection of sufficient observation data over many tasks. They also argue that the impact of classroom assessment can be evaluated through a consideration of the intended and unintended consequences of teachers' decisions, for example: Do students acquire deep understanding as a result of preparing for an essay test? Do students believe they are capable of learning new knowledge after self-monitoring of practice exercises? Does the class demonstrate needed skills or is remediation needed? (McMillan, 2003, p. 9). These new ways of looking at validity, reliability and impact in classroom assessment extend the constructs outlined earlier in the chapter (though some say, qualitatively change them) and contextualize them in the realities of formative assessment in the classroom. Research and thinking in this area are relatively new, especially in language assessment, and more research is needed to understand the relationships and differences between the constructs in formal and formative assessment. Meanwhile many would advocate that teachers keep a close eye on the characteristics of 'usefulness' as they go about their formative assessment, and at the same time accept that some yet-to-be-fully-understood adjustments are likely to be needed to accommodate the realities of formative assessment.

A framework of task characteristics: a framework to analyse individual tasks

Having considered some broader guiding questions about assessment tasks and procedures, we can now look at specific questions about individual tasks and check their characteristics. Is the task authentic, that is, does it reflect a real-life task that children are preparing for? Is it a suitable and fair task for all children? If the task is suitable for most children, are there some children who might need additional support if we use this task?

The following framework (presented in full in a checklist in Table 4.4; see Appendix to this chapter) guides teachers through a close analysis of the characteristics of a task, so that they can check exactly what is happening in the task and how it might influence the learners' performance. Children are vulnerable to task differences; there are cognitive, language, interactional, metalinguistic, involvement and physical characteristics of tasks that can influence the difficulty of a task (Cameron, 2000). In my experience, assessment tasks and procedures for young learners are rarely analysed to check for characteristics that may influence (often disadvantage) performance. Guides for young learner assessment tend to focus more on ways to assess, criteria for assessment and ways to record observations, without asking for more detailed analysis of the actual demands on children within those tasks.

Analysing tasks in this way takes time. The degree to which time is spent analysing an assessment task will depend on a number of situational factors. If the assessment is high-stakes, this type of analysis is essential. If a summative assessment is required with a clear reading of each child's abilities, then it is worth taking time to apply the framework to the assessment tasks during the task selection process. If a group of teachers is learning how to apply the framework, and are working together to reach an agreement on the selection of assessment tasks, this will initially take time. Once teachers have internalized the framework through professional development activities, they will be able to apply it to many of their classroom assessment tasks.

The categories of task characteristics are as follows:

Characteristics of the setting: The physical characteristics of the setting, for example the noise level and the seating conditions, are a component of the characteristics of the setting. Some tasks may be outside in the community – what are the physical characteristics in such cases? The participants in the assessment task (for example, the interviewer in an oral interview, or other children in a group task) are part of the characteristics of the setting, as is the time of the assessment.

Characteristics of the assessment task procedures (rubrics): The instructions that are used in an assessment task are a component of the characteristics of assessment task procedures. The way that instructions are given (for example, by the teacher, in writing, on a tape), the length and difficulty of the task are some variables that characterize the task. The structure of the task is another element in this category of characteristics, for example the number and length of parts in the task, the sequencing of parts, and time allotted to each task. Methods of judging performance – the criteria for correctness and the nature of the procedures for scoring are included in this set of characteristics. To cater for young learners, questions about the familiarity of the task structure, and the cognitive and social demands of the task are added to the original framework in this section.

Characteristics of the input: The input is the material contained in an assessment task that learners are expected to process in some way and to which they are expected to respond. In order to analyse the input in an assessment task, teachers and assessors need to ask questions about the format of the input and the language of the input. Questions about the language of the input are based on the Bachman and Palmer framework of language use described in Chapter 3 and relate to the areas of language knowledge described in this framework.

Characteristics of the expected response: The expected response is the response we are trying to elicit from children. We are trying to elicit a response through the instructions we have given, the task we have designed and the input we have provided. The actual response may be different from the expected response, as learners may respond differently because they have misunderstood something in the instructions, or may choose to do something in a different way.

The characteristics of the expected response may be described in terms of *format*, *type of response*, and *degree of speededness*. The format of the response may be analysed, for example, in terms of whether it is aural or visual, the expected language (first or target language) and its length. Type of response is concerned with the form of the response (does it involve choosing from among two or more responses provided? Is it an extended response?). We tend not to use degree of speededness in young learner language assessment; a speeded task is one where the score on the task depends primarily upon how quickly the test taker responds.

The language of the expected response, whether limited or extended, can be analysed in the same way as the language of the input, as above. This includes language characteristics and topical knowledge (components of language ability taken from Bachman and Palmer's framework of language use).

Relationship between input and response: In some tasks, the input from the adult will be determined or adapted by the nature of the response from the child. This happens in oral interviews, when the adult hears the response and responds accordingly, for example, acknowledging the response, adapting the content or level of difficulty of what he says next. There is no relationship between the input and response in extended listening tasks (for example a story on a tape), or in reading or written tasks – these tasks do not adapt to the child's response. A new type of reading or written task does, however, have opportunities for a relationship between input and response to exist. Adaptive computer tasks can select the next question or set of questions (easier or more difficult questions) based on the response of the child.

Under this task characteristic, there are questions about the scope of processing – the amount of input that needs to be processed before the child can respond, and about the directness of processing – the degree to which the child is expected to process the response primarily based on the information in the input (or will he be required to draw on further information from the context or from his own topical knowledge?).

In the checklist in Table 4.4 (see Appendix), these characteristics are presented as questions that teachers can ask as they analyse tasks. Since all questions will not be relevant for every task, teachers and assessors should select the questions that are relevant to the task in question. The questions should be checked against the characteristics of the learners. Thus, for example, 'How many parts or activities are there?' or 'How much time is allotted?, is checked with the question 'Is this suitable for the young learners who are being assessed through this task?'

Following are three examples of ways in which the framework can be applied to check the characteristics of the task. The first application of the framework (Task 1) shows how the framework helps teachers and assessors to check that a task is fair to all children involved in the task. The second application (Task 2) helps teachers and assessors to check if additional support is needed by some of the children in the class. Support involves modifying the task in some way to improve a child's chances to succeed; in assessment tasks support is noted and taken into account when the child's performance is judged. The third example (Task 3) is of a different order. It shows how the framework can be used to check whether the assessment task reflects a real-life task, that is, whether it is an authentic task. This kind of analysis is needed when assessment tasks are required to reflect the real world and are designed to check that children are able to use language successfully in an authentic task. The result of an analysis can bring surprising insights into an assessment task that on first consideration appears suitable.

In the examples different formats are used. A template for analysis is provided in the appendix.

Task 1: Using the framework of task characteristics to check fairness

The framework of task characteristics can be used to check that a planned assessment task will be fair for all the children being assessed, that is, that they will receive a score that represents their real abilities in the language, and that there is absence of bias.

Example 1: Description of assessment task 1

Planned assessment task:	Children respond to teacher's questions about pictures painted by children and pinned on the wall. (This task is adapted from Reilly and Ward (2000, p. 82).
Characteristics of learners:	Year 1, beginning EFL learners (aged 5).
Learning context:	The assessment task is embedded in the teaching task in which they are drawing pictures of their families and talking about them.

This assessment task is embedded in the teaching task in Table 4.2 and is highlighted in bold.

Analysis of characteristics of assessment task 1

Characteristics of the setting: The setting is familiar; the children will be in their classroom. The children will be settled and their attention will be on the teacher. It is a whole-class activity with their teacher whom they know well.

Characteristics of the task procedure (or rubrics): The teacher will give brief oral instructions in the target language, modelling what is required, and will not be collecting information on children's abilities until it is clear that the children understand what is required and are involved in the routine. A teacher aide will be available to assist.

There is only one section in the assessment activity: The time for the whole class activity will be ten minutes. Children will be asked either to volunteer (hands up) or to answer. They will be given time to respond.

Table 4.2 *Teaching task: Children draw pictures of their families and talk about them*

	Preparation	Core activity	Follow up
Language learning goals (other curriculum goals not specified here)	To learn/revise learnt lexis of family members. Practise 'This is . . .' 'Her/his name is . . .' Understand and respond to 'Who's this?' To listen to and predict meaning from context to other information about the family, supported by pictures/context.	Identify orally members of their family in paintings.	Identify members of family in photos brought to school.
Teaching activities	Children are shown photos of teacher's family, and are told 'This is my sister. Her name's . . ...', and further information in photos (with pointing, contextual support).	Children draw pictures of their families. Children tell the teacher individually who they are painting, and about their pictures.	Children are encouraged to bring in photos of their families and talk about them.
		Assessment task **In groups, children listen and respond to teacher's questions about the identity of the pictures on the wall. E.g. 'Who's this?' 'Whose picture is this?' and 'What colour hat is she wearing/is her hair/are her trousers?'** asked in contextualized ways (pointing to pictures, stressing important words).	

The teachers' judgment of performance will be by observation, with notes made, but backed up with an audiotape-recording. Children are not aware that this is an assessment activity.

Characteristics of the input: The input will be spoken target language, contextualized with pictures painted by the childen and pinned on the wall. The content of the pictures is familiar, as children will have just had the painting session. The vocabulary and contextualized structures will have been introduced and reinforced in the preparation activities. The teacher's language will be at the discourse level, but target vocabulary and structures will be stressed through her talk using contextualization strategies (relevant pointing, verbal stress, expressions, repetition). The topic of talk is personal, and within the conceptual capacity, interest and experience of the children.

Characteristics of the expected response: The children are familiar with the teacher–whole group questioning on pictures that all can see, and on raising hands/being selected to respond. Their expected response is that they will show that they understand the teacher's contextualized questions in the target language, and provide short spoken correct answers in the target language. 'It's/That's Mima's brother', 'That's my sister', 'It's green/red/blue', 'They are white', etc.' Sentence-level answers without cohesive devices are expected. (The emphasis is on understanding as these are beginning learners.)

The topic of the response is personal, and within the conceptual capacity and experience of learners.

Relationship between input and response: Talk is reciprocal – the teacher encourages and waits for a response, and provides feedback and comments on children's response. The topical knowledge needed is not all provided by the context of the activity i.e. children must rely on their own knowledge of who painted the pictures and what relationship they are to the painter. The task is appropriate to the cognitive, social and physical maturity of the children.

Findings of analysis of task 1: Is the picture-drawing task fair for all children?

The analysis of this assessment activity for young children reveals that even in such a seemingly simple assessment activity, where the teacher is evidently catering well to the physical, social, cognitive and language needs of young learners, two weak points in the planned task have emerged.

Firstly, this is a whole-group assessment activity and is 10 minutes long. The teacher is counteracting the possibility that only more confident children will volunteer, by also naming children and asking them to respond. However, it will be difficult for her to assess all children before their attention spans wane. She will need to find ways to ensure that all children are assessed. A practice effect will also emerge in a longer activity, that is, children will hear other children's responses as the task progresses, and this will mean that she may not be assessing children's understanding, but their memory of what others have said. This is a threat to the validity of the task she will not want if she is intent on checking each child's understanding (rather than teaching). The teacher may split the children into two or three groups, with other groups doing independent activities so that she can check all children in one group at a time.

Secondly, and much more seriously, the teacher is asking the children to identify the people in the pictures, but many children will not know who painted the picture or what their relationship may be to the painter. This expectation makes the activity much more difficult for some children in the group. Some children might not know all the children's names, or may not have been concentrating on who painted what. Some will have better memories than others. There may therefore be a potential threat to the validity of the task for some children because of unfamiliarity with the content of the task.

Experienced teachers would quickly redress this weakness in the assessment task by altering the task, building in ways to help the children to know who it is in the picture. For example, the teacher might plan to choose a limited number of pictures with a range of family memberships with which to ask questions so that children will know who painted each one and who is depicted. She might decide to assess in smaller groups, using the teacher aide to supervise the class while she does this.

This is a simple example of how an assessment task can be analysed to check that it will work fairly, in this case, so that all children will have an opportunity to participate and to demonstrate what they know and that the teacher will collect the best language sample from each child without over-supported performance.

Task 2: Using the framework of task characteristics to check additional support needs

For our purposes, *support* involves the modification of a task involving changes to the nature of the planned task or task-in-action in order to improve each learner's chances of success. Support is a complex issue in assessment but cannot be ignored in the assessment of young learners. As part of sound educational practice, teachers and assessors of young learners are generally committed to ensuring some kind of success for their learners. Therefore, where possible, they will include additional support during the task once they are aware that a child has reached his or her limit of ability or is distressed.

Additional support may be planned, so that the characteristics of the task are changed for the targeted children from the beginning. This is commonly called *task differentiation*. Task differentiation is a recommended assessment strategy in mainstream classroom assessment in England (SCAA booklet, UK) and is valuable when it is clear before the assessment takes place that some children will need support to be successful in the task. Another term for support strategies used in planned assessments, usually formal assessments, is *accommodations* (see Butler and Stevens, 1997; see also Chapter 9).

Additional support may also be given during the task; that is, the teacher adjusts the task once it is clear that the child is not successful. In a classroom assessment situation, the teacher may prepare the children as planned and set the the children to the task; he or she may then walk around and make sure, by observation, that children have understood the requirements of the task. The teacher can help those who did not understand what they had to do, making note of the fact that these individuals needed this additional help. In a role-play task, a child may need some prompting to get started.

In both types of situations, teachers and assessors must make professional judgments about the child's performance and take into account the additional support given in their judgment of the child's ability. This is not always easy. Although support adjustments appear unpalatable to measurement experts, who aim to see exact comparisons amongst learners, this practice reflects the essence of the reality of young learner teaching and assessment. In classroom assessment, the teacher's professionalism is critical; he or she must be relied upon to make the final judgment, balancing demand and support to come to a final decision about the ability of the child.

Providing additional support is also a teaching mechanism, and in teaching is aligned closely with strategies teachers use to *scaffold* learning as we have discussed in Chapter 2. The need to continue to apply support in assessment tasks for young learners when it is needed by individual learners or groups of learners is perhaps a reason why teaching and assessment are not easily distinguishable in young learner assessment contexts (Rea-Dickins and Gardner, 2000; Teasdale and Leung, 2000).

Some opportunities for additional support for learners in assessment tasks might be as follows:

• Characteristics of the setting: e.g. Support can be given to a child who is unsettled and nervous by placing him in a quieter setting.

• Characteristics of the assessment task procedures (or rubrics): e.g. Children who will clearly have difficulties with the instructions for the task might be given the instructions in their first language. A familiar task is chosen, so that all children can be successful.

• Characteristics of the input: e.g. The text used might be shortened for those with lower proficiency.

• Characteristics of the expected response: e.g. A child may be given extra time for the expected response.

• Relationship between input and response: e.g. A teacher prompts a child with additional questions and suggestions to help him or her to complete the task.

Providing too much additional support, in the sense that this makes the task too easy for the child, will not help the teacher to make informed judgments about the child's abilities, as we will discuss in Chapter 6. The degree of *familiarity* within each of the characteristics of the task will have an important influence on the type of support some or all children receive. Therefore, as researchers have observed (Nicholas, 1999), over-familiar, over-practised tasks may not challenge children to use language in purposeful and active ways, nor to extend themselves and show their true abilities in the tasks.

The following example of a task analysis is similar in many ways to Example 1 in that we are analysing the task to check for fairness; however, in this case we are checking for the suitability of the task for a particular learner (or learners), and then planning support needs.

Example 2: Description of assessment task 2

Planned assessment task:	Middle elementary children write a report about an Australian animal they have been researching. They will be expected to write the report independently, but the teacher will be at hand.
Characteristics of learners:	Year 4 ESL children in a mainstream class-room in Australia.
Learning context:	The assessment task takes place at the end of a teaching cycle, where learners have been revising their understanding about the purpose of reports, how to organize the text and content of report, and how to write appropriate language. They have undertaken a series of activities involving modelling of reports, joint construction, reporting to an audience and reflecting on processes.

Analysis of characteristics of assessment task 2

This analysis in Table 4.3 has been done jointly by a mainstream teacher and an ESL teacher, just as in more formal test situations groups of teachers and assessors might devise tasks together using the framework. The wording in Bold type indicates the areas of possible difficulty for the ESL learner.

Findings of analysis of task 2: Will the second language learner(s) need additional support in this assessment task?

The ESL learner has three areas of difficulty (see teacher's comments in bold above). He is very aware of the fact that results will contribute to a final mark and is aware that he is likely to do badly. He knows that his language proficiency in English is weak, and his knowledge of Australian animals minimal. His nervousness about this and about his parents' reactions to his marks means that he has difficulty concentrating.

The language of the input – the books that learners can refer to, is academically oriented, with difficult sentence structures, and nominalizations (*classification, habitat)* and science words that are unfamiliar.

Table 4.3 *Analysis of characteristics of assessment task 2*

Characteristics of the setting Physical characteristics Participants Time of task	In the mainstream classroom. Independent work. During morning language arts sessions over a week.
Characteristics of the assessment activity procedures (or rubrics) Instructions Structure Time allotment Scoring method	The instructions are given orally by the teacher. She explains in detail what is required, referring back to previous modelling and joint construction sessions, and showing models of completed reports. The teacher talks about a good piece of work (that is, outlines the criteria for success). Marks will be given and contribute to the final mark for the year. **The ESL learner is aware of the assessment and is nervous about his parents' reaction to his final rating.**
Characteristics of the input Format Language of input	The input is made up of reading texts from the library, found by the students themselves. Many have pictures to aid understanding; the language is academic (social studies) and is targeted to elementary age (mother tongue) learners. The topical knowledge required is concerned with animals, their description, classification, habitats etc.; skills in using the library are needed, as is a cultural understanding of how to work independently (that is, without teacher-centred input). **For the ESL learner the academic language is difficult, and so is the topical knowledge – he knows little about Australian animals. He is also not familiar with library research, nor with working without teacher direction.**
Characteristics of the expected response Format Language of expected response Topical characteristics	A two-page report is required, following a set format provided in models. (Classification [What is it?]; Description [What attributes does it have?]; Place/Time [Where is it? When is it?]; Dynamics [What does it do?]; Summarizing Comment). The report should exhibit the appropriate structure, and language features of a report

Table 4.3 *(continued)*

	genre, and contain relevant information, with pictures, about the animal chosen.
	The level of difficulty of the concepts is suitable for Year 4 age learners.
	For the ESL learner, the expectations for the response (genre, language, content) are very difficult.

Relationship between input and response
    Reactivity
    Scope of relationship
    Degree of relationship
    (degree of contextualization)
	There is no reactivity. The amount of information needed by students is mainly included in the books read, though most children will rely on previous knowledge of the animal to assist them to complete the report.

The report genre required is new to the ESL learner; this is not a writing task that he was familiar with in his previous school environment in his home country. He is unfamiliar with Australian animals, though he has read a little about them in his first language at home.

The analysis of the task highlights the ESL student's likely weak areas in the assessment task. The mainstream teacher and the ESL teacher can decide together what support can be given to the student. The fact that this is a formal assessment situation means that they should take note of the additional support they give, in order that they can come to a final result and report that gives the ESL learner and the parents an understanding of his progress in relation to the rest of the class. (In some assessment situations, it might be possible to give the ESL learner an independent mark based on his own progress. This, of course, is more pedagogically appropriate.)

The teacher can therefore plan to give the student the following additional support:

- Reassure the learner that his or her parents will also receive a profile report outlining his progress in ESL terms as well as in comparison to mainstream learners.
- Select texts (with pictures, and accessible language) for the learner (that is, avoid the need for library skills at this point).
- Give the learner guiding questions to answer reflecting the required stages in a report genre.

Task 3: Using the framework of task characteristics to check that an assessment task reflects the real-life task and is therefore relatively authentic

We will now turn to the use of the framework for a purpose of a different order. There are some assessment situations where assessors need to check that the task is an authentic one, that is, that it reflects the characteristics of a real-life task. Classroom teachers of young learners will not often have to do this type of checking, as most assessment tasks in the classroom come straight from the kinds of tasks usually carried out in the classroom – they are not required to reflect tasks 'in the real world' as they are 'authentic for the language learning classroom'. In contrast, teachers preparing second language learners for mainstream classrooms may sometimes need to check that a task reflects the characteristics of mainstream learning tasks (e.g., giving a presentation to the class about a social studies project; taking notes from a video on a science topic; interviewing a visitor). In a similar way, test designers in the United States are currently working on tests in which they will assess if children are developing the academic English language skills they need for participation in mainstream classes. These designers need to select test tasks that reflect the authenticity of the mainstream classroom, and the application of a framework of task characteristics can help them to do this. (I will describe the process of development of such a test in Chapter 9.)

To use a reasonably simple example to illustrate the analysis of tasks for this purpose, we might envisage a situation where young learners are being prepared by the teacher to go out and interview tourists in the city. This type of activity has been proved successful in Hong Kong where a teacher, Zoe Leung, has taken new arrivals from mainland China in the beginning stages of English, to interview English-speaking tourists near the tourist spots of Hong Kong. In order to assess children's ability to do this, the teacher sets up a highly comparable assessment task in the classroom before they go out and 'pester' tourists. The teacher is checking that her children are ready to attempt this activity, and that they are likely to experience some success. Note that this example of task analysis is focused on authenticity, not, at this point, on checking fairness or support needs.

Example 3: Description of assessment task 3

Planned assessment task:	Interviewing a tourist with prepared introduction and questions with limited, mostly predictable, responses 'May I ask you some

	questions?' 'Where do you come from?' 'How long have you been in Hong Kong?', 'Where are you staying?'
Characteristics of learners:	11-year-old beginning EFL learners in Hong Kong. (Students recently arrived from mainland China, with little experience talking to non-Chinese speakers.)
Learning context:	Students have been focusing on the language requirements, and practising this task for several weeks in their English classes. The teacher has taught ways to be polite in the situation, and prepared questions with them.

Analysis of characteristics of assessment task 3

Characteristics of the setting: In the real-life task, the interview setting will be in a crowded tourist area in Hong Kong, and there may be difficulties hearing every word that is spoken. The learners will be nervous because they will not know if they will be rebuffed rudely, or whether they will be able to make themselves understood, or understand what is said to them. They will also be 'on their own' without teacher support, though they will know that the teacher will be hovering nearby (but not within earshot). The teacher will advise them to make a beeline for tourists who look Caucasian, because at a guess they will speak English, but they may have a range of different English accents – American, Australian or English, perhaps South African, and they may not even speak English at all! The characteristics of the real-life setting are therefore quite unpredictable for the learners. The task involves students talking to unknown adults; this will involve certain expectations that arise when young people talk to older strangers (politeness, readiness to withdraw, formal questioning only, etc.).

In the assessment task, the level of anxiety will be difficult to duplicate. It may be possible to ask English-speaking visitors to come to the class to be interviewed. The noise level can be raised in the busy classroom by asking two or three visitors to come to be interviewed simultaneously.

Characteristics of the task procedures (or rubrics): In the real-life task, the procedures for the task will be informal in the situation once the approach has been made. However, the teacher will need to give careful instructions on how to approach the tourists, on the kinds of questions to ask (if the tourist is willing to participate) and on the way to thank the tourists and withdraw. The judgment of performance, even in the real-life task, will be through teacher judgment and student self-assessment of the success of the interaction. The teacher will talk to the students about and make formal the criteria for successful interviews, including politeness on the part of the students, use of English in a way that is understood, understanding and recording of the tourists' responses (if they were willing to take part), and polite withdrawal. Thus, to some extent, this real-life task has characteristics of a classroom teaching task – it is structured carefully by the teacher, will be assessed by the teacher and will be supported by the teacher if needed.

In the assessment task, the same procedures will be used. In this respect the real-life task and the classroom assessment task are comparable.

Characteristics of the input: In the real-life task, the language that the tourists use is somewhat unpredictable at the commencement of the interview, but at least structured by the questions the students will be asking. Thus once introductions have been made, and consent given, a question like *Where do you come from?* is likely to elicit a response *I come from Australia.* Accents may be unexpected, and angry, impolite or non-comprehending responses to *Do you mind if I interview you?* may happen. The language of the input and the topical characteristics will most likely be limited by the students' questions, and by the tourists recognizing the youth and beginning learner status of the students. It would seem that the real-life task is challenging, but related to the cognitive, social and emotional maturity of the students if the teacher is present for support.

In the classroom assessment task, the native-speaking visitors would need to be primed to be somewhat unpredictable at the beginning of each student's or group's interview with them. The questions and answers would probably match the real-life task. The reality of an unsolicited approach and introduction – *Excuse me, may I interview you for a school project?* – would, however, be difficult to reproduce in the classroom.

Characteristics of the expected response: In both the real-life task and the classroom assessment task, the expected response from students is the same, although they would have to deal with more unpredictability and anxiety in the real-life task. In terms of language use, they are required to ask prepared questions and to understand and record the tourists' or the visitors' responses to report back to the teacher. The teacher is close by but not within earshot, so conveying the responses to the teacher would be real meaning exchange in both situations. There may be some cultural aspects (topical characteristics) of the interaction in both situations that would need to be dealt with.

Relationship between input and response: In both situations, there is some potential for reactivity. At the beginning of the real-life task interaction will be more reciprocal, when the tourist may want to know more, or say something unexpected. Once the interview is underway, interaction will be less reciprocal as the interview follows the 'script' determined by the pre-planned interview questions. The scope of processing required from the learner is, once the interview is underway, only narrow. The processing of the response by the student will be supported by gestures (kind smiles, unfriendly frowns) and by other gestures, and perhaps repetition, so there will be a degree of contextualization to support the learner.

In the planned classroom task, the task will probably be less reciprocal at the beginning of the interview, since the visitor will already know why he has been invited. However, the teacher could take the step of priming the visitor to act as an unsuspecting tourist when he comes into the class, which will help to mirror the characteristics of the real-life task in the classroom.

Findings of analysis of task 3: Does the assessment task reflect the real-life interview task?

This is an example of how to analyse a task to check whether the assessment task reflects the characteristics of the real-life task. If English-speaking visitors were not able to attend the class (which is quite likely) then the task would need to be reanalysed using Chinese-speaking teachers or parents probably familiar to the students. Several more mismatches would then be likely to occur between the assessment task and the real-life task (the Chinese-speaking teachers would not be so intimidating; the children would know that they could resort to Cantonese, etc.)

Readers will hopefully have realized by reading this that analysing the task would help the teacher to clarify several of the task's characteristics, and improve the planning process for both the assessment task (check-ing if the students are ready) and teaching and learning (checking on further teaching requirements to prepare the students for the real-life task). Since the support for these students is high, the teachers will need to make complex decisions about the students' final marks for the task, as the task is now differentiated – the characteristics of the input and the expected response are different for the ESL learner compared to the mainstream students.

Since all classrooms around the world, whether foreign language or minority language learning classrooms, are made up of children with a range of abilities, backgrounds and needs, these types of decisions are regularly made by teachers in classroom-based assessment situations. Professional judgments balancing the nature of the task and the nature of support are at the heart of young learner assessment. The framework of task characteristics is therefore a tool that can help teachers and asses-sors to understand the way an assessment task will influence learners' performance.

Summary

Task-based assessment is a kind of performance-based assessment. Performance-based assessment involves the observation of behaviour in the real world, or of simulated behaviour in a real-life task. The principles of alternative assessment, authentic assessment, criterion-referenced assessment and divergent assessment reflect, with variations, the basic idea that assessment is best done through samples of learners' real lan-guage use, rather than through discrete-point items that assess aspects of the learners' knowledge of the language.

Tasks are defined as involving learners in purposeful, goal-oriented language use, specific to a certain situation. Many classroom activities can be used as assessment tasks. Selecting tasks and procedures for assessment involves great care, as bad decisions can cause disadvantage for all learners, or for a particular group of learners, or for an individual. Tasks and procedures should, for example, suit the characteristics of the learners, bias for best, engage the learners intellectually, assess the most relevant abilities and draw from multiple sources of information.

If teachers have an opportunity to analyse tasks more closely, prefer-ably with other teachers, they will gradually gain a professional frame-work that will help them to analyse assessment tasks more efficiently.

Assessment tasks and procedures need to be 'useful' (Bachman and Palmer, 1966). Tasks and procedures should be reliable (the learner should get the same results if another teacher were to assess their work, or if they were to be assessed in the same way again tomorrow); have construct validity (the interpretations that are made should be meaningful and appropriate), be authentic (the task should reflect children's real language use), be interactive (they should involve language ability in accomplishing the task); be practical, and have positive impact (a positive effect on the learners, teachers, parents and others affected by the assessment).

The analysis of tasks for 'usefulness' can be carried out using a framework of task characteristics (adapted from Bachman and Palmer 1966). Three purposes can be achieved using the framework – firstly, analysing to check if the chosen task reflects the intended real-life task, that is, whether it is authentic; secondly, to check fairness; and thirdly, to check for additional support needs amongst the learners. Examples of each of these types of analyses are provided.

The following chapter explores classroom-based assessment from the theoretical standpoint of this chapter – that the most effective assessment of language use is through performance in language tasks.

Appendix

Table 4.4 *Template for checking task characteristics for young learners (adapted from Bachman and Palmer, 1996, pp. 49–50)*

Task characteristics	Yes/No and comments
Description of the learner group:	
Task title:	

Characteristics of the setting

Physical characteristics
   Are there distractions in the environment?
   Is the setting familiar or unfamiliar?

Participants
   How many participants are there?
   Who are the other participants?
   Will the participants intimidate the child or cause a less
      successful performance?

Time of task
   Is the time of the assessment likely to influence the child's
      performance? (e.g., just before home time)

Characteristics of the assessment task procedures (rubrics)

Instructions
   Are the instructions in the child's native language or the
      target language?
   Are they aural or visual?
   Is the language at an appropriate level?
   Are the instructions conceptually appropriate for the age group?
   Is visual support given?
   Are examples provided?
   Other?

Structure
   How many parts or activities are there?
   How long are the instructions?
   Are the different parts of the procedure clearly distinguished from
      one another?
   Is there a fixed or variable sequence in the procedure?

Table 4.4 *(continued).*

Do the parts of the procedure differ in importance?
How many activities or items are there in the procedure?
Is the task structure familiar (Do children know what is expected)?
Are the cognitive and social demands of the task at the level
   appropriate to the age of the children?
What are the demands on the child's attention span, on the
   length of time he or she has to sit still? Is there any variation of
   physical requirement to ease demands?
Other?

Time allotment
   How much time is allotted? Will the activity be limited in time so
      that not all learners are expected to complete it or will it be
      long enough for all to attempt every task?
   Other?

Scoring method
   How will the task be judged as correct?
   Will an objective score be used (i.e., will there be a single correct
      answer)? Or will rating scales be used?
   Are all responses marked by the same teacher or assessor?
   If different teachers or assessors are used, are they involved in
      checking their decisions together so that the scores are
      comparable?
   Will the children know what the criteria are and how the scores
      will be given? How will this be done?
   Other?

Characteristics of the input

Format

• How is the input presented? In language form (written or
   spoken)? Or in non-language form (aural or visual including
   gestures, pictures, graphs, etc.)? Or both?
• Is the learner familiar with the form in which the activity
   is presented?
• To what extent are the format of the task and the language
   of the input appropriate to the cognitive and social maturity
   level of the child?
• What are the demands on the child's attention span, on the
   length of time he or she has to sit still? Is there any variation
   of physical requirements to ease demand?
• Will the format and input raise the interest of the child and
   encourage the child to participate in the task?
• Is the language of the input the learner's native language, the
   target language or both?

Table 4.4 *(continued).*

- Have the vocabulary, structures and genres been taught and practised in different contexts? Have they been taught or revised recently?
- Is the input made up of single words, phrases, sentences or extended discourse?
- Is the input an item (a chunk of language or non-language information) or a prompt (an instruction)?
- How fast does the child have to process the information in the input?
- Is the input delivered 'live' e.g. by the teacher in the classroom, or is it 'reproduced' e.g. via an audiotape or by both means?
- To what extent can children draw meaning from the context (from pictures, graphs, objects, the environment)?
- Other?

The language of the input

- To what extent is the language supported with teacher's explanations, with pictures, charts and realia? To what degree are the teacher's explanations stressing meaning through painting, stress, repetition, gestures and facial expressions?
- What is the nature of the organization characteristics of the language – the vocabulary, syntax, phonology (sound system) and graphology (writing system)?
- What is the nature of the pragmatic characteristics (what functions are being met, in the input? What dialect or language variety is being used? What register? (e.g., is the language formal or informal?)
- Is academic language being used?
- Is the language natural?
- Are there cultural references and figurative language in the input?
- What is the topic being discussed (personal, cultural, academic)?
- Other?

Characteristics of the expected response

Format

- Is the expected response aural, visual or both?
- What are the demands on the child's attention span, on the length of time he or she has to sit still? Is there any variation of physical requirements to ease demands?
- How is the response to be produced – in language form (written or spoken), or in non-language form (aural or visual including gestures, pictures, graphs, etc.)? Or both? Are fine motor skills required (e.g., to write or draw)?

Table 4.4 *(continued).*

- Is the expected response to be in the child's native language or his target language or both?
- To what extent is the child familiar with the type of response required (e.g., use of familiar actions and routines)? Has the child practised this test many times?
- Is the expected response to be made up of single words, phrases, sentences, or extended discourse?
- What are the demands on the child's attention span? Are fine-motor skills required (to write or draw)?
- To what extent is the child familiar with the type of response required (e.g., use of familiar actions, familiar routines)?
- To what extent has relevant language been taught and learned?
- Have they been taught or revised recently?
- To what degree can the children support what they say and do with reference to the context?
- To what extent is the format of the task at the appropriate level of cognitive and social maturity?
- Other?

Language of the expected response

- What is the nature of the organization characteristics of the language – the vocabulary, syntax, phonology (sound system) and graphology (writing system)?
- What is the nature of the pragmatic characteristics (what functions are being met in the expected response)?
- What dialect or language variety or register is to be used?
- Is the language expected natural?
- Are cultural references and figurative language expected?
- What is the topic being discussed (personal, cultural, academic)?
- Other?

Relationship between input and response

- Will the child be expected to give a one-off response (non-reciprocal), or will there be some processing of the input in relation to further information or feedback given (reciprocal)?
- Is the task adaptive (the task/the next question is adapted on the basis of the response the learner makes)?
- Does the child have to process a lot of input, or a limited amount of input? Will the child be expected to process the response based primarily on the information in the input, or will he or she be required to draw on further information from the context or from his or her own topical knowledge?
- Other?

CHAPTER FIVE

Classroom assessment of language use

Classroom assessment or **teacher assessment** refers to assessment carried out by teachers in the classroom. It may be **formative** when teachers are collecting information about children's strengths and weaknesses in order to provide feedback to learners and to make further decisions about teaching, or it may be **summative**, when teachers are collecting information at the end of a period of time, generally to report to others about children's progress. Summative assessment carried out by teachers may also inform their own teaching, if, for example, the learners return to them in the following school year. Formative assessment is also called **assessment for learning** (e.g., Black and Wiliam, 1998). Not all assessment in the classroom is classroom assessment. If teachers are administering tests in the classroom prepared by others, this is not considered to be classroom assessment because it is not prepared by the teacher but by others who are at least one step, and maybe many steps, removed from the learners and the learning situation of the classroom.

Teachers have opportunities to adopt performance assessment in its widest sense in the classroom, engaging children as active participants in assessment processes, assessing processes as well as products, collecting multiple sources of evidence over time, and working with parents and others in a collaborative assessment process. In classrooms there are many opportunities for assessment through language use tasks, when children are able to engage in language use in games, information gap oral tasks, story writing, question-and-answer tasks related to literature, project work and so on. Assessment can be embedded in instruction designed to achieve the curriculum objectives, and this enables teachers not only to check that learning is taking place, but also to use the feedback they receive through assessment to support learning. In this way, assessment is able to become, for a large part of the teaching year, an essential part of teaching and learning, rather than a separate process.

This chapter will begin by looking at influences on classroom assessment, on why some teachers of young learners are more ready and able to carry out classroom assessment than others. External influences are very real for some teachers, causing them to avoid a strong commitment to classroom assessment, whilst others are free to prepare and carry out their own assessment and to use assessment to support their teaching and learning (Rea-Dickins, 2001). Before outlining strategies that teachers use in the classroom, I will discuss some of the processes of classroom assessment – when it happens, how it is planned and how it is incorporated into teaching and learning. Classroom assessment is a continuous and integrated process that is both on-the-run and planned. **On-the-run assessment** is carried out by teachers for formative purposes to observe and note children's relevant abilities as they happen – the unexpected question from a quiet child, the engagement in pairwork by two children and the response to a comprehension question of a beginning learner in a whole-class shared reading of a story – often followed up with feedback or strategic intervention. On the other hand, **planned assessment** may be formative and summative and involves forethought to ensure that information is collected about children, on relevant abilities, and that that information is valid and fair or 'useful'. The role of **support** in classroom assessment is complex, since teachers need to offer help and encouragement in order for children to succeed and, at the same time, to assess their progress (see discussion in Chapter 4, pp. 125–6). A continuing theme of this chapter is that language use tasks are central to language assessment, and that the questions and frameworks described in Chapter 4 are relevant to classroom assessment, though with adjustments according to the purposes and context in which assessment is taking place.

Classroom assessment is dependent on record-keeping because there is so much that is observed during the course of teaching and assessment activities. Records need to keep track of the processes as well as the products of learning, and need to be easily interpreted when final reporting to parents and others is due. The final section in this chapter gives suggestions on how children's performance can be recorded, so that accumulated information can be used for either formative or summative purposes.

Influences on classroom assessment

The classroom is not an island, and teaching and assessment practices are influenced by the requirements of others for information about the children's progress. The following are three major influences on teachers' assessment practices in the classroom: system requirements, parental and student expectations and teacher expertise. Any of these influences might cause teachers to draw back from classroom assessment and to rely on others to carry out their assessment. For example, a group of teachers in Hong Kong have told me recently how they tend to avoid classroom assessment, even for formative assessment purposes. They say that their class sizes are too big, that classroom assessment takes too much time and is too difficult. External tests are devised in their school, external to their classrooms, to check pupils' progress on the request of the principal. These tests are used to report to parents. They therefore feel that their efforts are best placed in teaching children to pass the tests rather than carrying out classroom-based assessment that will be discounted. Apart from physical difficulties such as class size, the following are possible influences on teachers' approaches to classroom assessment.

System requirements

The education system in which children are learning will include three components that will influence teaching and assessment practice: standards, external tests and curriculum requirements.

Standards

The educational system may be organized around a set of standards that are mandated by a higher education authority (e.g., in the state or school district). These standards may be the reference point for curriculum requirements. The system may require that schools and teachers report to the system for accountability. Accountability may be measured by external tests or by student portfolios based on classroom assessment. These system requirements may drive parental expectations, as not only do parents want their children to do well, they want their children to go to schools where they get high test scores. Thus system requirements have a strong influence on teachers' flexibility with regard to classroom assessment.

External tests

An external test may be used in younger learner language programmes when an overall 'audit' of children's abilities is required by the education authority or school, or where a research programme is underway. Standardized tests are often norm-referenced. In **norm-referenced** tests, the information on how a child has achieved is compared with the achievement of the larger group of learners. This means that parents and schools are viewing the child's performance in comparison to other children. Whilst it is helpful for parents to know if a child is behind the normal range of performance for his or her age, it is not helpful if comparisons with other children's performance result in anxiety and pressure, and recriminations against the teacher and school.

The effect of high-stakes external testing on classroom-based assessment may be great. Teachers, parents and principals who are in such a teaching situation are anxious that the children pass the tests, and much of the teacher's energy may be focused on teaching to the tests. Tests are not necessarily the best way to improve learning (Shohamy, 1993) yet they have a strong hold on many language classrooms around the world.

Curriculum requirements

It may be that teachers are faced with very closely defined curriculum content to be covered, because they are obliged to aim towards detailed and explicit curriculum outcomes and standards. The curriculum may be delineated very inflexibly, with textbook chapters to be covered by set times. Teachers in these situations may find themselves teaching the required content or chapters regardless of the actual internalization of the content by the children. In these situations teachers might not assess in the classroom to check that children are learning and to diagnose their needs (since there is no time to go back to review), but rather to give a mark on children's work for accumulation towards the final mark at the end of the year. The nature of classroom assessment is fundamentally different in these situations to situations where teachers are using assessment to support learning. Education systems need to ensure that standards, external texts and other curriculum requirements are in alignment, so that teachers can be confident that their classroom assessment is relevant to their teaching and to the external tests that children are expected to take.

Parental and student expectations

If teachers' assessment decisions impact on students' life chances (e.g., admission into a good secondary school), then parents and students are usually anxious that assessment is valid and reliable. This often results in pressure for classroom assessment to be supplemented by, or overridden by, school or external tests. The classroom teachers' assessment may, in fact, be more valid than an external test – the teacher can, after all, observe performance over many tasks. However, in some high-stakes situations, classroom-based assessments lack credibility in the eyes of parents and children. Teachers, faced with pressure from parents (and therefore from the school administration) to make sure that their assessment is absolutely fair, often prefer not to be asked to make assessment decisions in the classroom.

In contrast there are situations in which the teachers' professional judgments of young learners are trusted, and their assessment decisions accepted by parents, learners and others. This is fortunate, as young learners are not advantaged by pressure to pass tests developed by others who do not know them. Children need time to learn and enjoy their study in a safe, nurturing and anxiety-free environment. Education systems need to work towards a situation where teachers' decisions have high status and are trusted in the community.

Teacher expertise

Many teachers have considerable training and experience in classroom assessment, whereas others are not trained and have not had experience in assessment. Given the essential role of assessment in teaching, there is clearly a critical need for classroom teachers to have training in assessment as part of their pre-service education. For teachers who have not had such training, it is important that they gain this as quickly as possible in their school. The amount of training and experience in classroom assessment that teachers can obtain depends, to a large extent, on the 'space' that they are given by the system (the education department, the principal, the parents) to learn how to use and develop their classroom assessment skills. Some teachers face more challenges than others in adopting classroom assessment strategies. The most effective way of improving classroom assessment skills is when teachers work collaboratively with other teachers, engaging in an 'assessment dialogue' with each other. Groups of teachers can help each other to develop classroom assessment skills when they plan assessment tasks together, share ideas on the procedures they have planned, try out ideas together, score children's work together and analyse patterns of data from the procedures. They can also share ideas on how to present the value of classroom assessment to principals and parents. Those who advocate classroom assessment value the support it gives to teaching and learning, and to the ultimate achievement of the stated curriculum goals and objectives. Teachers need to build up skills together to understand that classroom assessment is not a diversion from the 'real' business of teaching and learning, but a foundation for successful teaching and learning.

Purposes of classroom assessment

Teachers carry out classroom assessment continuously through the school year. Classroom assessment might occur in the following ways and for the following purposes:

- initial diagnosis at the beginning of the year (What are the strengths and weaknesses that need to be addressed from the start of the year?)
- ongoing diagnosis leading to decision-making about teaching during the course of teaching (How are they progressing? What feedback can I give right now? What do I need to teach next?)
- ongoing collection of evidence leading to information-sharing with children and their parents. What can I share with children about their ongoing progress and needs? What can I tell parents and others about children's ongoing progress?
- ongoing collection of evidence of progress leading to reporting against externally developed criteria (How are the children progressing towards the criteria?)
- summative purposes (What have they achieved? What do I report about their progress?)

Many assessment procedures for younger learners are embedded in classroom teaching and the purposes therefore reflect the purposes of teaching and learning.

Three assessment phases that underpin all assessment processes

I will start here by outlining the phases that underpin all assessment processes and then discuss how these are adapted and applied in classroom assessment. These phases are presented in more detail at the beginning of Chapter 9. These three phases are likely to be more interconnected, iterative and subtle in classroom assessment than in formal testing. For summative assessment, these processes are followed quite explicitly; for formative assessment they are embedded within the instruction-assessment cycle, as I will discuss below.

Design phase

This phase lays the foundation for the sound development of the assessment procedure. In this phase the teacher decides on the purpose for the procedure, checks that the assessment is appropriate for the situations and tasks that learners need in their actual language use context, or that are specified in the curriculum, and checks the characteristics of the learners. The constructs to be assessed (e.g., 'reading comprehension', 'writing a narrative') are defined clearly in this phase, and a plan needs to be considered to ensure that assessment will be 'useful'. (The qualities of 'usefulness' are discussed in Chapter 4.) The teacher also checks to ensure that the resources that will be required are available (e.g., the materials needed, the room space required) and plans how best to allocate these.

Operationalization phase

In the operationalization phase, the teacher prepares the assessment tasks, or blueprints for assessment tasks that may be adapted in different ways. Instructions are prepared, as well as scoring methods (see Chapter 8). The formal tools for analysis described in Chapter 4 become part of a teacher's professional framework and come into play in the selection of tasks.

Administration phase

In the administration phase the teacher is concerned with actually carrying out the assessment procedure and checking that the procedure has worked well. There may be a *try-out* of the assessment procedure first, when the test can be checked with individuals or with a group of children. For summative assessment, information on whether the procedure worked well or not can be done by collecting a variety of information, including marks from different teachers (to check reliability), information on children's emotional response to the assessment (to check impact) and so on. In formative assessment, teachers need to know other information, such as whether the assessment task was successful in checking the children's abilities and needs, and whether it was successful in promoting learning, as I will discuss below.

Embedding of these assessment phases in classroom assessment processes

These three phases of assessment inform classroom assessment, though the degree to which they are followed explicitly will depend on whether time is available, whether the assessment is planned (as opposed to on-the-run) and whether it is a high-stakes situation. The phases can be converted into a set of questions for classroom teachers as they follow through their classroom assessment processes.

- Why do I need to know, and who else needs to know? (The purpose the assessment will serve.)
- What do I need to know? (The constructs that will be assessed.)
- How can I find out? (The tasks and strategies that will be used.)
- What will I do with the information? (How information will be used, assembled and stored.)
- How will I know that the assessment has been effective and how can I improve it next time? (The evaluation of the assessment process.)

Whilst the principles and practices of assessment described in this book broadly apply to classroom assessment, there are some additional influences on assessment in the classroom, and particularly on formative assessment. Formative assessment processes are not simple and linear, but complex and iterative. McMillan (2003) reports from his research into classroom assessment that teachers tend to make their assessment decisions based on their foundational beliefs and values about education and learning. They also make decisions based on achieving goals for students that include non-cognitive outcomes (such as confidence and a sense of achievement) as well as those stated in the curriculum. They 'pull' for their students, in that they try to find ways that help their students succeed. They put great emphasis on promoting their students' understanding, and on accommodating individual differences among students. They vary assessments to accommodate these differences. Teachers believe it is imperative for students to be actively engaged in learning, and for them to be motivated to do their best work. These kinds of factors influence teachers as they undertake classroom assessment. Thus teachers undertaking assessment in the classroom need to understand the broader principles and practices of assessment outlined in this book, and at the same time, to adjust to the context of formative assessment and the needs of individuals in the busy-ness of the classroom. Further research is needed to help us understand these processes.

Two examples of classroom assessment processes in action

Teaching cycles can provide numerous opportunities for assessment. This is exemplified here in two different descriptions of how assessment works as part of a teaching cycle; both descriptions are concerned with the teaching of ESL in an elementary school context; the first is a teaching cycle that is being taught in an intensive language centre context and therefore relates closely to an EFL situation, the second is a study of teaching cycles in which ESL learners are learning English by participating in mainstream classroom activities.

In the first example, illustrated in Figure 5.1, Lumley and his colleagues (1994) describe a teaching cycle around the topic of maps; the activities in the teaching cycle are focused on the teaching of English (e.g., following instructions, giving clear directions in both spoken and written form) but this is done under a social studies topic, so that children are also learning the study skills (e.g., map-reading) they need to enter into the mainstream classroom. Assessment is strategically planned to take place, in different forms, throughout the teaching cycle.

The planned assessment activity 'Giving directions' is planned in more detail in advance, with descriptions of the activity itself:

> Using the map, students work in pairs to give each other directions from one point to a final location (e.g., from the school to the local shopping centre, from the school to one's home, from the shopping centre to the local swimming pool).
> (Lumley, Mincham and Raso, 1994, p. E15)

Target group: Middle elementary. **Proficiency level**: Intermediate. **Curriculum area**: Social education. **Topic**: Maps.

	Incidental observation	Focused observation	Discussion	Analysis of samples	Peer-/self-assessment
1. Following and giving directions – around the classroom/the school.	*				
2. Walking around/photographing features in local area, followed by building a simple model of the local area.					
3. Teacher models giving a series of instructions.					
4. Students follow instructions to move around the model.	*				
5. Pairwork: students give each other a series of instructions to follow.	*	*			
6. As a class, discuss features of clear instructions.					
7. Introduce street map of local area and familiarize students with map-reading.					
8. Planned assessment activity: Giving directions.		*	*		
9. Individual writing. Students write a series of directions to a 'secret' destination. Other students find the destination by following the directions.				*	*

Figure 5.1 Example of assessment embedded in a teaching cycle (Lumley, Mincham and Raso, 1994, p. E14).

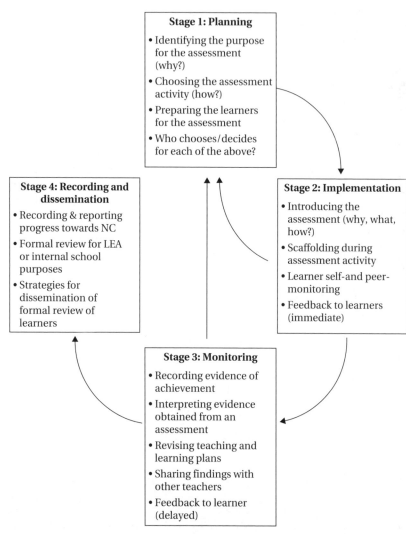

Figure 5.2 Processes and strategies in instruction-embedded classroom assessment.

The language to be assessed is also planned in advance:

- Inclusion of relevant and accurate detail
- Response to interlocutor (e.g., clarifying questions)
- Grammar and vocabulary: directions, time phrases, specific vocabulary (e.g., *intersection, parallel*)
- Use of verbs (e.g., imperatives: *turn, go*)

Lumley and his colleagues' teaching cycle describe assessment-as-plan, that is, the teacher's plans, in the design phase, for teaching and embedding assessment in the classroom.

The second example is from a study of good practice in a number of mainstream classrooms where second language learners are learning English and the mainstream curriculum together. Rea-Dickins (2001) describes assessment-as-action, showing how the phases of classroom assessment are incorporated into the assessment cycle. Rea-Dickins observes teachers carrying out assessment in the classroom and identifies four stages in the process (see Figure 5.2). In the first stage, the *planning stage*, teachers consider the purpose and the procedures they will follow. (This stage incorporates both the design and the operationalization phases of test development since planning is undertaken and the materials are prepared in this stage.) In the next stage, *the implementation stage*, teachers introduce the tasks to the children and engage in scaffolding as required. They encourage learner self- and peer-assessment and provide immediate feedback to the learners. In the third stage, the *monitoring stage*, teachers revise their teaching plans, share findings with other teachers, give delayed feedback to learners and record evidence. In the fourth stage, *recording and dissemination*, teachers record and report and make plans for the dissemination of the findings of their assessment procedures. (These three stages make up the administration phase in which the assessment procedures are put into action, and information analysed and used.) Rea-Dickins shows in this example how classroom assessment is integrally tied to teaching and learning, how teaching strategies are incorporated into the assessment procedure, how information from tests is shared with other teachers, and how teaching and learning plans are revised as a result of the assessment procedure. It also shows how information from the same assessment procedures is used for recording and formal reporting to others.

Rea-Dickins highlights several characteristics of classroom assessment processes.

- Teachers explain assessment tasks to children, introducing the purpose of the task, what the children will be doing during the activity. This reflects the procedures that are followed in teaching tasks.
- There is likely to be scaffolding and teaching during the assessment. It is rare that children are left to work alone on an assessment task in the classroom. Young learners are not usually left to struggle but are given help as they need it. Teachers do this to help children succeed in the

task (the need for help is noted in the judgment of the child's ability), and also because the teachers want to take up the opportunity to teach.

- Self- and peer-assessment is included in assessment; this helps children to learn and to take responsibility for their own learning.
- Feedback to learners is of two kinds. Feedback to individual children may be immediate, most likely during scaffolding within the assessment. Feedback may also be given to the child after records have been collected and evidence interpreted – perhaps in an individual conferencing session or in written form on the child's work.
- Record-keeping is an integral part of the assessment process. Records lead to delayed feedback for children but are also used for formal reporting purposes.

Only certain elements of the assessment process from these two examples have been outlined here, yet the full assessment process will involve design, operationalization and administration phases in some form. In the Lumley, Mincham and Raso example we see a procedure concentrating on the design phase, in which a variety of assessment methods are planned for a teaching cycle. In the Rea-Dickins example we see elements of the design, implementation and administration phases incorporated into the realities of classroom assessment. Both provide insights into classroom assessment at different phases of the assessment process. In these examples, processes of classroom assessment in young learner classrooms are closely tied to processes of instruction. As they do in their teaching, teachers transfer their knowledge of young learners' needs in learning (e.g., their need for clear explanations of procedures, for scaffolding when in difficulty, for immediate feedback) to assessment. It is this kind of teacher knowledge, coupled with informed instruction-embedded assessment processes, that characterize much of classroom assessment in young learner classrooms.

Strategies in classroom language assessment

In classroom assessment, there are opportunities for on-the-run assessment as teaching proceeds and for planned assessment when teachers make a conscious decision to target specific abilities or skills. This section describes assessment strategies that are commonly used by teachers of younger learners in the language classroom.

When language use is being assessed, the strategies available to classroom teachers pivot around the tasks that children are undertaking. When teachers are observing, they are observing children participating in language use tasks and other activities. What is the nature of the tasks children are involved in? Are the tasks in which they are engaged the best tasks to give the most helpful information about children's abilities? For the following strategies to be effective, questions about the selection of the tasks, discussed in Chapter 4, remain as an important backdrop to classroom assessment strategies.

Much classroom assessment is done through continuous assessment practices, combining many strategies over time to assess children's performance, of recording observations and of coming to a decision about progress from the use of these strategies. Observation (both incidental and planned) and on-the-run assessment are key components of continuous assessment, as are many of the strategies described in this chapter such as conferences, portfolios, contracts of work and the selection of specific classroom teaching tasks for planned assessment leading to an aggregated mark.

Incidental observation

Incidental observation happens as part of teaching, as teachers move around to observe and work with children during teaching activities. Incidental observation occurs as the teacher circulates among students who are engaged in classroom tasks and activities. Puckett and Black (2000) describe how teachers engage in incidental observation in the elementary classroom.

> During story time, for example, the teacher scans the listeners for facial expressions and body language and listens for verbal responses indicative of enjoyment, language development, and comprehension. . . .The children are also observed as they interact with one another and with adults. There are innumerable incidental observations inherent in day-to-day interactions with children. These incidental observations provide valuable information about what individual students are feeling, thinking, understand, and can do and guide the responsive teacher in setting appropriate expectations and experiences for them.
> (Puckett and Black, 2000, p. 217)

Incidental observation can take place, for example, during oral interaction, during the drafting process in writing, and during reading, when there is a feedback and support process about the reading, and when questions and discussions take place on reading. Observation might take place outside in the playground (are the second language learners able to hold their own in the new language during play), or in the school assembly (do they appear to be understanding or are they 'tuning out'?). Mental or written notes are made by the teacher to inform teaching decisions.

Planned observation

Planned observation can involve a number of techniques. Teachers may watch children's performance in tasks and activities in the classroom and take notes of what they see in a regular and systematic way. They may use observation checklists or rating scales. These checklists may be developed externally (see the following section) or may be developed by teachers for their own particular purposes.

Mason (1992) suggests that teachers should have a schedule for observing children:

> Be consistent and systematic with your observations because young children's learning about written language develops and changes very rapidly. Have a schedule for observing different children every day or every few days. In this way you will always have an up-to-date detailed record of every child's learning.
>
> (Mason, 1992, p. 117)

Observations become assessment only when they are recorded systematically over time so that characteristics and changes in student performance are noted (O'Malley and Valdez Pierce, 1996, p. 14). Figure 5.3 is a simple example of an observation checklist developed by a teacher reflecting the objectives for a unit of work she is teaching. Note that children might achieve at different levels.

Other terms could be used, such as 'low, high, not applicable', 'beginning, consolidating, established', or a space could be left open for comments. Planned observation of this kind could relate to any aspect of language learning – to sound–letter correspondence, word recognition, reading skills and so on. For a full discussion of observation checklists, see Chapter 8.

Figure 5.4 shows an observation checklist for a whole class. A recording sheet for observations can be a simple grid on one page, with the names

Name Term: Theme: The sea	Always	Sometimes	Rarely
Uses the target language in language activities (e.g., in games, in painting activities)			
Responds to questions and participates in whole-class discussions (Have you seen the sea? When did you go? What kinds of things were on the beach?)			
Follows with his/her eyes as teacher reads and points to words and pictures as he/she reads individually with the teacher			
Reacts to the story line in the storybooks about the sea read by the teacher to the whole class			
Follows instructions in the games and other activities for this unit			
Is able to write half a page about the sea without help			

Figure 5.3 A teacher-constructed observation checklist for a unit of work.

Date ....
Focus of observations (if applicable) ....

Annah	Annabel	Bella	Etc.		

Figure 5.4 A class recording sheet for incidental or planned observation.

of each child in the corner of each box on the grid. Teachers can write very small notes on the sheet that can be transferred later to the child's portfolio. For a full discussion of observation checklists, see Chapter 8.

Observing to check progress against externally developed criteria

Observing against externally developed criteria is often the basis for planned observation. Education Departments provide teachers with externally developed criteria. Teachers are asked to make decisions about children's progress – on which level they are performing – and to report during the school year to the school and the Education Department. Teachers will also take information from specifically designed assessment tasks and will combine this with observation data.

The following form (Figure 5.5) can be used by teachers to observe features of children's language. On the left are criteria, developed externally, and chosen specifically for the planned unit of work, or perhaps because they are salient in the children's learning at present (e.g., they may be working at Level 4, and the teacher is aiming to move them to Level 5).

Externally developed criteria	Dated comments and suggestions	Dated comments and suggestions	Dated comments and suggestions	Possible stage or level
Can respond briefly, with single words or short phrases, to what they see and hear.				
Can give short, simple responses to what they see and hear. They name and describe people, places and objects. They use set phrases (e.g., to ask for help and permission). Their pronunciation may still be approximate and the delivery hesitant, but their meaning is clear.				
Can understand the global meaning of short phrases clearly spoken.				
etc.				

Figure 5.5 Form for observing an individual learner against externally developed criteria (Qualifications and Curriculum Authority).

Teachers have space to write comments and suggestions over time as they observe specified criteria. The value of this pro forma is that it helps teachers to check that a criterion is well-established before deciding on the level at which the child is working.

The very best way to assess children' progress against externally developed criteria is for the teacher to get a picture of the child, make sure that she knows the child's abilities, *then* go to the checklist and fill in the form. Teachers observing against externally developed criteria might follow the guidelines set out in Figure 5.6.

Collect samples of the first drafts of student's writing. Use the format provided to analyse the student's work (two pieces per term is recommended). The performance indicators in the standards are valuable in providing information about what to look for in the student's work. Use the form provided on the next page. Record your observations and ideas. Attach the writing sample to this page with a copy of the analysis and keep in the student's portfolio.

Writing task _____
Teacher _____
Student _____
Date _____
Class _____
Other relevant information _____

Figure 5.6 Guidelines for teachers observing against externally developed criteria (adapted from Northern Territory Board of Studies, 1995).

On-the-run assessment

I have written so far about observation as though it were a separate activity from teaching, when teachers stand back and observe children's activity without immediate intervention. This does happen as part of assessment, but the reality is that teachers are often observing and teaching in one continuous process. This then becomes informal, instruction-embedded assessment, also called on-the-run assessment. Teachers engaging in on-the-run assessment have to take into account 'the interactive and contingent nature of student performance in the classroom which is dynamic and co-produced with the teachers and others' (Leung, 2004, p. 22). On-the-run assessment takes place as teaching and learning proceeds. Intervention might involve questioning, seeking clarification and pushing some learners forward in their understanding and language learning (Rea-Dickins, 2001, p. 437–8). Scaffolding of learning takes place during this process. The following checklist of scaffolding strategies shows the range of ways that teachers might be intervening as they teach, and thus the way that they can be both monitoring and responding to children's performance as they participate in on-the-run assessment.

Open-ended questioning – asking for descriptions, predictions and planning; explanations relating to the child's experience.

Providing feedback – encouragements; thinking aloud; interpretations of meaning; evaluations, clarification requests; acknowledgments and information talk.

Cognitive structuring – rules and logical relationships; sequencing; contradictions.

Holding in memory – restating goals; summaries and reminders.

Task regulation – matching interests and experience; rearranging elements; reducing alternatives; making more concrete.

Instructing – modeling; orienting; direction questioning; elicitations; co-participation.

Figure 5.7   Scaffolding Strategies Checklist (adapted from Notari-Syverson, O'Connor and Vadasy, 1998).

The teacher might construct a worksheet to deal with a particular problem (these children have not internalized enough vocabulary to do with the theme, and therefore they need to do picture-matching on a worksheet, and other activities with the teacher). Alternatively, the information may give the teacher enough information for her to realize that the whole class needs more revision and modelling of a particular genre (for example). These kinds of cyclical processes in the classroom indicate very strongly how teaching and assessment often work together as one process in classroom assessment, rather than as separate processes.

Conferences

Conferences involve the teacher engaging in a focused discussion with young learners about their work. Conferences can focus on individual pieces of work or reading selection, or a portfolio of work. Teachers ask questions to elicit children's responses, in order to assess their progress, and help children to reflect on their own performance. 'What reading did you do this week?' 'Why did you choose this story?' 'Read this piece for me and tell me what it is about.' Conferences are described further in Chapter 7 when we consider the assessment of reading and writing.

Other people in young learners' lives are sources of information; parents can give valuable information, for example, about children's use of their language at home, their interest in reading (in the first and second language) and their emotional well-being. Bilingual aides can share their observations about children's oral language and literacy in their first language. Bilingual aides and other teachers can also share their knowledge of the child's progress in other areas of learning. Conferences with such people provide invaluable sources of information on which to base decisions about children's needs, as well as their performance and progress.

Portfolios

Portfolios are collections of a student's work prepared over a period of time. They may include drawings, written pieces, audio tapes of performances, photographs of artwork (preferably with related language samples, for example, a written piece or a short interview with another child about what it is and how it was made); children's self-evaluation sheets, and so on. The use of portfolios becomes an assessment strategy when there are plans to select tasks for assessment and collection, and when materials are systematically collected.

Much has been written about portfolios (e.g., Genesee and Hamayan, 1994; Moya and O'Malley, 1994; Brown and Hudson, 1998; Puckett and Black, 2000). Portfolios are widely advocated by those involved in elementary education (e.g., Puckett and Black, 2000) and have formed a strong component of assessment in elementary education for many years. They provide a basis by which teachers can accumulate a record of children's achievement over time, motivate learning and discuss progress with others. Children should participate in the selection of portfolio content (following established criteria for selection), and there should be criteria for assessment of individual items and/or criteria for the whole portfolio. There should be evidence of student self-reflection. Using these tools, children are able to reflect upon their efforts and accomplishments, go back over past performances, and through this, become aware of what constitutes progress and how well they are progressing.

Moya and O'Malley (1994) summarize the literature findings about the strengths of portfolio assessment. Portfolios are able to do much more than provide a record of a child's progress. From a perusal of Moya and O'Malley's article, we gain an understanding that portfolios have the potential for:

- enhancing teacher professionalism through meaningful and active involvement in student assessment;
- establishing a sense of community among evaluators;
- encouraging thoughtful activity in the classroom;
- promoting serious discussion of criteria and what goes on in the classroom;
- creating instructional links at different grade levels;
- linking assessment more closely to classroom activities;
- allowing students to draw on the skills they learn in process-centred classrooms;
- allowing assessments to become a teaching strategy to improve learning;
- drawing on students' strengths rather than focusing on their weaknesses;
- involving both students and parents in assessment;
- making assessment more equitable.

The judicious use of portfolios can underpin classroom assessment, establishing greater learner and parental involvement in learning, more opportunities for explicitness in expectations and greater support for learning through assessment. These benefits will come if the philosophy of alternative assessment is linked to the use of portfolios.

Portfolios may be process portfolios, archival portfolios or aggregated portfolios (Puckett and Black, 2000). **Process portfolios** follow a student's growth from day to day, address short-term goals and evaluate current performance. It is work in progress. Process folders are also what teachers simply call their 'folders' on each child. **Archival portfolios** contain selected products from the process portfolio that are deemed to illustrate the child's ability. These are selected at regular intervals (three or four times during the year). This portfolio provides the basis for summative assessment (e.g., it can be used to check achievement of objectives, outcomes or performance standards) and can also be forwarded to the next teacher at the end of the year.

The **aggregated portfolio** is a class portfolio that includes, for example, representative work samples from each student's portfolio and summaries of class records. It is concerned with evidence for accountability and for evaluation of the programme. Weigle (2002) has evaluated the assessment of writing (of older learners) through portfolios in relation to Bachman and Palmer's six qualities of test usefulness.

> In academic settings in particular, portfolio assessment has the potential for greater construct validity, authenticity, interactiveness and impact, and thus may be an attractive choice for assessing writing. Portfolio assessment is also especially appropriate for internal [classroom] assessment where classroom teachers want as close a link as possible between instruction and assessment, and reliability is not a major factor.
> (Weigle, 2002, p. 211)

She states, however, that portfolios offer some drawbacks in large-scale, high-stakes assessment. Questions related to reliability (e.g., can we be certain that the learner will be given the same mark by another teacher for the portfolio?) and the availability of resources (e.g., will there be enough time to collect a portfolio that is representative of the learner's abilities?) need to be addressed. Since high-stakes assessment happens in classroom-based assessment (e.g., when teachers report to their education department, or when a decision is made about the second language child's placement in the mainstream), teachers and schools need to remain vigilant about making portfolios as 'useful' as possible, by, for example, planning samples of works, analysing tasks using the framework of task characteristics and group marking of portfolios.

Marking of portfolios can be done by adding up the marks from the individual pieces of work in the portfolio, by using a set of criteria for the portfolio as a whole (as in Figure 5.8), or through a combination of both. It is more valuable in terms of feedback to the learner to mark individual pieces of work with a separate criteria sheet or marking scheme, and not to just give one overall mark for the folder. Individual tasks need clear criteria both to guide the learner on what is required (and therefore to 'bias for best') and also to give specific feedback for further learning.

When teacher and child, or parents and child, look through the portfolio together, this can itself become a stimulating language activity. The portfolio once marked can be sent home for the parents to look at, and to return with their comments, or it can be produced at a teacher–parent interview and used to illustrate the range and quality of the child's work over the relevant period.

Name .... Date	Marks and comments
Does the portfolio contain the required pieces of work? (Note here the overall score for these individually marked pieces of work) To what extent has the learner presented the folder in an organized way? Is it tidy? Is it labelled in sections? Are drafts included? To what extent do they show that the learner has done the work himself, and has improved his writing in the process of drafting? Is the self-assessment sheet included in the portfolio? To what extent does this show evidence of critical reflection about (1) the quality of the contents of the portfolio? (2) what he has learned during the process? Overall mark and comment: Parents' comments:	

Figure 5.8 Sample criteria for a portfolio.

The European Language Portfolio

The European Language Portfolio aims to provide evidence of learning, in order to 'showcase' learning and progress. It is designed as an archival portfolio. Older learners are able to use the portfolio as a dossier to move between programmes, and to present to potential employers. Younger learners do not need portfolios for the latter purpose, though they may move between programmes and require documentation. The portfolio asks the children to give details about all the languages they can use, and where they use them, and asks them to record what they can do in the target language (colouring in speech bubbles, ticking checklists and filling in additional information about their course). It also gives them a chance to do some language activities.

Ingeborg (1998) writes about European Language Portfolios for pre-elementary and elementary foreign language learners in Europe:

> At this level, skills evaluation will be less necessary than providing information about introductory aspects characteristic of this form of teaching (songs, games, counting, rhymes, and sketches) and giving

children a sense of purpose. A portfolio for young children will require a special layout with space for children's activities e.g. drawing. It will act as a stimulus and as an introduction to knowledge-building, but it will also have informative value when pupils move from one school level to the next: pre-school to elementary school and elementary school to secondary school.   (Ingeborg, 1998, p. 214)

The European Language Portfolio can be downloaded from The Centre for Information on Language Teaching and Research (CILT) at http://www.cilt.org.uk.

Contracts of work and projects

Contracts of work comprise a set of tasks for children to perform over a period of time, agreed between the student and the teacher. The essence of a contract is that it is negotiated between the teacher and the child. Even young learners who cannot read can be given contracts with pictures and graphics (Puckett and Black, 2002, p. 252). Contracts are more suitable for young learners in the upper elementary grades who are able to negotiate the work, undertake to complete it and then carry it out. Contracts help children to organize themselves and begin to be responsible for their own learning. Contract work might be allocated to sections of the class time, for example an hour can be scheduled on a regular basis for children to continue with their contract work. Contracts of work can be assessed on both the process of completing the tasks (e.g., done on time, paced carefully) and the products (using language-related and other criteria). Learners should be provided with explicit assessment criteria for each task in the contract. These can be pinned to the back of the contract for easy reference. The criteria for the tasks in Figure 5.9 might relate to children's ability to work independently, the quality of the information collected from the Internet, their ability to select relevant information for their final report, and the quality (presentation and content) of the final report itself. (See Chapter 8 for a discussion of criteria and marking.)

Contracts of work such as this can be kept in a folder or portfolio by children. Teachers might include self-assessment procedures and/or a journal to include in the portfolio, where children can explore and explain how they felt they have performed, what they have learned, and perhaps what they think of the list of tasks in the contract.

Projects may or may not involve a negotiated contract but similarly involve a series of steps in the completion of a macro-task. Steps in

Name:	Date:	
I will complete the following tasks by the end of Week 3		
Tasks		**By date**
• Choose an animal to report on (see guiding questions attached)		Monday 15th April
• Search in the library/on the Internet for information on the animal		
• Write **a draft report** (using the model given by Ms. Jones) on the computer		
• Ask Ms. Jones to give me feedback on the report		
• Write a **polished version of the report**		
• Include some pictures downloaded from the Internet		
• **Prepare a plan for a presentation** about the animal to be given in front of the whole class		
• Check the plan with Ms. Jones		
• **Present the report** to the class		

Figure 5.9 Example of a contract for an extended or 'rich' task, for upper elementary learners.

projects might include guided library research on the topic, note-taking, drafting and re-drafting of reports and presentation of the report to others orally. Children may complete a project on a specific topic and/or exhibit their work. They may undertake the project individually or in pairs or groups. Their exhibit of the project may be a model, or a chart, a videotaped segment, or a simple website. For language assessment, it is important that language is involved in the exhibit – either through an accompanying description (a written piece, an oral presentation) or within the exhibit itself (a role play, a simulation, a video of a language event in which learners were involved).

Self- and peer-assessment

Self- and peer-assessment are strategies that can be used throughout classroom-based assessment. Children can be encouraged to be active participants in the assessment process if they are guided to think about

Name: .... Class ....

Task:

What I learned:

Problems I encountered:

How I can solve the problems:

Figure 5.10 Self-assessment sheet (Scarino, Vale, McKay and Clark, 1988, Book 3, p. 53).

their own performance, and the performance of their peers. Figure 5.10 shows an example of a self-assessment sheet that can help guide children to begin to focus on their learning and the problems they encountered in a task. If they are aware of the criteria being used, they begin to become more conscious of the quality of their work, and more responsible for their own learning. Teachers can help children to understand, reflect on and refer to criteria. A series of guided discussions about 'what makes a good piece of work', suitable for the age level, can help to make explicit what they should be aiming for. Children can complete charts about their performance and what they have learned. These kinds of activities, discussing pieces of work and filling in charts, can be conducted in the target language, giving another opportunity for language use. Self- and peer-assessment activities can also be very effectively conducted in the first language.

Another example of a self-assessment chart below (Figure 5.11) gives children a chance to check their abilities against set criteria or competencies. These criteria may come from the objectives of the course, and therefore raise awareness about what they should be learning, and how much they have achieved so far.

Teachers might sometimes use 'yes, mostly, a bit, no' as alternatives to guide answers. Interviews between the teacher and individual children can develop self-assessment skills, and also give feedback about the child's motivation and interests. ('What is the best thing you did this week?'). The use of contracts (see previous section) helps children to become more aware of their own plans and progress.

When SPEAKING I can	Not so well	OK	Quite well	Really well
• Ask questions • Answer questions • Introduce myself • Make a request • Talk about my family • Apologize when I do something wrong • Describe something Etc.				

Figure 5.11 Example of a self-assessment sheet.

Self- and peer-assessment forms can be used to guide children to think about their progress; they can be placed in children's portfolios or folders. The form in Figure 5.12 gives an idea how children can be encouraged to engage in peer-assessment before they ask the teacher to check what they can do.

Peer-assessment can be encouraged once criteria are developed and made known. Children need to be trained for peer-assessment, as with self-assessment. For peer-assessment they need to learn, for example, to follow the criteria, say positive things first, and not to laugh at others when they are experiencing difficulty. Children can gain awareness about what is required, or about a good piece of work, by reflecting on another child's performance using a simple set of criteria. Peer-assessment for younger learners is best used for formative purposes – their ability to stand back and give an abstract, independent assessment of a performance will be limited, and they will, of course, be influenced by their friends. Nevertheless, peer-assessment gives children another chance to gain awareness of what is expected, and an opportunity to learn how to help and learn from others.

Self- and peer-assessment is a teaching strategy as much as an assessment strategy. The benefits for the children can be, amongst others, opportunities to increase their language awareness and ability to talk about language (through discussions of what makes a good performance), increased responsibility for their own work and a strengthened sense of being part of a classroom community.

Name .... Class		
Topic: Food and drink		
I can . . . Unit objectives are listed in this column. Examples: **I can . . .** • express likes and dislikes about food • describe my favourite food • choose a meal from a menu • find out the preferences of my friends regarding food • draw a table to show my friends' preferences regarding food • negotiate activities	**Checked by my classmate (write the name of the classmate who checked you)**	**Checked by my teacher**

Figure 5.12 Peer-evaluation (adapted from Scarino et al., 1988, Book 3, p. 53).

Classroom tests

A classroom test refers to an individual task, or set of tasks, in which the conditions (e.g., support, interaction with others and time) are controlled. The scope of tasks that can be used in this way is very wide; they should be selected using a plan that reflects the objectives of the course, the content covered and the types of tasks used in teaching.

Teachers may also devise a classroom test that includes a number of tasks. There are various ways of working out the best balance or spread of tasks in such a procedure. An example of a multi-task procedure, in which the tasks are organized, with weightings, around speaking, vocabulary knowledge, listening and sound–symbol relationships, is given in Figure 5.13.

Quizzes (one word or short answers – e.g., 'Who won the running race yesterday?' 'What is the name of our principal?') and paper-and-pencil

TASK	Speaking	Vocabulary knowledge	Listening	Sound–symbol relationships	Weighting
1			Following directions given by teacher (sit down, stand up, turn around and touch your head, walk to the door).		40
2	Oral interview: Talking with teacher about a picture 'What can you see? What is the girl doing?'				40
3		Drawing pictures of objects as teacher tells the class what she can see in her picture (unseen to children).			10
4				Reading/ saying the sounds of selected letters/ characters on a page to the teacher.	10
					100

Figure 5.13 A planned assessment for young beginning foreign language learners.

tests can be used for a careful check on a child's progress, while ensuring that the work is all the child's own work, and giving him a chance to concentrate without interruption. The following chapters give many examples of tasks and items that can be used for the assessment of oral language, reading and writing.

The planning of a multi-task test reflects the processes followed in the planning of formal tests. (See Chapter 9 on the planning of tests.)

Keeping records in classroom assessment

Keeping records is an integral part of classroom assessment. It enables teachers to draw together data on children's performance from the range of assessment procedures that are used in the classroom. A folder or portfolio can be kept for each child, into which the teacher's notes of observations, samples of work, records of discussions with parents, and so on, can be kept. All these sources help teachers to gather together a picture of children's needs and abilities, and to report on progress to others.

Children can be involved in record-keeping, for example keeping records of their reading, or filling in charts about what they can do. Doing this helps them to reflect on their own learning; it also provides a record of their perceptions of their own learning for the teacher (Rivalland, 1992).

Record-keeping is important for accountability purposes. In most educational contexts there is an expectation that records on children's performance and progress will be kept.

After assessment tasks are carried out, scores need to be recorded in class books or in individual learner folders. Criteria sheets may be filled in and placed in the folder, together with samples of work. The result – a mark together with some qualitative comment if possible – might be noted in a class book with children's names down the left, and descriptions of the tasks along the top. An extract from a teacher's class record

Task	Morning talk (+ date)	Following instructions and drawing a picture	Recalling vocabulary	Etc.
Maria	*Very good. Needed little prompting.*	*Very good. Drew picture as per the instructions.*	*8/10 recalled.*	
Paolo	*Good. Showed a book about animals. Pointed out different animals.*	*Good, but hesitant.*	*5/10 recalled*	
Angela	*Poor. Only able to give one sentence. Shy.*	*Poor. Needed to follow Maria.*	*4/10 recalled*	

Figure 5.14 Class record sheet.

	Morning talk (+ date)	Following instructions and drawing a picture	Recalling vocabulary	Etc.
Date	. . ..	. .. ...		
Overall mark	*Very good.*	*Very good.*	*8/10*	
Comments	*Maria told about her experience at the zoo. Other children listened and asked questions. Needed little prompting.*	*Maria drew the picture from the instructions. She did this quickly and confidently, without glancing at others' work.*	*Matched words quickly and independently.*	

Figure 5.15 Individual record sheet – Maria.

sheet is given in Figure 5.14, with notes made for each child against criteria set out along the top of the sheet.

Some teachers may prefer to rely on the individual records they keep in each child's folder (see Figure 5.15), rather than to have an overall class sheet.

Teacher's assessments can also result in a descriptive record. In Figure 5.16, an ESL teacher's observation of a child's reading behaviour illustrates the degree of professional knowledge required in a well-executed observation of an ESL learner as a reader. This teacher has not only observed the child's performance in a range of tasks, she has also analysed the texts encountered in the mainstream class, and the possible problem areas for ESL learners. She has already completed a form about the child's background and language use at home. The observation record shows that the teacher knows a lot about the child's reading, including his attitude and reading behaviour at home. Her observations are based on an explicit construct of reading established through the National Curriculum in England and Wales.

Teachers' folders – building up a record of progress

A collection of children's work combined with field-notes, interview notes, mark sheets, anecdotal records and other data collected over time enables teachers to build up a record of progress, and to make decisions

Abbas is a 10-year-old boy in Grade 5 of elementary school

The following notes set the reader in context of his school learning environment

- **Type of texts encountered:** class novel, e.g. 'The Sheep Pig' by Dick King-Smith; free choice text – Abbas usually chooses nonfiction books often on the subject of Dinosaurs; Mathematical instructions and problem-solving texts; texts from other curriculum areas such as Science, Technology, History, Geography and Religious Education.
- **Purposes for reading:** to practise reading skills; to read for pleasure; to find out information; to gain access to curriculum knowledge.
- **Contexts for reading:** class novel – chosen by the class teacher, to be studied within a whole class context; free choice text – chosen by Abbas from school library; curriculum texts – chosen by the class teacher within the constraints of the National Curriculum.,
- **Associated activities:** 'The Sheep Pig' novel – comprehension exercises, cloze procedures, story telling and writing alternative endings of stories, word definitions, grammatical structures; free choice literature – book reviews; curriculum texts – answering questions, make something, set up an experiment, write about something.
- **Possible problem areas for ESL learners:** may have become familiar with some subject-specific vocabulary but understanding of meaning may remain underdeveloped; may have developed superficial coping strategies that mask underlying difficulties, e.g. decoding; comprehension of texts may be limited to the literal, therefore support and alternative strategies will be required to gain more thorough understanding; may have difficulty with the subject knowledge and/or the new language introduced.

Observations of Abbas as a reader

- **Reading silently:** (class novel) – fidgeted frequently, read a chunk of text and then looked around the room, looked out of the window etc. – seemed to need 'time out'. Did not seem to be really enjoying the reading process. Seemed relieved when teacher told the class to, 'finish the sentence they were reading'.
- **Reading aloud:** (class novel) – read adequately but tended to rush, ignore punctuation and mispronounce words. He did not go back and self-correct. He frequently looked up for approval and seemed slightly nervous. He had a good sight vocabulary which helped fluency. He used his Arabic–English dictionary to check unknown words. When asking questions based on the text, he answered correctly and had mostly understood the meaning.
- **Strategies used:** He had employed various strategies to help him establish meaning including: visual clues; sensible guesswork deduced from the context; asking questions about words/sentences he was unsure of; sounding out unfamiliar words; checking unknown vocabulary in his bilingual dictionary; using knowledge of wider range of reading strategies, e.g. digraphs, blends, magic 'e', prefixes, suffixes.

- **Areas to work on:** Fluency – more focus needed on punctuation in the text to help develop the flow of the sentence and fluency in general. Abbas needs to be encouraged to pause and self-correct after making a mistake.

Abbas' reading in general

Abbas does not read much at home unless he has to, e.g. for a homework task. He has access to both English and Arabic literature. In class he can read adequately, but has difficulty interpreting unfamiliar texts. He is able to make notes from his reading, but admits that he sometimes omits large quantities of knowledge due to lack of understanding. He handles nonfiction materials competently and is able to distinguish between the index and the contents pages to find information. He enjoys factual, scientific books much more than fiction and therefore has greater motivation to learn how to use them. He is able to gain superficial understanding of the text, by skimming to pick out some key words, but he needs to further develop this skill. He enjoys group reading tasks and gains far greater understanding of texts through working collaboratively with his peers. He enjoys talking to others about factual information discovered from nonfiction texts, especially books about dinosaurs. He frequently chooses these for his free choice texts. However, he prefers audio-visual presentations of nonfiction material, when he can access them (e.g., computers and CD-ROM). Abbas is able to use the library but only does so when he can perceive the need for a specific task. He is generally confident and will ask for help in using catalogues if unsure.

Figure 5.16 Observing an ESL learner as a reader (with permission, Bielby, 2002).

on children's progress based on a wide range of data. Teachers' folders are generally distinguished from portfolios because they are for the teachers' own records.

Rivalland (1992) suggests how records can be organized in folders which become profiles of children's performance. She suggests that teachers keep a manila folder for each child in the class. This folder holds all the various data collected about the child (completed criteria sheets from formal assessment, copies of work from formal assessment, field-notes, audiotapes, notes from interviews, etc). The folder provides easy access to the material for decision-making for a child's interim results for teaching and learning, or his or her assessment result for reporting purposes.

From this folder some key items representing major points in the child's progress can be transferred to a two-ring binder portfolio. It would then be accessible to the teacher, the child, the parents and other interested people. This selected portfolio can be taken home at regular intervals and can be a source for parent–teacher meetings.

Large classes and record-keeping

Teachers with large classes will have less time to manage detailed record-keeping for each child and will need to decide what is possible in their particular situations. An experienced teacher's hints are as follows:

- Do not try to record the progress of all students at the same time. Split the class into groups for the purposes of recording.

- Establish common formats to record learner progress.

- Follow suggestions below which relate in the main to effective use of time when monitoring progress.

  - Target your assessment. Eliminate assessment that doesn't serve a useful purpose, doesn't get used or doesn't justify the cost in teacher time, class time and so on.

  - Keep assessment at a practical level by involving learners wherever possible in devising assessment tools and collating results.

(Brown, 1999, p. 9)

These suggestions emphasize that teachers with large classes need to be realistic in what they can do, by targeting the essential record-keeping that is required. It is ineffective and inefficient if teaching and learning processes are overcome by the requirements of record-keeping, since assessment and record-keeping should support teaching and learning. It is helpful to discuss with other teachers what is practical and worthwhile record-keeping for the teaching situation (the time limits, class sizes, reporting requirements) in which teachers work.

Summary

Classroom assessment is the cornerstone of assessment for younger learners. It involves teachers observing children in a range of tasks over time, engaging in on-the-run assessment, recording data about the children's performance in class and individual record-sheets, and usually storing information in portfolios or folders for use in later review or for reporting to others. Classroom assessment of this kind can be carried out by all teachers of younger learners, to a greater or lesser degree, depending on their teaching and assessment scenario. Some teachers are in situations where system requirements and parental requirements and their own lack of expertise, may militate against the wide use of class-room assessment; however, classroom assessment is a vital tool in the achievement of the system requirements. Teachers can gain skills through collaboration and engagement in 'assessment dialogue' with other teachers, and with parents. Without the information they gain from classroom assessment, teachers would have little choice but to push onwards through the textbook or the curriculum, inevitably losing a number of children along the way. Classroom assessment is an integral part of a learner and learning-centred curriculum in which young learn-ers can thrive.

Assessment takes place throughout the year for different purposes, including diagnosis, collection of evidence to report against externally developed criteria such as standards (see Chapter 9) and summative, end-of-course purposes. Assessment involves three phases, as does formal assessment; a design phase, an operationalization phase and an implementation phase. These three phases are transformed into itera-tive and complex processes in classroom assessment. Early research tells us that teacher assessment is reflective, strongly driven by the teacher's beliefs about education and directed towards individual learning. Assessment may be planned within a teaching cycle and made explicit in a plan (assessment-as-plan). The realities of assessment as it happens in the classroom are becoming clearer as researchers observe and docu-ment the processes and characteristics of assessment (assessment-as-action). As Rea-Dickins (2001) has revealed, teaching practices are reflected in assessment in young learner classrooms, with explanations and introductions, scaffolding and feedback, involvement of other teachers and different uses of assessment information included in the process.

There are a number of classroom assessment strategies available to teachers. Incidental observation is used by teachers as they teach; teachers observe performance as it happens during the course of teaching and learning. Planned observation is usually carried out by teachers who are reporting against externally developed criteria. Other continuous assess-ment strategies include conferences, portfolios, self- and peer-assessment and contracts of work. Projects, tasks and assessment schemes and tests are also used in the classroom by teachers, for formative or summative purposes.

Keeping records is an integral part of classroom assessment. Teachers' folders and portfolios, together with records in the form of charts of observation and written reports of observations, support teachers' monitoring of children's progress and back up their reporting.

Classroom assessment carried out in these ways becomes the cornerstone of language assessment for younger learners. Employing a combination of these strategies helps teachers to build up a close and realistic knowledge of their learners' abilities. Classroom assessment can encourage children to participate in the learning process and can build motivation and confidence in children as they are given ongoing support to learn.

CHAPTER SIX

Assessing oral language

This chapter is devoted to the assessment of young learners' oral language. The assessment of oral language is challenging because of the combination of speaking and listening activities that may be involved: sometimes more speaking than listening (as in extended speaking tasks like news telling); sometimes a combination of both (as in conversations); and sometimes more listening than speaking (as in teacher-led class discussions). Teachers and assessors need to be able to assess children's language use ability in speaking and listening in tasks such as interviews, pairwork tasks and group interaction tasks that combine these activities. Teachers also need to be able to assess speaking and listening separately, especially in extended speaking and extended listening tasks.

Through oral language interactions with the teacher and with each other, young learners are able to try out their hypotheses about language, receive feedback and form new hypotheses. Through oral language children clarify their ideas about the world and from this base can move towards more formal expositions of their ideas in oral and written forms. Oral language is therefore the mainstay of both language learning and academic learning for young learners and a central tool in teaching and assessment in the classroom.

> Oral work not only leads to new learning; as a technique of revision it also reinforces the initial learning and prevents it from slipping away. Oral work can be used as an evaluation of pupil progress when teachers intervene in group work and become consultants. It can precede

any subject matter to reveal students' levels, interests and expectations, putting teachers in touch with the reality of their pupils (Freire, 1972).   (Corson, 1988, p. 28)

Oral language assessment is often avoided in external testing because of practical considerations; yet oral language makes up the core of young language learners' curriculum. Hence, to skip over oral language and to assess language learning through reading and writing is to deny the essence of young learners' language learning. Ways need to be found to assess oral language in external testing situations, if the impact of testing is to be positive.

In this chapter, I will outline the kind of oral language expectations that young foreign and second language learners encounter at school and then discuss the relationship between spoken and written language. This is followed by a description of the scope of oral language to be assessed, an overview of issues in oral language assessment, and then examples of types of assessment tasks in speaking and listening. Sections on assessing vocabulary and grammar in oral language complete the chapter.

Oral language at school

Children learning a foreign language in formal school settings learn best by communicating primarily through oral language; effective programmes give children early opportunities for practice of routine language and basic language patterns, but also for imaginative play, action rhymes and songs, response to narrative texts and participation in narrative and simple description. As they grow older (beyond eight) and become more proficient, young learners continue to learn best primarily through oral language, moving into conversations, narratives, simple recounts and reports. Written language is limited in its support of oral language learning in the early years, though a 'switch point', when written language becomes more supportive of oral language development, happens around eight or nine years of age (Cameron, 2001, pp. 66–7). In some foreign language programmes oral language activities move towards being content-based activities, when children move beyond social interaction in the classroom to academic use of language.

Most children in second language situations are engaged in primarily oral learning activities in the early years of school, but many will also be engaged in the serious business of learning how to read and write at the same time. For second language learners, a lack of oral language in the target language constitutes a major drawback for literacy development. However, oral language, once consolidated, provides an essential foundation for literacy development, and later, for academic learning (Bills, 1995). Oral language activities at school tend to become more and more content-based, mirroring the demands of the curriculum, as second language children progress through school. Second language children are generally expected to produce a wider range of genres and more extended talk incorporating more complex background knowledge as they progress through their primary years.

The relationship between spoken and written language

In this and the next chapter, listening, speaking, reading and writing are treated as separate language use activities for assessment purposes. Is this a legitimate thing to do? It is, if we recognize that these activities differ in many important ways. The features of language use in each activity depend on the purpose, the audience, the norms and expectations of the context (Weigle, 2002). School literacy educators have expressed these notions of sociocultural and cognitive differences between speaking and writing through a **mode continuum**. The mode continuum (see Figure 6.1) illustrates how language use differs according to the context and the nature of the cognitive demand on the child. **Mode**, in the continuum, refers to the channel of language use, which can be spoken or written.

At the 'action' of the mode continuum, we typically find oral language and literacy tasks that are 'face-to-face', like a conversation between friends, participation in a game, or writing a friendly e-mail. Meanings are

Face-to-face interaction	Non-interactive monologue
ACTION >> **REFLECTION**	
Language-Accompanying experience	Language-constructing experience
Typically oral language and literacy tasks that are 'face-to-face'	Typically written texts, but also oral texts such as formal debates and speeches

Figure 6.1 The mode continuum (Derewianka, 1992, p. 76).

created collaboratively since participants can use a fair amount of shared knowledge. They can refer to the immediate environment and do not need to mention things explicitly. There is give and take as participants build on each others' ideas. At the 'reflection' end of the continuum are oral monologues or written reflective pieces, where the onus to construct the meanings is on the individual, and these meanings must be self-sufficient. The text is more abstract; it is likely to be crafted, well-organized and dense (Derewianka, 1992).

Spoken and written language therefore have shared characteristics, which arise out of the purpose, audience and norms of the language use context. Yet there are also characteristics that define them as separate, not least of which is the fact that they require different cognitive abilities. Spoken language is transitory and must be processed in real time (unless it is written down in advance and read aloud); **prosodics** such as stress, intonation, pitch, volume and pausing are available to enhance meaning. Writing requires the knowledge and ability to write (orthography), lacks the devices available to speakers to enhance the message (Brown, 1994) (although punctuation such as exclamation marks can help in this regard) and requires careful planning and structuring of the text. Reading requires the ability to read, and interpretation strategies to make meaning available. Because of these differences, amongst others, it is legitimate to treat these language use activities separately for assessment purposes. However, the final decisions on the nature of the language use to be assessed (e.g., whether it is more action or reflection-oriented) need to take place at the task level.

The nature of oral language ability

In language use situations, when people speak, it is not the case that they simply open their mouths and speak the words and sentences. When people speak, they are doing so in a cultural context, they are speaking to another person or persons (perhaps friends, a teacher or a tester) who bring with them a relative degree of status and power and they are doing so in order to meet the purpose required of the interaction, which may be a conversation, or a task that needs completing.

Children use oral language either in conversations or in extended talk (Cameron, 2001). Conversations usually involve unplanned speech and are more casual in nature. Extended talk usually involves planned speech and is more formal. Assessment of participation in conversations is a challenge because conversation is 'dialogic' in nature; people take turns, finish off each other's utterances and build on each other's ideas: 'any attempt to unravel one pupil's spoken thread and regard it as a solo 'text' is doomed to failure. The meanings being worked on often hover uncertainly between the participants' (Des-Fountain and Howe, 1992, p. 140). In conversations, speakers are supported by feedback from **interlocutors** (other speakers) through nods, smiles, responses and by the kinds of responses, for example follow-up questions, incorporations (taking up what was said and using it), exclamations and so on. Scowls, interruptions and lack of eye contact deter even the most proficient speakers. The role of interlocutors is just as important in classroom interaction. As I will discuss below, in wider classroom interaction children's opportunities for participation depend on the nature of the classroom interaction that is set up by the teacher. Children's participation may be affected by the behaviour of one or several of the other participants, and by the kinds of interaction with the teacher. When teachers ask two-choice questions ('Do you like lettuce [or not?]') or display questions to which everyone knows the answer ('What colour is your hair?'), responses are more limited. When teachers ask referential questions to which they don't know the answer ('What do you think about that?') and add their own personal contribution, then children are likely to contribute more (Wood, 1992, p. 211). Children in second language classrooms may have difficulty participating in classroom interaction for more cultural reasons: they may not yet be familiar with the implicit rules of interaction in the classroom, for example, who should speak when, and to whom, and the degree of informality that is acceptable.

Spoken language often has incomplete sentences, non-specific words, and may contain relatively little information in any given chunk of language (Brown and Yule, 1983). This is because speech is made up of **idea units**.

> [Idea units are] . . . short phrases and clauses connected with *and, or, but* or *that* or not joined by conjunctions at all but simply spoken next to each other, with possibly a short pause between them.. . . Speakers are trying to communicate ideas that listeners need to comprehend in real time, as they are being spoken, and this means working within the parameters of the speakers' and listeners' working memory.   (Luoma, 2004 p. 12)

Speakers use fillers and hesitation markers (e.g., *kind of, sort of*) and will use periods of silence and repetition to give themselves time to speak. More mature speakers use phrases like *Now, let me see* and *That's a good question.* Therefore in informal conversation-type tasks speakers (even native speakers) are unlikely to produce language with complete sentences and precise word choice without hesitations and backtracks, slips and errors. Even in more formal, extended talk tasks, it is natural for speakers to stop in mid-sentence to begin a new sentence, hesitate, and to add '*ums*' and '*ahs*' as they think. The only time this will not happen (except with the most gifted speakers) is when speakers have detailed notes, or are reading a prepared speech word for word. This level of ability is not expected from young foreign/second language learners who, even when reading a prepared speech, will tend to hesitate because of their developing reading abilities, the demands of the foreign/second language and usually shyness about speaking in front of others.

In extended talk, there is also interaction; speakers must monitor their audience's response and adapt if necessary to convey the message more clearly; they need to meet their audience's expectations of the discourse structure (e.g., a morning talk), and their listeners need to be attentive and supportive.

The ability to use language for conversational interactions and oral presentations is not necessarily present in young learners. Cameron (2001, pp. 52–3) describes how, for example, children through to 10 years of age gradually develop the ability they need in oral language to estimate what other people will understand from what they say, and to ask for information if they don't understand. Thus complexity of oral language assessment of young learners is compounded by these maturational factors; children may not participate because they do not yet have the cognitive and social skills that are needed.

The scope of oral language to be assessed in young learner programmes

The scope of oral language to be assessed may be determined by a curriculum but may also be determined through standards or tests which may or may not be aligned with the curriculum. In some situations, where no curriculum exists, classroom teachers decide what should be assessed. Ultimately, the scope of oral language assessment depends on the purpose for the assessment, whether it is internal or external assessment, and whether it is for learning or accountability purposes. A curriculum will be influenced strongly by a number of factors, including the standards that it may be expected to meet, the aims of the programme, whether the programme is a foreign or second language programme, and the number of contact hours available. The curriculum may be written as goals and objectives (e.g., 'To establish and maintain relationships and routines in school and community situations') or as outcomes, that is, statements of expected achievement (e.g., 'Children make requests and interact with peers and familiar adults'). The curriculum may set out a list of genres. The following genres are typically found in oral language curricula for school learners:

- giving an account of what happened (Recount);
- arguing two sides of an issue (Debate);
- describing a significant incident (Anecdote);
- telling someone how to do something (Procedure);
- describing a person or a place (Description);
- finding out information from someone (Interview);
- maintaining relationships (Casual conversation);
- working out what to do (Planning).   (Derewianka, 1992, p. 72)

Children might be expected to engage in language use within these genres at various levels of language ability. An intermediate student may describe a procedure such as a simple science experiment, through a slot-and-filler task (having learned some simple phrases in order), while a more advanced student may be able to achieve the same purpose in a five minute 'free-speaking' demonstration. These differences in performance would be taken into account when the child's performance is judged.

A curriculum may also contain a list of functions. Functions are written as categories of behaviour (e.g., 'expressing thanks and gratitude; identifying and asking about people, places and things'). Functions give teachers and assessors the scope of oral language that is expected to be learned and therefore assessed. Grammar and vocabulary to be covered may also be listed as part of a curriculum covering oral language. A list of functions, and grammar and vocabulary leaves teachers with a list of decontextualized language that needs to be contextualized in tasks, both for teaching and for assessment.

A framework for oral language ability as a theoretical construct

What are the characteristics, then, of successful performance that teachers and assessors would look for as children's oral language develops?

Table 6.1 uses Bachman and Palmer's model of language knowledge (set out in Chapter 2) to describe the characteristics of oral interaction. The model can be used to provide a theory-based view of the characteristics of children's developing oral language, incorporating the range of knowledge that children need to be able to deal with the realities of interactive discourse in social and classroom contexts. The extent of language development that is sought after will depend on the curriculum requirements and/or the situations children will encounter in the target language.

Table 6.1 *Some characteristics of oral language ability (based on Bachman and Palmer's (1966) model of language knowledge)*

Depending on the curriculum requirements, and the situations children encounter, their development of oral language ability needs to include the following areas of language knowledge:

Organisational knowledge
Grammatical knowledge: Children's knowledge of vocabulary, syntax and phonology needs to grow and deepen. Their syntax needs to increase in accuracy. Their knowledge of phonology needs to improve – they need to utter sounds, words and sentences clearly with appropriate pronunciation and intonation. They need increasingly to understand others' pronunciation and intonation clearly. They need increasingly to be able to understand the different meanings implied by different intonation patterns (e.g., '*You're going home now? You're going home now.* ')

Textual knowledge: Children need to be increasingly able to speak in ways that are cohesive and well-organized; they need to do this both in conversational interactions and in extended speaking turns. For example, they need to be able to use and understand conjunctions that join sentences and paragraphs together (*but, then, and, though*).They need to improve in their ability to use relative clauses (*That is the house that my uncle lives in*). They need to learn how to refer back to other parts of the sentence (*That's my uncle's house. Let's go in and meet him*). In listening, children need to improve their ability to use textual knowledge to understand what is being said. They need to learn how to listen both to conversations and to extended texts.

Pragmatic knowledge
Functional knowledge: Children's ability to use language for many different functions needs to grow. They need to learn how to use language to get what they want, to learn, to imagine things, to think about things. They need to learn how to understand the purposes behind the language that is spoken to them, even when those purposes are not directly stated. (e.g., if the teacher says *You can go outside if you want to do that again,* does the child understand that she is really saying that she should stop? Experience of the context tells the child that no one goes outside the classroom unless they are in trouble.')

Table 6.1 *(continued)*

Sociolinguistic knowledge: Children need to learn to use oral language appropriate
to the language use situation that they are in. They need to learn to use and
understand the idioms and cultural references that they encounter in target language
situations (Do they understand, for example, that they can say *See ya* to friends, but
Goodbye to the teacher?) They need to learn how to appreciate the humour, the
attitudes, beliefs, ideals and values inherent in the talk of other people from different
cultures, and to communicate and act in ways that help them to reach out to people
from another culture.

Except in some large-scale assessment situations, where assessment is
designed to measure children's language use ability outside any particular curriculum (this situation is not common in young learner assessment), the scope of assessment mirrors the scope of the teaching and
learning programme. The scope of assessment should never be pulled
out of 'thin air'; what is assessed is always derived from the curriculum,
from the individual teacher's teaching objectives or from the teacher's
theory of language ability.

Contributing knowledge and skills

Curricula that are language–use oriented usually also list the contributing knowledge and skills that children need to learn. These are usually
assessed formatively in the classroom, and are checked through the
use of specially designed criteria in language use tasks (see Chapter 8).
Table 6.2 sets out a number of the contributing knowledge and skills that
would usually be included in an oral language curriculum statement, and
that would therefore need to be assessed. Some of these are embedded in
the theoretically based model in 6.1, but in curricula they are often listed
separately, alongside language use outcomes or objectives, intended as a
set of skills that teachers also need to attend to.

Teachers and assessors need to take account of the goals, objectives
and/or outcomes, and the range of contributing knowledge and abilities
in a curriculum, if it exists, and assess children's oral language skills
accordingly. Alternatively (and also additionally), theoretically based definitions of the constructs of oral language, such as the one described
above, are available to inform oral language assessment.

Table 6.2   *Examples of contributing knowledge and skills for oral language included in curricula*

- **Ability to discriminate sounds, stress and intonation:** For example, ability to recognize the stress in words and in connected speech. Ability to recognize differences in the use of intonation, e.g. to differentiate between questions and statements.

- **Knowledge of a growing range of vocabulary:** Ability to use and understand a growing range of vocabulary in their oral language. Knowledge of vocabulary growing in depth and accuracy.

- **Knowledge of a growing range of grammatical structures:** Ability to use and understand a growing range of structures. Improving accuracy in the use of grammatical structures.

- **Ability to predict meaning from a range of cues:** Ability to use the semantic, syntactic and graphophonic cues available in others' speech. Ability to use the context to facilitate understanding. Ability to draw on prior knowledge to facilitate understanding.

- **Ability to listen for explicit and implicit meaning:** Ability to listen for main ideas. An ability to listen for specific information. Ability to understand the connection between ideas by recognizing linking words and phrases e.g., *because, therefore, but, also, at last.*

- **Ability to take responsibility for their own learning:** Ability to seek out opportunities to speak to others, and listen to others talk in the target language. Willingness and ability to ask for help.

- **Ability to use communication strategies:** An ability to use strategies to join in and maintain conversations (e.g., using language to make sure they have a turn in groups, asking for repetition or confirmation when they don't understand).

- **Confidence and motivation:** Children show curiosity about situations where the target language is used. They enjoy using the language. They interact and listen with confidence.

Issues in the assessment of the oral language of young learners

Below, I discuss briefly a number of issues that arise in relation to the assessment of the oral language of young language learners.

Selecting oral language assessment tasks

Various factors need to be taken into account in the selection of oral language assessment tasks for young learners.

Motivation

Young learners need to see the value of participating in the assessment tasks that we use; therefore assessment tasks for oral language require a genuine need to communicate. To engage children, tasks usually have incorporated into them devices to maintain interest: colourful and interesting pictures, an action or doing component, a requirement for an immediate and compelling one-to-one interaction with another person, usually an adult. Puppets can also provide the gestures and to-and-fro interactions that keep children's attention in conversations. Incorporating an element of surprise or unpredictability into the task helps to keep a child's attention, as does the idea of a problem or mystery to be solved.

Determining the appropriateness and usefulness of oral langauge assessment tasks

How can teachers and assessors determine the appropriateness and use-fulness of oral language tasks? Oral language tasks will be more useful, and more likely to engage learners in language use, when more support is available – for example support from the things around in the environ-ment, visual support like pictures and objects, or conversational support such as gestures and facial expressions. Without these here-and-now features, oral language becomes more decontextualized and more cogni-tively demanding. And not only do objects and pictures that children can handle and look at provide support, they can help children to feel less anxious, drawing them into the task.

Oral language tasks are less likely to engage learners if there is not some introductory activity to 'tune' the child into the topic and into the lan-guage that is going to be used. In classroom assessment, teachers will usually introduce ideas and language to the whole group in introductory activities before children continue on with the assessment activity alone or with others. Oral language tasks are less likely to engage learners if no help is given along the way, and usually teachers will give support to help children to continue and be successful in the task. These introductory sessions, and the subsequent support, are taken into account when teachers make judgments about children's performance in classroom oral language tasks. Introductory sessions and in-task support are not possible in external tests, unless interviews or other one-to-one oral language tasks can be devised. Oral language tasks without introductory session and in-task support can be difficult for children.

Oral language tasks can be more, or less, engaging depending on the language that is being used by the interlocutor. Language use becomes more difficult, for example (as was discussed in Chapter 4), if a wider range of vocabulary is used, and if grammar is more complex. Language is easier if words are repeated, and if redundant information is given (Phillips, 1993). Oral language tasks that require more sophisticated communication strategies, like taking turns in group discussions and interrupting politely, are more difficult that those that are structured and supported closely by an adult. Expectations of register variation in the task (talking politely to a visitor, or talking in a friendly way to a peer) also affect the task difficulty.

Teachers and assessors need to be mindful of the cognitive requirements of the oral language task. If young children are asked to talk about something that happened last week, an element is being introduced into the task that may be beyond that child's cognitive capacity and may prejudice their performance. Older children in the upper elementary grades are more able to recount events in the past, imagine future events and describe abstract processes. However, most children of this age will still benefit from pictures and diagrams to assist them to talk in these ways.

Some expectations of oral language and listening tasks are more difficult for some young learners because of cognitive, social or emotional factors. Strangers may frighten some young learners, especially if the stranger is (for example) big and imposing or different. Cultural differences may cause some children to find some tasks more difficult than others, or indeed may cause teachers and assessors to judge their performance as weak. For example, young indigenous learners in Australia are unlikely to look an interviewer in the eye, because this is impolite in the Aboriginal culture. The framework of task characteristics in Chapter 4 can help to check the features of tasks to ensure that the selected tasks will be fair for all children.

Other dimensions of oral language tasks that influence performance, and therefore the selection of tasks

A task may involve conversational language or extended talk. Both have their own dimensions of cognitive difficulty. Conversational interaction requires children to listen to short turns in order to respond, to make split-second decisions about what to say, when to intervene and how to take a turn. Extended speaking involves a child giving a talk that is likely not to be interrupted and that requires its own internal coherence (e.g., the use of connectives which indicate the organization of the ideas, such as *then, after that).*

Other dimensions of oral interaction tasks are:

- the topic of the interaction
- the level of formality (informal, consultative, formal)
- the number of participants
- the relative status of the participants (high/low; low/high; equal)
- the familiarity of the participants with each other (stranger, acquaintance, friend)
- the gender of the participants

Each of these dimensions can make the task easier or more difficult, depending on the characteristics of the task and the personal characteristics of the learners.

The use of written texts

Finally, the use of written text as a basis for an oral assessment task should be avoided until literacy skills are known to be secure. For example, it would be inappropriate to ask children to read and answer questions on a story, when the child does not have the literacy skills to read that story well enough to gather the details of that story that are needed. Even though children's oral language may be progressing well, their performance on the oral task may be hampered by yet-to-be-developed skills in literacy.

Opportunities to assess oral language use in the classroom may not be available

An oral interaction task or tasks can be devised to assess oral language formally in the classroom. If the tasks are well chosen, this will give teachers and assessors an opportunity to assess the extent of children's oral language ability. However, oral interaction of young learners is often assessed informally through teacher observation in the classroom. Opportunities for assessment of oral language will not automatically be available in the classroom. Oral language can take place only if the 'pragmatic climate' (Cameron, 2001) of the classroom is right, that is, if the classroom approach is one that encourages language use, where children are using language creatively to exchange meanings for particular purposes.

In mainstream classrooms where second language children are learning the target language alongside first language-speaking peers, there is a real danger that second language learners are not given a chance to show what they can do. Harklau (1994) has observed that ESL learners in mainstream classes in the United States have little opportunity to talk (and therefore that they had restricted opportunities to learn how to use the language).

> In an average class, all other things being equal, individual students had only a 1:25 or 1:30 chance of being allocated a turn by the teacher during these activities. Even more significant for L2 learners, student participation in teacher-led discussion . . . was usually limited to a single word or phrase. (Harklau, 1994, p. 250)

Harklau's research was conducted in high schools, but her work serves to warn primary teachers of the danger of observation in the classroom; second language learners may be found to be weak in oral interaction possibly because they may not have an opportunity to show what they are able to do in the busy-ness of a classroom dominated by first language speakers. (Conversely, they may be weak because they have not had sufficient opportunities to interact.) As a principle of good teaching, teachers need to ensure that children have equal opportunities to participate in classrooms and, through interaction, to learn. Similarly, as a principle of 'useful' assessment, teachers need to ensure that they give children opportunities to show what they can do, and that they collect the best samples of children's performance.

Assessing pronunciation

When assessing pronunciation, teachers and assessors need to be concerned with the articulation of words and longer stretches of language in discourse rather than in isolation. Words change when they are used in sentences, for example in English in the sentence 'Please sit down,' 'please' and 'sit' become joined because the /z/ sound at the end of 'please' becomes devoiced or becomes an /s/ sound, when it is followed by the /s/

sound in 'sit'. In addition, the intonation, rhythm and stress of sentences change when sentences are combined to convey meaning in discourse.

In the main, pronunciation is best assessed in the context of language use. The central criterion for assessment should be *intelligibility* – can children be understood when they say something to others? If children cannot be understood, are there persistent errors that are being made that are causing this difficulty? Is the problem that specific sounds, for example the shortening of certain vowel sounds (as when 'dark' sounds like 'duck' in English) is consistently a problem? Or is the problem to do with prosody, that is, with features such as loudness, intonation, and word and sentence stress patterns?

Knowledge of the characteristics of the child's first language will help a teacher to know, in formative assessment, if a pronunciation error is due to the first language influencing the pronunciation in the target language. In young learners, pronunciation is not usually a long-term problem if children have good models in their input, and many opportunities to use language.

In external assessment, the main criterion for the assessment of pronunciation will be intelligibility.

Assessing vocabulary

Vocabulary can be assessed both through a child's oral language use and through literacy tasks. I include vocabulary assessment in this chapter because vocabulary development first takes place in oral language, and in the early stages of learning; it is only once vocabulary knowledge has established its foundations in oral language that it will be transferred to literacy. Once literacy is well established, vocabulary knowledge can increase through reading, and can be assessed through writing in some of the ways described below.

As children' language abilities develop to more advanced levels, assessors will be checking that children have the vocabulary they need to understand and use language for a range of purposes in a range of different contexts. They will be checking that children have, for example, vocabulary that helps them to describe things (*circular, straight)*, vocabulary that helps them to compare things (*better than, most exciting)*, idiomatic vocabulary and phrases (*Once upon a time*. . .), vocabulary that helps them to connect ideas (*and, then, however*), and vocabulary that helps them to modify the way things are said (*I think, maybe, sometimes*).

Even as children develop to advanced levels of language ability (as in second language contexts), they may not have full control of the nuances of meanings in their receptive and productive knowledge. However, children's ability to enhance meaning through vocabulary can be observed as they edit their written work, for example adding more words and phrases or changing words to achieve the exact meaning they want. The development of vocabulary knowledge is integral to the development of language ability; every component of communicative language ability (grammatical, textual, functional and sociolinguistic) relies on increasing knowledge of vocabulary, in all its definitions.

In the classroom, vocabulary can be assessed constantly and informally during the teaching and learning process. Teachers can use flashcards and pictures to teach and to check understanding ('Peter, what is this?'). They can point to objects and ask for words, and carry out oral gap-filling when they are reading stories (The man jumped onto the _____). Children may read a card aloud, or may respond with actions or by following the command (*jump, hop, skip, dance*). Adverbs can be added (*quickly, slowly*). Vocabulary games (e.g., finding the odd one out, picking up a word card from a pile, reading it and looking for a match) can help children to gain reading vocabulary, and also help teachers to check vocabulary.

Teachers can ask children to brainstorm vocabulary in a topic before a teaching task. 'What words can you think of that describe animals?' This helps to check which children have learned the words. As children progress, and in order to look at more depth in vocabulary knowledge, vocabulary networks can be used on the board to check if children can organise the words in their relationships. An example of this is provided in Figure 6.2 in which children are asked, 'What words can you think of that go with the topic word in the middle?' Additional spines can be added as children progress in their knowledge of the vocabulary.

When learners have developed some literacy skills, teachers and assessors can also check vocabulary through writing, using picture cloze ('Fill in the words in this story – the picture of the item is given'), word-matching tasks ('Draw a line between the words with similar meanings in the list') and picture labelling ('Label the parts of the body in this picture'). For more advanced learners, multiple-choice questions ('Choose the word that matches best the underlined word in the text') can be used. These are the kind of discrete-point vocabulary items that are sometimes used in external tests. Self-assessment strategies, such as the elicitation scale in Figure 6.3, can also be used, when children can look at words and fill in a self-report.

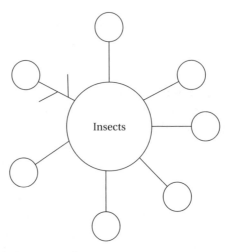

Figure 6.2 A Vocabulary network.

Self-report categories

I   I have never seen this word

II   I have seen this word before, but I don't know what it means

III   I have seen this word before and I *think* it means ___ (synonym or translation)

IV   I *know* this word. It means ___ (synonym or translation)

V   I can use this word in a sentence ____ (Write a sentence.)

Figure 6.3 The VKS (Vocabulary Knowledge Scale) elicitation scale (Paribakht, 1997, in Read, 2000, pp. 27–8).

To assess if vocabulary knowledge is indeed established in ways that mean that children can use the words with confidence and in different contexts, vocabulary is best assessed in an integrated way through language use in language use tasks. Criteria sheets or holistic rating scales that assess overall quality of the performance, one aspect of which is vocabulary, can be used. Alternatively, the assessment can use analytic scales that focus on vocabulary within the context of the language use task (see discussion of holistic and analytic rating scales in Chapter 8). In this way teachers and assessors can check if the vocabulary is learned to the point where it is being used appropriately to the topic, audience and purpose within the text and that it has range and depth, appropriate to the expectations of the child's age and proficiency development. For further discussion of vocabulary assessment, see Read (2000).

Assessing grammar

Grammar is also included in this chapter because assessment of grammar for young learners begins in oral language and continues in a more focused way in writing tasks only as children's language ability expands. There are different ways of looking at grammar. Grammar may simply be defined as accuracy (for example, *Is the child speaking the language without errors in word order and word endings? Is the child understanding what is said to him?*). Bachman and Palmer's (1996) theoretical definition of grammatical knowledge includes knowledge of vocabulary, syntax and phonology/ graphology; syntax refers to a range of features of syntactic structure depending on the requirements of the task, and grammar is assessed within the wider theoretical framework for language use that includes organizational knowledge, pragmatic knowledge and sociolinguistic knowledge. Purpura's (2004) more recent definition of grammatical knowledge is even broader because he introduces the notion of conveyance of meaning into the idea of grammar (rather than into the broader definition of language use as in Bachman and Palmer's framework). Thus, 'Grammatical knowledge is involved when examinees understand or produce utterances that are grammatically precise and contextually meaningful' (Purpura, 2004, p. 89). Learners have the grammatical knowledge they need when they can do this at the sentence and discourse levels. Purpura reminds us that the type and range of grammatical features required to communicate accurately and meaningfully will vary from one situation to another (Purpura, 2004, p. 84).

Young learners' grammar can be assessed in oral language through observation involving analysis of children's oral language as they engage in meaningful language use activities. Observation checklists, devised through a needs analysis, help teachers and assessors to check the grammar that is required for children's successful engagement in the task; these checklists usually describe a range of features of language that are required – not just grammar.

In the early stages of language learning, teachers and assessors need to be aware of children's propensity to employ formulaic expressions or chunks of language. Language chunks are unanalysed, in that children are unlikely to have the knowledge of the grammatical structure within the chunks. The use of chunks gives children a chance to engage in meaningful language use with the support of the context and other people (see Chapter 2). There may be some movement towards creative use of structure with the chunks as children's grammatical knowledge develops. This move to creative language use of structures often results in errors. Teachers and assessors need to understand that these creative errors are signals for growth rather than signs of non-learning. Assessment of grammar in these early stages of SLA must therefore be extremely cautious; there may be very little conscious awareness of the grammar within the language, both because of the use of chunks and because of limits in metalinguistic awareness. Assessment of grammar (in both oral and written language) in the earlier stages of language learning, and indeed beyond, should be informed by knowledge of SLA and designed to encourage, not stifle, this growth. This can be done by teachers praising language use and overlooking errors if meaning is conveyed. Errors can be scored as wrong as children's language progresses further; indeed, one of the skills of a foreign/second language teacher is knowing which errors should be corrected and when and which should be left until later.

As young learners progress in their language ability, and in their cognitive maturity, observations and analysis can look more closely at their knowledge of grammatical form at the sentence level and discourse level. At the sentence level, Purpura (2004, p. 91) lists prosodic forms such as stress and intonation, use of inflectional affixes, e.g., '-ed', use of voice, mood, word order. At the discourse level, he lists cohesive forms such as using personal and demonstrative references, use of logical connectors, information management forms such as using prosody and emphatic 'do' and interactional forms such as discourse markers like 'oh' and 'ah' and repairs and fillers. For an account of the range of grammatical features that may need to be assessed, see Purpura (2004, Chapter 4) or refer to other theoretical frameworks for grammar such as functional grammar (Halliday, 1994).

If the purpose is diagnostic assessment of contributing knowledge and skills, then discrete-point assessment may be appropriate. If the purpose of assessment is oral language use ability, then the grammatical requirements and expectations for a task are best combined with the wider range of features required to complete a language use task successfully. In this case, the grammatical features to be assessed are only some of the features to be assessed in an oral language use task. Examples of ways to construct oral language checklists and rating scales that incorporate grammatical knowledge can be found in Luoma (2004).

Classroom assessment of oral language

The following suggestions extend the principles and strategies of classroom assessment outlined in Chapter 5 to oral language assessment and
can be used in the classroom in conjunction with many of the oral language assessment tasks described in the following section.

Observation

Observation is a central tool for assessment of oral language in the classroom. Oral language is used in classroom management (e.g., when teachers tell children to settle down), in classroom instructions ('the next thing
I want you to do is . . . '), in group and individual readings of stories,
discussions, class surveys, literature-based tasks, games and so on.
Interaction with the teacher can occur in a group setting or on a one-to-
one basis. Interactions with other children, perhaps in problem-solving
tasks, can be observed by the teacher with or without intervening. When
literature is read to the class, teachers can check whether individual children are responding to the humour and/or the excitement at the expected
moments.

In the classroom, oral language assessment often occurs as part of a
cycle of teaching. Table 6.3 shows a teaching task that involves a set of
integrated teaching activities, some of which give the teacher the opportunity to observe and assess oral language. It may be that only a sample,
perhaps five children, are assessed in this one teaching task.

Table 6.3 *Big book activity with opportunities for oral language
observation*

1. **Teacher calls children to mat**
   Children listen to instructions and come to sit on the mat.
2. **Group reading of big book**
   Teacher reads to children, pointing out words as she reads . . .
3. **Group questions on the book**
   What happened to the . . .?
   What do you think . . .?
4. **Children draw pictures depicting the story and write under pictures**
   Teacher discusses with children what they are drawing and helps with
   writing.

Table 6.3   *(continued)*

5. **Second group reading of book**
    More teacher questions . . .
    Teachers asks children to choose a character and describe him/her/it.
    Children respond in the group with initial questions about this.

6. **Children draw and describe their character at their desk**
    Teacher comes around and asks questions
       Who is your character?
       Can you read what you have written?
       What else are you going to say about him?

Observation of oral language can take place in the first activity (listening and following instructions), the third (answering questions on the text – both literal and interpretive), the fourth (ability to describe and explain what they are doing), the fifth (answering questions on the text, and listening to instructions) and the sixth (answering questions about their character).

Observation of oral language in the classroom occurs from moment to moment in all teaching activities. It may be used for formative or summative purposes. Teachers use observation checklists for observation over many tasks, which may be teacher-prepared or externally developed (see Chapter 8). Gradually teachers build up knowledge, together with evidence in the form of anecdotal notes and completed criteria sheets, of each child's abilities. In Table 6.4, an experienced teacher has listed her guidelines for observing children's oral language ability in the classroom.

Table 6.4   *Guidelines for observing oral language (McKee, 1999)*

Selecting situations
*   Choose to observe children when they are involved in tasks that are part of the normal school activities and are familiar to the children
*   Where possible, choose situations in which children are interacting with each other
*   Morning sessions provide lots of opportunities for observing students in your class
*   Sit out in the playground during morning tea and lunch breaks
*   Arrive early at school each day, just to be available for interactions with the children

Points to remember
*   Do not despair if the child says nothing. Keep observing as much as you can during the observation period and observe interactions

Table 6.4   *(continued)*

- Observe your own behaviour. This is just as important as observing children's behaviour. Be aware of the extent you are relying on gestures, pointing and role playing to assist with the interaction or for children to respond to simple requests
- Be aware of how much knowledge of the home language the teacher has, to assist the child, in order to keep the interaction successful

Procedure
- Choose 2 or 3 children to observe each day
- Focus on each child for a period of time
- Keep a log of any informal interactions with any of the children, whether they are targeted for that day or not
- Complete the indicators on the Recording Format for each child

---

Oral records in portfolios

Oral records in portfolios can be collected by teachers as a means of closer analysis of performance and a record of progress. Taped recordings of children's speaking in different tasks (e.g., an interview with the teacher; describing something; giving instructions; narrating a story) can be collected over the year, analysed and stored (preferably with written transcripts) in a portfolio. This is a time-consuming assessment procedure, but a very valuable one. Many teachers have found that children's actual performance is not as good as they had thought; this may be because the children were over-supported by the teacher, or were using stock phrases together with good non-verbal communication strategies (what some have called 'fudging') to get through the demands of the task without in fact having said very much.

Assessment during teacher–student interactions

Teacher – student interactions on a task at hand, for example in reading and writing conferences, in excursions, as they focus together on a shared interest, provide opportunities for a close analysis of a child's oral language.

Self-assessment

Self-assessment strategies help children to monitor their progress. They may, for example, check a list of items of what they can do (*I can ask the teacher for help* ; *I can introduce myself)* or keep a record of their listening at the listening post.

Types of oral language assessment tasks for young learners

The following are examples of task types for assessment of oral interaction. Oral language tasks such as these may be integrated into classroom teaching tasks, may be used more formally for summative purposes or may be used in external tests. Each task requires refinement to suit the purpose of assessment, the context of assessment and learner characteristics.

Tasks involving speaking only

News telling

News telling is the first of the extended speaking tasks suggested here. However, if children in the audience are encouraged to ask questions, then the task becomes interactive. News telling involves children telling other children what they have done recently. It may be done in a whole-class setting, in a small group or in partners. This task assesses children's ability to do this in a way that conveys information to the audience with adequate detail, in an appropriate sequence. The abilities of children in the audience to listen critically for detail, and to generate questions can be assessed.

Selected children can be invited to tell news to the whole class, giving teachers a chance to focus attention on that child's abilities; alternatively, teachers can observe performance as they move around different groups. Tape-recordings can be made and performances analysed.

Storytelling

Children's ability to tell a story can be assessed with the use of illustrations cut away and laminated into a book. It is best to show the entire sequence of the pictures first, and ask for the story, because if children tell the story from page to page they tend to treat each picture as a separate unit, losing the sense of the connected story in their storytelling (Carpenter, Fujii and Kataoka, 1995). Children may know the story, having heard it in story-reading sessions, and therefore are likely to know the vocabulary and language they need. If the story sequence is new, they may need help to practise the vocabulary first.

Picture talks

Children can be asked to describe a picture. They can be given one or two minutes to look at the picture before they describe it.

Categorization tasks

A categorization task involves children sorting and finding patterns. Categorization tasks can assess children's descriptive language, and language of comparisons, as well as abstract explanations and academic talk and content. Children are asked to choose from a set of four pictures – which one is different or doesn't belong with the other three. There may not be a 'right answer' and children can be told this. The pictures are chosen according to the level of the children. For younger, less proficient children simple choices such as pictures of three plants and one person might be used. A **content-based assessment task** (that is, one in which children are being assessed on both language and content) for more proficient learners might involve, for example, the classification of animals in science.

Oral presentations

Oral presentations are also extended speaking tasks. Children may be talking about their own experiences without preparation, or they may be delivering a report on a project that has been prepared over a number of weeks. The task will be easier if children are able to hold and show objects or pictures or other artefacts. The task will also be easier if an adult is available to assist them when they need help.

Other speaking-only genres

Depending on their age and level of proficiency, children may be asked to do the following in a speaking-only situation: argue two sides of an issue (Debate), describe a significant event (Anecdote), tell someone how to do something (Procedure) or describe a person or a place (Description).

Tasks involving both speaking and listening

Question-and-answer tasks

Simple one-word answer questions are useful to elicit vocabulary and formulaic expressions in beginning learners. In the following example from a beginning seven-year-old, the answer 'I am seven years old' will have been learned as a formulaic expression. (The teacher's or assessor's knowledge of the children will ascertain whether this is the case.)

Q.   What's your name?
Ch.   Mimi
Q.   How old are you?
Ch.   I am seven years old

Question and answer tasks should move beyond simple learned question- and-answer routines as soon as possible, since learned routines only help to assess that children have memorized the language taught. Since we are looking for communicative language use, where children call on their language resource, we can extend question and answer tasks by doing the following:

- adding an element of surprise and unpredictability
- increasing the complexity of the questions (even though the expected response may remain simple)
- including new vocabulary (sometimes unknown) into the questions
- supporting new language in questions with gestures, objects, pictures to help children to predict from the context

- supporting new language by asking simpler or explanatory follow-up questions where needed

A skilled English teacher in China whom I observed added the element of surprise and unpredictability to his questions and pushed his children to call on their language resource quickly and creatively. He walked around the class, picking up children's bags as he found them, and then randomly asked children in the class to answer his questions.

> Whose bag is this?
> What colour is it?
> What about this one? Whose is this?
> Is it your bag, Li?
> Is it Li's bag, Xiaomei?
> Xiaomei – ask Li if it is her bag.
> What do you think is inside Li's bag, Mei?

Question and answer tasks like this can be extended according to the proficiency level of the children, and can be used in individual or whole-class sessions.

Extending the language of questions, and adding supporting visual aids and questions, alters the characteristics of the task, and the changes should be noted by teachers and assessors in their judgment of performances.

Carpenter, Fujii and Kataoka, (1995) asked questions, using the support of toys in an activity they called 'Toybox'. After some initial questions requiring actions only (pointing, nodding, moving things), they introduced questions requiring language production responses ('What colour are the sunglasses?' 'Which is bigger, the boat or the airplane?') moving on, according to the proficiency of the children, to more complex commands and questions like 'Put the airplane which is bigger inside the truck which is closest to the rabbit'; 'How many people do you think could fit inside the biggest airplane?'.

It is easy to see how a question-and-answer task can be used to assess more proficient children on subject content knowledge. For example, a diagram showing aspects of the food cycle could be shown to the child and questions asked around the diagram.

Oral interviews

Oral interviews assess children's ability to interact using both listening and speaking skills. Oral interviews typically involve teachers talking on a one-to-one basis with a child. However, group oral interviews, where children prepare their own questions with support, can also be success-ful with children in the upper elementary age group. A script for the inter-view may be prepared, with guidelines on the questions to be asked, the stages of the interview and ways to close the interview. Interviews work best if there is a *warming up stage* when the child is made to feel com-fortable while easy questions are asked ('What's your name?' How old are you?'), a *level check*, to determine the child's level of proficiency, a *probe* when questions are asked that push the child to show the limit of his or her skills and then a *wind-down* to bring the child back to a level when he or she is able to talk comfortably and finish with a feeling of success. Interviews with children need to be short, depending on their age and proficiency level.

Oral interviews are not an ideal vehicle to elicit young learners' best performance, especially if they are classic face-to-face question-and-answer interviews. Observations of language use in familiar settings, in tasks suited to their everyday learning environment, are more likely to be more effective. However, with a familiar adult, and with the use of objects and pictures, a sample of the child's oral language may be elicited. Children often go quiet in interviews with adults, especially strangers. The interviewer can use a puppet to talk to the child, and perhaps the child can also talk through a puppet. Picture tasks, manipulation tasks and role plays can be incorporated into oral interviews, turning the child's attention to the colourful pictures, and the manipulation of objects ('Can you put the horse in the field?').

An oral interview needs to be planned carefully, with a check that the language to be elicited is broad enough to represent what the child is expected to do. It is best to follow the planned pattern of questions, though some deviation away from the plan and then back again helps interviewers to probe children's abilities further. In high-stakes situa-tions assessors should be trained and made aware of the degree to which they are able to adapt their responses to the child's performance, or should adhere to the set questions. Hughes (2003) advises interview-ers to give as many 'fresh starts' as possible, to encourage participation. He suggests that a second tester should be available if possible to help to observe and make decisions on the performance without being distracted by the need to elicit language. Interviews should be carried out in a quiet room.

Mini-dialogues and role plays

Mini-dialogues and role plays are commonly used to assess children's learning of learned routines. Two children (or more) are often asked to perform the mini-dialogue in front of the class.

Child 1:	*How are you?*
Child 2:	I'm fine thank you. And you?
Child 1:	*I'm fine thank you. What's your name?*
Child 2:	My name is Lucilla.

These types of pre-learned dialogues are useful for teachers to check children's rote learning of the dialogue, but they do not help to establish if the child is able to use the language. It is valuable to build in to mini-dialogues and role plays an element of unpredictability and surprise, even in small ways. Figure 6.4 shows how a pre-learned dialogue can turn into a real language use task.
Children getting on a bus

Child 1:	*A ticket to the city please*
Child/bus driver:	*That'll be 50 cents*
(Money is exchanged)	
Child 2:	*I need to go to the high school.*
Child/bus driver:	*That'll be 25 cents*
(Money is exchanged)	
Child 3:	*A ticket to the town hall please*
Child/bus driver:	*(Prompted by the teacher) I'm sorry, this bus doesn't go to the town hall*

Child 3 has to respond to this unexpected statement from the bus driver.

Figure 6.4 An example of a role play involving unpredictability.

In the early stages of creativity language learners begin to use whole structures in creative ways, choosing items to fill one or two slots in language that is fixed and known. In **slot-and-filler** role plays, children are asked to create and perform a dialogue using some of their own words or ideas. They might be asked to do this by using puppets in a puppet theatre

First puppet:	*Hallo.*
Second puppet:	Hallo. What's your name?
First puppet:	*My name is. . . .. [child chooses name]*
Second puppet:	What are you wearing today?
First puppet:	*I'm wearing . . ..[child names something the puppet is wearing, selecting from known vocabulary for clothes]*
Second puppet:	It's very nice. What colour is it?
First puppet:	*It's . . .. [child names colour]*
Second puppet:	How are you feeling today?
First puppet:	*I'm feeling . . . [sad/happy]*
Second puppet:	Show me what you feel like.
	[the puppet mimes the feeling]

Figure 6.5 Example of a slot-and-filler role play.

set up as a particular context (see Figure 6.5). The teacher might manipulate one of the puppets.

Carpenter, Fujii and Kataoka (1995) used a slot-and-filler role play to assess children's ability in a Japanese immersion programme to vary role and register through Japanese. They used hand puppets to elicit language in two different simulated situations. In the first, the child played a role essentially identical to themselves, telling a new student about their school. In the second situation, the child acted the role of the teacher, and the tester spoke for two puppets who were students. The first situation was designed to elicit very informal language, whilst the second was designed to elicit more formal, classroom language. The role play lasted from two to four minutes, and was one of a series of short tasks assessing oral interaction.

Role plays are not only suitable for children at the beginning stages of language learning. They can be used for more proficient learners as the example in Figure 6.6 shows.

Oral information gap tasks

Oral information gap tasks are also called **barrier tasks.** They require children to interact and use language to complete the task. They usually involve children having a board between them and one or both having information that the other needs. One child has to tell the other what to draw, construct, assemble, match or notice.

Questions are asked ('Is there a red car in your picture?') and commands given ('Put the green balloon in the basket'). Children can

Each learner is given a card with the role that they will take up, and the reason why they are talking to each other. They are also given a calendar to check days and dates.

Student A	Student B
Student A You want to go to the movies, but you have a lot of homework to do, so your parents say you can only go on the following nights. Try to find a time when you can go to the movies with your friend. (Do not show this list to your friend.) Wednesday October 15th Friday October 17th Wednesday October 22nd	**Student B** You really want to go to the movies, but you are busy with sports practice on Wednesday and Friday nights. Try to find a time when you can go to the movies with your friend.

Figure 6.6 Example of a role-play assessment task for more advanced learners.

Table 6.5 *Types of oral information-gap tasks (adapted from Education Department of Western Australia, 1997, pp. 110–11)*

Simple sequence or pattern making
Describe successive items in an array or sequence such as bead threading or a clothes-line.

Matching Pairs
Take turns describing objects or pictures. One player describes an item until the other locates and displays its matching pair. Repeat the process until all items are paired.

Assembly
Assemble pictures or objects from a choice of component parts, e.g. making a clown's face.

Construction
Describe the steps in building a particular construction; e.g. a block construction.

Location
Choose and place items in relation to each other on a picture board.

Grids
Describe the position of marker objects on a picture grid; e.g. attribute blocks on 3 x 3 grid. Older children can use local road maps.

Route finding
Describe how to get from one point on a map to a specified location. The listener draws the route on the corresponding map.

Spotting differences
Give pairs of children pictures that have slightly different details. The children describe their pictures to each other and identify the differences.

also be asked to ask questions and give commands to the teacher or their peer. As with all tasks, the level of language used will depend on the proficiency and age of the children. A similar task might be used with more advanced, older learners and might deal with subject content.

Oral information gap tasks assess children's ability to give and receive instructions, whether they can give explicit and complete information to their partner, and whether they can monitor information they hear and use questions to clarify or gain further information. Children can work with an adult, or with a peer.

Oral information gap tasks are easy to produce. They can be made with pictures, blocks, beads, models or toys, for example. Table 6.5 lists eight types of information gap tasks that can be constructed.

Information gap tasks can be used as games in a classroom, with some children being selected for closer assessment. Their interaction can be taped and analysed later, or the teacher can observe and note the quality of children's performance.

Partner and group discussions

Partner and group discussions can be used for assessment if children are trained to take turns and to listen to each other, and have had practice taking part in discussions. Teachers can train children by allocating turns:

> *John, I want you to ask Michael what he watched on TV last night.*
> *Michael, now it's your turn.*
> *John, now I want you to ask Michael a follow-up question about what he said.*

Groups also need to be trained to take turns and listen to each other.

Topics that can be discussed include exchanging personal information, sharing likes and dislikes, recounting experiences, expressing opinions, describing and explaining, swapping stories and jokes, using your imagination (what if . . .?) (Education Department of Western Australia, 1997b).

Partner and group discussions assess oral language use related to the different functions (e.g., expressing opinion, describing, imagining) as well as the ability to encourage others, give feedback, negotiate and to work together.

Other speaking and listening genres

Children may be asked to find out information from someone (Interview), maintain relationships (Casual conversation), or work out what to do (Planning). Other genres mentioned above in the speaking-only section, for example telling someone how to do something (Procedure), may also be conducted in an interactive situation.

Assessing listening only

In my own experience, listening assessment is often combined with speaking in 'oral language assessment' and is then largely ignored. However, there are many situations in which listening needs to be assessed explicitly, especially in school learning contexts where listening plays an important role, not just in language learning, but in learning itself. Children need to be able to listen to texts (e.g., teacher talk and peer talk around activities in the classroom, and extended texts like teacher input on learning topics, and stories) to learn about the world, to pick up new vocabulary and to connect language with what they see and do. For these reasons, listening needs its own profile in assessment.

A child's listening ability is strongly influenced by the nature of the spoken texts that are being encountered, and spoken texts, as I discussed earlier in this chapter, vary according to the purpose, topic and context. The spoken text may be part of a conversation, it may be an extended talk or it may be teacher talk made up of extended input with questions, responses and asides incorporated. It may be accompanied by gestures, pictures or actions or it may not. Stress and intonation may help children with their understanding, but different accents, fast speech and long stretches of input may hinder understanding. If there is a gap in listeners' understanding in a communicative situation, they will compensate by using other available information from the context, or from their background knowledge. This may be harder for those listening in a foreign and second language, because of differences in backgrounds and culture. (See Buck, 2002, for more on listening and listening assessment.)

Listening is more difficult to assess than speaking because it is 'invisible' and has to be assessed indirectly. Evidence of listening comprehension can be readily observed in conversations, where children's responses and participation can be used as evidence of understanding. In listening-only tasks where the aim is specifically to assess listening comprehension, teachers and assessors need to find evidence of understanding in children's reactions and in subsequent activities. Thus in the examples of listening-only tasks given below, the tasks often involve listening and doing – carrying out actions, answering questions, retelling and so on. In listening-only tasks, children need to concentrate, to try to grasp the overall meaning of what they are listening to and to monitor the structure of the monologue. They have to listen to decide what the main points are, and identify signals that indicate the structure of organization of the ideas (Derewianka, 1992). The cognitive load can therefore be high.

Listening-only tasks surround children in classroom learning. For example, the teacher is constantly giving instructions, showing pictures and telling stories. Mixed in with this will be opportunities to interact, to respond and ask questions. Thus the classroom is a rich site for listening-only assessment.

Selecting listening-only tasks

As in oral interaction tasks, there needs to be a reason for listening to the task beyond being told to do so (because otherwise they might simply choose not to). Children need to be prepared for listening tasks. They need to know beforehand why they are listening 'Listen to the story and try to find out why the monster ran away'.

Teachers and assessors should give children every chance to show they have understood. In a conversation, the evidence will be in their participation. In listening-only tasks, there should be a 'product': for example, they should be asked to perform an action, to draw a picture or fill in a diagram, to build a model or to do a short piece of written work. Listening is an 'invisible' skill without these products.

Pictures, simple charts, puppets and other visual materials might be required as a support in assessment tasks for listening comprehension, especially with younger and less proficient children. If there is suitable visual support, the text can be slightly beyond the children's current comprehension level; this will check children's ability to use the context as they listen. We should be careful that interpretation of the picture or diagram does not substitute for the need for listening, and that the cognitive demand in the visual material and in the text is appropriate.

What kinds of texts should be used for listening tasks? Teachers and assessors should avoid using very familiar texts, because using familiar texts will only give an assessment of children's accumulated knowledge of the text in question, but not of their ability to comprehend new language. Texts should introduce some new knowledge, or an element of unpredictability. As early as possible, it is valuable to move towards using authentic samples of spoken language, involving the stops and starts, backtracks and interruptions typical of real interactions. Authentic samples of language might also include 'noise' – elements in the text such as someone else talking, or music playing in the background. Second language children require the skill to deal with noise as they listen – how many subject content classes are not carried out without group work going on around them, interruptions from children in the class, or a football match going on outside in the playground? (For a discussion of the 'listenability' of texts see Read, 2000).

Other skills should not be expected in the children's response unless their other skills are known to be secure enough for the task. Writing a response may require literacy skills the child does not yet have. Some responses may require a good memory; it is important not to overload the children's capacity to process and retain information. Multiple-choice tasks require skills beyond listening, and children need to learn additional strategies to deal with these tasks. Children can be asked to respond in their first language if a response in the target language would interfere with their ability to show they understood (Read, 2000). Bilingual aides can help to check the response for understanding.

The following ideas for assessing listening comprehension draw on the teaching techniques of Brewster (1984) and Ur (1994).

'Listen-and-do' tasks requiring action responses

In these tasks, a minimal (usually non-verbal) response is required to demonstrate understanding. The following are types of assessment tasks requiring a short response. Children enjoy responding with actions. Through actions, nods or shakes of the head, pointing, moving around, they can show they understand. As long as children see a point to following the questions and commands (we need to make sure that they do), then the evidence for their comprehension can be clearly seen in their actions.

Action tasks

Action tasks are excellent ways to assess listening comprehension, as are games like 'Simon Says'. Assessors need to keep in mind that children might be copying each other, and checks with individual children may be needed. Instructions can also be given, for example to draw something or, to build something with building blocks.

Total physical response tasks

Total physical response or TPR tasks are action tasks that involve children in a physical response to a request or command. The requests can be simple, or become more and more complex depending on what is to be assessed (see Figure 6.7). Understanding of cohesive devises, as in the following example, can be included for more advanced students.

> Baohua, stand up and sit down again.
> Simon, draw a picture of a car on the blackboard, and *when* you have finished, ask John to come and draw three people in *it*.

These tasks are good fun for observers. If teachers want to assess each child without immediate prior practice, it will be necessary to remove observers who are also to be assessed, as they will learn quickly from listening and observing others complete the action.

'Further afield requests', which are requests that take children beyond the immediate proximity of the teacher, perhaps to do something at the other end of the classroom, or even outside the classroom, can be used by teachers to check children's understanding of the request, but also of other knowledge and understandings. The following request assesses the child's knowledge of the school surroundings, and also her confidence to go out of the class and ask a relative stranger for something. (Thanks to Anne Mackay for the following examples.)

> Mimi, go and see Mrs Jones in the front office and give this note to her.
> Or, for more advanced learners, because they have to come back with something,
> Mimi, go and ask Mrs Jones in the front office to lend me a pair of scissors.

Classroom commands (adapt these to your own routine)	Stand up. Sit down. Give X a pencil, please. Open/close the door. Put up your hand.
Body	Touch your partner's back. Put your hand on your head. Hold up seven fingers.
Verbs in general (mime)	Eat an orange. Drink a very cold fizzy drink. Go to the shop and ask for some chewing gum.
Prepositions	Put your pencil on the floor. Put your book under the chair.
Abilities	If you can swim, clap once. If you can play the recorder, stand up.
Physical descriptions	Hold hands with someone with brown eyes. Touch someone who is wearing a red jumper.
Comparatives	If Y is taller than Z, put up your left hand. If my chair is bigger than yours, clap your hands twice.
Likes and dislikes	If you like bananas, pretend you are eating one. If you don't like eggs, make a face.
General knowledge (These can reflect topics the children are working on.)	If ice is made from water, nod your head. If a spider has eight legs, clap eight times.

Figure 6.7 Suggestions for total physical response (Phillips, 1993, p. 20).

'Listen-and-do' tasks requiring short language responses

'Listen-and-do' tasks might require a short language response, meaning that some skills in speaking or writing will be required.

True/false tasks

In a class assessment activity, children can be asked to respond physically, for example by raising a different-coloured piece of paper for true or false. For more formal assessment, children can be asked to circle 'true' or 'false' on an answer sheet, or tick/check the correct item.

Aural cloze

Aural cloze is suitable for children with appropriate literacy skills. A written passage is provided with words deleted at regular or irregular intervals and learners are asked to listen to the text and write in the missing words. Teachers and assessors need to be careful to balance the number of gaps with the time available for filling in the gap. This task does not focus on learners' ability to predict meaning from context; more on their ability to distinguish the words being used. **Story cloze** is the same task using a story as the text. This task is assessing reading as much as listening.

Noting specific information

In these tasks, children are asked to listen for specific information ('What did the mouse do when it saw the elephant'?) and to note the answer. The answer might be set out in written form as multiple-choice items.

Grids and charts

Grids are often used in children's textbooks to stimulate language use. They can be used successfully in tasks to assess listening comprehension. Grids are usually rectangles marked off into squares, which children fill in as required (as in Figure 6.8). Teachers and assessors need to monitor closely that the cognitive demand is suitable for the age group, and that the texts are at the appropriate proficiency level.

In this task, the text can be made simple or complex (e.g., information can be given in order or out of order; less or more redundant information can be given) depending on the proficiency level of the learners.

Matching tasks

Children listen to a description of a picture – which picture is being described? They can point to the picture, or circle the picture.

Learners listen to a text about four students, Alice, Johannes, Gerhardt and Michel. They have to fill out the details about the students as they hear them.

	Alice	Johannes	Gerhardt	Michel
Name				
Country				
Boy or girl				
Age				
Appearance				
Likes				
Dislikes				

Figure 6.8 A listening grid task.

Spot the mistake

Children listen to a familiar story, but there are errors in the story. They need to signal there is a mistake and explain it. Alternatively, children can be given a picture sequence depicting an event; they listen to the description of the event and check if there are any mistakes in the picture sequence.

Listening tasks requiring longer responses

As we move into listening assessment tasks which involve making longer responses, we move into a zone where very careful consideration is needed concerning the cognitive and literacy demands placed on the children. Asking children, for example, to paraphrase or summarize what they hear, to fill in gaps in a conversation, or to answer comprehension questions based on a spoken text should be treated with care for elementary-age children.

Responding to a series of comprehension questions

Children listen to a text (or view a video text) and answer a series of oral or written comprehension questions. The text and questions should be very carefully chosen to ensure that children are able to deal with the cognitive load, the literacy requirements, and that they have the background and cultural knowledge required. In these tasks children should be given the questions first before they hear the text. Assessors have to be careful that this kind of task does not become a memory test.

Dictation

Dictation involves children listening to a text and writing it down as they hear it. The reader may pause after a phrase or after a sentence or even longer, depending on the proficiency level of the students. A dictation task enables teachers and assessors to check children's perception of the sounds and words, and also their understanding, as it is difficult to write down a series of sounds that you don't understand.

Dictation texts should be chosen carefully to suit the literacy, proficiency level and concentration span of the students. Dictation does not give assessors any indication of the children's writing ability beyond the mechanics of writing, because children have not creatively produced the language themselves. Dictation is best used to provide some indication of listening perception and comprehension.

Summary

Oral language, consisting of speaking and listening in different combinations, is the foundation for language learning. It is through oral language that children develop literacy skills. This is so, both for first language learners learning their first language, and for foreign and second language learners learning a new language. Oral language also establishes the foundation for learning through the foreign/second language, when children are able to interact with new ideas and establish new concepts through interaction with others and with the world through the language.

Whilst this and the following chapter are organized around oral interaction and literacy, there are many complex differences between the notions of spoken and written language, and any simplistic division between oral and written modes is inappropriate. A 'mode continuum' (Derewianka, 1992) helps to illustrate that there are closely shared features of language in face-to-face oral language tasks and literacy tasks (e.g., conversations and personal notes), and also closely shared features between extended spoken and written tasks (e.g., formal debates and formal written pieces). The differences are not simply spoken and written. In the final analysis, however, it is the task, rather than the skill, that will determine the nature of the language to be used (Bachman and Palmer, 1996), and it is most appropriate to analyse the task and its demands, rather than the skill involved.

The scope of oral language to be assessed depends on the curriculum which may be influenced by sets of standards. Curricula may describe oral language in terms of objectives or outcomes, as genres or functions; underlying skills are described and are also assessed in formative assessment. Teachers and assessors can also refer to theory to inform oral language assessment; the Bachman and Palmer (1996) framework is one theoretical perspective that helps to define the components and characteristics that define successful oral language use. Teachers and assessors need further knowledge of child development and language acquisition and the characteristics of learners (their language programme, their current age, their first language literacy development, etc.) to know what exactly should be expected. With this, they will know which tasks to select, and the characteristics of performance that indicate both quality and growth.

There are many issues for teachers and assessors to consider in relation to oral language assessment. Assessment of oral language requires knowledge of, amongst other aspects, the quality of classroom interaction (is it giving children opportunities to show what they are capable of?); understanding of the issues in task selection including task difficulty; and knowledge of the best ways to assess grammar, vocabulary and pronunciation in oral language.

This chapter describes a range of assessment task-types that can be used in oral language assessment, in speaking-only, speaking and listening, and listening-only categories. There are many influences on children's performance in an oral language task, a number of which are highlighted in this chapter. It is important for teachers and assessors to apply the framework of task characteristics described in Chapter 4 to an oral assessment task whenever possible, especially in high-stakes assessment situations.

The assessment of oral language is at the centre of language assessment in a young learner programme; oral language provides the foundation for literacy development. Assessment is able to help build this strong foundation if principles and practices of language use assessment, as outlined here, are followed. The next chapter is dedicated to the assessment of young language learners' foreign/second language literacy.

CHAPTER SEVEN

Assessing reading and writing

Introduction

In this chapter we turn to the assessment of the abilities of young learners to read and write in their foreign or second language. To many, assessment of reading and writing is more pressing than the assessment of oral language: this may be because these skills are more readily associated with learning and academic progress by parents and administrators, or because they are more likely (often because of testing costs) to feature prominently in high-stakes external tests. Yet, as was emphasized in the previous chapter, oral language is the foundation for reading and writing, and to promote reading and writing assessment over oral language assessment 'because it is important' or 'because it is less expensive' is to do the young language learner a disservice. Even though writing can support oral language development to some extent, the more oral language that children can bring to their reading and writing assessment tasks, the more successful and motivated they will be. This is just one area of knowledge that teachers and assessors bring to the assessment of young learners' reading and writing; they also require a range of professional understandings about the expected developmental progress, the influence of first language literacy abilities, and the role of the cultural and background knowledge in reading and writing in a foreign or second language. These are briefly summarized at the beginning of this chapter.

The chapter then turns first to the assessment of reading, and then to the assessment of writing; each section presents examples of task types

217

and tasks suitable for young learners. As Alderson (2000) reminds us, there is not a best method for reading (or, in my view, writing) assessment. No single assessment method can fulfil all the varied purposes for which we might test, despite claims that some procedures, such as cloze, are a panacea, widely used in tests. For young learners there are many alternative ways to assess reading and writing that combine teaching with assessment.

As a further introductory comment to this chapter, it is noted that, in many educational circles, reading and writing are commonly combined and thought of as *literacy*, with literacy dealt with through a range of theoretical positions, often sociocultural (e.g., Luke and Freebody, 1990; Gee, 1996). Whilst these theories underpin broader understandings of literacy taken up in this chapter, it is more helpful, for assessment purposes, that reading and writing are dealt with in separate sections (this mirrors, for example, the separate treatment of the assessment of reading and writing in this assessment series). As I discuss in this chapter, there are many further ways to categorize activities that involve reading and writing; reading and writing are simply a first broad categorization. In order for the assessment of young learners to be as accessible as possible, I have chosen to take reading and writing, rather than the broader concept of *literacy*, as starting points for assessment.

Reading and writing in a foreign or second language at school

For children learning a foreign language in regular foreign language programmes, reading generally begins early, often incidentally, as they learn sight words and as they are exposed to simple reading texts (labels, posters, messages, stories) in the foreign language classroom. Young foreign language learners in the early primary school years are in the process of developing their literacy understandings and skills, whether in their first or their foreign language. They are in the process of becoming part of a new discourse community and developing a series of new identities (see Chapter 2). Very early readers (and writers) in a foreign language tend to concentrate on code breaking (e.g., working out sound–symbol relationships, alphabet knowledge and so on) at first, and this can take a great deal of their attention. The texts that they read and write vary from short passages, poems, questions and instructions in beginning years, to passages and narratives and academically oriented texts related to content areas in later years (depending on the type of programme and the extent of contact with the language). Children are likely to be restricted in their literacy skills development in the foreign language by their oral language skills in the language which can only progress according to the contact hours they have with the language. If they are learning a language that has a different script from their first language, this too may affect their progress, at least initially (Bartlett, 2001).

Children learning a second language are immersed in their second language, and will need to learn subject content (such as social studies; maths) through the language, necessitating an early engagement with reading and writing, with expectations of achievement targeted to children who have spoken the language for at least five years or more of their lives. Second language children read a wider range of texts as they progress through school and are expected to use different styles of writing for different purposes. Despite these advantages, second language learners can be in a precarious position when their literacy skills are assessed. If the education system or school ignores their second language learning status and assesses them alongside their peers with the same tests or the same observational criteria, then they are in danger of being assessed unfairly. The criteria may be based on expected progress of first language learners (McKay, 2001); the result can be that second language children can be wrongly assessed as falling behind or even slow (Cummins, 1984).

Three key factors in the development of literacy skills in a foreign or second language

The influences on the foreign or second language literacy skills development of young learners are many. The nature of the learning environment is central: does it give children opportunities for using oral language in the target language? Are there opportunities to read and write in ways that involves the exchange of new meanings? Research into second language reading is summarized by Valdez Pierce (2001, pp. 65–67), and second language literacy is also addressed in depth by Cameron (2001). From the many influences on foreign/second language literacy success, the following three are emphasized here: first language literacy, cultural and background knowledge, and oral language.

First language literacy

Many children have developed some literacy skills and understandings in their first language and are ready to proceed into transferring these skills and understandings to literacy in their new language. Children learning how to read and write in a foreign language are likely to be adding skills to those already developing in their first language. Cameron (2001) describes the development of reading and writing skills and the influence of the first language on children's foreign language development. There are knowledge, skills and strategies that can be transferred across the two languages and new understandings that need to be gained about the particular cues to meaning in the new language. For many children, explicit teaching of reading strategies is required. Children developing literacy skills in their second language may not have a strong literacy foundation in their first language. Cummins (1981) has found that children's progress in literacy can be influenced detrimentally by lack of age-appropriate competence in either their first or their second language. When this is the case, children have no opportunity to develop the cognitive systems they need to function academically. His 'threshold hypothesis' suggests that if children have this ability in one language, it is possible to transfer it to the new language. Children can take up to four years to develop age-appropriate social language in the new language in a second language situation, but up to seven years or more to develop age-appropriate academic language in the new language.

The relationship between first language and second language literacy development is evident in children's second language reading and writing development. Those with little or no literacy in their first language will be adversely affected and their second language reading and writing will inevitably be weak. Alderson (2000, p. 39) suggests from research into adult reading, however, that second language knowledge is more likely ultimately to predict success in second language reading than are first language reading abilities. First language reading abilities are still important if readers have crossed a linguistic threshold in their first language (that is, they have gained a sufficient level of reading ability in their first language that enables them to transfer their first language reading ability to the second language reading context), but this will have a different effect depending on the characteristics of the task (e.g., text topic, text language, genre) and task demands. Knowledge about the expected development of first language literacy (even though there may be some differences across cultures) helps the teacher and assessor to understand the reasons for children's progress or lack of progress, and the types of errors that they make in the second language.

Cultural and background knowledge

In a constructivist view of reading (see Chapter 1), children bring meaning to the text when they read. They bring their own background and cultural knowledge, or **schemata**, into play as they read, and therefore they construct their own meaning. The text has no meaning other than that which the reader has given it (Selly, 1999). A child whose schemata do not accord with the ideas in the text will have greater difficulty reading than a child who brings the same knowledge and cultural background as the text. Vocabulary carries a large part of a language speaker's cultural and background knowledge; for example, children may understand a word such as 'home' in ways that relate to their own culturally based understandings and experiences. A word may therefore be 'learned' (can be read out loud; can be glossed) but in fact may only just be beginning to be understood fully. In summary, research suggests that the processes of reading in first and additional languages are similar except for the shared prior (and cultural) knowledge that language learners bring to literacy development, and their lower proficiency in the target language in which they are learning to read (Chamot and O'Malley, 1994).

An oral language foundation in the target language

In both foreign and second language situations, the ability to use language orally in the target language is the foundation for reading and writing. Phonological awareness, vocabulary knowledge, and other knowledge and skills required for reading and writing develop from oral language. Knowledge of oral vocabulary speeds up recognition, and known words are easier to hold in short-term memory (Cameron, 2001). Oral language used in language use tasks becomes a tool for thinking and learning for second/foreign language learners in the same way as for mother-tongue speakers (Barnes, Britton and Torbe, 1986; Wells, 1989). Through talking, children are able to construct new understandings, to represent knowledge for themselves and to share it with others. In addition, ideas become explicit and thoughts become clearer through talking. This may happen in more limited ways for foreign language learners than for immersion and second language learners, but the principles are the same. Without a foundation of oral language, in which are embedded the grammatical and vocabulary knowledge and cultural understandings they need, children's ability to read and write will be severely hampered. They may be able to 'skim the surface' of reading and writing but will be robbed of the deeper understanding and knowledge that make up literacy. This is not to say that reading and writing cannot also provide support for oral language developments if handled carefully and in a limited way. Once a good base of oral language is established, this can provide a foundation for further reading and writing in an iterative or repeating cycle of growth. Teachers and assessors therefore need to plan overall assessment of language learning so that reading and writing are not emphasized over oral language. This iterative approach applies throughout the primary years.

Assessment of young learners' second language literacy skills therefore requires specialist knowledge. The selection of tasks, decisions on the quality of performance, and subsequent teaching intervention are dependent on, amongst other knowledge, awareness of at least these three key influences. A section follows on assessing through computers: the remainder of this chapter deals first with the assessment of reading, and then of writing.

Assessing reading and writing through computers

Assessing young learners' literacy through computers has advantages and disadvantages. The main disadvantage is the requirement that children have the requisite computer and keyboard skills. For the assessment of writing through short or extended texts (a narrative, a report), children need to have mastered the keyboard and at least some elementary word-processing skills. Computer assessment for extended writing would be selected only if children are known to have these skills.

It is possible to assess reading, grammar and vocabulary knowledge through selected-response and discrete-point assessment, when children are expected to click the mouse only (yes/no; select the right response; connect the correct statement to the picture). **Computer adaptive** assessment (in which the computer decides, based on the child's responses, what level of item difficulty should be presented next) can be used to advantage with these kinds of items. We need to keep in mind the limitations of selected-response and discrete-point assessment items, but they can be useful for diagnosis, for assessment of some kinds of reading, and for assessment of some contributing knowledge and skills. One advantage of commercial computer-based programmes containing these kinds of assessment items is that in the classroom children can gain valuable practice, and perhaps motivation, by completing them. As they, individually, complete a level successfully on the commercial programme (perhaps when they have finished their set work), they move to a new level and are often motivated to continue to work on the programme to compete with their classmates.

It may be that computer-writing skills can be the content of the assessment, rather than language use itself. That is, children can be assessed for their ability to employ multimedia techniques, for example combining graphics, audio-recordings, scanned documents and hypercard techniques into their writing product. These kinds of skills are valuable 'multi-literacy' skills, and enhance children's engagement with texts and with learning. They are of great importance in children's repertoire of literacy skills today. However, teachers and assessors need to recognize that these kinds of skills should be included in assessment decisions about language performance and progress only when they are part of the curriculum and when all children have equal opportunities to extend their abilities in these areas.

Assessing reading

The nature of reading ability

Reading involves making meaning from a text. Readers employ three main cueing systems when they read; they rely on **graphophonic cues** at the word level (i.e. cues from the way a word is written and how it 'sounds out'), **syntactic cues** at the sentence level (i.e. cues that give information about the role of any one word within a sentence or clause of words) and **semantic cues** at the whole text level (i.e. cues that relate to the meaning of a word or words in relationship with the whole text, and also with associated pictures or photographs that accompany the whole text). A theory that maintains that reading evolves from a knowledge of the graphophonic and syntactic cues upwards takes a **bottom-up** perspective of reading, and a theory that maintains that reading begins with semantics and discourse organization takes a **top-down** perspective. It is currently believed by most theorists that reading is an **interactive** process, in which bottom-up and top-down skills work together in the reading process (Carrell, Devine and Eskey, 1991).

> We can think of a reader working within a written text as like a satellite searching information about a landscape, and zooming in to different levels of scale to get information of different types at different scales. Pictures of the earth from space show it as a mainly blue sphere with continental masses set in oceans, while, at a much larger scale, British railways use satellite pictures to identify dangerous piles of autumn leaves that have fallen on railway tracks. To really understand the Earth, information is needed from all scales, from the leaf to continental masses; to really understand a text, information has to be integrated from the various scales at which a text can be 'read', from individual letters to discourse organization.
>
> (Cameron, 2001, p. 129)

Reading is both process and product. The process of reading involves the interaction between the reader and the text – how the reader is deciphering the writing on the page, what he or she is thinking about while reading, and how the reader is monitoring his or her reading, if at all (Alderson, 2000). The product of reading is reading comprehension, or an internal construction of meaning; that is, there has been understanding (at least to some degree) of what has been read. Both need to be assessed. Processes of reading are usually assessed through continuous, formative assessment in the classroom, and reading comprehension is generally assessed through both formative and summative assessment.

Readers bring their schemata into play in order to interpret the text. Because children's schemata vary greatly, especially if they come from diverse cultural backgrounds, it is very likely they will interpret the text differently and gain different meaning from the text. This is true of all readers, young and old. Underpinning all of these processes, a large part of learning to read is to gain those literacy understandings we discussed in Chapter 2, that is, to come closer to the shared understandings of the discourse community in which the written text belongs. Readers are referred to Cameron (2001) for an extensive discussion of the knowledge and skills children need when developing literacy skills in a second language.

The scope of reading ability to be assessed in young learner language programmes

The scope of the young learners' reading ability that is to be assessed is usually determined by the curriculum and the theoretical perspectives underpinning that curriculum. The curriculum may list the reading texts or text types that children should be reading. Basal readers (reading books chosen to be read by all children as core, base texts) may be listed, or there may be text types described, for example simple, illustrated children's narratives, simple information texts, short stories, picture-book stories, or as children gain more skills, fables, legends or science fiction. The class textbook may provide reading matter, drawing from the range of texts that are specified in the curriculum. The curriculum is also likely to set out the child's expected growth in reading ability, reflecting children's ability to become independent readers, being able to read a growing range of texts and text types for a range of different purposes. It may set out expected accompanying growth in contributing knowledge and skills (such as those listed in Table 7.2 below) and growing consciousness about using these to gain control over what they read. Hopefully, the curriculum would concentrate on reading whole texts and gaining meaning from those texts. There should be reference to an expected growth in ability to reflect critically on what they read, and to respond to the different interpretations that are possible in texts (e.g., what may be some of the underlying messages behind the story of 'Red Riding Hood'?). The nature of the reading curriculum therefore depends on its theoretical perspectives, and the scope of reading ability to be assessed will depend on this to some extent.

A framework for assessing reading ability as a theoretical construct

Most teachers reach beyond the curriculum and draw on their professional perspectives to teach and assess reading. Teachers and assessors also bring their theoretical perspectives to decisions about what to assess, especially in formative classroom assessment, and in assessment that is not tightly determined by a curriculum. Theoretical perspectives frame what we look for in assessment, for example what the children should be able to do when they read, the kinds of contributing knowledge and skills that help children to read and how children should be developing in their reading.

There are many frameworks that teachers can draw on to define their constructs for reading assessment even if curricula are available. Table 7.1 sets out components of reading ability following the Bachman and Palmer (1996) framework of language use, focusing on the areas of language knowledge that are brought to reading. In reading, these areas of language knowledge are activated with the other components of language use – their individual characteristics, topical knowledge and strategic competence when children read. The framework provides a theoretical checklist for teachers and assessors with regard to the scope of children's reading knowledge.

Teachers and assessors need to establish the types of texts that children read, for what purpose and at what level. Professional texts, developmental continua and other guidelines are available to assist in these decisions. Many younger language learners already have some developing reading skills and understandings in their first language that they are able to transfer to their reading in the target language, and this can help their reading in the target language. Others begin their schooling and learn how to read in their second and weaker language. Thus the scope of reading expectations may not be achievable for all at the same time, and teachers and assessors must, wherever possible, construct assessment tasks that enable children to succeed at their own level.

The curriculum may also list the contributing knowledge and skills that need to be learned and therefore assessed. These skills are usually assessed by teachers in the classroom; usually through observation and analysis of reading behaviour. Examples of contributing knowledge and skills are set out in Table 7.2; whilst many of these skills are embedded in the integrated theoretically based model in Table 7.1 above, this is a separate list for teachers to teach and monitor over time. (For a discussion about contributing skills in reading, see Alderson, 2000, pp. 9–13.)

Contributing knowledge and skills form an important part of teacher assessment of reading in primary classrooms; teachers need to look

Table 7.1 *Some characteristics of reading ability (based on Bachman and Palmer's (1996) model of language knowledge)*

Depending on the curriculum requirements, and the situations children encounter, their reading ability needs to develop with the following characteristics:

Organizational knowledge

Grammatical knowledge: Children need to decode letters and words, and/or recognize words/characters by sight. Their vocabulary knowledge needs to broaden and deepen. Their syntax needs to increase in accuracy. They need to be able to understand a range of structures.

Textual knowledge: Children need to be able to read a range of texts, for the range of purposes for which they need to write in the target language. They need to employ textual knowledge to understand the meaning of the text. (For example, can they understand the meanings of conjunctions that join sentences and paragraphs together (*but, then, and, though*)? Are they aware of different text structures or genres, and if so, do they use this knowledge to predict the purpose and meaning of the text?)

Pragmatic knowledge

Functional knowledge: Children need to understand the purposes behind the language they read, even when those purposes are not directly stated.

Sociolinguistic knowledge: Children need sufficient knowledge and experience of the target language culture to understand the cultural references in the text. (Are their schemata expanding through experience in the new culture towards understanding the cultural references in their reading? Do they understand when language is appropriate or inappropriate to the context (perhaps leading to humour or embarrassment for the story character)? Do they understand the humour in the text? Do they understand the attitudes, beliefs, customs, ideals and values inherent in the text?) Children need to begin to analyse the text, that is, to look for assumptions and biases in the text.

back at the curriculum, at standards and reading observational schedules, to help them to establish what is required at different developmental levels.

Issues in the assessment of the reading of young language learners

Below I briefly discuss some issues that arise in relation to the assessment of the reading of young language learners.

Table 7.2 *Examples of contributing knowledge and skills for reading*

- **Ability to decode** *(for phonic-based languages)*: Ability to match sounds with letters, with phonic blends. An ability to sound out words. Ability to use these graphophonic cues as support but without over-reliance on them.
- **Knowledge of a growing range of vocabulary**: Ability to read and understand a growing range of vocabulary.
- **Knowledge of a growing range of grammatical structures**: Ability to understand a growing range of structures in their reading.
- **Ability to predict meaning from a range of cues**: Ability to use the semantic, syntactic and graphophonic cues in the text. Ability to use the range of cues (e.g., titles, illustrations) that are available to gain meaning from the text.
- **Ability to draw on prior knowledge, and knowledge of different genres**: Ability to use their personal experience, and their knowledge of the context, for example, when they meet an unknown word in the text (The wolf is outside the door – he *knocks* on the door).
- **Ability to understand main ideas and connections**: Ability to identify the main ideas in the text. An ability to locate specific information.
- **Ability to take responsibility for their own learning**: Ability to seek out opportunities to read in the target language. Keeping a reflective diary of their reading. Ability to ask for help. Ability to follow through after reading conferences.
- **Confidence and motivation**: Showing curiosity about print. Enjoying reading. Being self-motivated to read. Talking about their reading and sharing it with others. Being confident when they read a new text.
- **Ability to critically analyse and interpret**: Ability, usually in more advanced children, to understand that some characters are stereotyped in the story, or that there may be other levels of meaning in the text (for example, that there is a message for people to be friendlier to each other).

Selecting reading texts and tasks for young learners

Assessing reading is not straightforward because reading, like listening, can only be measured through other skills. Judgement of children's ability is made through their actions, speaking or writing. Care needs to be taken that the assessment task is assessing reading and is not 'contaminated' by high levels of writing or speaking requirements.

For reading to take place successfully, there must be motivation on the part of children to read: 'the reader will not concentrate on the words unless there is some expectation of reward such as enjoyment or use-fulness' (Selly, 1999, pp. 58–9). The interest level of the text will have considerable influence on the motivation of the child, and therefore possibly on the quality of the child's performance. Texts should be selected with knowledge of the learner characteristics: their interests, age, cognitive maturity, language proficiency and reading ability level. Authentic materials from the child's environment provide valuable texts for assessment. Food packaging, greeting cards, advertising material, magazines, internet games are examples of authentic materials for foreign language learners. Second language learners are surrounded by authentic materials. Teachers and assessors can use materials from the primary classroom (texts on social studies topics, children's project reports, stories and poems, instructions, invitations, diagrams and charts, maps, myths and legends, etc.) as authentic materials for reading assessment tasks.

Children's literature is central to the development of reading in young learners (Jalongo, 2000) and therefore can play a central role in reading assessment. Children naturally enjoy stories. Children's literature arouses feelings and provokes reflection and sometimes opposition (Selly, 1999). Children's literature is very suitable to use as assessment, especially since texts, especially for younger learners, are generally accompanied by colourful and motivating illustrations.

Children should also be interested in *giving a response* to the task. Why should he or she answer this question or complete this task? Young children may decide to move on to another more interesting activity, if the response seems too difficult or irrelevant to them.

The difficulty of a reading text is an important factor in text selection. Difficulty relates to many features of the text, including the familiarity of the vocabulary, the length and complexity of the sentences in the text, the presence or absence of illustrations, the spaces between the lines, the size of the letters and so on. Readability formula are discussed by Read (2000). However, the level of difficulty of texts is best decided by a group of experts who are able to gauge the suitability of the text for the age group in question, as well as the appropriateness of the vocabulary (and other features) for the proficiency level of the children being assessed. Together, the difficulty of a reading text (an input characteristic) and the reading ability level of the child (a learner characteristic) will strongly influence the 'usefulness' of a task (Alderson, 2000).

Children's performance is likely to be negatively influenced if they are not able to bring their own background and cultural knowledge, or schemata, into play as they read. Texts should therefore be chosen to be sure that all children can draw on their background knowledge or, at least, to ensure that children are not excluded by the specifically cultural content that they are unlikely to know.

The familiarity of texts needs to be taken into consideration in the selection of tasks. Classroom texts can become very familiar to children. Teachers read them to children many times over as part of the recycling and re-reading process that helps children to read, and often they are available in the reading corner and perhaps at the listening post for individual reading. Familiar texts are helpful for formative assessment, but from time to time it is valuable to bring out a new, unfamiliar book for informal reading assessment. This gives teachers a clear idea of how children are able to read without the support of a familiar text.

Children may be asked in the assessment task to respond in their first language (Alderson, 2000). This may encourage children who are not confident to respond. The issues here are the same as in listening comprehension tasks (see Chapter 6). The use of the first language in a response does not negate the validity of the response; however, in many teaching and assessment contexts, the use of the first language is not always possible, because there is not a speaker of the first language available.

Choosing which comprehension questions to ask and how to ask them

Questions that teachers and assessors ask in order to check for comprehension can differ, and this can affect the nature of the task. Comprehension questions may be literal, interpretative, critical or creative (Education Department of South Australia, 1973). **Literal questions**, like 'How many people were in the boat?' are asking for the direct literal meaning of a word, sentence or idea in context. Literal questions may ask for details (locating or identifying facts), main ideas, sequence (order of incidents or actions) and recognition of character traits. Interpretive questions probe for greater depth than literal comprehension, asking for meanings not directly stated in the text. **Interpretive questions** ('Do you think the people will be safe in the boat?') include questions that ask for generalizations, cause and effect, anticipation of endings and the sensing of motives. **Critical reading questions** like 'Do you think it was a good idea to go out in that boat?' asks for evaluation and personal judgment. They may also be concerned with underlying assumptions in the text. 'Why do you think the author has chosen to write about girls (and not boys) sailing the boat?' In **creative reading questions** like 'What would you do if you were in the boat?' the reader goes beyond the author's text to obtain or express new ideas. Teachers can encourage children to go beyond direct implications gathered from the text.

There are also text-based questions that can be asked about grammatical and vocabulary knowledge. 'What does *it* refer to here?' 'What does *surprising* mean in this context?' 'What is another word for *unhelpful*?' as well as questions about attitude, enjoyment, speed of reading and support for reading at home.

It is possible for children to answer the range of questions if the questions are graded appropriately for the age and reading ability of the reader. Asking questions that span these five types helps teachers and assessors to ensure that the broad construct of reading described in this chapter is assessed.

Should children's reading vocabulary be assessed separately?

Vocabulary plays an important role in a learner's performance on a reading test; vocabulary knowledge appears to be an indication of the learner's subject matter or topical knowledge and is important to text comprehension (Alderson, 2000). Vocabulary is a significant element in several categories in the Bachman and Palmer framework of language knowledge (knowledge of vocabulary, sociolinguistic knowledge including 'natural or idiomatic expressions', 'cultural references' and 'figures of speech').

Vocabulary can be assessed either in an embedded way, during an assessment of a child's reading, or it can be assessed discretely. Since children are learning how to read for meaning, it makes most sense to assess children's vocabulary in the context of their reading. This can be done in informal assessment by questioning children about the meaning of selected words, or through checklists which alert teachers and assessors to check the required reading behaviour as part of the wider assessment (*Has the child been able to understand the range of vocabulary in the text?*). In formal assessment tasks vocabulary can be targeted through the task itself, but still within the context of language use, as in the following example for beginners (targeted vocabulary is underlined).

Draw a red circle around the picture of the antelope.
Draw a blue square around the picture of the elephant.
Colour the giraffe yellow and black.

If discrete assessment of vocabulary is needed, it is best done in informal classroom situations: a spot check of children's understanding of vocabulary with flash cards; a request to point to pictures; a worksheet matching pictures to words and so on.

How do we know if it is a second language reading problem or a learning problem?

If a child is having problems with reading in the target language, how do teachers know if that child's problem is reading in a second language, or whether that child has learning difficulties? The best person to answer this question is the child's classroom teacher(s) who can take time to:

- check the child's reading development in his or her first language. Through a bilingual aide it is possible to check if the child is at the expected level of literacy in his or her first language.

- talk to parents about the child's involvement with reading at home. Is the child interested in books? Is the child reading in the first language at home?

- observe the child in classroom activities, and talk to his or her other teachers. Is the child involved in class activities and gaining some meaning from texts? Most importantly, is the child *progressing* in some way in his or her skills development?

It is possible that the child has had disrupted first language literacy experiences because of migration or other reasons. Teachers have to be careful in these situations; a delay in first language literacy does not mean that the child has learning difficulties. Over time, through exposure to oral language experiences, and gradually to simple written texts in the target language, most children with first language literacy delay will improve in their literacy in the target language. They will improve even more in their literacy development in the target language if their first language literacy skills are also enhanced at the same time. If a teacher has carried out all the checks over some period of time and yet seen very little improvement in reading, it may then be necessary to refer the child to a learning difficulty specialist.

Classroom assessment of reading

The following are some of the assessment strategies that teachers can use to assess reading in the classroom. They are supplementary to the principles and strategies of classroom assessment set out in Chapter 5, and can be used with the types of reading assessment tasks in the section following this one.

Observation

In the classroom there are many opportunities for assessment of reading, and teachers observe children constantly as they read. Are they reading independently? Can they follow through after a conference? Are they keeping their diaries? Are they responding to teacher questions on the mat, and do they have some enthusiasm as they pick up a book? These kinds of observations can be noted in anecdotal records or on checklists. Teachers can also be guided in their observations by externally developed criteria that map children's expected development in reading.

Interviews with parents

Interviews with parents provide valuable information on the child's attitudes to reading, and engagement in reading at home.

Teacher–student reading conferences

Teacher–student reading conferences involve the teacher listening to reading, asking comprehension questions, analysing errors, and checking on the child's attitude and motivation. Children's reading strategies can also be checked. Do they predict from the context? Can they sound out unfamiliar words? Do they self-correct?

Teachers can observe children's reading abilities more closely by splitting the class into small groups, setting the children a set of tasks to follow and moving between the groups. Children need to be trained in group work and working independently without teacher supervision.

Oral reading

Oral reading involves children reading aloud for the teacher, individually or around a group. Oral reading should not be overused as an informal assessment tool in the classroom, as it can be disadvantageous to children's confidence and motivation when they are not successful in a highly visible situation. When oral reading is used as an assessment tool, skills such as word pronunciation, recognition of punctuation, speed of reading (checked through pace), understanding of meaning (checked through intonation, stress and voice modulation revealing shades of meaning) can be assessed. Teachers should watch out that children do not 'word call' or 'bark at print', that is read word by word in a meaningless stream. This is common in foreign/second language learners who have learned to recognize the words or characters but do not have a sufficient oral language foundation to gain meaning from their reading.

Group reading sessions are useful to check individual children's reading. Figure 7.1 shows how a teacher can organize to listen to group reading in a class.

Informal diagnostic procedures

Informal diagnostic procedures are procedures that may be prepared commercially or by the teacher. Informal diagnostic procedures may contain tests of contributing skills such as visual discrimination, listening comprehension, alphabet recognition, letter–sound correspondence and may also include tests of oral reading, silent reading comprehension, literary appreciation, and attitude and interest. Collections of diagnostic procedures can be useful for language teachers if they are checked for usefulness by the teacher. Are they, for example, suitable for foreign/second language learners? Is the expected background and cultural knowledge appropriate for foreign/second language learners?

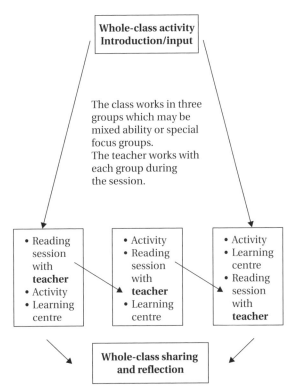

Figure 7.1 Working with smaller groups in the classroom to observe reading (adapted from Education Department of Western Australia, 1997a, p. 11).

Miscue analysis

Miscue analysis is a type of diagnostic procedure. It is commonly used to analyse the reading ability of beginning first language learners and has also been applied to second language learners (Davies, 1995). Miscue analysis involves the recording of differences between the children's response and the actual words on the page. A type of miscue analysis used widely with young English-as-a-first-language learners is Marie Clay's '**running records**' (Clay, 2000). Miscue analysis can take time, and as Alderson points out, the analysis is necessarily subjective. Miscues are analysed at the graphemic, phonemic, morphological, syntactic and semantic level.

The following is an example of a miscue (Education Department of Western Australia, 1997a, p. 132).

| Text: | The man painted his *house* and then sold it. |
| Child: | The man painted his *horse* and then sold it. |

The child has made an error or miscue. The child's substitution of *horse* for *house* shows that he/she has probably used graphophonic information to arrive at the word *horse* which looks and sounds similar to *house*.

It shows also that the child has not used meaning to help decode (it is unlikely that a man would paint a *horse*).

There are several criticisms of miscue analysis. Children's wrong predictions may be a normal part of reading, and may be wrongly analysed as miscues. The method also focuses on word-level information, and should not be taken to assess reading comprehension (Freebody and Austin, 1992).

Portfolios

Portfolios help teachers gather a range of items: information about what has been read, impressions and feelings about reading in journal entries, records on interviews with parents, observation schedules, pupil self-assessments and results of informal diagnostic testing. The portfolio may be established by the teacher as a literacy portfolio, in which both reading and writing items are collected together. Students may or may not be involved in collecting items for the portfolio, or they may develop their own.

Self-assessment

Self-assessment is an important and integral component of informal teacher assessment (see Chapter 5). Are children able to evaluate their own reading? Can they reflect on their progress? With the help of self-evaluation question sheets, progress charts, reading logs and journals (in which they enter, for example, the details of texts they have read and whether they could read it easily or with difficulty, and whether they enjoyed it), they can become responsible for their own learning. In the right environment, they can progress successfully towards being independent and fluent readers.

Types of reading assessment tasks for young learners

There are a number of types of tasks that can be used to assess young learners' reading. These might be used in informal or formal assessment situations. Decisions on the types of tasks that can be used to assess depends on a range of factors; an analysis of task (and text) characteristics might be carried out, as described in Chapter 3.

As with most assessment tasks for young learners, an introductory activity may be needed to 'set the scene', reminding children of the relevant vocabulary, of the concepts involved, and of the requirements of the task.

'Read-and-do' tasks requiring action responses

Children may be required to follow instructions – for example, read and draw, read and build, read and follow instructions. See a discussion of these types of tasks under listening comprehension in the previous chapter.

Reading and retelling

Children can be asked to retell or rewrite as much as possible of the text they have read. The task may be free or prompted. Story retells are valuable for beginning learners as children do not need to reinvent a plot. Both free or prompted recalls are a common measure of both comprehension and memory of text; we would not expect word-for-word accuracy in the retellings, but rather amalgamations, extensions and distortions from the original text (Freebody and Austin, 1992) Since background and cultural knowledge plays a critical role in reading, children will recall more of a text on a familiar topic because they are using this knowledge to process and recall a text. For example, readers recalling a text about a family celebration in another culture remember much less than those who were of the same culture. In addition, the perspective of the reader can influence recall: different recall has been observed by older readers who read a description of a home and its contents from the point of view of burgling the home, compared to buying the home.

Only a short time should elapse between when students hear or read a story and their opportunity to retell. To help children recall, they can be encouraged to fold a paper into three and draw pictures of the beginning, middle and end of the stories, and as they gain more skills, they can be encouraged to write brief notes to use as a guide (Coles and Jenkins, 1998).

According to Freebody and Austin (1992), ways that retelling/rewriting tasks are judged include the following:

- the number of pieces of information, or 'idea units' that have been recalled. An idea unit is a unit containing a separate idea. Thus, in the following sentence 'The school holidays are coming soon', there are four idea units – 'school', 'holidays', 'are coming', and 'soon'
- ordering of events if a story, or ideas if an argument
- certain key expressions (like the phrase 'the big brown teapot' which was repeated several times in the story)

It is important to let learners know how their recall will be evaluated in advance.

'Read-and-do' tasks requiring a short written answer

Short-answer written tasks are an alternative to multiple-choice tasks. Children are asked to respond in a few words, not just choose a correct response (as in multiple-choice, or True/False tasks). A more objective task would be one where the right answer is clearly set out in the answer key, and where children are likely to respond with anticipated answers. These tasks are not easy to construct, and need to be pre-tested with children, and perhaps colleagues. If a range of answers is possible, these must be anticipated in the answer key. Short-answer tasks may be constructed around a variety of texts, for example pictures with captions, paragraphs, whole texts such as short stories or information pieces, or texts such as advertisements, recipes and so on. Figure 7.2 gives an example of a short-answer task for Grade 3 children in Singapore.

'Read-and-do' tasks requiring a longer written answer

Children can be asked to respond to their reading with longer written answers. The difficulty of using this type of task for assessment is that a

Read the passage carefully. Then answer the questions that follow.

The air we breathe in these days is polluted and it is getting worse. Air pollution causes all kinds of breathing problems. It also makes us feel tired and gives us headaches and sore eyes. Many children suffer from asthma because of pollution in the air.

Air pollution is caused mainly by harmful gases from motor vehicles and factories. Cigarette smoking and the use of some detergent, furniture paints, air fresheners and insecticides also cause air pollution.

To control air pollution, the government has passed laws to make sure that vehicles do not give out harmful gases and factory owners reduce the amount of fumes that are given out from their factories. Nowadays, drivers are encouraged to use unleaded petrol which makes the air less polluted.

We can also help to keep the air clean by using fewer insecticides, air fresheners and detergents, which contain chemicals that are harmful to the environment. We can grow more trees and plants. A greener environment will make the air fresh and cool.

The Earth is a beautiful place to live in. It is our duty to keep it clean.

1. What are the **two** main causes of air pollution?

_____

_____

2. What do many children suffer from because of polluted air?

_____

_____

3. What can a driver do to help reduce pollution?

_____

_____

4. How can we help to make the air fresh and cool?

_____

_____

Figure 7.2 Example of a 'read-and-do' task requiring a short answer (Yat, 2001 Practice 7, p. 5).

child's writing ability may interfere too much with his or her chance to show what he or she has understood in the text. Memory may also come into play. Children may be asked to write a letter to a character in a story, to write a summary of what they have heard. These types of tasks may give a teacher a good idea of whether a child has understood a text in the classroom and can be combined with written assessment in the classroom. However, for high-stakes assessment, it is more valid and fair if tasks are used that are less dependent on writing or other skills.

Reading and answering true or false questions

True–false items give children two choices (these kinds of items are called 'dichotomous items'), and therefore children have a 50% chance of getting the right answer. To counteract this, it is important to have several items in a formal high-stakes test. As with all assessment tasks, the cognitive (and cultural) demand of true–false items for younger learners needs careful thought.

Read the story

A one page story is given about a boy called Tom and a lost Teddy.

True or false

Here are some sentences about the story.

Some of the sentences are true and some are false.
Put a ✓ next to the sentences that are true.

- The giant locked Tom inside the cupboard.
- The giant's teddy was on the pillow.
- The giant cried because he lost his teddy.
- Tom found the giant's teddy.

Figure 7.3 Example of true/false reading comprehension task (Mahon, 1994).

Reading and picture-matching

Matching techniques where children match a word, a short phrase or paragraph with a picture (and perhaps a diagram for children in upper elementary years) are appropriate for younger learners. In matching tasks, young learners may be distracted by characteristics of the pictures that we would not have thought of; for example, a car in the background may attract one child's attention and he or she may see a connection with the car rather than the elephant in the foreground, and connect the statement 'I can move and make a loud noise' to the car. This highlights the need for very careful pre-testing of a task if it is used in high-stakes situations.

Draw a line from the picture to the sentence that describes it.

Part 1
– 5 questions –

Listen and draw lines. There is one example.

Alf   Fred   Daisy   Sally   Kim   Paul   Jim

The children are playing at the beach.

The dog is running after the ball.

The children and the dog are swimming in the sea.

Figure 7.4 Example of picture-matching task.

Reading and answering multiple-choice items

Multiple-choice tasks are very common in commercial tests but tend not to be used by classroom language teachers, who are aware of the need for careful preparation and pre-testing of tasks to ensure usefulness.

'Multiple choice tasks allow testers to control the range of possible answers to comprehension questions, and to some extent to control the students' thought processes when responding' (Alderson, 2000). There are pitfalls in using multiple-choice tasks, particularly related to the role that **distractors** play (the options other than the correct answer). Do they trick children into answering? Are there clues, like the length of the answer? The **test-wiseness** of learners (the familiarity of the learners with the multiple-choice task itself) will influence the result; children who have practised other multiple-choice tasks are likely to do better. Multiple-choice questions involve skilled and time-consuming preparation. Answers do not always show *why* the learner responded in the way he or she did – that is, they may be right for the wrong reason.

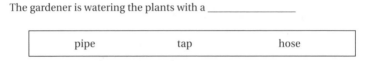

The gardener is watering the plants with a _____

pipe	tap	hose

Figure 7.5 Example of a multiple-choice vocabulary item, Primary 2 (Yat, 2001).

Reading and completing charts – information transfer

Information-transfer tasks are very popular as teaching tasks in course books, where children are often asked to conduct a survey and then convey information to a simple grid. Careful scaffolding by teachers is required to assist children under eight to understand charts such as these, and therefore the use of charts in formal assessment for children of this age should be used with caution.

Simple diagrams, charts and tables may be used with upper elementary-age learners to present information; children are then asked to respond to questions about the information provided in diagrammatic form.

Alternatively, older children may be asked to read a text, and to complete a grid-based information-transfer table as in Figure 7.6.

Cloze and gap-filling tasks

Cloze and gap-filling tasks are of a different order from the above task types. They usually have a contrived text and depend on a theory of reading that suggests that predicting meaning and filling in gaps indicates that understanding is achieved (Alderson, 2000).

What is the name of the animal?	What does it eat?	How big is it?	Where does it live?

Figure 7.6 Example of a grid-based information-transfer table.

In **cloze** tests every n-th word is typically deleted (traditionally every fifth, sixth or seventh word). One or two sentences are usually left intact at the beginning and end of the text to provide some degree of contextual support. If cloze tests have targeted words deleted (adjectives, or grammar words, or any selected words), these are considered by Alderson (2000) to be gap-filling tasks. In **gap-filling tasks**, the teacher or assessor decides, on a rational basis, which words to delete, leaving no fewer than five or six words between gaps to make sure that readers have sufficient contextual clues.

Cloze and gap-filling tasks check children's abilities to focus on semantic, syntactic and graphophonic cues in the text, and therefore, if carefully constructed, can provide useful information about a child's reading ability. However, children need to 'learn the method' or become test-wise for this type of task. If they have not been trained in the way that the task works, they may be disadvantaged, and the task will not be a 'useful' one.

There are many examples of cloze and gap-filling tasks in tests for younger learners. Figure 7.7 shows one of these.

There are 12 blanks in the passage below. Fill in each blank with a suitable word.

When I was little, I liked to go to the zoo very much. I often _____ there with my father. We always go in the _____ and return at midday. Sometimes _____ would go by trishaw, and _____, in a borrowed car. As I _____ animals, I found the zoo _____ interesting.

When I was old enough, I often _____ to the zoo with my friends. We usually climbed _____ the fence in order to avoid _____ the entrance fee. The ticket to _____ in was cheap enough, but it seemed _____ to spend the money on buying _____ for ourselves.

Figure 7.7 Example of a gap-filling task (adapted from Phang, 2001b, pp. 11–12).

Alderson (2000, pp. 207–11) discusses issues with regard to the use of cloze and gap tests. Cloze tests that have different choices of deletions (for example, every fifth or ninth word) lead to significantly different test results. It is not possible to predict with confidence what a cloze test will measure: what the test measures will depend on the individual words deleted. The gap-filling procedure, on the other hand, is much more under the control of the teacher or assessor. For example, she may delete selected content words to test an understanding of the overall meaning of the text, or function words to test mainly grammatical knowledge, or connecting words which carry the text's coherence. Alderson reminds us that pre-testing of both cloze and gap-filling tasks is essential. Responses should be carefully checked to see how learners have responded and to check whether they reveal what is required about their understanding of the text.

It is possible to construct **multiple-choice cloze tasks**. For each word that is missing, children are given three possible words to choose from. For example, in Figure 7.7 the first gap could be numbered (1), and below the children find they have a number of options to choose from:

(1) go
     think
     fall

Multiple-choice cloze tasks give children a little more help in their predictions. (See Read (2000) for a discussion of the relative effectiveness of cloze and gap-filling tests at the sentence and at the text level). It is also possible to construct picture-cloze tasks that place a picture in the gap and therefore check children's vocabulary knowledge. However, picture cloze does not necessarily assess predicting skills, since children are able to label the picture without reading the sentences.

Assessing writing

The nature of writing ability

In Chapter 6 I pointed out the relationship between spoken and written language use. There is not a divide between spoken and written language use; rather there is a continuum from contextual factors and demands, from face-to-face interaction to non-interactive monologue. In the former kind of situation, conversations and friendly e-mail interactions are jointly constructed; in the latter kind of situation, meanings must be self-sufficient, usually more abstract and certainly well organized to hold the attention and understanding of the reader. Writing thus requires different kinds of ability depending on the type of writing that is being engaged in.

I emphasized the sociocultural nature of language learning in Chapter 2. This theme is reiterated by Weigle in relation to writing. It is important to view writing not solely as the product of an individual, but as a social and cultural act (Weigle, 2002, p. 19). Writing is also a cognitive activity. Weigle (2002: pp 23 ff.) discusses the complex cognitive processes, or mental activities, involved in writing, the sources of knowledge writers draw upon in writing and other factors that influence the writing process. To second language writing we must add the three key factors I mentioned above, that is, first language literacy, cultural and background knowledge, and the need for an oral language foundation in the target language.

Writing, like reading, is both a process and a product. Writing as a process involves the pre-writing, writing, revising and editing processes that writers go through to produce a piece of writing. The 'products' of writing are numerous, and in many forms, determined by different purposes and audiences and contexts for writing, for example the illustrated sentences, letters, narratives and shared books that children produce in the classroom and elsewhere. Young learners not only have to work towards learning the processes and products involved in 'mature' writing in the target language, but also have to deal with the physical and cognitive demands of early literacy, either in their first or the target language, or in both. Readers are referred to Cameron (2001) for a valuable account of the knowledge and skills children need when learning how to write.

The scope of writing ability to be assessed in young learner programmes

The construct of writing assessment may be determined by the curriculum, and/or by theory, in the same way as discussed for reading. As children's ability to write in the target language develops, it will be expected that they will be able to write longer and more independently produced texts that are appropriate to their purpose, and that have greater accuracy and a wider range of vocabulary (as required). They will also be expected to use writing

for other purposes that do not require length, but require specialization –
for example, to write notes, to fill in forms, and to write arguments and
science experiments.

Descriptions of the expected writing ability to be learned, and therefore assessed, are often presented as written genres to be mastered.
Genres are used in many young learner writing education programmes
to organize teaching and assessment. The range of major forms of
writing are narrative, recount, procedure, report, explanation and
exposition. Some specific examples of genres are provided in the following list:

- Write a story, fable, myth, fairytale, poem or play. (Narrative)
- Write a newspaper account, a letter or a journal. Write about how I
  solved a problem. Write a record of exercise and food for the day.
  Write how chickens hatched. (Recount)
- Write instructions on how to build a model. Write how to read a
  map. Write a recipe. Write an experiment. (Procedure)
- Write a report on elephants. Write a report on deserts. Write a report
  on life in a desert, after reading a story about a camel. (Report)
- Explain how you come to school. Explain how a caterpillar grows.
  (Explanation)
- Write about an issue: Does language learning help me to understand
  other people better? Should we wear school uniforms? (Exposition)
  (Education Department of Western Australia, 1997d)

Children can succeed in writing genres at a range of different levels, and
assessment is related to the gradual development of features of successful
writing within each genre. Thus, assessors will look for the appropriate
characteristics of the appropriate genre when they mark children's
writing. The following example shows a simple, successful recount for a
beginning learner.

> *Class 4B went to the zoo.*
> *There were many different animals.*
> *Peter and I walked a long way.*
> *We saw lots of animals.*
> *I liked the tigers best.*

This example of a recount is successful because it has the basic features of
a recount: setting, events in time order, and concluding statement/
ending.

A framework for writing as a theoretical construct

As with oral language, and reading, teachers bring their own theoretical perspectives to the teaching and assessment of writing and draw on these perspectives to define the constructs that they are assessing in writing. In classroom assessment, many teachers assess formatively, informed by their beliefs about what writing is, and how it develops in young foreign/second language learners. They do so with an eye on the goals and objectives or outcomes that they are expected to achieve in the curriculum. Teachers may be guided by the textbook they are using; good textbooks set out teaching and assessment according to theoretical perspectives usually stated in the introduction.

By defining the characteristics of young learners' writing knowledge in Table 7.3, using the framework of language use (Bachman and Palmer, 1996), the components of second language writing are aligned with those of oral language and reading in this book. The use of a second-language-based framework highlights those components of language knowledge that foreign/second language learners need to be able to learn to write successfully.

A theoretical framework such as this helps teachers and assessors to establish the construct that is being assessed, helping to establish the scope of what it is to be an effective writer, and therefore what to look for in children's writing performance.

Contributing knowledge and skills

Classroom teachers are continuously assessing the underlying skills that contribute to the writing progress. They regularly do this as diagnostic and on-the-run assessment. Examples of the contributing knowledge and skills that underpin the ability to write are set out in Table 7.4. Some of these are embedded in Table 7.3, but here they are listed separately, intended as a set of skills that teachers need to attend to.

Issues in the assessment of writing of young language learners

Below I briefly discuss some issues that arise in relation to assessing the writing of young language learners.

Table 7.3 *Some characteristics of developing writing ability (based on Bachman and Palmer's (1946) model of language knowledge)*

Depending on the curriculum requirements, and the situations children encounter, their writing ability needs to develop with the following characteristics:

Organizational knowledge

Grammatical knowledge.   Children need to form letters or characters. Their spelling needs to become increasingly correct. Their vocabulary knowledge needs to broaden and deepen. Their syntax needs to increase in accuracy. Their knowledge of grammar needs to increase. (Are they able to produce more complex texts, building cohesion across sentences and parts of sentences with appropriate connectors to make complex verbal meanings (relationships of time, expressing tentativeness and subtle intention with *might* and *could*) and using subordination (*After the rain came, the river broke its bank*)?)

Textual knowledge.   Children need to write across the range of texts that they need in the target language. They need to write using appropriate text structures for different audiences and purposes. (Do they know the different genres that are required? Do they have explicit knowledge of these different genres; for example, can they talk about the different stages in different genres? Are they able to use connectives appropriately to denote relationships between sentences and paragraphs (cause and effect, consequence, etc.)?)

Pragmatic knowledge

Functional knowledge.   Children need to be able to write to achieve the purposes they wish to achieve. (Do they know how to achieve their purposes by changing their writing (style, formality, text structure, etc.) to suit their purpose and audience?)

Sociolinguistic knowledge.   Children need the required knowledge and experience of the target language culture to be able to convey their meaning to their audience. They need knowledge of vocabulary to help them to convey this meaning. They need confidence in their own background and experiences to convey information and ideas from their own cultural background in their writing. They need to be able to reach out to people from other cultures in their writing. They need to understand when language is appropriate or inappropriate to the context (perhaps leading to humour or embarrassment for the story character). They need to understand the humour in the text. They need to understand the attitudes, beliefs, customs, ideals and values inherent in the text. They need to develop skills to analyse texts, that is, to look for assumptions and biases in the text.

Selecting writing tasks for young learners

Teachers and assessors will select writing assessment tasks that help them to assess children's achievement of the objectives or outcomes that

Table 7.4 *Examples of contributing knowledge and skills for writing*

Ability to write to suit purpose and audience.   Ability to write to meet the purpose and audience, that is, according to the appropriate genre.

Ability to organize paragraphs logically.   Ability to write paragraphs logically and in accordance with the expected stages of a genre (e.g., for recounts, orientation, events, evaluative comment or concluding statement).

Knowledge of a growing range of vocabulary.   Ability to write using a growing range of vocabulary. Ability to use vocabulary accurately. Ability to take some risks and try new vocabulary.

Knowledge of a growing range of grammatical structures.   Ability to use a growing range of structures in their writing. Ability to use structures accurately. Ability to take some risks and try out new structures (making some errors because of this).

Ability to punctuate. Ability to use the appropriate punctuation for the target language. (e.g., for English, can they use basic punctuation marks accurately? Can they use capital letters for proper nouns, and to start sentences? Can they use full stops to end sentences? Can they use apostrophes for possession?)

Ability to employ connectives appropriately.   Ability to employ a range of connectives to express sequence (e.g., *next, then, finally*).

Ability to follow through a drafting procedure.   Ability to draft and revise their work for improvement. (Can they reorder text to clarify meaning (moving words, phrases and clauses)? Can they correct their own punctuation and spelling?)

Explicit knowledge of text structures (genres).   Ability to identify purpose and audience for a writing task. Ability to identify which genre is needed for a particular purpose.

Ability to write independently.   Ability to look for and use words displayed in the classroom. Ability to use a dictionary or glossary. Ability to concentrate on the task, and work alone.

---

need to be checked in the curriculum, and/or of their progress according to their theoretical perspectives about writing development.

As with all assessment of language use, it is important to encourage the writing of new meanings in tasks rather than old meanings that are evoked, for example when children copy, write memorized sentences and write down what is heard, as in dictation. Writing is a complex activity requiring children to think about a number of factors simultaneously – for example, the formation of letters or characters, vocabulary, grammar and punctuation, layout, organization and selection of appropriate content for the intended audience. If the assessment task requires neat writing, correct punctuation and perfect spelling, then the likely result might be short boring texts written by children who have no interest in the message only in what the teacher demands

(Education Department of Western Australia, 1997d). Therefore in some assessment tasks it may be wise to make new meanings less important, and the mechanics more important. In other assessment tasks, new meanings may be brought to the forefront, and in these tasks teachers and assessors should be ready to accept less accuracy in the final product. Different expectations should be conveyed to the children, and help given to children to focus on different aspects of writing.

Tasks need to be selected that avoid anxiety and motivate. Writing anxiety can be an issue for writers (Weigle, 2002). This is particularly so for second language writers, who, unless they have more advanced proficiency, require more support and more time than their mother-tongue-speaking peers to write. Weigle (2002) also emphasizes the important role of motivation in successful writing. The writer's goals, predispositions, beliefs and attitudes about writing will influence the way the writer will tackle a writing task. The writer estimates the 'cost/benefit' of writing, and will decide on the investment he or she is willing to make in the task. Older learners, most of whom understand the stakes involved when they are assessed, generally decide that the investment is worth it. For younger learners, the 'cost/benefit' is often not external to the classroom or to the present time. Younger learners need to find motivation in the task for its own sake. I have argued this point in different ways through each of the four skills. Teachers and assessors cannot rely on younger children's extrinsic motivation to complete an assessment task.

Giving writers a choice of tasks can have advantages, in that writers can write about what they are interested in. But in external assessment situations, a choice of tasks can have disadvantages in that time may be taken up choosing, and the equivalence of the tasks becomes difficult to determine. In external testing situations these disadvantages need to be overcome.

Another issue in the selection of writing tasks is the degree to which children's skills in other areas will impinge on their ability to complete the task. It is more than likely that children will require a degree of reading ability to complete writing assessment tasks, and it is possible that a source text or instructions will need to be read. If instructions are misunderstood, then the child's writing performance can be affected. If a source text is used, then difficulty level of the reading text may also influence the difficulty level of a writing task.

The selection of writing tasks is aided by the use of the framework of task characteristics described in Chapter 4.

Prompts and preparations for writing assessment

In external and formal assessment tasks, prompts and preparations for writing tasks are important. Clear instructions are needed, with an indication of the audience and purpose for the task, and some indication of how the writing will be scored. Length should be specified in pages (for example, 'write half a page', 'write one page'), otherwise writers will tend to think within the limits of shorter structural units such as words or paragraphs (Carson, 2000). However, prompts such as these are a poor substitute for the kind of preparation that young learners usually receive in the classroom before they undertake writing. In the classroom, teachers invariably tune children into a writing task; this will be done even in more formal assessment tasks where children will be expected (after the introduction) to write independently and for an allotted time. Children need to be reminded of the topic of the writing task, perhaps through brainstorming – 'What do you know about giraffes?' or 'What did we find out about cockatoos last week?' They need to be reminded about the vocabulary that relates to the topic and, depending on their explicit knowledge of genres, to be reminded about the genre ('What kind of text do we need here? What does a report look like?'). This type of preparation is needed for young learners who are not yet at mature levels of abstract thinking.

These types of introductory sessions for writing tasks constitute support, as does individual one-to-one support given to children who need it as they try to complete the task. Rather than deny assistance that can give support to learning and avoid failure, teachers need to give the support and then take account of the degree of help given in the judgment of children's progress. The difficulty level of writing tasks in the classroom can be adjusted according to whether they are guided, modelled or independent, and whether support is given during the task.

Meanwhile, in external tests and those formal tests where teachers require students to write without an introductory session and without one-to-one support, it is inevitable that unless they are highly practised in the type of task, a number of children will not be able to show their full abilities, and a number may fail. This is one of the central reasons why educators of young learners dislike and hope to avoid external and formal assessment of young learners.

Does dictation assess writing?

Dictation is commonly used in some parts of the world as a regular assessment procedure to check the writing of young learners. In some cases, the dictation scores, perhaps together with grammar and vocabulary scores, are given to parents each week, and parents anxiously wait to hear how their child has scored in comparison to other students. But parents are being misled if they believe that dictation assesses writing progress. Dictation assesses children's ability to distinguish sounds and words in a stream of sounds, and to write these words (or characters) down with the correct spelling or character formation on paper. There is some assessment of children's understanding involved – they need to be able to understand what is being dictated in order to remember and write down what they hear. But writing a dictated passage does not involve writing in the sense that we have adopted here – there are no new meanings involved. Rather than assessing writing, dictation assesses children's listening ability coupled with the ability to record mechanically and accurately the words and sentences they hear. Checking this ability is helpful for diagnostic purposes, but should not be seen as an indication of writing ability.

Should vocabulary, grammar and spelling be assessed separately from written tasks?

Vocabulary, grammar and spelling can be assessed separately from language use written tasks, but the appropriateness of doing so will depend on the purpose for assessment. In writing, more than in oral interaction and reading, knowledge of vocabulary and grammar, and spelling ability are regularly separated out for assessment. If the purpose of assessment is children's ability to write, then assessment of contributing knowledge and abilities such as these is best done through checklists in which teachers and assessors are reminded to look out for these abilities within the context of the language use task. Table 7.3 above shows how vocabulary, grammar and spelling are only some of the components of writing ability that may need to be assessed. If the purpose of assessment is to assess the contributing knowledge and skills for writing, usually for diagnostic purposes, then it is appropriate to assess them separately. (See also my discussion in Chapter 6 on the assessment of grammar in oral interaction.)

Assessing vocabulary and grammar separately

It is the case that on many occasions, especially in large-scale tests, vocabulary and grammar are assessed separately. Items such as the examples given below are used in large-scale tests because they are easy to administer and to score, and because they do give an indication of children's knowledge of vocabulary and grammar. However, if these kinds of items are used in place of language use tasks, then it would be necessary to question the theoretical construct for writing held by the test developers; their construct for writing would not be language use in writing, but rather knowledge of grammar and vocabulary. As was explained in Chapter 3, discrete-point items isolate vocabulary and grammar from a wider context (though they may have a sentence-level context) and therefore will always be less helpful than tasks which connect the vocabulary and grammar to the wider context of language use.

Figure 7.8 shows some examples of ways that vocabulary and grammar can be assessed separately from language use in writing tasks.

Matching items (vocabulary)
Children match a picture with a word, or a word with a definition.

Matching words with meanings:

> You have two of these, and you can hear
> through them.   _____

Pictures of the items can be provided with words attached, for beginning students.

Picture gap-filling (vocabulary)
Children fill in a gap in a sentence after identifying the name of an object in an accompanying picture.

Choose the correct answer and write the answer in the spaces

Credit: Captain Budd Christman, NOAA Corps

The w _ _ _ _ is the largest animal in the world.

Multiple-choice item (vocabulary)
Choose the correct answer and write its number in the brackets provided.
My father has just bought a new set of *chairs, tables, cupboards and beds*
(1) laundry   (2) decoration
(3) furniture   (4) draper

Multiple-choice gap-fill item assessing grammar (Yat, 2001)
Jane and Peter _____ late for school
(1) was   (2) were
(3) had   (4) being

Sentence completion (grammar)
Complete these questions with 'Who', 'Where', 'What', or 'How.'

Question: _____ is your father doing?
Answer: He is washing the dishes.
Question: _____ are you going?
Answer: I'm going to school.

Figure 7.8 Types of discrete-point vocabulary and grammar assessment items.

Assessing spelling or character-writing separately

Learning to spell or to produce characters involves more than rote learning of lists of words or characters. Teachers need to check that children are employing strategies that enable them to sound out (if appropriate) and recognize the graphophonic relationships in the words they are learning and to see the visual patterns and meaning. They need to check that children are learning to classify, hypothesise, generalize and look for patterns and relationships (Education Department of Western Australia, 1997e). Teachers also need to check that children are learning strategies of self-monitoring and self-regulating, that they are taking responsibility for getting their own spelling or character-writing correct. The following quote relates to both spelling and character writing. 'Good spellers are not perfect spellers. They are people who can say, "No that doesn't look right", and then check to see if the word is correct: (Education Department of Western Australia, 1997e, p. 15). Assessing spelling or character-writing as it develops, in the classroom, is therefore much more than checking whether selected words can be spelt or characters can be formed correctly. Some children bring knowledge of word or character formation from their first language. There may, however, be differences that might interfere with the children's learning, sometimes because the two scripts are deceptively similar, causing confusion for the child expecting words to be spelt or formed the same.

Spelling may also be assessed in formal classroom tests and external tests. However, once again, spelling is best assessed in language use tasks.

Assessing language and content

The principles and practices in the assessment of language and content, that is, the learning of a target language alongside and integrated into a subject content area, are no different from those outlined for language use assessment throughout this book. There are, however, some additional issues that are raised when language and content are assessed together. These issues are addressed under 'writing' because it is often most evident in writing in the school context; however, it is an issue that is just as pertinent to oral language and reading assessment.

In the foreign/second language profession, content refers to subject or curriculum knowledge. Content is topical knowledge; however, content is a more specific form of topical knowledge since teachers use it to refer to the type of formal knowledge that children learn at school. Very young learners deal with content when they are participating in activities in, for example, cooking, art and science activities. They talk about, and perhaps read and write about, their observations and knowledge. What happens when you have a cup of water and a cup of sand on a balance? What has changed when we mix ingredients for a cake? What are the names of different animal groups? How can different colours be mixed? As children progress through primary school the content that they talk, read and write about extends beyond themselves and their immediate environment out to the wider world. As children get older, content becomes more closely related to the formal subjects of the curriculum and begins to become more abstract and complex.

Children learning in foreign language programmes may study topics from content areas, but these may be less directly connected to content areas. They may be organized through themes; for example, 'Our neighbourhood', 'Our classroom', 'There's no place like home' or 'The five senses'. These are themes around which content can be developed in the classroom. Themes bring content, and content provides children with an opportunity to talk, read and write *about* something. Content-based tasks are likely to be more interactive and authentic, and more likely to stimulate participation and interest.

The language that is used in a content-based language task is closely tied in with the subject content area and the purpose and audience for the task. This influence of content on language becomes stronger as children grow familiar with the subjects they are studying. There are typical subject-specific patterns of language in each different discipline. These patterns are evident in the words and sentences that are used, and also at the paragraph and whole text or genre level. In these formal content areas, patterns of language represent knowledge in particular ways (Cope, Kalantzis and Wignell, 1993; Halliday, 1994).

Assessment of language and literacy in content areas therefore requires assessment of the learners' ability to use the language specific to the subject area in question, or more specifically to its purpose and context. The expectations for this ability will increase as children learn more in the subject area. It is beyond the scope of this book to outline the differences in the language of different content areas; indeed differences and similarities across subjects are still very much under investigation. In addition, each target language needs to be studied for its own variations. The genre movement, in which spoken and written texts are analysed and categorized according to the purpose and audience of the text, has taken us a long way towards understanding how language varies in different contexts, and this knowledge can be readily applied to assessment, as I have illustrated in this and other chapters. Mohan and Slater (2004) have described how language and content can be assessed using systemic functional linguistics (see Chapter 3).

Mohan's (1986) 'knowledge framework' is an approach that can be applied to the analysis and understanding of the type of content-based activity and the language within it. Mohan categorizes knowledge into three broad categories, and then ties different types of language to these categories.

What we have, then, when young learners engage with language and content tasks are two central components – language ability (appropriate to the content) and content knowledge. Should these two components be assessed together, or should they be assessed separately? To obtain the most 'useful' information about the child's language ability, it is best to assess each component separately (Bachman and Palmer, 1996). When teachers and assessors are primarily concerned with children's language ability, rather than their knowledge of the content, this is the best course of action. Assessing language and content separately involves having separate criteria for the language ability and for content knowledge in the task, though the criteria may be listed together on one sheet (see an example of this in Figure 8.3 in Chapter 8). Separate marks may be given for each component, or one mark may be given for the total performance. The issue, then, is what will be the weighting between the marks for language and content? When the relative weighting between language and content is made explicit, this helps teachers and assessors to be reliable and fair in their marking. However, it is somewhat inevitable that there will be different interpretations of the relative mix between language and content. 'the reality of language testing is that a given test task will involve varying degrees of language ability and topical knowledge for different test takers' (Bachman and Palmer, 1996, p. 198).

Another reality is that even if the intent is to separate language and content in order to be fair, this is not totally possible. Children's spoken or written responses on a topic may not show their true language ability if they do not know much about the topic. They may not have the relevant content knowledge because they come from a different cultural background, are new to the school or, indeed, have not understood the content in previous lessons. To reiterate, assessing language and content is not a new type of assessment, but an application of the principles and practices of assessment outlined in this book. Added to these principles should be a heightened awareness of the nature of language expectations relative to different subjects and contexts and of the issues involved in judging language and content in the same performance.

Classroom assessment of writing

The following are some specific classroom writing assessment strategies and tasks to supplement the classroom assessment strategies in Chapter 5.

Observation

Observation of children's writing ability involves ongoing checks of children's writing processes as well as their writing products. Children's writing processes involve, for example, their abilities to plan their writing, to concentrate on the writing task, to evaluate their own writing and to undertake a drafting process. Once writing pieces are completed or 'polished' after a series of drafts, teachers are able to check the product of writing, perhaps as they 'publish' the pieces on the wall or in a class book. For diagnostic and feedback purposes, weaknesses and strengths are noted in records and discussed with the child. Whenever possible, included in the observation records should be a note on the amount of support that was needed as children wrote their drafts, and as they completed their final polished piece.

Writing conferences

Teacher–student writing conferences and interactions are perhaps the main informal assessment strategy used by teachers for writing. Writing conferences involve teacher and student in one-to-one extended discussion of the writing that has been or is in the process of being done. Conferences, and the shorter one-to-one interactions that take place as the teacher moves from student to student, are essential opportunities for scaffolding of learning. As a child asks and answers questions about the writing in front of them, the teacher gains crucial insights about their writing processes and understandings.

Portfolios

Portfolios lend themselves very well to writing assessment. Samples of work can be collected in chronological order with completed criteria sheets attached to them; observation sheets can be dated and kept together with records of writing conferences with children. Parent interviews and children's self-assessment sheets can also be kept in the portfolio. The content of the portfolio will eventually depend on the purpose and audience for the portfolio (see Chapter 5).

Self-assessment

Self-assessment gives children an important opportunity to develop their awareness of the nature of their progress and needs in writing. With awareness can come a degree of ownership and control of their own writing development. Children can record their writing experiences in writing logs, setting out the date, the form of writing, who the intended audience was, and whether or not they completed the writing. Writing journals can be more detailed, when children write reflectively about their writing, setting out, for example, the things they can do, or what they are finding hard. Logs and journals can be written in the child's first language in the early stages, though they do provide an opportunity for communicative writing in the target language. Opportunities to share writing with peers and parents, to gauge the understanding and reaction of others, helps children to gain further insights into their writing.

Types of writing assessment tasks for young learners

This section suggests a number of writing assessment tasks that can be used for formal writing assessment, either in the classroom or in external assessment procedures. Readers can also refer to a range of valuable references that deal with the teaching and assessment of first and second language literacy for further ideas (e.g., O'Malley and Valdez Pierce, 1996; Education Department of Western Australia, 1997d; Puckett and Black, 2000; Weigle, 2002).

Writing in speech bubbles

Early writers might be asked to fill in speech bubbles in a cartoon story. This kind of task can be supported by oral language, and can reflect mini-dialogues and role plays used in the assessment of oral interaction. (See issues related to these task types under assessing oral interaction.)

Writing in response to a picture

Pictures such as familiar scenes in which, for example, young children are involved in some action are commonly used to stimulate children's writing.

> **H.   Look at the picture. Write a story of at least 50 words about it. You may use the helping words given in the box. (10 marks)**

umbrella	lightning flash	newspaper	heavily
bus stop	thunder roar	cover	wet

A Rainy Day

_____

_____

_____

_____

_____

_____

_____

Figure 7.9 Example of picture-stimulated writing. (Yat, 2001).

Completing a story

Children may be asked to complete a story, as in the following task.

Complete the story about **Staying with Aunt May**. You may use the points given to help write the story.

- Why you were visiting Aunt May
- Why you were carrying a big bag
- How long you stayed there
- What you did there
- Whether you enjoyed your stay

'What a lovely big house,' I said to myself as I walked into the living room, dragging my big bag of clothes and books. Aunt May was ....

Figure 7.10 Example of a guided, story-completion task (Phang, 2001a).

Open response writing

Open response writing is the main type of task used in classroom writing, and therefore plays a key role in classroom writing assessment. Open response writing tasks may be guided in that some structure and/or vocabulary may be given, or they may be quite open. Guided writing tasks are helpful for young learners, as they give some structure and support as to what is required. (The task in Figure 7.10 above is a guided writing task, giving prompts to help the children's response.) In the main, children are asked to write about something, or to someone, or for some purpose. There may be a picture or a reminder about something that has happened or been done recently. Promptings such as these help to stimulate children's ideas, and to help recall. A reminder about vocabulary helps children to write, and for those who have learned about different genres, an explicit reminder about the appropriate genre can also help them to get going. The following topics set children working on four different genres.

> Our trip to the zoo! (Recount)
> Making a cake. (Procedure)
> Frogs. (Report)
> How the rabbit made friends with the tortoise. (Narrative)

Re-forming a text

Once children know the form of some genres, they can be asked to re-form a text into a new genre. This is not an easy task but it can be used with more proficient students. Children may, for example, read a story, and then be asked to write the story from a different point of view – perhaps from the villain's point of view. An event in a story might be rewritten as a newspaper report. A diary may be rewritten as a recount.

Summary

As children become literate they are engaging in a social and cultural act. Current theories of literacy help teachers and assessors to see that literacy is a complex social and cultural endeavour, and that assessment of foreign and second language learners' literacy needs to take young learners' cultural journey into account. There are also many cognitive challenges in the development of literacy; children are confronted with new understandings about print, with new problems to solve about meanings in words, sentences, paragraphs and texts – how to understand them and how to construct them.

Key influences on the development of foreign and second language literacy are first language literacy, oral language in the target language, and cultural and background knowledge. Teachers' and assessors' selection of tasks and interpretation of performance in those tasks (and the subsequent teaching required) should be informed by knowledge of these influences.

Assessment of reading and writing is guided by the curriculum and/or by theoretical perspectives. In this chapter, the scope of goals and objectives in languages curricula for reading and writing is outlined, and reading and writing are mapped out following Bachman and Palmer (1996). Several issues in the assessment of reading and writing are discussed, including selection of texts and tasks, and the place of vocabulary, grammar and spelling assessment are discussed. Ways of assessing reading and writing are suggested, including classrom assessment strategies and task types that can be used in both the classroom and formal tests.

CHAPTER EIGHT

Evaluating young learners' performance and progress

Introduction

This chapter is concerned with the phase of assessment in which teachers and assessors evaluate the quality of children's performance in language use tasks. How do teachers and assessors of young learners know what to look for in children's performance? How do they establish the qualities of a good performance? What scoring methods do they use to guide their judgment about quality? And how do they do this in ways that make sure that the decisions that we make as a result of the assessment are as 'useful' as is required?

In this chapter I discuss the characteristics of good scoring rubrics, with examples of common types of rubrics that can be used in young learner language assessment. **Scoring rubrics** are the instructions for marking or scoring that are prepared for and by teachers and assessors. There are ways that scoring rubrics can be constructed to maximize their potential for effective scoring. Finally, in this chapter, some examples of standards are given and discussed, since standards are used more and more commonly to evaluate young learners' performance and progress over time.

A note on evaluating performance during classroom formative assessment

The kinds of assessment decisions classroom teachers make about children's performance are often embedded in the busy-ness of teaching and are mainly aimed at improving learning. Some commentators suggest that there are qualitative differences between the decisions that teachers make to evaluate performance in this kind of assessment, compared to decisions made by teachers and assessors to evaluate performance in more formal assessment tasks. They suggest that to make formative assessment decisions in the classroom, teachers generally rely on their internalized set of understandings about what kind of performance they should expect to see. The internalization of criteria is vital for teachers if they are to give instant feedback as part of formative assessment, and to follow it up with scaffolding and further instruction. Teachers' criteria are gleaned from a range of sources – from the curriculum, from standards or benchmark documents, from the textbook or from externally devised criteria such as those from standards, or from external tests that will be used to measure their children's (and, indirectly, their own) performance. This teacher's comment shows how she learned to internalize the criteria from standards rather than deal with them all on paper.

> Well, I used to use these sheets and I used to spend hours ticking this off and ticking that off and trying to work this in. It helped me look for things. I used to hear teachers saying 'Oh, it's all up here, it's in my head.' I used to wonder how they just knew where the child's at and what they can and can't do. But I can actually do that now and working through all the checklists and all the information that I thought I had to collect was far too much. (Leigh)
>
> (Breen, 1997, p. 119)

Another line of thinking is that rather than internalizing criteria from checklists and standards, teachers tend to use their own constructs, or those shared by the community of practitioners, rather than those established through standardized assessment criteria (Leung, 2004, p. 24). Leung (2005), following the work of Wiliam (2001) and others, suggests that teacher assessment might best be described as 'construct-referenced' assessment. In construct-referenced assessment the construct is held in the mind of teachers when they make judgments about performance. There is a common understanding of what is required; the criteria are not necessarily all written out and made explicit. This suggestion is made because there is some question about how formal and how 'measured' formative, and particularly on-the-run, assessment can be.

We do know that formative assessment is a complex and individualized process. Teachers hold in their minds the current performance of each child and are looking for the next expected gains for that child. Teaching occurs, and records are completed based on that child's individualized learning progress. Records tend therefore to be positive notes of gains in learning ('can now label all the parts of the body'), rather than negative based on generally expected gains for the whole class ('is not yet able to write a short letter to a friend').

Researchers in teacher assessment are suggesting that validity and reliability in formative classroom assessment processes need to be viewed in different ways from those in formal assessment. They suggest that validity in this type of assessment rests in the construct held in the teacher's mind being shored up by sufficient teaching experience, and by evidence that learning has taken place. They propose that reliability is best gained through the collection of sufficient observation data over many tasks (McMillan, 2003; Smith, 2003). It is also suggested that teachers can best evaluate the assessment process in formative assessment by checking on the learning that has taken place as a result of their assessment and feedback (Torrance and Pryor, 1998). We need to know more about the nature of the kinds of evaluations teachers make of children's performance during formative assessment (Leung, 2005). Meanwhile, the principles behind the following procedures are still thought to form an important basis for evaluating children's performance in the classroom. For example, even with formative assessment it is valuable for the classroom teacher to make explicit, from time to time, the criteria being used and decisions being made, and to check their appropriateness with colleagues. This is especially so when stakes are high.

The scoring method

In order to evaluate children's performance in the most appropriate way possible, a scoring method is needed. The **scoring method** consists of (1) the criteria by which students' responses are evaluated and (2) the procedures followed to arrive at a score (Bachman and Palmer, 1996, p. 194).

1. Deciding on the criteria by which students' responses are evaluated

The definitions of performance that assessors look for when they are deciding what constitutes successful performance are generally called **criteria**. When criteria are written in scoring rubrics they are often also called **descriptors**. Criteria may be written as headings (Fluency; Accuracy), as statements (Can participate in group activities) or as questions (Is the learner able to write a short letter to friends with appropriate informal language?). Criteria may be broadly defined ('Can write a letter') or more specifically defined ('Can pronounce final consonants clearly'), depending on what criteria assessors are looking for. The criteria that teachers and assessors select as part of the scoring method relate back to the definition of the construct they are assessing, and those criteria they select 'operationalise the construct' for the performance (Bachman and Palmer, 1996, p. 194). Well-defined sets of criteria should therefore be theoretically based and not just randomly selected. Thus, the criteria for an oral presentation in class need to come from a theoretical understanding of what constitutes a successful oral presentation in class.

The more specific the criterion, the clearer and more objective can be the decision about the child's performance, but this may mean that the information that is gleaned may be very specific and therefore not particularly informative for an assessment of language use. Thus, if the criteria are correct/incorrect as follows:

"Does the child answer 'Yes, that is a dog'?"   Yes/No

or

"Does the child draw a line between the horse and the field?"   Yes/No

the teacher or assessor has an easy, objective decision to make. The criteria are absolutely specific, and the answer is either yes or no. The child will probably have participated in a certain degree of language use to complete these assessment items (in the first, the child identifies the dog and answers a question; in the second the child has understood a question and followed a command), but there is a limited amount of language use possible in assessment items of this kind. Language use tasks that are likely to assess and promote language use involve interactiveness and authenticity (Bachman and Palmer, 1996), as described in Chapter 4, and are less likely to be tasks that can be marked as simply 'correct' or 'incorrect'. Objective criteria, with yes/no decisions, are not very appropriate for language assessment. As Davidson and Lynch (2002) point out,

> In practice, this approach . . .[using specific criteria] . . .works only with domains that can be narrowly defined, such as basic mathematical operations or discrete point grammatical features, and is impossible to use with broader, more complex areas of achievement, such as communicative language ability.
>
> (Davidson and Lynch, 2002, p. 12)

To assess language use, we have to accept a lesser degree of specificity in the criteria, because language use involves a number of different elements that together render the language use successful or not. For example, it is much more difficult to answer the following criteria with correct/incorrect. The marker has to make a personal, or subjective decision to answer the question because there is a complex decision to be made about whether all the elements came together effectively into successful language use.

> Did the child describe what she did on the class outing successfully?
> Did the child retell the main events in sufficient detail?

Criteria such as these are more generally used in assessment of language use; they are often combined into groups of criteria, as the examples of scoring rubrics in this chapter illustrate. Assessment criteria for most language use tasks can never be made fully explicit (Brindley, 2001). The wording of criteria for language use tasks is rarely precise, and a decision on performance inevitably requires some interpretation by teachers and assessors. To work towards promoting children's ability to use the language, teachers and assessors therefore have to find ways to work with less-specific criteria, and to work with some imprecision in marking (as is discussed in the next section).

2. Deciding on how to arrive at a mark or score

To determine the second component of the scoring method, deciding on how to arrive at a mark or score, teachers and assessors need to decide how the child's response will be marked or scored. Will there only be a right or a wrong answer to each question or item, and thus a set of marks that will be added up? Or will there be varying degrees of correctness? There are different ways that a performance can be scored. If the task is a picture-matching task, a multiple-choice or a true/false task, then **dichotomous scoring** is likely to be used, that is, each response will be marked as either correct or incorrect. The final mark is arrived at by adding the correct responses together. Cloze and gap-filling task items are usually marked correct/incorrect; there may sometimes be two or three acceptable responses (e.g., 'home' and 'house') listed in the marking schedule, but in the end the answer is considered correct or incorrect. There are also ways that correct/incorrect scoring can be used effectively with multiple criteria, that is, scores can be reported separately for different areas of language ability by using a method of **partial**

credit scoring (see Bachman and Palmer, 1996, pp. 199–202). When dichotomous and partial credit scoring items are carefully constructed, teachers and assessors can quickly score the child's performance and gain valuable information about a child's needs, strengths and weaknesses.

In language use tasks, where the quality of the performance is to be evaluated, scoring procedures are usually constructed in ways that enable markers to select a level at which children are performing. Markers choose amongst groupings of criteria that are designed to represent as well as possible the performance level of the language user. There are weaknesses in this kind of scoring procedure, as I will point out below, but the grouping of criteria into levels is considered to be the most effective procedure found to deal with the complexity of scoring of language use.

Scoring rubrics and reporting scales

Scoring rubrics are 'instruction sheets' guiding the scoring of performance and may be designed and used by teachers for their own classroom assessment, or by assessors for use by many markers involved in, for example, the scoring of a large-scale test. In some parts of the world, scoring rubrics are also known by teachers of young learners as **criteria sheets** (for certain kinds of rubrics) or **scoring guidelines**. Scoring rubrics generally provide the framework for the scoring method; that is, they contain both the criteria that are to be used (reflecting the construct to be assessed) and guidelines on how a mark or score will be arrived at. Scoring rubrics for language use tasks may be written for performance on a single task, or they may be written for performance across a range of tasks. Different types of scoring rubrics are used by teachers and assessors depending on the purpose, the audience and the context of the assessment. The type of scoring rubric that is used is determined on the basis of the construct definition; that is, on what is to be assessed. Thus, if the construct to be assessed is the ability of the young learners to perform a letter-writing task to a friend, then the rubric will be constructed around the nature of the expected ability of the young learners in question to write an informal letter to a friend. Once scores are decided, they are reported to parents, learners and others. **Reporting scales** provide general descriptions of performance against which teachers and assessors can report on children's achievement. These same reporting scales can also provide general descriptions that can inform and guide the development of scoring rubrics. Performance standards, which I discuss below, are commonly used reporting scales in education departments.

A framework for the evaluation of scoring rubrics and reporting scales

How do we know if a scoring rubric and reporting scales are effective and appropriate? The evaluation of scoring rubrics can be complex, as a range of considerations about purpose, validity, reliability, practicality and use come together in scoring rubrics as they do in the selection of assessment tasks. This section sets out some of the main considerations in the evaluation of scoring rubrics for young learners. Alderson (1991) has referred to three distinct purposes for rating scales: **Constructor-oriented scales** (designed to guide the construction of tests), **assessor-oriented scales** (designed to guide the rating process) and **user-oriented scales** (designed to provide useful information to users who will be interpreting the test scores). The first purpose is not relevant to the discussion here; I refer to the last two categories of scales: assessor-, or marker-oriented, and user-oriented purposes, with a general category, to organize a set of considerations for the evaluation of scoring rubrics and reporting scales.

Marker-oriented considerations are those that relate to the needs of markers (both classroom teachers and external assessors) as they evaluate children's performance through scoring rubrics. User-oriented considerations are those that relate to the needs of users such as the children themselves, parents, other teachers and administrators as they read about performance described through reporting scales. General considerations are relevant to both scoring rubrics and ratings scales. Table 8.1 summarises these considerations, which are then discussed briefly below. Some assessment tools, such as rating scales, can be used as both scoring rubrics and reporting scales; they should then be evaluated according to the purpose(s) for which they are being used.

General considerations

Are the scoring rubrics and reporting scales appropriate for young learners?

Scoring rubrics and reporting scales used to evaluate and report on young learners' performance need to reflect the language use characteristics of the learner group in question and their learning context. In the case of

Table 8.1 *Considerations in the evaluation of scoring rubrics and reporting scales for young learners*

General considerations (for scoring rubrics and reporting scales)

- Are they appropriate for young language learners?
  - Do they reflect the developmental needs and first and second language literacy growth characteristics of young learners?
  - Do they reflect the curriculum and the learning opportunities that children have?

Marker-oriented considerations (for scoring rubrics)

- Do they reflect the purpose for assessment?
- Do they reflect the construct that is to be assessed?
- Are they clear and logical and therefore as unambiguous as possible for markers?
  - Are they written in clear and objective language? Do markers have sufficient guidance on what mark should be given for what kind of performance?
  - Are the numbers of levels feasible? Are they accompanied by samples of work?
- Are they practical, in the sense that they do not make unreasonable demands on markers' time?
- Will they promote a fair assessment of all young learners?
  - Do they avoid descriptions or procedures that advantage or disadvantage some children because of their culture, sex or socioeconomic background?
- Will their use promote markers' professional understandings about learning?

User-oriented considerations (for reporting scales)

- Do the reporting scales reflect their purpose?
- Are they meaningful to those who will use them (learners, parents, other teachers, administrators)?
  - Can users handle the language of the descriptors, the different dimensions and levels?
- Will the reported scores generated from the scoring rubrics serve users' needs?
  - Will they provide the information that is needed (e.g., about what to teach; about what to report to others, about resource allocation)?
- Will they have a positive impact on users?
  - Will users' understandings about the nature of second language learning be enhanced?
  - Will they have a positive impact on the learning, and more broadly, on the lives of young learners?

young learners, scoring rubrics should therefore reflect the characteristics of the expected language performance of young learners in the programme in which they are learning. They should reflect the developmental and literacy features that we know about young second learners' language use, and they should reflect the curriculum and learning opportunities to which children are exposed.

Marker-oriented considerations

Do the scoring rubrics reflect the purpose for assessment?

Scoring rubrics should reflect the purpose for the assessment. They might be prepared for formative or summative assessment in the classroom, where the classroom teacher is marking children's performance, or they might be used in external tests that are to be marked by assessors. The purpose for the assessment will influence the degree of precision and detail that is required in the scoring rubric. The appropriateness to purpose will be reflected in the kind of information that is generated. If the purpose is to provide diagnostic information for teaching purposes, then detail about children's performance will be required. If the purpose is to place the child on a level for purposes of comparison with other children in the cohort (say, of Grade 6 children in the state), then less information needs to be generated. In classroom informal assessments, criteria sheets and checklists can be prepared quickly enough to guide scoring; for summative assessment and in large-scale tests, more preparation and more detail, perhaps in analytic rating scales, is likely to be needed. For diagnostic assessment, analytic scales provide more information and therefore might be more suitable than holistic rating scales, as I will discuss below with regard to rating scales.

Do the scoring rubrics reflect the construct that is to be assessed?

Scoring rubrics need to reflect the construct that is to be assessed. Thus, if they are to be used to evaluate children's second language performance in an interview, then the characteristics of young learners' interview performance need to be established and identified through descriptors. The attributes that underlie successful performance should be identified in the scoring rubric, wherever possible based on a theoretical basis about the nature of that performance. Whilst, ideally, all the important characteristics of expected performance should be included, it is often not practical to include all aspects of performance, and it is better to indicate the salient characteristics that markers should be looking for. If all features of performance are included, the scoring rubrics become too complex to use (Greatorex, 2003, p. 128). It is therefore best if rubrics *exemplify* the performance rather than describe every feature of performance required (Black, 1993, in Greatorex, 2003, p. 128). Salient characteristics may be criteria that represent the core features of that performance, or new understanding and achievements that teachers are looking for from the learner group in question.

Are the scoring rubrics understandable and logical, and therefore as unambiguous as possible for markers?

Without scoring rubrics of some kind, teachers are likely to be reliant on tacit knowledge, or on 'expert notions' of quality to evaluate and assign a mark to the piece of work. The use of expert knowledge is an important contributor to classroom assessment activities and can have some reliability of its own if there is 'sufficiency of information'. However, as I pointed out above, a lack of guidance in the evaluation of performance may lead to threats to reliability. Scoring rubrics play a valuable role in making explicit the criteria by which the performance should be evaluated. It is important, therefore, that criteria are clearly defined and that levels are well articulated (Bachman and Palmer, 1996; Weigle, 2002). However, because scoring rubrics rely on verbal description, there is often some 'fuzziness' or vagueness in descriptors (Sadler, 1987, p. 202). According to Sadler (1987, p. 202) there are two types of descriptors; **sharp descriptors** describing features that are either present or absent (return address, date, greeting) and **fuzzy descriptors** that are matters of degree (*clear* solutions, *superior* writing ability, *neat* appearance). Scoring rubrics are likely to include both types. Fuzziness is seen in scoring rubrics when writers attempt to establish progress across levels using relative terms (*none, little, some, much*) and when they combine these relative terms with words like 'coherent' that require interpretation (*incoherent, somewhat lacking in coherence, reasonably coherent, highly coherent*). Despite these difficulties, Sadler suggests fuzzy descriptions should not be seen as inferior to sharp ones, or that they should be avoided if at all possible because of their lack of precision and their inability to guide assessment in a definitive way.

> Verbal description cannot . . . be sharper or more precise than language will allow. In particular, fuzzy standards cannot be transformed

into sharp standards simply by using more detailed or elaborate language, for much the same reason that there are practical limits to the degree of improvement that can result from using a magnifying glass on a blurred photograph. The element, whether it be a group of words or a cluster of silver particles, needs a context for it to be properly interpreted.   (Sadler, 1987, p. 206)

For this reason, Sadler suggests that samples of work should be used with verbal descriptions to exemplify the meaning of the descriptions, and that the number of exemplars can probably be made fairly small provided they are accompanied by explicit annotations of the properties of individual samples of work (Sadler, 1987, p. 207). Brindley, too (1998, p. 70), suggests that a library of exemplars of student performance can be built up to accompany scoring rubrics, in this case outcomes-based reporting frameworks, to help teachers to interpret and understand (Gipps, 1994) the assessment criteria. I discuss below ways in which reliability can be maximized in the use of scoring rubrics.

An important issue in scoring rubrics that have levels of performance is how many levels of performance there should be. The number of levels that are chosen depends on considerations of 'usefulness' (Bachman and Palmer, 1996, p. 212). The number of levels in a scale will depend on whether markers can reasonably be expected to distinguish performance at each level. It also depends on impact. If the purpose of the assessment is to place children into three different learning groups or classes, then three levels may be sufficient. If the purpose is to map children's progress in enough detail to help teachers understand the nature of their performance and thus their need for teaching support, then more levels are likely to be needed.

Will the scoring rubrics promote a fair assessment for all learners?

Both markers and users hope for a fair assessment for all learners. As I discussed in the framework for the selection of tasks in Chapter 4, scoring rubrics should avoid descriptions or procedures that advantage or disadvantage some children because of characteristics such as their culture, sex or socioeconomic background. As an example, if criteria in the scoring rubrics are asking for performance that may favour boys over girls (e.g., a criterion that children write at least a page on a football game showing evidence of understanding about the game, and using appropriate football-related vocabulary), then there is likely to be some bias, both in the task and in the scoring rubrics. By being appropriate for young learners and their context, appropriate to their purpose, and reflecting the construct to be assessed, they are also more likely to be fair for all learners.

Are the scoring rubrics practical?

Scoring rubrics need to be practical for the time and context in which they will be used. In the classroom context, teachers need rubrics that can be developed and used within the limited time available in classroom teaching. In this context, rubrics that are generalizable to several tasks save the time and energy required for their development. Brindley reports, however, that teachers will not necessarily reject assessment systems that increase their workload, if they perceive value in the information they gain for learners, teachers and parents (Brindley, 1998, p. 65). In formal testing situations, when scoring rubrics are developed by teams, and groups of markers are brought together to be trained and then to mark collaboratively and under supervision, more complex scoring rubrics may be considered practical.

Will their use promote professional understandings about learning?

All materials to which teachers refer are bound to have some influence on their thinking. Scoring rubrics, especially in classroom teaching contexts, are able to inform professional understandings. Therefore, scoring rubrics that are prepared with proper attention to learner group, purpose and construct, as well as to clarity and fairness, are more acceptable in terms of influence on professional thinking, than those that are not.

User-oriented considerations

Do the reporting scales reflect their purpose?

Reporting scales are designed to establish the range of possible performance, and thus to establish and facilitate reporting of the level of children's performance. Large-scale reporting scales in the form of performance standards carry complexity in their purpose, since they can have many purposes; they set out to establish the curriculum (what should be learned), to provide a hierarchy of achievement for reporting purposes, and are often also used for accountability. There may be tension between these purposes, and this can cause confusion for users and weaknesses in the standards, as I will discuss below.

Are the reporting scales meaningful to those who will use them (learners, parents, other teachers, administrators)?

Reporting scales should be meaningful not only to markers, but also to others who use them. Thus, children (depending on their age and the complexity of the criteria in the reporting scales) can be guided to understand what is required in a task to judge their own performance, and what aspects of their performance need to be improved. Parents can be given a better opportunity to understand the expectations of tasks, or the requirements across a term's work, when scoring rubrics are available to them. Administrators prefer straightforward measurable scoring rubrics that provide them with the answers they are looking for, without making the evaluation too complex.

Will the reported scores generated serve users' needs?

Some reporting scales are not designed for other users, but simply for the classroom teacher. Some are designed with the learner in mind; they can help children to understand the strengths and weaknesses of their own performance. Other reporting scales are shared with parents, or other teachers. Yet again others, such as performance standards, are written for teachers, parents and administrators to understand. Thus, it depends on the purpose of the reporting scales as to whether they will serve users' needs, and, as I discuss later in this chapter, in some cases conflicting purposes result in tensions in the way reporting scales are presented and used. The report also needs to meet users' needs. In some cases, for example when parents are receiving a report, profile reporting might be best; in others, for example when administrators are making resourcing decisions, a single score or a set of scores is more likely to be required. Administrators need reporting scales that will generate the kind of information they need to make administrative decisions, related to resourcing, reporting on trends, and accountability. For this reason, administrators like certain kinds of performance standards, as I will discuss in the last section of this chapter. Developers of reporting scales need to decide on the users' tolerance for discrepancies (Weigle, 2002, p. 127) and to be as clear as possible about purpose and user needs.

Will the reporting scales have a positive impact on users?

In many cases, reporting scales will only be seen by markers, that is, by classroom teachers and assessors of external tests. In some cases learners, parents and other teachers (for example, mainstream teachers) are shown reporting scales, and performance is discussed with them. Administrators are presented with patterns of performance of cohorts of learners as they monitor data from tests and teacher reports. The messages that learners, parents, teachers and administrators receive from the assessment process should aim to have a positive impact, promoting, in a broad sense (that is over cohorts and over time), understanding and notions of strengths and progress rather than weakness and failure. If assessments, of which reporting scales are a part, result in disempowerment of young learners, perhaps through a loss of self-concept or a sense of inferiority in the community, then the assessments are not 'useful' and have failed (Cummins, 2000). This can happen, for example, when children are observed erroneously to be failing over several years when first language reporting scales are used to monitor their second language and literacy progress (Davison, 1999; McKay, 2001; Davison and McKay, 2002).

Types of scoring rubrics and reporting scales used with young learners

This section presents some different kinds of scoring rubrics used in the evaluation of young learners' language performance. Some of these are intended to be used mainly by classroom teachers, while some could be used both in the classroom and in large-scale assessments. Observation checklists are commonly used by classroom teachers of young learners as they observe, note and check off children's performance during classroom teaching and learning activities. Criteria sheets are often teacher-constructed and are regularly used by classroom teachers for classroom assessment, though they may also be constructed by assessors for tests. **Rating scales** setting out worst to best performance to guide assessment decisions are more likely to be used in planned assessment tasks in the classroom, and in external tests where scales are prepared and used to reflect the range of performance (from weak to strong) that is expected by the particular group of children taking the assessment procedure. Rating scales may be used as reporting scales to report on achievement. Standards are also a type of reporting scale but are generally designed to report on performance across abilities and over time. Standards set out expected curriculum-related performance and progress over a number of years. Some examples of standards are given and discussed in a section at the end of this chapter.

Observation checklists

Classroom teachers often devise their own observation checklists to check that their learners are achieving the objectives they have set for learning, over a unit of work, or a length of time. An observation checklist is usually made up of points of observable behaviour that can be checked off, such as in the checklist in Figure 8.1.

When observation checklists are teacher-constructed and based on previous observations of learners, they are more likely to be appropriate

Name: Term: Theme: My favourite animal			
	Yes/No	Comments (When? Where? How well?)	Teaching points to follow up
Can name their favourite animal			
Can label the parts of the anima			
Can describe the colours and shapes of the animal			
Can ask someone else about their favourite animal			
Can tell a story about their animal, with the help of a paper model and pictures			

Figure 8.1 An example of an observation checklist.

to the learner group and learning programme. The decision regarding the observation may be a **competency** decision, that is, either children are competent or they are not in each criterion to be checked, or it could also be a profile rating, in columns under relative terms such as 'emerging', 'developing' and 'consolidated'. It is very unlikely that teachers require a final mark to be tallied; the checklist is a profile that gives the teacher a sense of what each child can and cannot do, and this is sufficient for the information that is needed for teaching purposes, and for verbal descriptions of progress in reports to parents and others.

Teachers may also select descriptors out of developmental continua, place them in their checklist, and observe children's progress against these indicators over time. **Developmental continua** are usually written by educational professionals attached to Education Departments or sometimes by commercial organizations. They describe the expected progress of learners, which are usually a combination of developmental and curriculum-related growth. The 'First Steps' materials, an extract from which is given in Table 8.2, are materials that provide developmental continua in oral language, writing, reading and spelling for first langauge learners.

Table 8.2 *Extract from developmental continuum for first language reading development (Education Department of Western Australia, 1997c)*

Making meaning at text level (early reading level)

The reader:
- is beginning to read familiar texts confidently and can retell major content from visual and printed texts, e.g. language experience recounts, shared books, simple informational texts and children's television programmes
- can identify and talk about a range of different text forms such as letters, lists, recipes, stories, newspaper and magazine articles, television drama and documentaries
- demonstrates understanding that all texts, both narrative and informational, are written by authors who are expressing their own ideas
- identifies the main topic of a story or informational text and supplies some supporting information
- talks about characters in books using picture clues, personal experience and the text to make inferences
- provides detail about characters, setting and events when retelling a story
- has strong personal reaction to advertisements, ideas and information from informational texts, making links to own knowledge
- makes comparisons with other texts read or viewed
- can talk about how to predict text content, e.g. 'I knew that book hadn't got facts in it. The dinosaurs had clothes on.'

Teachers may also refer to performance standards to select relevant observation criteria. They add selected descriptors from the developmental continua and/or the performance standards to their observation checklists, usually checking off criteria as they see evidence of the stated behaviour in classroom activities or assessment tasks. Foreign and second language teachers need to be cautious about selecting descriptors from developmental continua and performance standards designed for first language learners. Depending on their background experience and age on entry into learning the target language, second language learners' literacy development can differ quite markedly from that of first language learners. For example, young language learners will make grammatical 'errors' in their structures that do not appear in first language learners' writing, yet these 'errors' are indications of the creativity essential for healthy language learning progress in foreign and second language learning (see McKay, 1998). Developmental continua designed for first language learners also may not consider different cultural backgrounds in their criteria. In these cases, the criteria that are included in teachers' observation checklists may not be appropriate for young learners and their learning programmes, and may not reflect the construct of the assessment (that is, second language learning). The clarity, practicality and fairness of observation checklists depend on factors such as the kinds of descriptors teachers select and how they make their decisions about competency (e.g., how many times should teachers observe the behaviour in question before it is considered a competency?). When teachers list the characteristics of performance to be observed in collaboration with others, and with reference to appropriate documents, this is likely to assist their professional understandings.

When observation checklists are used primarily for formative assessment purposes, there are no other users' needs to be met other than the children's, who may, with help, have a chance to understand more about what is required and how they are progressing. When teachers' observation sheets become the tool for evaluation and reporting of children's progress to administrators, the stakes are raised. Administrators require a simpler report such as an indication of the child's level(s) on performance standards. Interpreting data from observation checklists into levels on performance standards requires a high degree of teacher subjective judgment, and administrators find this difficult to accept as reliable. Conversely, this kind of reporting requirement can have a negative impact on the use of checklists for their original purpose, formative assessment.

Criteria sheets

A criteria sheet is a one-sheet table of descriptors, accompanied by a marking scheme, that guides markers to evaluate the quality of performance in a particular task. Criteria sheets are commonly used by classroom teachers of young learners for both formative and summative assessment purposes. In both the following examples, the overall construct to be assessed is the completion of the task (Can the child complete the task successfully?) and a set of criteria, organized into **dimensions** (categories of criteria), which define the constructs or contributing knowledge and skills to be assessed. These criteria are usually prepared by the teacher or by assessors with close consideration of the knowledge and abilities that are considered to make up successful completion of the task. In the first example in Figure 8.2, the dimensions considered relevant to an oral presentation to a class are 'text context and organization', 'vocabulary and sentence structure' and 'responsiveness', and specific criteria are listed within these dimensions. In the second example in Figure 8.3, dimensions and criteria for process report writing have been conceptualized with reference to systemic functional linguistics. Because criteria sheets are constructed for specific tasks, and usually with a particular learner group and learning programme in mind, they are more likely to meet the evaluation criteria for appropriateness for the learner group, the learning programme and the construct. Because they contain detail within the dimensions and criteria, they are appropriate for formative assessment and also, in more formal assessment, can give clear guidelines on the construct, or the characteristics of the performance required.

In both the examples, the scoring procedure is on the right hand side: teachers rate children's performance as low, medium or high, as in Figure 8.2, or, as in Figure 8.3, 'very competent' to 'not yet'. The example in Figure 8.3 has a scale at the bottom for teachers to give a final score. This type of scoring device is generally considered suitable for formative and low-stakes classroom-based assessment, since teachers use their own 'expert notions' or internal criteria (developed over time and based on shared understandings and experience) to establish what is low, medium or high performance. For some teachers, though, their internal criteria may not be well established, and their decisions about low, medium or high performance may not be appropriate. In these cases collaboration with other teachers in discussions of marks for different samples of work is beneficial.

Student's name _____ Level/stage_____Date_____

Characteristics of the student to note:

Description of task (including characteristics of setting, input, etc.)

News telling: Oral presentation to class

Additional support given to this student

Assessment criteria	Comment	low ◄──► high		
Text content and organization • includes key information (where, when, who, what) • provides appropriate elaboration and detail • maintains fluency • concludes appropriately				
Vocabulary and sentence structure • connects ideas using appropriate conjunctions (and, but, then, unless, so) • uses adjectives • uses varied and specific vocabulary • is generally accurate in structure • articulates words clearly				
Responsiveness • is aware of interest needs of other children • makes appropriate eye contact • responds appropriately to questions				

Comments

Final mark:

Figure 8.2 A criteria sheet for a news telling oral presentation to class.

Description of the activity: Students share or report on a process they used to complete a task in an individual or group activity					
Name of student: Name of school: Title of narrative:	Year level/class: Teacher:		Date:		
Criteria [Tick appropriate box]	Very compe-tent	Compe-tent	Limited compe-tence	Not yet	Comment
Ability to carry out the task: Did the student • share or report willingly • share or report with minimal teacher support [questioning or prompting]					
Structure and organization: Did the student • set the context, e.g. 'For the plant project we . . .' 'Our experiment was called . . .' • give sufficient detail • sequence information, e.g. 'First we did x . . . then we . . .' • keep on the topic					
Language features: Did the student • use a variety of time phrases, e.g. 'then, next' • use specific vocabulary, e.g. stiff, beat, beaker, apparatus • use verb tenses accurately and consistently, e.g. 'when it was added . . .' • use pronoun references accurately, e.g. it, this, these, those					
Communication skills: Did the student • speak fluently without too many hesitations, e.g. 'um, er' • speak clearly, e.g. pronounce words accurately, sound plurals and verb endings					

• self-correct, e.g. 'then he poured . . stirred' • refer to finished product to enhance meaning [optional]					

General comments:

Global rating: [circle]	lowest 1_____2_____3_____4_____5 highest

Note: This example is designed for second language learners who are in upper elementary and who have written a science experiment.

Figure 8.3 A criteria sheet for a report on a written process (based on the genre approach) (Education Department of South Australia, 1990).

If the purpose for assessment is formal and high-stakes, then this type of scoring rubric is not sufficient; criteria sheets should be supplemented with rating scales that establish more clearly what 'low', 'medium' and 'high' performance looks like. Samples of work exemplifying the levels can also support the rating process. This then helps the criteria sheet to be as clear and unambiguous as possible for markers. Criteria sheets, as many teachers know them, are related to a more formal approach to task-based assessment called **primary trait scoring**.

> The philosophy behind primary trait scoring is that it is important to understand how well students can write within a narrowly defined range of discourse (e.g., persuasion or explanation). In primary trait scoring, the rating scale is defined with respect to the specific writing assignment and essays are judged according to the degree of success with which the writer has carried out the assignment.
>
> (Weigle, 2002, p. 110)

In primary trait scoring a number of components are required.

(a) the writing task
(b) a statement of the primary rhetorical trait (e.g., persuasive essay, congratulatory letter) elicited by the task
(c) a hypothesis about the expected performance on the task
(d) a statement of the relationship between the task and the primary trait
(e) a rating scale which articulates levels of performance
(f) sample scripts at each level
(g) explanations of why each script was scored as it was.

(Weigle, 2002, p. 110)

These components are required in high-stakes assessment situations. However, it should be noted that this becomes a time- and labour-intensive exercise (Lloyd-Jones, 1997, cited in Weigle, 2002, p. 110).

Criteria sheets, like observation checklists, have many strengths in teacher assessment situations, and for the same reasons. They can be developed to reflect the learner group, the learning context and the specific constructs in question. They differ from observation sheets in that they may be used in summative testing, and in external tests. Their fairness then rests in the employment of strategies to maximize reliability in marking, as listed above by Weigle, and as discussed below. The main users of criteria sheets are learners who can be guided to understand the requirements of tasks and to self-assess where their cognitive maturity allows for this.

Holistic rating scales

A holistic rating scale provides descriptions of ability at a number of different levels. These levels are provided on a single scale, which is divided into bands or levels labelled in various ways, for example from 'needs improvement' to 'good' to 'outstanding', or from 'Level 1', to 'Level 5'. Holistic scales can be constructed from curriculum or theory-based definitions of language ability. Holistic scales are generally used when groups of teachers or assessors can work together to produce them and then to share them. They are often borrowed from publications or from each other by teachers and adapted to fit the tasks they are assessing. Figure 8.4 gives an example of a holistic rating scale designed to guide teachers and assessors to score a literature response.

The marker selects which of these levels best describes the child's performance, in order to arrive at a decision about the quality of the performance. It may be that the child's performance doesn't meet every criterion in the level that is chosen; the usual practice is for the marker to select the level that reflects the performance most closely.

The second example of a holistic scale, in Table 8.3, is designed to assess writing across a number of writing samples. This scale has also been constructed around unarticulated dimensions through each level; organization, grammar, vocabulary and mechanics.

The advantages and disadvantages of holistic and analytic scoring are discussed by many writers, including Weigle (2002, pp. 112–14).and Bachman and Palmer (1996, pp. 219–22). Holistic scoring is faster (and

Outstanding	Describes most story elements (characters, setting, beginning, middle and end of story) through oral or written language or drawings Responds personally to the story Provides an accurate and detailed description of the story Develops criteria for evaluating the story
Good	Describes most story elements through oral or written language or drawings Responds personally to the story Provides an accurate description of the story with some details Analyzes something about the story (plot, setting, character, illustrations)
Satisfactory	Describes some story elements through oral or written language or drawings Makes a limited personal response to the story Provides an accurate description of the story Explains why he or she likes or does not like the story
Needs improvement	Describes few story elements through oral or written language or drawings Makes no response or a limited personal response to the story Provides a less than accurate description of the story States that he or she likes or does not like the story

Figure 8.4 Example of a holistic rating scale for a specific task (a primary trait rating scale): A Literature Response (O'Malley and Valdez Pierce, 1996, p. 113).

therefore less expensive) than analytic scoring (discussed below) because markers can make an overall assessment quickly; their attention is focused on certain aspects of the performance, and this can guide them to know what is salient or important for a successful performance. It is argued that holistic scoring is more authentic, because it reflects more closely on a personal reaction of a reader to a text, or of an observer to a performance, than in analytic scoring methods (Weigle, 2002, p. 114). Some disadvantages of holistic scoring are (1) that holistic scoring provides a single score, and therefore useful diagnostic information may not be collected about the performance, and (2) holistic scores are not always easy to interpret, as raters may not use the same criteria to arrive at the same scores; for example, some markers may put more store into grammatical accuracy than others. Markers may also develop their own internal rating scale and this may drift away from the intended scale.

Table 8.3 *Sample holistic rating scales for writing samples (Adapted from a rubric drafted by the ESL Teachers Portfolio Assessment Group, Fairfax County Public Schools, Virginia, O'Malley and Valdez Pierce, 1996, p. 22)*

Rating	Criteria
6 Proficient	Writes single or multiple paragraphs with clear introduction, fully developed ideas and a conclusion Uses appropriate verb tense and a variety of grammatical and syntactical structures; uses complex sentences effectively; uses smooth transitions Uses varied, precise vocabulary Has occasional errors in mechanics (spelling, punctuation and capitalization) which do not detract from meaning
5 Fluent	Writes single or multiple paragraphs with main idea and supporting detail: presents ideas logically, though some parts may not be fully developed Uses appropriate verb tense and a variety of grammatical and syntactical structures; errors in sentence structure do not detract from meaning; uses transitions Uses varied vocabulary appropriate for the purpose Has few errors in mechanics which do not detract from meaning
4 Expanding	Organizes ideas in logical or sequential order with some supporting detail; begins to write a paragraph Experiments with a variety of verb tenses but does not use them consistently; subject/verb agreement errors; uses some compound and complex sentences; limited use of transitions Vocabulary is appropriate to purpose but sometimes awkward Uses punctuation, capitalization and mostly conventional spelling; errors sometimes interfere with meaning
3 Developing	Writes sentences around an idea; some sequencing present, but may lack cohesion Writes in present tense and simple sentences; has difficulty with subject/verb agreement; run-on sentences are common; begins to use compound sentences
2 Beginning	Begins to convey meaning through writing Writes predominately phrases and patterned or simple sentences Uses limited or repetitious vocabulary Uses temporary (phonetic) spelling
1 Emerging	No evidence of idea development or organization Uses single words, pictures, and patterned phrases Copies from a model Little awareness of spelling, capitalization, or punctuation

Misinterpretations of holistic rating scales are common sources of imprecision in judging and reporting students' performance (e.g., North, 1993). There are ways that reliability can be maximized in the use of rating scales, as will be discussed later in this chapter.

Analytic rating scales

Analytic rating scales differ from holistic scales in that they split up the specified criteria so that markers make a decision about the level of performance on each dimension (or criterion) and then come up with a final score, single composite or profile, by checking across the overall pattern of levels achieved. They are made up of the same number of separate scales as there are distinct components in the construct definition (Bachman and Palmer, 1996). Like holistic scales, analytic scales can be constructed from curriculum or theory-based definitions of language ability. To make decisions on scoring as unambiguous as possible, the weighting of each level for each dimension or criterion can be stipulated. Weighting can be equal, or different percentages are allocated. Thus a pattern of weighting can then be used to establish (if this is what is wanted) that the theoretical construct is strongly concerned with language use and less so with vocabulary and accuracy. Grammar, vocabulary, pronunciation and other features of language can be assessed through analytic scales. Purpura (2004, 254) suggests that analytic scoring rather than holistic scoring helps us to estimate the relative contribution of the grammatical (or other) knowledge to the assessment.

In Table 8.4, I have transposed the same criteria from Table 8.3 into separate categories for an analytic rating scale. In this scale, the dimensions are explicitly labelled as 'Description of the story elements'; 'The nature of the personal response'; 'The accuracy of the story description'; and 'Evaluation of the story' and presented as separate scales within the analytic scale.

To use this scale, markers circle the descriptors that describe the child's level on each of the criteria, and from there can make a 'profile' report on the child's ability either by presenting the marked rating scales as a profile or by coming to a decision about the most prominent level. The profile method helps to show in which areas the child is weaker or stronger; thus information set out in this way is more immediately useful for diagnostic purposes than the single score that is obtained from a holistic scale.

Table 8.4 *Example of an analytic rating scale (adapted from Table 8.3)*

Categories of criteria	Needs improvement	Satisfactory	Good	Outstanding
Description of the story elements	Describes few story elements through oral or written language or drawings	Describes some story elements through oral or written language or drawings	Describes most story elements through oral or written language or drawings	Describes most story elements (characters, settings, beginning, middle, and end of story) through oral or written language or drawings
The nature of the personal response	Makes no response or a limited personal response to the story	Makes a limited personal response to the story	Responds personally to the story	Responds personally to the story
The accuracy of the story description	Provides less than accurate description of the story	Provides an accurate description of the story	Provides an accurate description of the story with some details	Provides an accurate and detailed description of the story
Evaluation of the story	States that he or she likes or does not like the story	Explains why he or she likes or does not like the story	Analyses something about the story (plot, setting, character, illustrations)	Develops criteria for evaluating the story

Analytic criteria are considered to help teachers and assessors to be less subjective and less prone to variability in their marking than holistic criteria. They take more time to complete than global scales, but they provide clear guidance to markers on what they are looking for. It is harder for markers to ignore aspects of performance. The decisions that markers make are also very clearly set out for all to see. They give assessors the opportunity to acknowledge uneven development of sub-skills in individual children's performance. Analytic scales are therefore particularly useful for second language learners because uneven performance across different criteria is typically a feature of second language development; this helps to profile learners' strengths and needs in the performance (Hamp-Lyons, 1991, cited in Weigle 2002, p. 120). In addition, analytic scales have been found to be more useful in rater training, as inexperienced raters can understand the criteria more easily when they are set out in separate scales rather than in holistic scales (Weigle, 2002, p. 120).

A second example of an analytic rating scale, designed to score oral proficiency, is presented in Figure 8.5 to illustrate that not all rating scales are suitable for young learners. The scale describes performance in the lower levels in negative terms, as incorrect and weak: 'Speech is so halting and fragmentary as to make conversation virtually impossible'; 'Errors in grammar and word order so severe as to make speech virtually unintelligible'. For positive impact, criteria and descriptors for young learners are more suitable when they describe strengths and progress rather than errors. Without positive descriptions of growth, teachers may look for errors rather than instances of growth and resulting negative feedback to children and parents may result in loss of self-esteem and motivation.

Student Oral Proficiency Rating

Student's name   Grade   Language observed
School
City   State
Rated by   Date

DIRECTIONS: For each of the 5 categories below at the left, mark an "X" across the box that best describes the student's abilities.

	LEVEL 1	LEVEL 2	LEVEL 3	LEVEL 4	LEVEL 5
Compre-hension	Cannot understand even simple conversation.	Has great difficulty following what is said. Can comprehend only 'social conversation' spoken	Understands most of what is said at slower-than-normal speed with repetitions.	Understands nearly everything at normal speed, although occasional repetition may be necessary.	Understands everyday conversation and normal classroom discussions without difficulty.

	LEVEL 1	LEVEL 2	LEVEL 3	LEVEL 4	LEVEL 5
		slowly and with frequent repetitions.			
Fluency	Speech is so halting and frag-mentary as to make conver-sation virtually impossible.	Usually hesitant: often forced into silence by language limita-tions.	Speech in everyday communi-cation and classroom discussion is frequently disrupted by the student's search for the correct manner of expression.	Speech in everyday communi-cation and classroom discussion is generally fluent, with occasional lapses while the student searches for the correct manner of expression.	Speech in everyday conversation and in classroom discussion is fluent and effortless, approxi-mating that of a native speaker.
Vocabulary	Vocabulary limitations are so extreme as to make conver-sation virtually impossible.	Misuse of words and very limited vocabu-lary make compre-hension quite difficult.	Frequently uses the wrong words; conver-sation somewhat limited because of inade-quate vocabulary.	Occasionally uses inappro-priate terms or must rephrase ideas because of inadequate vocabulary.	Use of vocabulary and idioms approxi-mates that of a native speaker.
Pronun-ciation	Pronun-ciation problems so severe as to make speech virtually unintell-igible.	Very hard to under-stand because of pronun-ciation problems. Must frequently	Pronun-ciation problems necessitate concen-tration on the part of the listener and	Always intelligible, though one is conscious of a definite accent and occasional inappro-priate	Pronun ciation and intonation approximate a native speaker's.

	LEVEL 1	LEVEL 2	LEVEL 3	LEVEL 4	LEVEL 5
		repeat in order to be under-stood.	occasionally lead to misunder-standing.	intonation patterns.	
Grammar	Errors in grammar and word order so severe as to make speech virtually unintell-igible.	Grammar and word order errors make compre-hension difficult. Must often rephrase or restrict what is said to basic patterns.	Makes frequent errors of grammar and word order which occasionally obscure meaning.	Occasionally makes grammatical or word order errors which do not obscure meaning.	Grammatical usage and word order approximate a native speaker's.

Figure 8.5 An example of a scale more suitable for older learners. Student Oral Proficiency Rating (adapted from the Student Oral Language Observation Matrix (SOLOM)) developed by the San Jose (California) United School District (Thompson, 1997, p. 176).

Holistic and analytic rating scales can be prepared and used effectively as scoring rubrics for learner language. They can be used for formative and summative purposes. They can be written to reflect the construct being assessed, and to reflect the young learner curriculum. Clarity can be achieved for markers in the descriptions, though samples of work and marker training are needed to maximise reliability and thus fairness. Once they are written, they are practical to use; however, their preparation can take time and collaboration with other teachers and experts is desirable in both their preparation and in their use for marking. If judiciously shared with children, they can give guidance on what is required. Teachers gain valuable professional understandings through such collaboration and marker training. The use of rating scales, backed up with moderation, tends to be accepted by parents and administrators and rating scales are com-monly used in high-stakes testing: 'ratings provide greater opportunity for assessing the effectiveness of the test task, as well as its impact on test takers. For such reasons, we believe that ratings are well worth their relatively high cost in human resources' (Bachman and Palmer, 1996, p. 200). Rating scales can also be used as reporting scales, that is, they can become reference points for the reporting of achievement to students, parents and others. If they are used as reporting scales, then they need to be evaluated against the user-oriented criteria for reporting scales in Table 8.1.

The following section gives guidance on developing scoring rubrics, and on maximizing reliability in their use.

How scoring rubrics are constructed

In order to prepare scoring rubrics so that they present the most appropriate criteria and guidelines to arrive at a mark, classroom teachers carrying out low-stakes assessment can construct their own rubrics according to their own knowledge and expectations of children's performance, and according to the curriculum requirements. The degree of work required in developing scoring rubrics depends on the purpose for assessment, and in particular how high the stakes are. The following steps can be taken in both low- and high-stakes assessment, though in low-stakes assessment the degree to which the steps are followed will depend on time and collegial support available.

- Determine what the characteristics of quality performance are. (Refer to earlier sections of Chapters 6 and 7 in this book for theoretical frameworks, genres and contributing skills to inform what these characteristics might be in oral language, reading and writing.)
- Gather sample rubrics that were developed for a similar purpose, for children of a similar age in a comparable learning context.
- Gather samples of children's work that demonstrate the range of performance from ineffective to very effective.
- Discuss with others the characteristics of these models that distinguish the effective ones from the ineffective ones.
- Write criteria (in levels, if required) for the important characteristics.
- Gather another set of samples of students' work.
- Try out the rubrics to see if they help you make accurate judgments about children's performance (and that you agree with others on these judgments).
- Revise your criteria, if necessary.
- Try it again until the score captures the 'quality' of the work.

(adapted from Herman et al., 1992, p. 75)

Careful checks like this are necessary if the rubrics are to be considered valid and reliable. Decisions on the nature of the criteria, on the degree of detail in the criteria and on the number of levels are an integral part of this process. In high-stakes situations, it is preferable to base scoring rubrics on empirical evidence, rather than simply on agreements about what criteria should be used, and on what 'looks right'. Empirical evidence should be based on actual student performance and may include analyses of actual samples of work, and also analyses of teachers' comments about what constitutes performance at different levels (Greatorex, 2003, p. 127).

How to maximize reliability in scoring

Reliability refers to the extent to which the child would get the same results if another teacher or assessor were to assess their work, or if they were to assess it in the same way again another day, or if they were assessed through different tasks and with different rubrics. Reliability is an essential quality of 'useful 'assessment, but the level of reliability needed is dependent on the importance of decisions to be made. The amount of time and resources allocated to achieving reliable ratings will be a function of the importance of the decisions to be made. For very low-stakes decisions (e.g., diagnosis), fewer resources need be allocated, and we can settle for lower levels of reliability; for medium to high-stakes decisions (e.g., progress, grades), we need to allocate more resources to ensure reliability.

The following example illustrates the difficulties some teachers have using rating scales without training. At the beginning of a professional development workshop (that is, before teachers had been trained in the use of the scoring rubrics), elementary teachers of French in Australia were asked by their advisory teachers how they would rate an upper elementary student's writing, reproduced in Figure 8.6. The teachers were given the rubrics and asked 'Can you indicate the level qualities of this piece of work?' (The English translation was not provided for the teachers; it is provided for this example only.)

Table 8.5 shows the ratings and comments from the teachers in the professional development activity. Teachers wrote the notes for themselves, to help them with their discussion on the ratings given and why (as in a moderation session); however, they were kindly submitted and collected by the advisory teachers and are reproduced here to show how different teachers judged the piece of work.

Famous people: Kylie Minogue

Elle s'apple Kylie Minogue. Elle est née le mai 1968. Elle est allee Comberville Lycee, Melbourne. Elle aime jouer la comedie. Elle n'aime pas le sport. Elle a une soeur qui s'apple Danii et elle a un frere qui s'apple Brendan. En 1979 gagna le role en The hendersons. *Elle aussi Gagna le role de Charlene. En Avril Kylie gagna le TV Logie pour la meilleure actrice pour le role de Charlene. En aout 1986 elle chantait 'Locomotion' qui gagn numero uno en Australia a Londre au mois de Septembre 1981 recordai, 'I should be so lucky'. Elle a dix-neuf ans. Kylie devait choisir entre chanter et jouer. Elle chantait. Elle est chante devant la reine a la* Royal Command Performance.

[Grammatical errors cannot be included in the translation]. Her name is Kylie Minogue. She was born in May 1968. She went to Comberville School, Melbourne. She likes to act comedy. She doesn't like sport. She has a sister who is called Danii and she has a brother who is called Brendan. In 1979 she won a role in *The Hendersons*. She also won the role of Charlene. In April Kylie won a TV Logie for the best actress for the role of Charlene. In August 1986 she sang 'Locomotion' which won number one in Australia and London. In September 1981 she recorded 'I should be so lucky'. She is 19 years old. Kylie had to choose between singing and acting. She sang. She has sung in front of the Queen at the *Royal Command Performance*.

Figure 8.6 An upper elementary student's writing in French, assessed independently by a group of teachers in Table 8.5 (Dodd and Butler, 2002).

This example of teachers' assessment decisions shows how teachers can make widely different judgments about the qualities of a piece of work, even with the same set of scoring rubrics. It is evident that the constructs that are to be assessed in the piece of work are not at all clear to teachers; they are picking up on different qualities described in different levels, and placing the piece of work at different levels. Teacher 5 has placed more weight on accuracy and rated the piece of work as a low 3.5. Teacher 1 could see many positive features in the text, including cohesiveness and spontaneity, and rated it as a high Level 6. Teacher 2 was looking for colloquial expressions and register change, following the criteria in Level 6.

Researchers have found that assessment criteria are commonly interpreted differently by markers (North, 1993; Gipps, 1994; Chalhoub-Deville, 1995). Markers' ratings can be different for a number of reasons:

- the scoring rubrics may not be valid descriptions
- the scoring rubrics may not be clear enough
- markers may not be familiar enough with the scoring rubrics (and may need more training on how to understand the constructs within the guidelines)

Table 8.5 *Teachers' ratings of the piece of written work in Figure 8.6 (Dodd and Butler, 2002)*

Teacher	Mark assigned	Teachers' comments
Teacher 1	6	'The student is writing a personal recount/text of Kylie Minogue whereby his/her ideas are developed and presented logically. There are a few errors with grammar, spelling etc. but there is evidence of being able to write a lengthy text with a fair bit of cohesiveness and spontaneity. Use of formal/informal language, frequency of expression, common colloquial expression.'
Teacher 4	5.5	'Has tried to generate original language (emerging) with some complex elements. Has used model.'
Teacher 2	5	'Use of imperfect/perfect. No problem understanding despite grammatical errors. No really colloquial expressions to warrant level 6. No difference in register but no opportunity to show. Could be "simple cohesive text" re level 4 but I think it's beyond.'
Teacher 3	Between 3.5 and 4.5	'The student has shown manipulation showing structure and linguistic features. The text constructed is simple and cohesive. It has been taken from a model. Prepositions/tense, recount, sentences/to be/to have.'
Teacher 5	3.5	'Linked sentences on a familiar topic, but hasn't manipulated sentences accurately.'

- markers are using their own conceptualization of the criteria, rather than interpreting the written criteria
- markers are bringing unconscious expectations and subjective preferences regarding the relative importance of different criteria
- markers need samples of work to assist them to make a decision
- the scoring rubrics cannot provide sufficiently useful criteria to make a judgment on one piece of work (they are not, after all, intended for this purpose)
- teachers (in formative assessment situations) assume different degrees of support for the learners

If teachers and assessors are to mark in a consistent manner, it is essential that they agree on the meaning and application of the criteria (William, 1996, cited in Greatorex, 2003, p. 130). The following procedures can help to maximize reliability: (1) the careful development of the scoring rubrics; (2) working with markers to reach consensus or agreement on the meaning of the rubrics; and (3) training markers.

1. Careful development of scoring rubrics

Reliability of marking is more likely when the scoring rubrics are carefully developed, that is, when assessors follow the steps described above and check their rubrics against the characteristics of effective scoring rubrics listed above.

2. Working with markers to reach consensus

When markers have the opportunity to work together to reach a consensus on their scores, this also helps to raise reliability. In classroom assessment, for example, a teacher may ask another teacher to check his marking. Two teachers may mark work (or chosen samples of work) independently and check their findings together. When markers have opportunities to discuss criteria and levels together, and have access to each other's opinions and experience, especially with reference to work samples, they can come to a shared understanding of the scoring rubrics and the appropriate final scores. Group sessions when markers come together to share their understanding of the scoring rubrics and to reach consensus on final scores are called **moderation sessions**. A further marker can be asked to assess the same sample of work if there is still a discrepancy, and further moderation sessions may be organized to ensure that markers do not gradually slip away from the agreed understandings and expectations. These same kinds of procedures are used in formal assessment situations and are supplemented with statistical moderation procedures (that is, statistical procedures are used to compare and adjust the patterns of markers' scores) where high stakes are involved and resources for this are available.

3. Training markers

Markers can be trained through the same kinds of moderation procedures described above. In school assessment, training can occur over time through professional development activities. Markers study the rubrics, then independently give sample texts a score with reference to the scoring rubrics. Some markers are invited to tell others their score, and why they arrived at that score. Other markers do the same, in particular those who disagree, until a consensus is reached. Markers may take the samples with agreed scores away with them to refer to when they are marking.

Hasselgren (2000) reports that in a national assessment project in Norwegian elementary schools, teachers have opportunities for training in a variety of centrally supported classroom assessment and professional development procedures. Teachers are provided with rubrics with levels of performance, on which they are encouraged to write comments. Pupils have their own evaluation sheets. Professional development activities are provided so that teachers are familiar with how to use the material, and how to interpret results. In the project, professional development was found to be both popular and effective, as the following extract from Hasselgren's account outlines.

> Scoring instruments are provided both for pupils and teachers. Pupils' self-assessment forms are filled in at the end of each subtest. Pupils use a four-point scale ('yes, mostly, a bit, no') to rate various aspects of their own performance, salient to the particular macro-skill being tested, as well as their overall performance. They are also asked to rate the material, and to say what they have learnt, using English as far as possible.
>
> The teachers have a range of scoring forms. For the first three sub-tests, scores are entered on a score sheet. However, teachers are encouraged to add comments, which may be influenced by the pupil's own assessment. For the speaking and writing tests, teachers fill in a profile form for each pupil, choosing one of three level descriptors for each of five different aspects, roughly corresponding to the components of communicative language ability . . . In the case of speaking, observation forms for classroom use are provided . . . There is some correspondence between the questions on pupils' self-assessment forms and those in the teachers' materials.
>
> The material is photocopiable and the profile, self-assessment and observation forms are intended to be used on a regular basis in class-room activity. It is anticipated that this ongoing, more comprehensive and multiple perspective assessment will yield a more reliable profile of a pupil's ability than a one-off test battery could ever achieve, besides providing a means of tracking and documenting progress. Moreover, it gives training to both pupils and teachers in the

areas of assessment, providing them with a metalanguage for describing their language abilities.

Teachers are instructed not only in how to use the material, but also on how to interpret results and, equally importantly, on how to act on them to develop their pupils' skills. It is emphasized that scores and profiles should only be regarded as an indication of ability, which should be pursued further. The assessment results should always be interpreted alongside the pupils' self-assessment comments.

While the handbook is intended to be self-instructing, it is recognized that teachers benefit from active training in the use of the test material and accompanying forms. For this reason, county authorities have been invited to arrange in-service training courses in assessment using the EVA material. This activity is currently ongoing and has proved to be popular among authorities and teachers alike.

(Hasselgren, 2000, p. 266)

In teacher assessment situations, professional development activities such as those created in the Norwegian project make reliability more likely. However, as is recognized in the project, the appropriate construction of scoring rubrics remains as a central condition for reliability.

Standards

As I described in Chapter 1, standards are descriptions of curriculum outcomes, usually described in stages of progress; they give descriptions of how much, or at what level, students need to perform to demonstrate achievement of the content standards, or descriptions of what students should know and be able to do. There is a growing body of literature on standards for language learners (Brindley, 1998; Clair, Adger, Short and Millen, 1998; McKay, 2000) to which readers can refer. The following section attempts to provide some sense, in summary, of the issues in the development, use and evaluation of standards for young second language learners.

The development and use of standards

There are different ways that standards are presented (see, for example, the three standards presented below). Some standards are lists of bullet points of curriculum-related outcomes, some are set out as staged descriptions of developing ability. Some are organized around goal statements ('To use English to achieve academically in all content areas: Students will use appropriate learning strategies to construct and apply academic knowledge' (TESOL, 1997, p. 91), and others around language use activities such as listening, speaking, reading and viewing, and writing. Some stand alone, others are accompanied by exemplar tasks, and others by vignettes and instructional sequences. The differences depend on a variety of factors such as their purpose and philosophical framework.

Standards are used for a variety of purposes, including the following:

(1) to establish expected standards of achievement;
(2) to provide system-wide reference points to assist teachers in assessing individual progress;
(3) to provide a common framework for curriculum development;
(4) to provide more comprehensive information for reporting to interested parties outside the classroom, such as parents, employers, and educational authorities;
(5) to provide a basis for identifying needs and targeting resource allocation;
(6) to clarify the kinds of performance that lead to academic success;
(7) to provide a resource for teacher professional development.

(adapted from Brindley, 1998, pp. 49–50)

One advantage of standards is, amongst others, that assessments can be closely aligned with instruction. Teachers and assessors can design assessments with reference to the outcomes statements and can compare students' performance with the statements to evaluate that performance. The standards provide a common reference point for teachers, assessors and administrators, facilitating communication about learning and progress. Standards also provide a rational and objective basis for administrators' decisions about programme needs and resource allocation (Brindley, 1998, p. 52).

There are different ways that standards are developed, depending on their purpose. Some are developed *a priori*, meaning that they are designed without reference to empirical data, but more with reference to the curriculum requirements and what is generally expected of students as they progress through their stages of learning. Some standards are designed *a posteriori*, that is, they are designed following examination of the outcomes that students actually achieve. There are examples of both in the three examples of standards below. The advantage of the former is that the outcomes are usually closely aligned with the curriculum, though they may be developed primarily through subjective and experience-based judgments. The advantage of *a posteriori* development is that there is less likely to be a mismatch between developmental pathways and the descriptions contained in the standards since empirical and psychometric methods are used. A disadvantage, however, is that there may not be a close match in the stages and descriptors with the published curriculum (Sadler, 1987, p. 3). In some cases, a combination of approaches is used.

How is students' performance assessed and reported against standards? In many situations around the world (e.g., the United States), standardized tests are used; that is, large-scale, statistically normed tests, devised to assess students' performance against the official standards, are administered to cohorts of students across a state or nation. In other situations (e.g., England and Wales), standard assessment tasks are administered by teachers and marked by external assessors at certain assigned stages of schooling. In other countries around the world (e.g., Australia), classroom teachers are expected to observe and record progress against the standards over time and, through their reporting, pass on to parents and administrators a report on children's progress against the state standards. (However, in Australia, there has been a gradual introduction of other national standardized tests designed for accountability purposes.)

The impact of standards on young second language learners

Standards can have a positive impact in that they can give administrators and teachers a common understanding about what should be taught; parents can become clearer about what should be taught and learned, and they can find out how their child is progressing in relation to other children and the expected progress of children of this age. However, there can also be a negative impact when parents begin to believe their child is 'falling behind', when in fact the issue may be a developmental 'lag', common with young children, who often 'catch up' at a later stage of development. Young second language learners may also be behind because they are being assessed against unrealistic and invalid first language learner expectations. Standards may have other negative impacts, especially when they are tied to external tests (McKay, 2004). Teachers may become obliged to teach to the standards, instead of to the developmental needs of children; the curriculum may become assessment-driven; assessment requirements take up time that could be devoted to teaching. Teachers can become focused on the need to move children up the scale, rather than to meet current needs (McKay, forthcoming). Lastly, teachers can be judged accountable based on the results of tests tied to standards. This accountability measure is believed by some administrators to cause teachers to teach 'even harder' to advance the children along the scale. However, it can cause stress amongst teachers and a loss of individualized teaching appropriate to children's needs. Children come to teachers from a range of different starting points and developmental levels, and they develop at different rates and have different needs.

There are continuing issues to be resolved concerning tensions in the use of standards and of the impact of standards and accompanying testing regimes on learners. Research into the impact of standards was discussed in Chapter 3; there is a continuing need for research in the area, particularly in relation to the impact of standards and their accompanying external tests on young learners.

Three examples of performance standards

This section briefly describes three performance standards and evaluates them using the framework for evaluating scoring rubrics and reporting scales in Table 8.1 above.

Example 1: The Illinois Foreign Language Learning Standards

The foreign language learning standards of the Illinois State Board of Education are a good example of standards mandated by a large educational authority. These standards set out the expectations of content and performance of learners being taught through the state curriculum. As is common in an education department's standards documents, these standards combine both the content and performance standards within one document. The statement of what should be learned also becomes the statement of criteria (the descriptors) that guide teachers' and assessors' assessment of what has been learned. Standards are provided under three goals across five stages. Table 8.6 shows the Learning Standards for foreign language learning under the first goal, Goal 28 *Communication*. A general learning standard is listed on the left, and then more specific standards are listed (with connection by numbers to content standards) across the page in five stages of progress.

Table 8.6 *Illinois Foreign Language Learning Standards: Standards under Goal 28 Communication (Illinois State Board of Education, 2003)*

As a result of their schooling students will be able to:

Learning standards	Stage 1 Beginning	Stage 2 Beginning intermediate	Stage 3 Intermediate	Stage 4 Advanced intermediate	Stage 5 Advanced
A. Understand oral communication in the target language	**28.A.1a** Recognize basic language patterns (e.g., forms of address, questions, case) **28.A.1b** Respond appropriately to single commands in the target language	**28.A.2a** Comprehend illustrated stories, audiovisual programs or websites **28.A.2b** Follow instructions in the target language, given one step at a time, for a wide range of activities	**28.A.3a** Comprehend main messages of simple oral and audio presentations with assistance from resources (e.g., glossaries, guided questions, outlines) **28.A.3b** Follow instructions in the target language as given in multistep segments for assignment and activities in and out of the classroom		

303

Table 8.6 *(continued)*

As a result of their schooling students will be able to:

Learning standards	Stage 1 Beginning	Stage 2 Beginning intermediate	Stage 3 Intermediate	Stage 4 Advanced intermediate	Stage 5 Advanced
B. Interact in the target language in various settings	**28.B.1a** Respond to and ask simple questions with prompts **28.B.1b** Imitate pronunciation, intonation and inflection including sounds unique in the target language	**28.B.2a** Pose questions spontaneously in structured situations **28.B.2b** Produce language using proper pronunciation, information and inflection **28.B.2c** Comprehend gestures and body language often used in everyday interactions in the target language	**28.B.3a** Respond to open-ended questions and initiate communication in various situations **28.B.3b** Produce language with improved pronunciation, intonation and inflection **28.B.3c** Use appropriate non-verbal cues common in areas where the target language is spoken		
C. Understand written passages in the target language use setting	**28.C.1a** Recognize the written form of familiar spoken language and predict meaning of key words in a	**28.C.2a** Comprehend directions, read simple passages, infer meaning of cognates and recognize loan words	**28.C.3a** Comprehend the main message of a variety of written materials with the help of resources (e.g., dictionary, thesaurus, software, Internet, e-mail)		

304

D. Use the target language to present information, concepts and ideas for a variety of purposes to different audiences	simple story, poem or song. **28.C.1b** Infer meaning of cognates from context **28.D.1a** Copy/write words, phrases and simple sentences **28.D.1b** Describe people, activities and objects from school and home	**28.C.2b** Decode new vocabulary using contextual clues and drawing on words and phrases from prior lessons **28.D.2a** Write on familiar topics using appropriate grammar, punctuation and capitalization **28.D.2b** Present a simple written or oral report on familiar topics **28.D.2c** Present an original production (e.g., TV commercials, ads, skits, songs) using known vocabulary and grammatical structures	to expand vocabulary **28.C.3b** Compare word use, phrasing and sentence structures of the target language with those used in one or more other languages **28.D.3a** Write compositions and reports with a specific focus, supporting details, logical sequence and conclusion **28.D.3b** Present findings from research on unfamiliar topics (e.g., the Roman army, the French chateaux, origins of chocolate) **28.D.3c** Present a simple, original poem or story based on a model

The Illinois standards were written *a priori*, as many education depart-ment standards are written, that is, the writers have set out hoped-for outcomes, rather than nominate outcomes based on research data of learner performance. The layout of these standards reflects their admin-istrative purpose – they are designed to collect system-level data on stu-dents' progress. However, in order to clarify the meaning of the standards for teachers, the state has provided other material such as sample class-room assessment tasks and performance descriptors. These are for use at the local level, on a voluntary basis, to support classroom teaching and assessment. The first three stages in these standards reflect to a limited extent the types of abilities pertinent to young learner foreign language learning, for example 'Copy/write words, phrases and simple sentences', but probably because of the need to cater for all age groups in the early stages, the characteristics of young learners are not prominent in these descriptions. Classroom assessments and performance descriptors may elaborate young learner performance criteria beyond what is shown in this broad statement of the standards. However, a separate set of state-ments for young language learners, reflecting the special nature of their language learning, and language learning outcomes, would ensure that the standards reflected the construct of assessment. Those devising tests would be better guided towards testing appropriate for young learners. Those monitoring children's progress in the classroom would have less ambiguity to deal with in the descriptions. Nevertheless, as I discussed above, the minimal nature of the descriptors would be likely to continue to present a challenge for teachers involved in day-to-day assessment. Questions regarding the positive impact on the learning of young learn-ers of these standards (as they stand without specific statements for young learners), and whether teachers' professional understandings and involvement in the learning process are enhanced through the use of these standards, with their accompanying materials, can best be answered through research.

For users, parents, other teachers and administrators, it is likely that the standards present meaningful descriptions of progress. The descrip-tors and levels more than likely provide valuable information for users. A report would be generated from these standards that will give parents an understanding of their child's progress through the required curricu-lum, and (even though performance assessment avoids normative judg-ments) an idea of their child's progress in relation to that of others of their age group. A report can also provide administrators with an overview of the performance of cohorts of students, individual schools and individual teachers if needed. The impact of the standards on users is likely to be positive, since there is possibly a greater understanding of the nature of the curriculum.

Example 2: The Common European Framework of Reference

The Common European Framework of Reference 'provides a common basis for the elaboration of language syllabuses, curriculum guidelines, examinations, textbooks etc. across Europe'. It defines levels of proficiency 'which allow learners' progress to be measured at each stage of learning and on a life-long basis' (Council of Europe, 2001). The purpose for this framework is to bring together the different language learning programmes in Europe by setting out a common understanding of pathways and levels. There is a global scale (Figure 8.7), and illustrative scales for different skills, an example of which is presented in Figure 8.8. These scales can be used to organize and monitor progress across groups and programmes, as well as to check individual learner progress. For our purposes, the earlier levels of proficiency only are presented in Figure 8.6 and Table 8.5, since the upper levels move into the type of language performance expected of adults. The levels were developed mainly *a posteriori*, in that the development of the final descriptors were based on empirical analysis of teachers' perceptions of development (see North, 1995), and on theories of language competence, made explicit throughout the Common Reference Levels publication (Council of Europe, 2001).

Many illustrative scales are also provided in the document. Illustrative scales give more detail about levels of progress in specific skills. Figure 8.8 shows the illustrative scale for 'Interviewing and being interviewed'.

Those who constructed the Framework of Reference did not write a specific scale for young learners. Many of the descriptors in the 'Common Reference Levels: global scale' are inappropriate for younger learners beyond B1 Independent User as the topics of discussion become more abstract, specialized and technical, and texts become longer and more detailed. The first three levels are suitable for use with young foreign language learners, though they are skeletal, designed to describe development of beginning learners of all ages. The descriptor in Level C2 of the Common Reference Scales expects that the language user 'Can keep up his/her side of the dialogue extremely well, structuring the talk and interacting authoritatively with complete fluency as interviewer or interviewee.' In the illustrative scale above, learners at B1 are able to 'use a

Proficient User	C2	
	C1	
Independent user	B2	
	B1	Can understand the main points of clear standard input on familiar matters regularly encountered in work, school, leisure etc. Can deal with most situations likely to arise whilst travelling in an area where the language is spoken. Can produce simple connected text on topics which are familiar or of personal interest. Can describe experiences and events, dreams, hopes and ambitions and briefly give reasons and explanations for opinions and plans.
Basic user	A2	Can understand sentences and frequently used expressions related to areas of most immediate relevance (e.g., very basic personal and family information, shopping, local geography, employment). Can communicate in simple and routine tasks requiring a simple and direct exchange of information on familiar and routine matters. Can describe in simple terms aspects of his/her background, immediate environment and matters in areas of immediate need.
	A1	Can understand and use familiar everyday expressions and very basic phrases aimed at the satisfaction of needs of a concrete type. Can introduce him/herself and others and can ask and answer questions about personal details such as where he/she lives, people he/she knows and things he/she has. Can interact in a simple way provided the other person talks slowly and clearly and is prepared to help.

Figure 8.7 First three levels of Common Reference Levels: global scale (Council of Europe, 2001, p. 24).

prepared questionnaire to carry out a structured interview'. Young learners might therefore be restricted to the lower levels of the Common Framework Scales, unless ways of describing advanced proficiency can be found that do not require advanced cognitive and social skills. Children might connect back into the same or further levels (B2 and

B1	Can provide concrete information required in an interview/consultation (e.g., describe the symptoms to a doctor) but does so with limited precision.
	Can carry out a prepared interview, checking and confirming information, though he/she may occasionally have to ask for repetition if the other person's response is rapid or extended.
	Can take some initiatives in an interview/consultation (e.g., to bring up a new subject, but is very dependent on interviewer in the interaction.
	Can use a prepared questionnaire to carry out a structured interview, with some spontaneous follow up questions.
A2	Can make him/herself understood in an interview and communicate ideas and information on familiar topics, provided he/she can ask for clarification occasionally, and is given some help to express what he/she wants to.
	Can answer simple questions and respond to simple statements in an interview.
A1	Can reply in an interview to simple direct questions spoken very slowly and clearly in direct non-idiomatic speech about personal details.

Figure 8.8 Example of the levels A1–B1 of an illustrative scale: interviewing and being interviewed. Common European Framework of Reference (Council of Europe, 2001, p. 82).

onwards) on the original scale as they advance in cognitive maturity and in their foreign language learning.

Therefore work is required by elementary language educators to adapt the Common Reference levels to young foreign language learners. Hasselgren's (2005) scales for young learners, developed within the framework of the Common Reference Scales, are of interest in this regard. The value of a common framework such as the Common Reference Scales is very great, and educators of young learners have a common reference point from which to build up a set of standards for young learners that can be adapted for different languages, and that can later connect into levels for older learners.

The Common Framework Scales reflect their stated purpose, providing a basis for the elaboration of textbooks and programmes, and for the monitoring of learners' progress at each stage of learning, though this purpose is not, in reality, attained for young learners without further research and interpretation. The construct to be assessed, language proficiency, is well outlined in theoretical terms, and empirical procedures used help to ensure that the scales reflect this construct. However, the construct of language proficiency for younger learners is not sufficiently addressed; young learners are not mentioned throughout the document and it therefore must be assumed that they are not included in the learner group. The lack of attention to young learners means that young learners' needs may not be met by teachers who use the scales to guide their assessment, and teachers' professional understandings about young learners' language learning may not be enhanced. Similarly, users involved with young learners (young learners themselves, parents, teachers, curriculum developers, administrators) may find that these scales do not meet their needs unless there is further research and development targeted towards the language learning of young learners.

In summary, the Common European Framework has provided language educators in Europe with an important theoretically and empirically based framework, but young learners would have benefited most if their particular learner characteristics and needs had been included in the original project.

Example 3: The Australian (NLLIA) ESL Bandscales

A set of Australian ESL Bandscales (McKay, Hudson, and Sapuppo, 1994), known in Australia as the NLLIA (National Languages and Literacy Institute of Australia) ESL Bandscales, are examples of performance standards. Their purpose is to provide ESL teachers with a common reference tool for assessment and planning for ESL learners in ESL and mainstream programmes. They are written in the form of holistic rating scales in Listening, Speaking, Reading and Writing. The ESL Bandscales reflect the multiple entry points of ESL learners into Australian schools (see Figure 8.9). There are three Bandscales reflecting three broad age groups; junior primary (approximately ages 5–7), middle/upper primary (approximately ages 8–11) and secondary (approximately ages 12–18). The scales describe progress from beginning to advanced English language development in the mainstream context for each of these broad age groups. There are separate junior primary and middle/upper primary scales and secondary scales, giving a strong profile to young learners' language learning pathways. A young learner who is near-equivalent to native-speaking children of his/her own age, in the upper levels of the junior primary and middle/upper primary Bandscales, is therefore not 'made invisible' as they move closer to but have not yet attained native speaker-like language abilities.

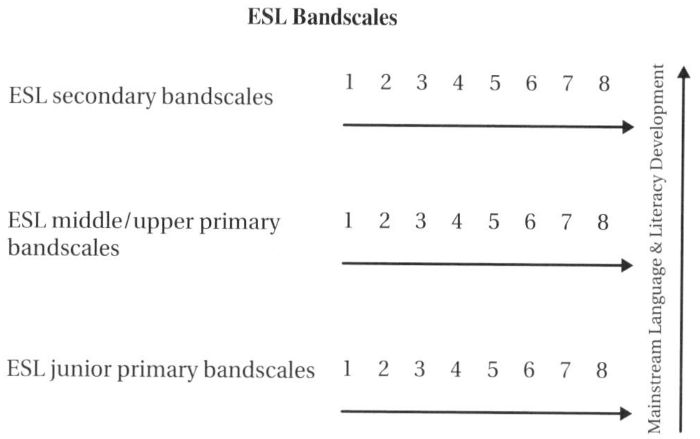

ESL Bandscales

Figure 8.9 The three levels of the Australian (NLLIA) ESL Bandscales (McKay, Hudson and Sapuppo, 1994, p. A17) accommodating multiple entry points.

In Figure 8.10, Levels 4 and 5 of Junior Primary Listening are reproduced as examples of two levels for young learners in the ESL Bandscales. The first bolded statement is an overall statement designed for first reference. The remainder of the descriptors follow a theoretically based structure outlined in the introduction to the materials (McKay, Hudson and Sapuppo, 1994, p. A27).

The purpose of the NLLIA ESL Bandscales was primarily to improve teachers' professional understandings about second language learning, and therefore to inform their teaching and assessment decisions as they work with mainstream teachers in Australian schools. They were written with this clear purpose in mind, and therefore are not written in bullet-point lists, include more 'messages' for teachers, and describe, in holistic descriptions, the typical language behaviour of children moving through the levels. They include reminders about the characteristics of second language acquisition of young learners (e.g., of the possible presence of the silent period), and reminders about the role of the first language in second language learning. They reflect the cognitive demand and the maturity of each broad age group, and also the types of tasks that young learners are expected to carry out in their mainstream classrooms. Because of this clarity of purpose, the ESL Bandscales can be said to be appropriate for young learners, to reflect their purpose, and their construct (that is, the

---

Listening: Level 4

Are able to comprehend social English in familiar contexts (e.g., in general school contexts: in classroom interaction around activities, in playground interactions, on excursions etc.) with ease, with only occasional help given by the interlocutor. Are able to follow instructions within a classroom learning activity if explained and presented clearly (i.e. with clear steps, modelling of the task, logical sequencing of steps) though will often rely on further repetition of instructions on a one-to-one or small group basis.

Require intensive concentration to comprehend fully. Are likely to lose comprehension with high background noise present (e.g., other children talking). May use strategies which give the impression that full comprehension has taken place (e.g., nodding; smiling; copying actions of others: silence) which can be misleading in learning activities.

Need time for processing of language experienced (e.g., before having to answer a question; during teacher talk; during class discussion). Have short concentration span if topic of lesson is unfamiliar.

Will lack precision in understanding, e.g. will miss many details of the language they hear, e.g. may not understand a wide range of prepositions, e.g. between, below, beneath and will have difficulty with complex structures, e.g. although . . . how often . . . etc. Are restricted by a limited vocabulary.

Listening: Level 5

Are able to comprehend English in a range of social contexts pertinent to their age level. Are less dependent on extra help from the interlocutor, and have little need to ask for repetition or reformulation, especially if the topic is familiar. Will comprehend main points and most detail in learning activities on familiar topics if activities are language-focused (i.e. teacher is aware of language demands of the task); will continue to have some difficulty comprehending extended teacher talk at normal speed and with more complex ideas in learning activities when they are expressed through complex language.

Can comprehend gist of new topic-specific language if contextual and language support is given, and time is allowed for processing. Will miss some specific details because of lack of 'depth' of language, e.g. limited range of vocabulary, lack of understanding of complex structure and relationships such as degrees of certainty/uncertainty (i.e. modality) e.g. (might, could), problem/solution (if. . . then), before and after, compare/contrast (similar to; different from).

Lapses in comprehension of spoken texts can be caused by gaps in vocabulary, overload of new vocabulary, and gaps in concepts because of previous lapses in understanding. May lose the thread once a lapse occurs.

May lose concentration if topic and language of the lesson are unfamiliar.

Figure 8.10 Extract from The Australian (NLLIA) ESL Bandscales (Junior Primary Listening Levels 4 and 5).

language learning of young learners in the mainstream). They can be said to promote a reasonably fair assessment for young learners.

For markers (that is, mostly ESL teachers in schools, often in conjunction with mainstream teachers), the ESL Bandscales can be said to avoid ambiguity in the sense that the clarity of purpose, the assessment of young learners in mainstream classes, helps observation of learning and assessment of learning outcomes. The validity and reliability of the ESL Bandscales, the assessment practices of ESL teachers around the ESL Bandscales, and the impact of the ESL Bandscales on teachers' professional understandings is currently under review. Research to date in Australia, together with anecdotal feedback, strong sales of the document and adaptation of the materials for indigenous learners, indicates that many ESL teachers use and can relate to the ESL Bandscales (Breen et al., 1997; Davison and Williams, 2002).

In contrast, there are mixed signals about the value of the ESL Bandscales for users. Whilst ESL teachers (the markers) have found them to be appropriate and useful, ESL teachers have needed to simplify the descriptions for the mainstream classroom teachers they work with. They have also needed to adapt and simplify them for students and parents. This is not necessarily a problem, since the adaptations can be carried out to suit the particular learning groups and learning contexts. At the system level, although some education systems have taken them up for administrative purposes, many education departments have chosen to use more administrative national or state-developed outcomes-based ESL frameworks rather than adopt the ESL Bandscales, because they are seen not to meet the needs of administrators, nor to follow the requirements of outcomes-based reform. They have, however, been taken up for administrative purposes by smaller, more flexible education departments. In relation to their impact on learners and their parents, it is believed that the impact of the NLLIA ESL Bandscales on ESL learners and their parents has been positive, firstly because of the increased understanding on the part of teachers about ESL learner progress, and secondly because students and parents can understand progress in positive terms against second language pathways, rather than only in negative comparison with first language literacy development.

Summary

Teachers and assessors need to determine the scoring method they will use; to do this, firstly they need to decide on the criteria by which children's responses are evaluated, and secondly to decide on how to arrive at a score. Criteria tell teachers and assessors what they should be looking for in a learner's performance and operationalize the construct that is to be assessed.

Good scoring rubrics reflect the construct(s) to be assessed and are created by teachers and assessors who are familiar with the curriculum, how the curriculum is taught and the characteristics of the young learners in question. They also give clear guidelines on how to arrive at a score. In language use assessment, it is difficult for criteria to be specific, and even when they are, they are interpreted differently by teachers because of their different experience and background, and orientation to the subject and the children. There are therefore a number of strategies that need to be followed to try to ensure reliability of assessment, including the careful development of rubrics, working with markers to reach consensus and training markers. It may be possible to use correct/incorrect or partial credit scoring, depending on the type of question. A number of principles are given in the chapter to guide the evaluation of scoring rubrics and reporting scales for young learners; scoring rubrics for young learners generally take the form of observation checklists, task-based criteria sheets and holistic and analytic rating scales. Rating scales may also be used as reporting scales. Each of these has strengths and weaknesses. Scoring rubrics are best constructed by groups of professionals working together and are best based on empirical evidence rather than simply on agreements about what 'looks right'.

Many education departments around the world have introduced content and performance standards setting out what should be taught and assessed over time. Professional bodies have also produced performance standards setting out expected stages of growth. There are a number of ways that standards are constructed. Performance standards are a type of reporting scale and their effectiveness can be evaluated using considerations appropriate to reporting scales. Three examples of language standards from around the world show different ways that the construction of standards has been approached, how well this has been done and in particular how they meet the requirement that the characteristics of young learners' learning are addressed.

CHAPTER NINE

Testing young language learners through large-scale tests

Introduction

In this chapter we will look at the development and use of large-scale tests for young learners. Large-scale tests are externally developed tests that are administered to many learners, usually across school districts or school systems. They are usually standardized, that is, they follow a consistent set of procedures for designing, administering and scoring. Standardization is required when scores will be used to compare individuals or groups. If children take the same test under the same conditions, then the scores in the tests are believed to have the same 'meaning' and are therefore comparable.

Large-scale standardized tests are employed for many reasons. They can save time and money as resources are pooled in one place, and efficiencies are maximized through shared development and administration processes. Paper-and-pencil tests, often used in large-scale standardized tests, are easy to administer and score, and are therefore less costly. Standardized tests have credibility when they are developed through research techniques. Facts and figures are impressive and can be reported to the public as evidence of effectiveness. They also have anonymity; schools and teachers do not need to be the bearers of bad news to parents and children but can refer to the impartial third party, the test, to convey a judgment. Lastly, standardized tests have comparability. With standardized test data, one school can be compared with others, locally, regionally and nationally (Jalongo, 2000). Comparable data from large-scale standardized tests provides administrators with what they believe is non-refutable evidence for accountability purposes when other, perhaps more qualitative, evidence is, in their opinion, not acceptable or trusted.

Many young second language learners are assessed through large-scale testing. They may be assessed on language-specific tests or on content-area tests designed for the majority. In the USA, ESL learners, or English Language Learners (ELLs), have, for many years, been tested on content-area tests designed for all students. Recently, yearly monitoring of English language proficiency of these learners has been legislated.

However, advocates of alternative assessment techniques discourage the use of large-scale testing with young learners. Nevertheless, testing of young language learners is taking place around the world. I therefore begin with an outline of the main criticisms of the large-scale testing of young learners. The main steps in test development that are outlined in this chapter, following Bachman and Palmer (1996), apply to both large-scale and smaller-scale assessment. However, a full and thorough application of the many test development steps is most likely to occur when a high level of resources, including research facilities, is available. The Cambridge Young Learner English Test provides the basis in this chapter for an illustration of a large-scale foreign language test with full resources to conduct the many steps in standardized test development.

In the second major section of this chapter, I examine approaches to the large-scale testing of the English language of second language learners and emphasize the need to ensure that these tests focus on academic language proficiency, that is, the language of school. Alternatives to standardized testing are advocated by many educators, even in large-scale testing situations, and these are reviewed in this chapter.

How appropriate is large-scale standardized testing for young language learners?

One of the main criticisms of large-scale standardized testing is pedagogical: that such tests do not usually provide immediate feedback for test takers to improve their learning, or to teachers to improve their teaching. They are designed primarily for administrative purposes; that is, to monitor children's learning to inform teachers and parents about children's relative progress (Is this child slipping behind?), and to inform the central authorities about progress patterns for policy and administrative reasons (Is this school meeting its targets?). Indeed, Shohamy

(2001) has pointed out how there has been a shift in recent years in the primary role of test from measuring knowledge to enabling centralized bodies to control the content of education, and learning and teaching. Teachers argue that they prefer classroom performance-based assessment because they can gather information about performance and progress, give immediate feedback and adjust their teaching accordingly, thus immediately influencing the learning process.

Opponents of large-scale tests suggest that a test is a sample of one type of behaviour in one type of context (a testing context) and since children perform in different ways in different contexts, a child's behaviour in different settings can be radically different. The artificiality of a testing situation will influence what kind of a sample is collected, and it is therefore best to assess language use ability in a natural setting, rather than relying on the contrived situations required by standardized tests.

Some educators argue, too, that there is little value in comparing the progress of young learners with others at the early stages of their learning. Young learners mature at different rates and their individual progress is best monitored with reference to broadly expected developmental norms, and with expectation of difference, not in direct comparison to others. Loss of self-esteem and confidence can result from negative feedback in these vulnerable early years. Many argue it is the teacher who can give the best feedback to the child, and the most informed and detailed reports to parents.

Some educators argue that not only can large-scale standardized tests be of little direct use in the pedagogy of the classroom; in some situations they can have a negative impact on teaching and learning. In high-stakes testing situations, schools and teachers can become nervous about test results (schools' future funding or teachers' careers may depend on good results) and may systematically teach to the test. This inevitably leads to a narrowing of the curriculum.

> The issue here is not whether children can learn to be better test takers. Of course they can. The question is: What has been sacrificed in the process? If the test begins to dictate the curriculum and severely restrict teachers' innovative teaching practices, then the test – a mere sample of behavior – has become far more influential than it should be.
> (Jalongo, 2000, p. 294).

Most large-scale standardized tests, for reasons of practicality, have a pencil-and-paper test format, that is, learners are asked to complete various tasks and items on paper. Preparing children to take a paper-and-pencil test is likely to be at the expense of real experiences with the language. Similarly, a large-scale standardized test might be a test of language knowledge, tested through discrete-point items such as grammar or vocabulary items, rather than language use tasks. Discrete-point items do not reflect the construct that should be assessed in language teaching – that is, language use. As I have argued through this book, young learners need a breadth of experiences with the target language. They need to combine the use of the language with physical encounters with their environment, and they need opportunities to encounter the language in a range of social situations.

There is no doubt that the characteristics of young learners cause them to have some difficulties with large-scale standardized tests. Young learners are often unfamiliar with test procedures and may not realize the importance of the test. While adults will address themselves to a test, knowing the way tests work, and how important they are, children may not be able to give the test the attention it needs to show what they can or cannot do. The length of tests can put children at a disadvantage; children are used to short, concentrated, often physical tasks and find it difficult to concentrate for very long. If the test is only short to accommodate this, the lack of breadth of sampling is likely to affect the score: for example, a child's reading proficiency may be assessed on just one or two items. Response formats (e.g., circle the correct answer) may confuse children, especially when they are in an isolated situation without adult help that could quickly put them right. Children may not give an answer to an item; this may not necessarily be because they don't know the answer, but because they are not sure of what to do or are afraid of making a mistake. These are some of the characteristics of young learners that need to be taken into account in testing situations.

Yet, others argue that large-scale standardized tests play an important role in education, and that such tests, developed appropriately, can be of value in the education of young learners. Standardized tests can be attached to the mandated or published curriculum, thus reinforcing the teaching of that curriculum, and perhaps the expected progress rate through that curriculum. Data from standardized tests help administrators to find out where additional resources are needed to improve learning, or where programmes should be extended or curtailed. Current managerialist ideologies in education require administrators to have reliable information about achievement in the range of schools and classrooms under their jurisdiction. With data from standardized testing, data administrators are able to ascertain accountability, and to provide rewards and sanctions accordingly. Parents are more aware of how their children are progressing in relation to other children and can make decisions about where to send their children based on the published achievements of their schools on tests. For all these reasons, standardized tests are likely to stay with us.

Ultimately decisions on whether a standardized test for young language learners goes ahead must depend on the nature of the impact of the test on those young learners involved. Impact is one of the factors to be considered when a test's 'usefulness' is evaluated. Systematic procedures should be followed to maximize the test's 'usefulness' if it does go ahead. The procedures described below give guidance on how to develop both large-scale and smaller-scale tests, and how to ensure that they will be 'useful' for young learners.

Processes of test development (for both large- and small-scale testing)

This section provides a brief overview of test development processes. The next section illustrates these test development processes through a case study description of a large-scale test for young learners, the Cambridge Young Learners English Tests. Full details of test development processes can be found in specialist testing volumes; several writers have outlined these processes in detail (for example, Alderson, Clapham, and Wall, 1995; Bachman and Palmer, 1996; Davison and Lynch, 2002; Weigle, 2002). Test development processes should be followed in all test development, whether for large-scale tests or smaller-scale tests in a school or classroom. In small-scale situations there are likely to be limitations on resources which will influence the degree to which each step can be followed in depth, though all steps should be followed if a 'useful' test is to be devised.

Bachman and Palmer (1996) identify three phases in test development: a design phase, an operationalization phase and an administration phase. These phases are likely to be followed in a linear fashion but may be followed in an iterative way, when developers return back to previous steps as they find out something new, or as they realize they need to rectify a problem. The phases are summarized below. Figure 9.1 shows an overview version of Bachman and Palmer's model of test development.

Design phase

Describing purpose, TLU (target language use) domain and task types,
    and characteristics of test takers
Defining construct(s)
Developing a plan for evaluating the qualities of usefulness
Checking available resources and planning their allocation
    and management

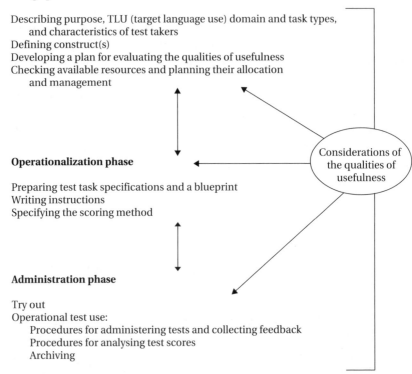

Operationalization phase

Preparing test task specifications and a blueprint
Writing instructions
Specifying the scoring method

Considerations of
the qualities of
usefulness

Administration phase

Try out
Operational test use:
    Procedures for administering tests and collecting feedback
    Procedures for analysing test scores
    Archiving

Figure 9.1 Model of test development (adapted from Bachman and Palmer,
1996, p. 86).

In the **design phase**, test developers gather information that will
provide the foundation of information and theory required for the next
phases of test development. Test developers establish the test purpose by
communicating with those requesting the test, for example teachers,
schools or education systems. These requirements form the mandate for
the test (Davison and Lynch, 2002). The task types in the TLU domain
(that is, the situations and tasks that learners use and need in their actual
language use context), and the characteristics of the test takers are
described in detail; these provide a basis for developing test tasks, and to
check the 'usefulness' of the test. To do this, test developers draw on direct
knowledge of the children and their curriculum or learning context, or
they find out information from informants (usually teachers). In the
design phase, test developers also define the constructs that are to be
assessed. They do this by referring to the curriculum specifications, to a

theory of language or to both. The constructs need to be defined clearly, as these provide the basis for the development of test tasks and also provide the basis for considering and investigating the construct validity. The design phase also involves the development of a plan for evaluating the qualities of 'usefulness' of the test. Also in the design phase, developers need to check the resources (human, material and time) that will be available for the test development process, and to plan how they will be allocated and managed.

In the **operationalization phase** test developers are concerned with preparing test task specifications and a blueprint. *Test task specifications* will describe the types of test tasks that will be included in the test; the relevant task characteristics for each task in the test will be described in detail as part of this process. (For an example of test task specifications see Table 9.5 later in this chapter). A *blueprint* for the test consists of information about the structure, or overall organization of the test, as well as test task specifications for each task type to be included in the test. Writing instructions are prepared in this phase; these instructions give information to test writers about the structure of the test, the nature of the tasks and how learners are expected to respond. Also in this phase, the scoring methods are specified: firstly the criteria are defined, and then the procedures that will be followed to arrive at a score are determined.

The **test administration phase** involves administering the test, collecting information and analysing this information. The plan for evaluating the qualities of 'usefulness' determined in the design phase is put into operation in this phase when developers analyse the relevant qualitative and quantitative information that comes to them through the administration of the test. There are typically two phases in the test administration phase: a try-out phase and an operational test use phase. A *try-out*, which is like a pilot phase, gives developers information about whether aspects of the test need to be altered. A try-out can be done with small groups or larger groups, and even in classroom testing is highly recommended. It is highly recommended that the try-out phases be iterative. Ideally, before full tests are assembled for piloting, individual tasks or sets of items should be tried out and revised if necessary. In the *operational test use phase*, the test is administered as a test. The testing environment is prepared; test materials are collected, examiners trained and the test is given to the intended test takers. Performances are scored and results analysed, and at this time further information can be collected about test 'usefulness'. Procedures for these processes are prepared. Test scores might be analysed, for example to determine the quality of a test item, or the reliability of a test score, using statistical procedures. Also in the test administration phase, archiving procedures are determined and carried out, so that tasks and other information can be easily retrieved as needed.

Considerations of qualities of 'usefulness' run throughout the above three test development phases; design, operationalization and administration. As outlined in Chapter 5, there should be an appropriate balance amongst the six qualities of 'usefulness': 'This is done by determining minimum acceptable levels for each and recognizing that what constitutes an appropriate balance and appropriate minimum acceptable levels will vary from one testing situation to another' (Bachman and Palmer, 1996) Plans to evaluate 'usefulness' are drawn up in the design phase. Plans will stipulate data collection to be carried out quantitatively, for example through the collection and analysis of test scores, and qualitatively, for example through the collection and analysis of observers' descriptions, and verbal self-reports from students. Data collection and analysis will mostly take place in the test administration phase. Questions will be asked through all development phases to carry out a logical evaluation of each quality. For example, 'Is the language ability construct for this test clearly and unambiguously defined?' See Bachman and Palmer (1996, p.149) for a checklist of questions for evaluating the qualities of 'usefulness'.

Illustrating the test development process: The Cambridge Young Learners English Tests

The Cambridge Young Learners English Tests is a set of large-scale tests developed and administered by the University of Cambridge ESOL (English for Speakers of Other Languages) Examinations. At the end of 2001 the worldwide candidature had reached nearly 200,000, with large numbers of candidates in countries such as China, Spain, Argentina and Italy. Preliminary work on the Cambridge Young Learners test took five years. Work commenced in 1993, and the test was first taken by candidates in 1997. The following description of, and details of the development of, the Cambridge Young Learners Test are drawn from Cambridge ESOL publicity materials, research notes and sample tests, published articles and interviews with Cambridge ESOL personnel (Taylor and Saville, 2002; University of Cambridge ESOL Examinations, 2003). The three phases of test development – test design, operationalization and administration – provide the framework for the presentation of information.

The test design phase

Describing the purpose: The purpose of the Cambridge Young Learners English Tests is described in test publications. The overall purpose is to assess the English language ability and progress of young English as a foreign language learners, in many countries around the world. The stated aims of the Cambridge Young Learners English Tests are to:

- sample relevant and meaningful language use
- promote effective learning and teaching
- encourage future learning and teaching of English
- measure accurately and fairly

(University of Cambridge ESOL Examinations, 2003, p. 6)

The three tests together build a bridge to take young learners of English from beginner to the beginning level of the Key English Test (KET) in the Cambridge Main Suite exams.

Describing the TLU domain and task types and the characteristics of the learners, and defining the construct: The TLU domain and task types for young foreign language learners were established in the design phase for the test. Researchers conducted a close examination of curriculum design and pedagogy for young learners, recent textbooks and other resource material (e.g., a CD ROM, developed by Homerton College, Cambridge University's teacher training college). Textbooks and teaching materials in classrooms around the world were reviewed, in order that the main content areas (topics, vocabulary, etc.) which frequently occur in young learner programmes were reflected. Theories of children's foreign language learning (the way they learn, but also the pathways they take) were also examined. The presentation of these materials was also reviewed, in order to inform the way that tests might be presented. There is now about an 80% overlap with textbooks in the test syllabus. Item banks, that is, sets of items which have been developed and trialled, were built up, and this process continues. These item banks are drawn upon in the development of individual tests.

The test takers for the Cambridge Young Learners English Tests are children learning English as a foreign language around the world, ranging from ages 7 to 12 (with some children accepted at 13 years of age if they are learning alongside 12-year-olds).

Cambridge ESOL has paid particular attention to the educational consequences of using a language test with young learners, and the following areas were carefully considered:

- current approaches to curriculum design and pedagogy for young learners, including recent textbooks and other resource materials (e.g., CD ROM);
- children's cognitive and first language development;
- the potential influence of test methods, including the familiarity and appropriacy of different task types, item formats, typography and layout;
- probable variation between different first language groups and cultures.

(University of Cambridge ESOL Examinations, 2003, p. 5)

Taylor and Saville (2002) describe how extensive literature reviews were undertaken into children's socio-psychological and cognitive development, the second language teaching and learning of young learners, and issues in second language assessment of young learners. This helped the developers to form close knowledge of the children that would be taking the test, and to identify the nature of the constructs to be assessed. The handbook states that the test samples 'relevant and meaningful language use'. The four macro-skills (listening, speaking, reading and writing) are covered, though there is emphasis on oral/aural skills 'because of the primacy of spoken language over written language among children' (Taylor and Saville, 2002). Writing is largely at the word/phrase (enabling skills) level 'since young children have generally not yet developed the imaginative and organizational skills needed to produce extended writing' (Taylor and Saville, 2002).

A syllabus was subsequently devised to indicate the nature of the construct and the range of knowledge and skills to be tested. These are described through lists of topics, notions and concepts, structures and vocabulary for each level. As part of the structure list, language use (communication) items are itemized, connecting to the language (grammar and structures) and language items (examples). The syllabus for each level is provided in a free handbook, and is also available on the Internet. Table 9.1 shows an extract from the structure list for the first level, Starters. Other lists of topics, notions and concepts for each level are also provided, along with an alphabetic vocabulary list. Thus, the construct for assessment is clearly established, and also openly available to all stakeholders.

Table 9.1 *Extract from Starters Structure List (University of Cambridge ESOL Examinations, 2003, p. 13)*

LANGUAGE (GRAMMAR AND STRUCTURES)	LANGUAGE USE (COMMUNICATION)	LANGUAGE ITEMS (EXAMPLES)
THE ALPHABET	Writing down spelling	That's W-H-I-T-E.
NOUNS		
Singular and plural, including limited, specified, irregular plural forms (Proper nouns)	Asking who people are and identifying people	*Are you Bill?* *It's Pat.*
(Common nouns) Possessive forms: /'s /s'	Responding to requests for information about objects Talking about ownership	*They're oranges, not lemons.* *That's Ann's bike.*
ADJECTIVES size, age, colour	Describing and identifying objects, people and animals	*He's a small boy.* *Your face is very dirty.*
	Identifying colours	*It's a red car.*
DETERMINERS a, an, the, some	Identifying objects, animals, fruit, vegetables, etc. (with countables and uncountables)	*It's a banana.* *Who's eating an egg?* *Put the tomato on the table.* *He's got some apples.*
my, your, his, her, our, their	Talking about possessions and relationships	*It's my brother's birthday.*
(list continues)		

The constructs, that is, the expected language use and language knowledge as identified above, become more complex in the specifications for *Starters*, to *Movers*, to *Flyers*, the three levels of proficiency in the test.

Developing a plan for evaluating the qualities of 'usefulness':   Plans were put into place to check that the test would have the qualities of 'usefulness' or its equivalent theoretically. These included plans for ongoing qualitative and quantitative data collection and analysis in the test administration phase, such as surveys of test users (centres, teachers, examiners) in different markets to ask for feedback on various aspects of the tests; analysis of test papers to ascertain the skills focus in individual tasks and balance across papers, and trialling of task types with different learner groups.

Checking available resources and planning their allocation and management: Plans for the allocation and management of resources were put in place in the early stages. Resources were needed to cover the costs of test development, for the planned research to establish 'usefulness', for publicity materials for the test, handbooks that described the specifications of the test, and reports that reported research findings and information about candidate performance from year to year. The development of a large-scale test such as the Cambridge Young Learner English Tests involved initial outlays that would not be recouped for several years.

In the test design phase, the groundwork was therefore set for the test.

The operationalization phase

Preparing test specifications and blueprints for tasks: The Cambridge Young Learners English Tests are structured around three levels of proficiency, *Starters*, *Movers* and *Flyers*. The three levels of the test can be taken by any age group, depending on their hours of English tuition. However, *Starters* is designed for children from the age of 7. *Movers* is typically taken by children aged between 8 and 11, and *Flyers* test takers are typically aged between 9 and 12 years.

In order to focus on success and to motivate children to continue to learn English, the test developers established that all candidates who complete the test would receive an award. The award would focus on what they can do, rather than what they cannot do, and would give credit for having taken part in the test. This aspect of the test addresses the vulnerability of young learners.

A blueprint for each test component (listening, reading/writing and speaking) and for each level was prepared. These are published in the handbook. There is therefore a clear, explicitly stated expectation of the types of tasks or items that will be in each test, available for teachers, parents and test takers.

Following the definition of the construct in early phases of the project, tasks in the test focus on meaning rather than form: they are based on the kinds of task-based communicative activity, often interactive in nature, which are already used in many primary classrooms around the world.

A guiding principle for the project has been a desire to close the distance between children's experience of learning and testing (Taylor and Saville, 2002, p. 3). The age of test takers is taken into account in the task types. Tasks are brief and 'active' or 'game-like', e.g. colouring activities, and there are frequent changes of activity or task type. Test takers' cultural differences are taken into account in the development of test tasks. Items that may offend, or might not be understood, are screened out. Skin tones in pictures need to be varied; words used may be regional (should 'armchair' or 'sofa' be used?). Tasks are presented in a clear and attractive format to meet the interests of young learners. Colourful illustrations help children to relax and feel less nervous. The tests are 'topic-led' like many popular course books (Taylor and Saville, 2002).

An example of a blueprint for tasks appears in Table 9.2. It is the blueprint for the Starters Listening test tasks:

Table 9.2 *Summary of Starters Listening Test Components (University of Cambridge ESOL Examinations, 2003, p. 31)*

I've updated this to show changes in the 2003 version of the YLE Handbook

PARTS/ TASKS 1	MAIN SKILL FOCUS	INPUT	EXPECTED RESPONSE/ ITEM TYPE	NO. OF ITEMS
	Listening for lexical items and prepositions	Picture + dialogue	Carry out instructions and position things correctly on a picture	5
	Listening for numbers and spelling	Illustrated dialogue	Write down numbers and spelling	5
	Listening for information (present tenses)	Pictures + dialogue	3-option multiple-choice (pictures; tick the correct picture)	5
	Listening for lexis and relative position	Picture + dialogue	Carry out instructions, locating and colouring correctly	5

Each of the tasks or parts is described in further detail, for example:

Part 3:
This task consists of five questions, each a three-option multiple-choice with pictures. The information is conveyed in a series of

five self-contained dialogues. The speakers are always clearly differentiated by age or sex. There is a focus on the use of verbs in present tenses. (University of Cambridge ESOL Examinations, 2003)

Specifications are precise. For example, for the speaking test, an interview, the child is met by an usher (preferably someone who is known to them) who explains the test format in the child's first language then takes them into the exam room and introduces them to the examiner. The interview is three to five minutes long for Starters, five to seven minutes for Movers and seven to nine minutes long for Flyers. The interviewer is trained to follow an 'interlocutor frame', a script on which the interview questions (and responses) are based. The interlocutor can correct the child if the child is misinterpreting the task, but not in his performance in the task. Examiners are told to be encouraging, and actively praise children taking the tests, in order to put the children at ease and help them to do well in the speaking tests. Children need the reassurance of knowing they are doing the right thing to feel confident about tackling a task such as a problem-solving activity or describing a series of pictures. These instructions for the interviewer are part of the blueprint. The components of the interview are also written out for each level, as Table 9.3 illustrates.

Table 9.3 *Components for Movers Speaking Component (University of Cambridge ESOL Examinations, 2003, p. 23)*

PARTS	INPUT	EXPECTED RESPONSE/ITEM TYPE
1	Greeting and name check: two similar pictures	Identify four differences between pictures
2	Picture sequence	Describe each picture in turn
3	Picture sets	Identify the odd one out and give reason
4	Open-ended questions	Answer personal questions

Each level of the test has different procedures and tasks in the interview, in order that the developing proficiency level of children can be tapped.

Specifying the scoring method: Scoring methods were developed. The scoring methods were determined by the task type. Thus the speaking component is scored with the use of a rating scale that includes interactive listening ability, pronunciation and production of words and phrases.

The task in Part 4 of the Starters reading and writing component is a gap-filling (prompted) task with one-word answers; therefore guidelines for scoring on a correct/incorrect basis are given. A test is made 'easier' if misspellings are accepted. Cambridge ESOL has decided that, since they are looking for meaning in language use, there can be some acceptable misspellings. 'Spellings which are nearly correct, rather than completely correct, will be accepted, e.g. "trea" would be accepted if the expected answer was "tree" '. (University of Cambridge ESOL Examinations, 2003). Examples of marking keys are available. Mark distribution is specified, for example, 5 marks for each part. The following is part of a sample task.

Movers Reading and Writing Task (this is the third of three pictures in story sequence. Each picture has part of the story and questions beneath it).

Jane said, 'Look at this! There's a cupboard here!' Jim carefully opened the cupboard door. He saw two green eyes looking at him. 'Help!' he shouted and they all ran outside and stood behind a tree. Jane was afraid and she climbed up the tree. Then the door slowly opened, and a black cat walked out.

7 What did Jim see?   ....

8 Where did they stand outside?   ....

9 Why did Jane climb up the tree?   because ....

10 What came outside after the children? ....

Figure 9.2 Movers Reading and Writing Task, Part 5 (University of Cambridge ESOL Examinations, 2002, p. 20).

The marking scheme for the whole task is presented as follows. The unbracketed words are needed to complete the answer correctly; the bracketed words are also acceptable in the answer.

Part 5	10 marks
1	(an)(old) house
2	play (in it)
3	(the) door
4	Jane (and) Peter
5	Jane (did)/(wanted to)
6	(the) bedroom
7	(two)(green) eyes
8	Behind (a) tree
9	(she was) afraid
10	(a)(black) cat

Figure 9.3 Marking key for Flyers Reading and Writing, Part 1 (University of Cambridge ESOL Examinations, 2002, p. 22).

Specifications for the final scores for the test are that shields will be presented to children, with five shields as the top score on the test.

Thus, in this phase, the specifications for the test tasks and the test as a whole have been established, in preparation for the final test administration phase.

The test administration phase

In test writing, test writers on the Cambridge Young Learners English Tests follow the task specifications exactly, keeping, for example, within the vocabulary list and characteristics of the input (gender of speakers, number of speakers, etc.). Illustrators play a critical role in the development of tasks, since most tasks have pictures. These are adapted on computers as test writers require changes. As a test developer explained, the illustrators (with the task writers) have to 'see into the child's world, and see how they think'.

Try-out: In the developmental phase of the test, sample tasks were prepared according to each blueprint. Versions of the test were trialled in 1995/6 with over 3,000 children in Europe, South America and South East

Asia. Feedback from teachers was collected, and children's answers were statistically analysed. This information was used to construct the live test versions. The trialling and feedback confirmed, for example, that questions should be in colour (Taylor and Saville, 2002).

Operational test use phase: The administration of the Cambridge Young Learners English Tests is done through test centres around the world. Centres can apply to be a Cambridge Young Learners testing centre. Schools can apply, if they have the required facilities. Cambridge ESOL visits, checks and approves each centre. Guidelines exist for testing centres in relation to confidentiality, requirements for destruction of papers and other procedures. Approved Cambridge Centres are able to administer tests at times that suit them. They order versions of the test from Cambridge ESOL and administer them to fit in with local conditions (school terms, holiday periods, etc.) The administration department 'manages' the versions of the Reading, Writing and Listening papers to ensure security according to what the centre has administered in previous sessions. The Speaking Test materials are supplied in sets of 10 (from 2004) and are sent out once the notification of intention to hold a test is received. This allows increased choice in different markets and also improved security. The completed question papers and mark sheets are returned to Cambridge to be marked. Results are issued within two weeks of receipt of the scripts by Cambridge ESOL. Papers are double-marked, checked (sometimes three times) and then put into the computer twice. Candidates' numbers are checked in the computer. Specific arrangements are made with some countries, for example China, for timing of testing, and marking of scripts.

To recognize one of the purposes of the test (to encourage future learning and teaching) the developers decided to emphasize predictability over authenticity in the tests. To ensure authenticity in tasks, a degree of unpredictability in language of the input and the expected responses (e.g., the length of the text, the grammar and vocabulary items) is needed. The construct of the tests aims to ensure adequate authenticity by mirroring tasks and approaches used in young learner classrooms around the world. Yet the developers believe that predictability is more important than authenticity for younger learners. Predictability is needed to bolster chances of success, and to ensure that the test is fair. Therefore they chose to strengthen predictability by publishing clear specifications for tasks and providing vocabulary lists that needed to be learned. The chances for children to be successful are bolstered by the accessibility of blueprints, sample tests, handbooks and research articles.

Considerations of the qualities of 'usefulness':   or its equivalent were and continue to be an integral part of the test administration phase. Monitoring and evaluation, which are essential for test validation, are ongoing for these tests (Marshall and Gutteridge, 2002). An empirical process of calibration, using Rasch analysis, is used to check difficulty of items. However, since these are high facility tests, that is, they are designed so that most test takers can do well, there can be a lack of discrimination and the statistics can become unstable. Data are also collected through anchor items. These anchor items are then cross-compared with other tests, for example the KET (Key English Test in Cambridge Main Suite exams). It is possible to identify candidates, and to follow and observe their progress as they move up the three levels, and into the KET. Their rate of progress, that is, the time they need to progress, is monitored. Progress would be expected to be lock step – if not this provides feedback on difficulty of each level and items within them.

Ongoing research is integral to the test. For example, the following areas of research are relevant to the Cambridge Young Learner Speaking Test (Ball and Wilson, 2002):

- Developing a corpus (audio-recorded database) of speaking tests, made up of a representative sample of Young Learner Speaking Tests from around the world. These can then be searchable by a range of variables including the age or first language of the candidate or the marks awarded.

- Undertaking qualitative analyses of transcriptions. For example, the following questions can be asked about the storytelling task:

  - How do candidates perform in the storytelling task compared to other parts of the test?

  - Are there qualitative and/or quantitative differences between the language produced in the storytelling task and other parts of the speaking test?

  - Do candidates hesitate or display uncertainty or nervousness in the storytelling task?

  - How do examiners use back-up questions in the storytelling task?

- Validating the rating scales. Are the assessment criteria for the Young Learner Speaking Tests appropriate? Results of a special re-rating project and questionnaires/protocol analysis with examiners will help Cambridge ESOL to evaluate the effectiveness of the assessment criteria and rating scales.

Summary: the test development process

Large-scale testing of young learners inevitably requires attention to the special characteristics and needs of young learners. The Cambridge Young Learners English Tests provide an example of a set of large-scale language test for young learners. The test development phases and ongoing research help to ensure that children have a fair but also an enriching (rather than a discouraging) experience in the taking of the tests.

The design phase establishes the purpose of the test, young learner characteristics, the TLU domain in which they are learning, the typical tasks they learn through and the constructs that are to be assessed. This step is critical to the rest of the test development process. Once the design phase is established, the test is targeted for young learners and their needs and interests. The operationalization phase requires developers to prepare young learner-related specifications and blueprints that match the requirements set out in the design phase. The test administration phase follows through to actual use of the test with young learners, and an ongoing evaluation of the test for 'usefulness', specifically in relation to young learners. Young learners are at the forefront in each development phase.

The remainder of this chapter is concerned with issues in the large-scale testing of young second language learners, that is, of children who are being tested in the majority language of school, and often simultaneously in subject content. These children are in a different situation from foreign language learners who are usually assessed in the foreign language at the levels of achievement appropriate to the foreign language curriculum they have been studying.

Large-scale standardized tests for school-age second language learners

The test development processes described above underpin all language test development, whether the test is for foreign or second language learners, and whether it is for younger or older learners. Differences in test purposes, the TLU domain, the characteristics of learners and so on will influence the final nature of the test. Thus, the multiple points at which second language learners enter into language learning, the requirements of the academic language of schooling in their TLU domain and the rapid progress that second language learners are likely to make are just some of the many factors that make test development decisions different for second language learners. This section is concerned with the macro-decisions that are made around large-scale testing of second language learners, and will then examine how test development processes are applied to testing academic language proficiency. Most of the issues in this section apply to all learners at school, whether they are older or younger, though issues related to academic language proficiency become more and more salient as children progress through into upper primary school and beyond.

There are two main scenarios in which second language learners are tested on a large scale. The first scenario is by far the most common; this is when second language learners are tested on large-scale content-area tests normed on the general population of students and taken by all students. Thus, second language learners take tests in maths, science and other subjects designed to test all students' achievement. In some countries, the content-area tests that young learners are expected to take are limited to literacy and numeracy tests, again normed on the general population. In these testing situations, second language learners are simply counted as part of the general population and assessed accordingly. The second, less common, scenario for large-scale testing of second language learners is when a specifically designed second language test (rather than a majority-normed) test is used to monitor the language proficiency of second language learners.

These two large-scale testing scenarios for second language learners feature in different ways in different countries around the world. The first scenario is played out in most countries. For example, in the United Kingdom, second language learners are assessed through National Curriculum tests; that is, their progress is assessed through the common content-area testing procedures for all children. In Australia, second language learners are assessed through common large-scale literacy tests although in most States and Territories further teacher-based monitoring of their language progress using ESL standards is also conducted. In the United States, large-scale content-area tests, based on curriculum standards, are commonly administered to all learners. All students are expected to take these tests, though early second language learners have sometimes been excluded. A federal policy initiative, the No Child Left Behind Act (2001), has meant that the second scenario, the testing of learners on specifically designed second language tests is also being pursued in the United States. The act requires the use of a uniform state-level data set for second language learners, collected through yearly large-scale English language proficiency assessments of second language learners. This initiative has resulted in the development and use of a number of English language tests specially designed for early second language learners. The data from these tests are available to be used for a number of purposes:

- collecting baseline data on academic language proficiency to determine annual growth and annual yearly progress
- monitoring student progress in academic language proficiency achievement on a summative basis
- reclassifying, redesignating, or transitioning students from support services
- determining accountability for student learning
- measuring maintenance of student progress after transition from support services
- providing feedback to all educational stakeholders

(Gottlieb, 2003 , p. 3)

In the following sections we look at the pitfalls in tests in the first scenario – that is, where school-age learners are tested in content-area tests designed for majority, first language learners. There are, of course, many pitfalls in tests in the second scenario, those designed specifically for second language learners. These generally relate to the pitfalls that are encountered in every test development process; Abedi (2004, p. 12), for example, has commented on the weaknesses of many English language proficiency tests used for second language learners in the United States, suggesting concerns with their operationalization of language proficiency, with validity and reliability, with the adequacy of scoring directions, and with the limited population on which test norms are based. Ways to include academic language proficiency in the operationalization of language proficiency in tests for second language learners are addressed in the final section of this chapter.

Pitfalls in testing second language learners through large-scale content tests normed on first language learners

Pitfalls in the design phase

Much has been written about the pitfalls of assessing second language learners on tests normed on majority group, first language learners (Cummins, 1983; Garcia and Pearson, 1994; Valdes and Figueroa, 1994;

Butler and Stevens, 2001; McKay, 2001; Bailey and Butler, 2003). When tests are normed on majority first language learners, right from the design phase in the test development process, learner characteristics and the expected performance (the construct to be assessed) are more likely to be invalid for second language learners. The TLU domain and tasks are generally the same for both first and second language learners (they are learning in the same mainstream classrooms) unless they are in intensive language centres, but the expected performance in large-scale content-area tests is normed on the language performance and academic achievement of the majority. In addition, the nature of, and expected levels of, content-area knowledge will be normed on mainstream first language students, thus creating **content bias** in tests. Young learners who speak a dialect of the majority language and/or who come from a non-mainstream culture will also experience the same difficulties with regard to the expectations and content bias in tests.

In addition, when second language learners take content-area tests, their developing language proficiency is likely to have an influence on inferences that are made on the basis of the test scores, especially when the tests are made up of performance assessment tasks (Bachman, 2002). That is, the tests may be invalid for second language learners because they may not be able to show the extent of their topical knowledge relevant to the assessment tasks. This is also a form of content bias. In a similar vein, test tasks may have content bias because they are cultur-ally inappropriate for students from different cultural backgrounds. Culturally appropriate tests may need to be informed by research with different cultural groups; this research, including interviews and think-aloud protocols with students, would help to reveal students' difficulties, from interpretation of questions because of different communication styles, to differences in contextual understandings that influence performance. Solano-Flores and Trumbull (2003) give an example of mis-taken contextual understanding in which a student from a low-income family misinterprets a math 'Lunch Money' problem, understanding that the mother has only $1 instead of in fact having multiples of $1. They conclude: 'understandings of non-mainstream language and non-mainstream culture must be incorporated as part of the reasoning that guides the entire assessment process' (Solano-Flores and Trumbull, 2003, p. 12). Each pitfall that arises in the design phase inevitably resurfaces in the next two phases, emphasizing the need for an appropriate foundation to be established in the design phase.

Pitfalls in the operationalization phase

In the subsequent operationalization phase of test development, large-scale content-area tests normed on first language learners are shaped by the learner characteristics and constructs defined in phase one. The criteria for scoring will reflect the construct established in the design phase, that is, the language achieved by successful first language learners of this age group. In the marking of the test it is likely, then, that second language and literacy characteristics will be regarded as errors, rather than recognized as evidence of creativity, risk-taking and progress along second language learning pathways. Students' cultural misunderstandings and linguistic approximations will also be marked as incorrect.

Pitfalls in the administration phase

In the administration phase, statistical analysis in the try-out stage is likely to eliminate items that do not represent the majority.

> To create a final test, those items that have the lowest correlation with the total test score are eliminated on the grounds that they provide a poor estimate of the phenomenon being measured. In other words, those very items on which low-scoring students do comparatively well disappear! If we remember that low-income and ethnic minority students are overrepresented in the set of low-scoring students, then it is almost inevitable that minority students will perform relatively poorly on final versions of tests built through this process.
>
> (Garcia and Pearson, 1994, p. 343)

When a test is administered, it may have prescribed time limitations, and these are problematic for second language learners taking standardized content-area tests. Early second language learners take longer to process both the questions and their answers. As a result they are deprived of the time they need to show what they are able to do. Unfamiliar vocabulary and paraphrasing and expressions written in academic language may 'throw' students who know the correct answer (Garcia and Pearson, 1994). Thus in each stage of the test development process, there are factors militating against the valid and fair testing of second language learners.

It is possible to control for content bias, that is, for differences in students' knowledge of topics by, for example, making sure that a variety of topics are covered in the test, and by eliminating questions that can be answered without having to read the information provided in the task (Garcia and Pearson, 1994). Garcia (1991) found that when topical knowledge was controlled statistically in a standardized test, the comprehension differences between Latino and Anglo children disappeared. Garcia and Pearson (1994, p. 349) also report that it is possible for second language learners to demonstrate their understanding of a text more effectively when they are allowed to use their first language in the assessment task. Research of this type is informing large-scale test developers that there are weaknesses in large-scale content-area tests for second language learners that need close attention. Other solutions recommend that early second language learners are not included in standardized content-area tests at all until they have reached a certain level of proficiency in the second language. These types of solutions are gaining credibility in the United States; details of such proposals are discussed below.

Concerns about impact

The above concerns about large-scale tests normed on majority first language learners relate in particular to their validity as tests for second language learners. An aspect of validity is the nature of impact of a test on teaching and learning, and on young learners' lives. In large-scale testing, the scores of second language learners are inevitably lower, especially in the first several years of their schooling in the new language. The scores of indigenous children in Australia, for example, on national literacy and numeracy tests are consistently reported as significantly lower than the norm. Many of these children live in communities in the outback, though many also live in country towns and cities. Many of those who live in the outback speak their own language(s) at home and have little contact with English until they come to school. Some speak Aboriginal English, a dialect of standard Australian English. They are expected to achieve as well on the literacy and numeracy tests as all Australian learners, but this is not always possible, especially in the early years of school. The impact of low results for individuals, and for the group (since the results of indigenous learners are generally combined in analyses of results), are feelings of low-esteem felt by indigenous children and their parents, and a sense of discouragement felt by their teachers. Many second language children from a range of cultural and linguistic backgrounds in countries around the world may not be as visible as indigenous learners in

Australia, but the impact of standardized content-area tests normed on their majority-language-speaking peers may be negative in similar ways. Yet the reality is that in second language terms, many learners are achieving strongly in the target language at their own level. Large-scale content-area tests do many second language learners a disservice; they ignore the huge advances they are making, hinder them from showing what they know in the content area and then deliver results that can cause distress to the learners, their families and their teachers.

In addition, in high-stakes situations, tests can have a 'disproportionate curricular influence' (Garcia and Pearson, 1994) in that teachers may teach to the test to gain the best results from their students. The test becomes the teachers' main reference point, with the result that the curriculum may be narrowed to the scope of the content covered in the test. Second language learners may be deprived of the many experiences they need in the language to help them to progress. Writers who deal with the negative impact of standardized content-area tests point out that many of these effects are also felt by students of lower socioeconomic status who also experience dissonance with the dominant culture.

Important research is taking place, especially in the United States, designed to counteract the negative influences of standardized content-area assessment on second language learners. The following section outlines some strategies that can be used to avoid some of the pitfalls of large-scale content-area tests.

Strategies to avoid some of the pitfalls of large-scale content testing normed on first language learners

The reality is that in current managerialist (or economic rationalist) educational environments, the pitfalls of large-scale content testing are outweighed, in administrators' minds, by the need to gather overall, comparable data about the achievements of all students, teachers and schools. Given this situation, can large-scale testing be made to be more valid and have a more positive impact on second language learners? This section outlines two strategies that have been proposed or are being used; though their effectiveness is not yet fully established. They are that the education system:

• introduce accommodations into large-scale tests
• restructure testing pathways for second language learners

Introduce accommodations into large-scale tests

Accommodations are additional support mechanisms provided in a test
for a designated group of test takers who need help to access the content
or to demonstrate what they know. Butler and Stevens (2001) suggest that
there are two categories of test accommodations: modifications to the
test itself and modifications to the test procedure (see Table 9.4 below). In
each category there are a number of ways that the test can be modified to
help second language learners. Some accommodations are likely to be
less valuable for young learners than others (e.g., the use of dictionaries
and glossaries with younger learners) but most can be applied easily to
young learner assessment. Many accommodations make the text and the
questions more accessible and give test takers a better chance to show
what they know.

Table 9.4 *Two categories of accommodations for English language
learners (Butler and Stevens, 2001, p. 413)*

Modifications of the test	Modifications of the test procedures
• assessment in the native language	• extra assessment time
• text change in vocabulary	• breaks during testing
• modification of linguistic complexity	• administration in several sessions
• addition of visual supports	• oral directions in the native language
• use of glossaries in native language	• small-group administration
• use of English Glossary	• separate-room administration
• linguistic modifications of test directions	• use of dictionaries
• additional example items/tasks	• reading aloud of questions in English
	• answers directly in text booklet
	• directions read aloud or explained

Results of research on whether accommodations make any significant
difference in the performance of second language learners on content-
area tests is mixed; that is, that significant improvements are not always
evident, and importantly that improvement depends on the student's
level of language proficiency (Butler and Stevens, 2001; Gottlieb, 2003).
In some cases improved performance of English language learners in a
large-scale test have been evident, for example Abedi et al. (2000) found
there were differences in the performance of fourth-grade students who
were and who were not given an English and a bilingual dictionary
during a test.

More research is needed into the idea of tailoring accommodations to the nature of students' language proficiency and knowledge. Because learners will benefit from accommodations differently because of differences in their proficiency, it is important that standard accommodations are not simply added to tests to 'solve the second language learner problem'. As Gottlieb points out, add-on accommodations might not be valid for many second language learners.

> Accommodations generally apply to intact or off-the-shelf school district or state tests, some that are high stakes in nature, that have not been conceptualised, piloted, or normed on English language learners. In that case, accommodations become the means of retro-fitting assessments that, by their very nature of development, are invalid for English language learners. (Gottlieb, 2003, p. 31)

We are not yet sure how valid or effective accommodations are in helping second language students in standardized content-area tests. Test accommodations are therefore one alternative to large-scale content-area tests, though further research is needed to explore how accommodations can be used most effectively. (See Koenig and Bachman (2004) for a detailed discussion of issues of accommodations for ELLs and research needed.)

Restructure the testing pathways for early second language learners

Gottlieb (2003) addresses the problems of large-scale assessment of second language learners in the United States by proposing a framework to restructure the large-scale assessment of second language learners. She argues that it is important that assessment should be sensitive to longitudinal, individual student growth and not rely solely on large-scale, high-stakes tests that look for commonalities across large learner groups. She also argues, as I have done above, that it serves no purpose to include second language learners in large-scale assessment crafted for first language English speakers; more often than not, this practice results in penalties for second language learners and their schools.

Gottlieb firstly redefines large-scale testing. Large-scale testing, she suggests, can be carried out in the classroom, at grade levels/departments, at the school level, at school district level and at the state level (p. 21). Then she proposes a framework in which large-scale testing of ELLs occurs at three stages:

a 'alternate' (or alternative) school-based assessment

b school district or state assessment with accommodations

c school district or state assessment.

'Alternate' assessment is Gottlieb's term for standards-based measures specifically designed for early second language learners, carried out at the school level in ways that produce defensible data (p. 25). This kind of assessment is non-standardized and is carried out at the classroom or school level. It may take a number of forms, including the following:

- a specific test reflective of ESL, content-based instruction
- an achievement measure in the students' native language parallel to another large-scale tool
- a set of content-based tasks interpreted with standard rubrics
- a standard, student portfolio of academic performance

Gottlieb suggests that teacher-based assessment can be used as 'a form of large-scale testing' for second language learners, that is, that it can take the place of large-scale testing, at least for second language learner groups, when they are at the beginning stages of language proficiency. At the same time she recognizes that large-scale testing is useful at certain points in a child's educational career to provide confirmatory evidence for administrative purposes. She advocates that classroom-based assessment can produce data for large-scale assessment under the following conditions:

- when standard prompts (blueprints) appropriate for students' age and development are made available to teachers
- when content-related language samples are collected (a) in the fall to establish an initial baseline, (b) at mid-year to monitor progress and (c) at the end of the year to measure growth
- when samples of performance are collected and held in the student's records

School-based assessment should have certain characteristics if it is to be incorporated into a state's repertoire of large-scale assessment. It should be conducted in educational contexts that are appropriate for ELL education (e.g., support services should be in place; sufficient teaching resources should be available; the political climate of the school should be supportive); there should be use of language in the classroom that

facilitates students' opportunities to demonstrate their content knowledge (this may be in their first language); and the technical quality of the
assessment should be equal to that of other large-scale assessments and
of comparable rigour. Technical quality is covered when, for example,
standard prompts, or tasks, appropriate for students' age and development and anchored in specific content standards across grade levels are
made available to teachers; when content-related language samples are
collected by classroom teachers on a regular basis; and when samples of
performance are collected and held in students' record offices. In addition, there must be strong inter-rater agreement in scoring (at least 85%)
and standard guidelines for the collection, analysis and reporting of data.
A reporting scheme that maps both the academic achievement of ELLs
and their language proficiency should be followed. In addition, ongoing
validation studies and evaluation efforts should be carried out to ensure
that the scheme is functioning optimally for ELLs. Thus Gottlieb is suggesting that school-based assessment can be made rigorous enough to
replace or work alongside large-scale, standardized content-area assessment, at least in the students' early stages of second language learning.

As ELL students progress in their English language proficiency (and in
some cases, content knowledge), they will progress through two thresh-
olds, at which point changes can be made to the testing they undergo.
Students reach Threshold 1 when their school-based assessment indicates they are ready. Once they have reached Threshold 1, they are able to
be tested through the school-district/state content-based assessment in
which accommodations are provided. Students reach Threshold 2 when
they are ready to take content tests without accommodations. Ideally,
decisions are made about whether students have reached Threshold 2
based on their previous performance on tests with accommodations, and
also on other indicators of academic language proficiency.

Gottlieb's staged approach provides an alternative to large-scale
content-area assessment for early second language learners. It reduces the
dangers that large-scale content-area assessment bring for learners who
are unable to show what they know because of their developing language
proficiency. It recognizes that school-based assessment is of higher pedagogical value for early second language learners, and by introducing the
imperative of technical quality is attempting to win administrators over to
her side to support school-based assessment at this point of their learning.

Large-scale testing is a reality in the United States, and therefore
Gottlieb provides a stepping-stone, through school-based assessment,
and through tests with accommodations, to full unsupported testing.

The idea of a staged approach to full content assessment is relevant to all countries and situations where second language learners are expected to be included in a large-scale content-area testing regime; it is also applicable to young second language learners wherever they are included in a large-scale testing regime.

Ways to address the assessment of academic language proficiency in large-scale tests

Second language learners require both social and academic proficiency in order to succeed at school (Collier, 1992; Cummins, 1980, 1984), therefore tests for second language learning should include academic proficiency, though this is not always done (Bailey and Butler, 2003). The academic language proficiency that should be assessed should be that language which is required in students' real-life world – that is, it should be based on the mainstream content-based curriculum that they have to study. In the early elementary school years, the academic language that children use in school is tied closely to classroom activities (the language of instructions, the language of doing and talking about the physical things around them). Activities such as art and mini-project work, e.g., building models, checking what happens with water and sand, all require early academic language that will become more sophisticated as they go through primary school. In the middle and upper elementary years, children need to describe objects and processes, report on what they have discovered, summarize their findings from a library project, and so on. An effective test for second language learners should reflect the language children need in their real-life world at school, and through this, alert teachers and schools as well as parents and the children themselves, to the areas of language they need to master in order to participate fully in the mainstream classroom.

A group of researchers in the United States has been researching the nature of academic language proficiency for test development purposes (Butler and Bailey, 2002; Bailey and Butler, 2003; Bailey, Butler, LaFramenta and Ong, 2004; Butler et al., 2004). The researchers Bailey and Butler have concentrated in some components of their work (Stevens et al., 2000; Bailey and Butler, 2003) on the design phase of academic language test development. They have been determining the nature of the TLU domain and the task types that young learners at upper primary level are expected to perform in mainstream classrooms and in standardized content tests. Their first task was to establish the definition of academic proficiency, to capture the language that students actually encounter in school. They did this by collecting language data in classrooms, and also by examining the following through a range of subjects and grade levels:

- empirical studies of student performance and the language demands of content and English language assessments
- the language prerequisites assumed in national, state and ESL content standards
- teacher expectations for language comprehension and production
- classroom exposure to all, including teacher talk and textbooks and other print materials.

Bailey and Butler's (2003) approach to defining academic language proficiency draws on research by Mislevy and his colleagues in what they call 'evidence-based design' (Mislevy, Steinberg and Almond, 2002). Their analysis has enabled them to move towards a detailed and explicit account of the academic language needs of students. Analysis of four state content standards showed that elementary students are required to *analyse, compare, describe, observe* and *record*; at middle school level, students are required to *compare, explain, identify* and *recognize*. Analysis of the TESOL K-12 ESL standards gave further information about the kind of language necessary to achieve each TESOL goal. From observations of classrooms, the researchers found that teachers used primarily four language functions – description, explanation, comparison and assessment – and two repair strategies, clarification and paraphrasing. They found that student talk data revealed five predominant functions of language – explanation, description, comparison, questioning and commenting (Bailey and Butler, 2003). The working definition of academic language that the research group has adopted describes academic language at the lexical (vocabulary), syntactic (forms of grammar) and discourse (rhetorical) levels, with a central focus on the functions of language (Bailey et al., 2004). The work has made it clear that many English language tests are not assessing whether students have the English language skills necessary for success at school.

From the clarification of the construct (the academic language proficiency that primary-age learners need in mainstream classrooms), Bailey and Butler proceed to the development of task specifications that will reflect the construct. Table 9.5 is an example of a test specification for academic language proficiency assessment based on Bailey and Butler's research. The specification follows Butler et al.'s (1996) framework for test specifications.

Table 9.5 *Example of test specification components applied to a draft prototype academic language proficiency task (Bailey and Butler, 2003, p. 27)*

Domain: Oral Language: Comprehension of *Description* (input) and production *Explanation* (output).

General description: The task will test the test taker's ability to *listen and comprehend* the language of description and in turn *produce* the language of explanation.

Prompt attributes: The test administrator will read aloud to the test taker a short passage with specified attributes that give sentence length and complexity, breadth and depth of vocabulary, etc., as determined by textbook and classroom discourse analysis. The passage and explanation text question will be crafted to elicit the language of elaborated explanation. The task will have an academic theme or focus, but all information to provide an accurate response to the prompt will be included such that no specific content-area knowledge outside the prompt will be required.

Response attributes: The test taker will respond orally and will produce the necessary language to achieve the goals of the task, which include (1) demonstrating understanding of the language of description via responses to a series of comprehension questions, (2) using cognitive processes to infer relevant information from the descriptive passage, and (3) producing a fully elaborated explanation in response to the explanation question (see scoring guidelines under specification supplement below).

Sample item/task read aloud by test administrator:

I am going to read you a short passage and then ask you some questions about it.

> *A teacher specifically told a group of students to carefully place their experiments in a safe location in the classroom. One student placed his glass bottles very close to the edge of his desk. When the teacher turned around she was angered by what she encountered.*

Who told the students to place their experiments in a safe location? (comprehension question)
Where did one student place his experiment? (comprehension question)
Who was angered? (comprehension question)
Explain as much as you can why the teacher was angry. (explanation question)

Specification supplement (scoring guidelines):

(1) Test taker will need to accurately answer comprehension questions about the description heard (scored correct/incorrect regardless of language sophistication and fluency), (2) test taker will need to infer that the teacher in the prompt was angry because she saw that the student put his experiment in the wrong place and (3) test taker will need to use the language of explanation (vocabulary, syntax, and discourse) to demonstrate that understanding to the tester.

Table 9.5　*(continued)*

Rubric for scoring explanations:

Level 1: Response is characterised by an incomplete and/or incorrect answer.

> **Example response 1a:**　The teacher was angry
> **Example response 1b:**　The teacher was angry because the student put the bottle on his desk.

Level 2: Response is characterised by a generally correct answer but the test taker has failed to elaborate how the inference (the bottle is in a dangerous position and could fall easily) was drawn

> **Example response 2a:**　He didn't follow directions.*
> **Example response 2b:**　The teacher was angry because the student did not follow directions.*

Level 3: Response is characterised by use of appropriate language to demonstrate a fully elaborated explanation. The test taker is able to infer that the teacher in the prompt was angry because the student put his experiment in the wrong place. The test taker demonstrates the use of the language of explanation to demonstrate that understanding (e.g., use of conditional tense for hypothetical events).

> **Example response 3:**　The teacher was angry because the student did not follow directions. He put his bottle very close to the edge of the desk, which is a dangerous place because the bottle could fall and break.

* Note from authors:
1 This example is for illustrative/conceptual purposes only and should not be seen as an operational test item. It is not a prototype to be modelled.
2 Note that in casual conversation, the explanations in Response #2a and #2b would be considered adequate. This highlights the difference between social uses of language and academic uses of language that hold speakers accountable for their claims, requiring them to verbally construct an argument citing evidence or logical conclusions to back up such claims. Moreover, these responses may be acceptable in many classrooms. Teachers may not require students to elaborate on their explanations in a way that overtly demonstrates to the teacher the necessary inferencing processes or steps in logical thinking.

Because this is a draft prototype of how academic language task specifications might be presented, the task in Figure 9.3 is necessarily short, both in its prompt and in the examples of expected responses. In reality, the prompts and the length and nature of expected responses in an academic task are likely to be longer and more complex, particularly for students in upper primary school. The test specification in Table 9.5 illustrates some important points. Firstly, the test developers are not expecting content knowledge outside the prompt to be demonstrated; this is to ensure that content knowledge does not override knowledge of the academic language they are assessing. Secondly, they are expecting cognitive processes to be activated in this task when students infer relevant information from the descriptive passage. And thirdly, they make sure that the top score (Level 3) goes to a response that has the characteristics of academic language, that is, one that requires students to use the language of explanation in which the conditional tense might be used for hypothetical events.

A close analysis of the construct of academic language proficiency and a careful development of test specifications lead to a more likely outcome of test 'usefulness'. Certainly, a test of academic language proficiency, if used to further the academic language skills of young second language learners, is likely to have a positive impact on their future success at school and on their life chances.

Alternatives to large-scale testing for young language learners

Many educators have written about the advantages of alternative assessment over standardized assessment (Herman, Aschbacher and Winters, 1992; Genishi and Brainard, 1995; Huerta-Macias, 1995; Brown and Hudson, 1998). As we discussed in Chapter 5, proponents of alternative assessment advocate performance-based assessment in the classroom, tapping into what children can actually do in a natural and familiar language use situation. They turn away from large-scale tests that are usually paper-and-pencil, often made up of multiple-choice and discrete-point items, with children under pressure to show what they know in a limited space of time and in unfamiliar surroundings.

For young second language learners, teacher-based alternative assessment techniques have many advantages; for example, they can be assessed in familiar surroundings with familiar teachers, and tailored accommodations can be administered (and noted by the teacher) to help children show what they know and what they can do. This type of assessment has a major advantage for all stakeholders – children, parents, teachers, schools and education systems; assessment is carried out by those who spend time with the children and are able to witness the range of abilities they have. Immediate feedback is provided to children and to the teacher, and assessment runs as an underlying and supportive thread through learning. If the assessment is to be used for high-stakes decisions, then steps like those proposed by Gottlieb and Brindley, and described in the previous section, need to be taken to ensure that the assessment procedures produce 'defensible data'. If administrators are able to accept the data that are given them through these processes, then all are winners, because the data are likely to be more 'useful' than those collected through large-scale tests. The result is more trustworthy data for administrators, principals and parents, and a fairer and more positive assessment experience for children. Brindley (1998; 2001) has written in depth about maximizing validity and reliability in outcomes-based assessment conducted by teachers. To standardize assessment procedures more closely, banks of prototype or actual assessment tasks can be made available for teachers to use in classroom assessment, and engaging teachers in moderation activities with trained personnel can check consistency of marking. Portfolios have also been suggested for use in systematic ways as an alternative to standardized tests (Salinger, 1998). A clear specification on what is required in the portfolio and how it will be scored, accompanied by professional development and moderation, is essential if portfolios are to be used systematically to collect comparative data over large populations.

Finally, many educators believe that large-scale testing of young learners need not necessarily be high-stakes. I refer once again to the EVA Project (Evaluation of English in Schools), conducted in Norwegian Ministry of Education schools by the University of Bergen (Hasselgren, 2000). (See Chapter 3 for more details of this project.) The project is different from many large-scale assessment endeavours in that the assessment procedures are not designed to provide data to administrators and parents, but rather to improve formative assessment in the classroom. It is therefore low-stakes for all participants. As part of the project, teachers are given tasks to use. Scoring instruments are provided to guide children to carry out self-assessment, and to teachers to help them to conduct their assessment. Teachers are given professional development on how to use the material and also how to interpret the results. Scores and profiles that are produced as a result of this assessment are regarded as indicative of ability which should be pursued further by the teacher (p. 266). Research is conducted into test results and, for example, pupils' responses, to provide insights into the assessment process and its value. The purpose of this large-scale assessment is to improve teaching and learning on a large-scale.

> In the absence of any tradition that smacks of grading in primary schools, both teachers and pupils are able to approach assessment

> without prejudice and put it to positive use. It seems that, in some ways, we have got it right. There are, so far, no 'victims' of testing in the Norwegian primary school, and the principal challenge to those involving themselves in this area will be to ensure that the situation remains that way!   (Hasselgren, 2000, p. 267)

Thus assessment materials and guidelines are produced centrally to give teachers a common set of assessment procedures from which they can learn, and around which they can engage in collegial professional development. The ultimate purpose is to support teachers in their class-room assessment. Whilst these procedures do not provide data for administrators, principals and parents, they would be able to provide low-stakes information to centrally based advisory teachers about students' progress, who would be made aware of support needs. They are worth considering as an alternative to large-scale high-stakes tests for young learners who are vulnerable to failure and unlikely to understand the full repercussions and requirements of the test-taking process.

Summary

There are many challenges in large-scale testing of young learners. Many educators object to the use of large-scale testing, particularly with young learners, for a number of reasons, in particular because of their vulnerability to failure, their lack of maturity which may lead to misconceptions about the test requirements, and their need for immediate feedback and subsequent adjustments to teaching.

Test development is undertaken in three phases, the design phase, the operationalization phase and the implementation phase (Bachman and Palmer, 1996). These processes help to ensure that tests are valid, reliable, practical, interactive, and have a positive impact (that is, that they are 'useful'). The Cambridge Young Learners English Tests are foreign language tests that provide a case study of the test development process. They indicate how procedures must be systematic and in order to ensure a large-scale test for young test takers is as valid, fair and motivating as possible.

Second language learners are often required to take large-scale content-area tests normed on first language speakers. The reference point for these tests is the expected achievement of their first-language-speaking peers. Bias in these tests is created immediately from the start of test development, that is, in the design phase when the expectations for language and content achievement are set in relation to another learner group. The operationalization and implementation phases of test development perpetuate this bias. The result can be that the tests are invalid and unfair for many second language learners, and hence, the negative impact can be great.

Two strategies can be used to avoid the pitfalls of large-scale content tests. Accommodations included in tests help some learners, but their effectiveness is not yet established by research. A framework strategy has been proposed by Gottlieb (2003) in which second language learners proceed through a staged process, in which they are first assessed in the classroom by their teachers before reaching the first threshold, then introduced to large-scale content-area assessment with the support of accommodations within the test. Finally they move into large-scale content tests without support. Gottlieb's strategy illustrates how complex solutions are needed to provide suitable tests for second language learners in a mainstream testing context.

Large-scale tests for young second language learners require the same test development processes as those described above. As with all test development, there are special considerations for each group of learners: second language learners are learning in mainstream classrooms and testing is concerned with language and content knowledge. Tests of language for young learners in these situations need to consider children's academic proficiency; even for young learners in mainstream classrooms, there are early academic proficiency requirements in schooling. The work of researchers in the United States (Bailey et al., 2004) illustrates how academic proficiency for young second language learners is being defined and operationalized through an 'evidenced-based' approach, in which data is being collected directly from curriculum documents, teachers and classroom observations about the nature of academic proficiency in the primary years.

Alternative assessment is advocated by many educators as a replacement for large-scale testing. Teacher assessment that is strongly guided, supported and coordinated by centrally based advisory teachers, as in the Norwegian EVA project (Hasselgren, 2000), can provide a strong alternative to large-scale standardized testing for foreign language programmes, and can be particularly beneficial for young learners.

CHAPTER TEN

The way forward

Introduction

This final chapter sets out some broad directions which require further concentration and attention in the field of young learner language assessment. Young learner assessment as a coordinated entity is a relatively new field of endeavour, characterized by a limited number of research articles, chapters in edited books concerned primarily with teaching, some resource books with practical assessment suggestions and, more recently, dedicated conferences. So where do we go from here? Two broad mutually supporting themes help to establish key areas requiring consolidation in the field: firstly, theories, frameworks and connections; and secondly, but no less important, professionalism and research.

Consolidating theories, frameworks and connections

This book has pursued a number of themes in relation to young learner language assessment. Each of these themes, listed below, also suggests an area for future consolidation.

Promoting the best assessment of language use

Arguments and exhortations for the assessment of language use have been made in earlier chapters in this book. Young learners' natural desire and need to use language means that it is not a major challenge to engage children in language use, especially when the environment is conducive to doing things with others and with things around them. The natural corollary of teaching through language use is to assess language use. When this is not happening (and this might be for many reasons beyond the teachers' scope of influence as I suggest below), changes should be considered, not only to assessment, but to the curriculum or standards in place, to professional development activities and to teaching and learning in the classroom.

Textbooks play a vital role in the promotion of language use. However, Rea-Dickins and Rixon (1999) report that there is an absence of language use tasks in textbooks for young foreign language learners around the world. The researchers suggest that because of this textbooks may be hampering teachers' opportunities to teach children to use language in communicative ways, and to develop this ability over a reasonable time.

> One source of the problem could lie in the 'playing it safe' practices of authors and publishers whose work has such a big influence upon what many teachers feel to be feasible. Course books for YL vary tremendously in how they treat continuous discourse rather than isolated sentence-based work, but the tendency is on the whole to offer very little development over time . . . the length, and coherence, of both reading and listening experiences in many course books for YL remains low from book one to book three, and often even beyond.
>
> (Rea-Dickins and Rixon, 1999 p. 98)

Young learners and their teachers will rely on publishers of foreign language textbooks to introduce more language use tasks into their textbooks in the future, and importantly, to integrate language use assessment tasks throughout the textbooks.

For second language learners, language use is less of an issue in their learning environment but is still a critical issue in assessment. Are assessment procedures designed in ways that recognize second language learners' actual language use needs in the community and at school? Do the assessment procedures take account of the characteristics of the way they develop language proficiency? Are early second language learners only ever assessed on language use ability in conjunction with content-area knowledge, with the result that they succeed with neither? We need ongoing exploration of ways in which assessment of young second language learners can be successful, that is, with positive impact, around the world.

Once language use assessment is established, appropriate language use assessment of young learners, whether for foreign or second language learners, requires that systematic procedures are followed and that these procedures are systematically refined. The process of learning about language use assessment of young learners is unlikely to end, as each assessment situation presents a new group of young learners, a new learning context and particular stakeholder needs. For this reason, the sharing of experiences and initiatives in young learner language use assessment is an important way forward for the foreign language and second language fields.

Drawing on theory, research and pedagogy from young learner education

Any educational endeavour with young learners must have as its foundation the theories of growth and learning that are relevant to the age group in question. It is no less important that those who assess the language of young learners underpin their assessment decisions with knowledge of child development and learning, as well as first and second language acquisition and their interrelationship. The way forward in this regard is that those who assess young language learners continue to draw on these areas of knowledge and to emphasize the need to do so.

Building on established assessment frameworks and reaching out to the general assessment field

A central strategy in this book has been to draw significantly on one established assessment framework (Bachman and Palmer, 1996). This framework, which was not developed specifically for young learners, sets out systematically considerations for language assessment. By drawing on this framework, and adapting the framework where necessary for young learner assessment, the approach in this book has been to deal with many aspects of young learner assessment in a coordinated and comprehensive way. Other frameworks might be adapted in the same way. It is possible, with reference to a framework, to check that all facets of assessment are considered in the classroom and in large-scale test development (from identifying the characteristics of learners, to task selection, to decisions about children's performance and progress). It is possible to be confident that the assessment procedures are as 'useful' as possible and, as part of this, will have a positive impact on the children involved. This concept is as relevant to the classroom teacher as it is to the educational administrator. Without doubt, for the sake of the young learners involved, the way forward must involve further pursuit of young learner assessment through a framework approach, in order that the best possible result with regard to 'usefulness' is achieved.

There is a wealth of assessment knowledge in the general assessment field that may not have been fully tapped by assessors of young learners' language. This is understandable to a degree, since the general assessment field is almost always addressed to teachers and assessors working with older learners. This book has attempted to reach out to the general assessment field and to remind teachers and assessors that many of these perspectives and research findings are relevant and important to the young learner field. It is essential that researchers and writers continue to undertake this kind of translation for teachers and assessors.

Bringing foreign and second language young learner assessment closer together

There are clearly many points of connection between foreign and second language assessment. In this book I have been able to bring the two fields together at many points in the assessment framework (e.g., in the principle of language use, in principles of task design, in decision-making on performance, in the principles of test development) because the underlying considerations and thinking in assessment theory are constant. At the same time, however, there are differences between the two groups based on different purposes for assessment, the characteristics of the learners and the context in which they are learning. Yet these differences exist between any two sets of assessment procedures – the purposes may be different, the learner characteristics and the context may be different and so on. Each assessment procedure must be considered on its own basis. Thus the differences between foreign and second language learner assessment are less than many may think – in both, procedures should be designed according to common considerations established in assessment theory and as described in this book.

The connections between the two fields with regard to research into assessment will be important, but also mixed. Common principles and research findings about young learner assessment in general (e.g., ways to assess the language of young learners; task types that are effective; children's responses to taking large-scale tests) will produce some areas of common research interest. This type of interchange should be encouraged. However, in particular the different constructs being assessed (the language that children need), and their learning context (foreign language versus ESL and mainstream classrooms), will make many of the research findings very different, and the foreign language and second language assessment fields will part at these points. The way forward is to look for connecting points and to build on them, perhaps through shared young learner assessment journals, books, professional development activities and conferences, and to recognize and acknowledge differences when they are relevant by also sharing in more separately defined professional groupings.

There are therefore theories, frameworks and connections suggested in this book that the young learner language assessment field should take further to promote effective assessment practices, and become further established as a vital and viable branch of language assessment. In order for this to happen, professional expertise and research in young learner assessment needs further consolidation.

Consolidating professional understandings and research

A clear weakness in young learner assessment is first the lack of expertise of teachers in relation to assessment, and secondly their low interest in spending time with assessment. In research into young learner language teaching programmes, teachers were found to be fully occupied developing teaching knowledge and skills, and most were less interested in assessment. Yet assessment is an integral and essential component of teaching and learning; teaching is diminished considerably if assessment is not integrated into it. To go even further, one cannot exist without the other. Therefore, an imperative for the field is for language teachers of young learners to improve their professional expertise in the area.

Improving professional expertise

Professional development in assessment for teachers of young learners may be one of the most pressing issues for the immediate future. Projects like the EVA project in Norway (Hasselgren, 2000) have shown ways in which teachers' 'assessment literacy' can be strengthened; with centralized support through standardized assessment tasks, carefully developed to suit the needs of young learners, and scoring guidelines together with moderation and professional development support, teachers have opportunities to gain knowledge and skills that immediately enhance teaching and learning in the classroom. Other successful professional development initiatives such as the Australian Language Levels project (Scarino, Vale, McKay, and Clark, 1988) and the development of the TESOL standards in the United States (TESOL, 1997) give the profession not only examples of how assessment is conducted, but also how it is an integral part of the language curriculum. Yet these projects are expensive in terms of resources and personnel. Professional development may be provided in university pre-service teacher education programmes, in districts by advisory teachers, and through local conferences. In whichever way professional development is possible, it should be a priority for teachers of young foreign and second language learners (including mainstream teachers of second language learners). Assessment need not be the main focus of professional development initiatives, but its place in a healthy curriculum should be emphasized, and teachers' knowledge and skills in assessment strongly promoted.

One of the possible alternatives to large-scale standardized assessment that we discussed in Chapter 9 was teacher assessment with guidance, support and coordination from centrally based education personnel. For this to be a real alternative, which many educators would hope for, then teachers need to have the knowledge and skills to carry out their part of the assessment process appropriately. This is another potent argument for teachers to have high-level skills in assessment.

When education personnel take on the responsibility for the development of external tests (tests for the whole school, or school district, or state, or nation), the importance of training personnel in test development procedures, and in the special characteristics and needs of young learners, is critical. Given young learners' vulnerability and the complexity of the influence of their developing maturity and literacy-related knowledge and skills (in both the first and second language), the importance of training cannot be overestimated.

Building on new understandings about teacher assessment

In recent years researchers in general education have been breaking new ground in the area of teacher assessment (see, for example, Issue 4, Vol 22 of *Educational Measurement, Issues and Practice*), and researchers in second language education have followed this lead (Rea-Dickins, 2001; Leung, 2005). Researchers are considering, for example, that the nature of validity and reliability in classroom assessment needs to be treated differently; that the main yardstick for validity in classroom formative assessment is the success of the learning that takes place (Brookhart, 2003), and that reliability can be strengthened through 'sufficiency of information' (Smith, 2003). The assessment practices that teachers use as they teach are therefore coming into better focus, and with the new requirements for standards-referenced assessment and reporting, further insights are also being gained into how teachers make decisions using externally developed criteria. New understandings in this area will help teachers and teacher-trainers not only to strengthen the teaching and learning process in language classrooms, but also hopefully to strengthen administrators' and parents' trust in classroom teachers' assessment expertise. With trust in teachers' abilities to assess and report on young learners' progress may come a lessening of reliance on standardized testing. Improved knowledge of, and expertise in, teacher assessment is therefore a priority for the young learner assessment field.

Exploring contextual influences on teachers and assessors around the world

Those involved in young learner language assessment around the world live and work in different contexts that result in possibilities and constraints that are specific to that context. There are many possible reasons why teachers in different teaching contexts around the world may or may not be able to (or wish to) assess through language use tasks. These include:

- The nature of the set curriculum and learning texts: When the curriculum establishes that children will learn to use language in communicative ways, and when the textbooks follow through with this, setting out language use tasks and assessing their progress through language use tasks, then clearly language use assessment in the classroom is more likely.

- The nature of external testing or externally imposed assessment requirements: If external testing is employed in the system, there will be an impact on the teaching and learning in the classroom. There will also be an impact on the assessment procedures. Thus, if a teacher is preparing for an external test that is known to assess through discrete-point assessment items, the teacher is more than likely to replicate this type of assessment in the practice-time before the test and, inevitably, through the teaching period. Likewise, if teachers are required to assess against externally developed criteria, for example standards, then teachers assess according to the way these criteria are conceptualized. Externally developed criteria that are based on language use will result in teacher assessment of language use.

- The nature of the 'curriculum space' teachers are given by the educational system: If teachers are given the responsibility to plan their programmes, to make decisions about which tasks they will use and how they will teach, to choose their own resources, and to plan and carry out their own assessment, then they are being given a large amount of curriculum space. If the educational system provides a set textbook, expects the textbook to be followed closely, and sets the assessment procedures, then the curriculum space is small. There are varying degrees of curriculum space.

  If the curriculum space is small but the system provides appropriate language use curriculum and assessment guidance, then this can be positive. If, however, the teachers are provided with curriculum and assessment materials that are more concerned with language knowledge (grammar, vocabulary and correct pronunciation), then it is difficult for them to introduce language use tasks into their teaching and assessment procedures. This must be done by the education system. If the curriculum space is large, there is more scope for teachers to introduce new ideas.

- The degree to which the teachers' beliefs about language learning match the principles behind teaching and assessing through language use: If teachers believe that children learn language through language use, then given support and professional development when they need it, they are likely to adopt language use assessment. Despite their importance, belief systems are only one reason why teachers may not adopt a particular approach to teaching or assessment; they may not do so because the school culture is resistant to change, because of time constraints and lack of opportunities to work through new ideas with others and/or because of individual teachers' own entrenched and safe patterns of teaching (Markee, 1993). Teachers' belief systems, however, usually reflect their broader sociopolitical context.

> Assumptions about 'active' and 'passive' students, about the use of
> group work and pair work, about self-interest as a key to motivation
> 'tell us about yourself'), about memorization being an outmoded
> learning strategy, about oral communication as the goal and means
> of instruction, about an informal atmosphere in the class being most
> conducive to language learning, about learning activities being fun,
> about games being an appropriate way of teaching and learning – all
> these, despite the claims by some researchers that they are empir-
> ically preferable, are cultural preferences.
>
> (Pennycook, 2000, p. 98)

This means that teachers do not hold their beliefs simply because they
agree with the theoretical principles and are convinced by the research.
They do so because of broader cultural beliefs that underpin their views
of language learning. Teachers' beliefs about language learning may or
may not match principles behind teaching and assessing through language use.

- The degree of collegiality and team work in the school environment: In
  high-stakes assessment situations, devising language use tasks and
  making summative decisions about children's performance in tasks
  requires collegiality. Teachers meet together in moderation meetings to
  establish that they have made the right decisions about children's performance. They gain confidence from this procedure and also learn
  from each other. The full procedure is able to strengthen the trust of the
  administrators and parents in the teacher-based assessment procedure. Collegiality and team work also supports formative assessment in
  the classroom; in particular in situations where teachers are developing new skills (Meister, 2000).

- The extent of teachers' ability to use the target language: For foreign
  language teachers who do not have a good level of communicative proficiency in the target language, the introduction or implementation of
  language use teaching and assessment in their classroom can be con-
  fronting to their professional status and confidence.

These are just some of the many, interrelated influences on teachers'
decisions and actions in the classroom. Recognition of contextual influences helps local decision-makers to consider the appropriateness or
viability of assessment practices. Figure 10.1 sets out the range of powerful influences on whether a teaching innovation or procedure is taken
up by teachers. Work on contextual influences on assessment necessarily incorporates recognition of the sociopolitical forces at work in a

society; that is, how education in general, and assessment practices in particular, work to maintain the social, economic, cultural and political status quo (Shohamy, 2001). How these forces are addressed in young learner language programmes – by teachers, principals, curriculum-writers, test developers and administrators – is worthy of exploration and certainly of wide dissemination amongst educators and assessors of young language learners.

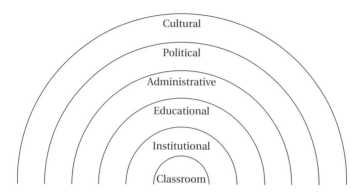

Figure 10.1 The hierarchy of interrelating subsystems in which an innovation has to operate (Kennedy, 1988, p. 332 cited in Markee, 1993).

If changes are required at the education system, institutional or class-room level, then principles of curricular innovation and teacher change may be followed (Fullan, 1993; Hargreaves, 1994; Meister, 2000). The experience of innovation and change in young learner assessment in different contexts also needs to be documented and disseminated. Sharing experiences of the successes and failures of changes in assessment practices, and in particular of the impact of these changes on young learners' lives, will enhance the knowledge in the field of what works and why in different contexts.

Researching further, disseminating more widely, and making connections

Research is fundamental if the young learner assessment field is to move forward. An account of research in the field is presented in Chapter 3 of this book; current research is categorized under four main purposes, and these purposes provide an organizing principle for further research needs. The purposes are:

- to investigate and share information about current practices
- to find ways to ensure valid and fair assessment practices
- to find out more about the nature of young learner language proficiency and language growth
- to investigate and improve the impact of assessment on young learners

Research into young learner language assessment is relatively new and is not always widely published. *Language Testing* and *Language Assessment Quarterly* are two journals that do, from time to time, publish articles and special issues on young learner assessment. A dedicated journal for young learner language assessment, one that combines foreign language and second language assessment research, will add to the venues for publication and sharing. The disadvantage of a dedicated journal may, however, be a sense of being separate from the general assessment field. However, mentoring of research and publications in the field through a dedicated journal, edited publications and conferences would be valuable for a new field such as this. Contributions to general assessment publications and conferences by researchers working in the young learner area provide a connection with the general assessment field.

Finally, researchers need to maintain the same connections that I have suggested above for the field. There needs to be ongoing communication between researchers involved in elementary education and in general assessment; and a consolidation of contact between researchers in second language and foreign language education. Part of the ability to make connections is probably to know where fields connect and where they differ, because there are indeed some areas where they come together closely, but others where they move apart.

Summary

In this chapter I argue that the way forward is to consolidate young learner assessment in two broad directions. Firstly, there is a need for consolidation of the theories, frameworks and connections, and secondly there is a need for consolidation of professional understandings and research. Young learner language assessment is broad in its conceptual base, taking theories from general education and from language education and assessment. Its scope is also broad, in that it encompasses both foreign language and second language assessment. There are therefore many sources for guidance as well as opportunities for connections. This will involve, indeed require, consolidation of understandings about ways in which teachers can strengthen their assessment practices, about the way in which teachers and assessors can develop their professional knowledge about assessment and about the way the contexts in which they work influence their ability to take up appropriate assessment practices for young learners. It will also require research and dissemination of research findings, with connections strengthened with the general assessment field, and between the foreign and second language assessment components of young learner research. In order to establish connections, those involved in young learner assessment need to be able to identify where their field connects with other fields and interests, and where it should remain separate. This is an issue of identity for those involved in young learner language assessment.

References

Abedi, J. (2004). The No Child Left Behind Act and English language learners: assessment and accountability issues. *Educational Researcher*, 33, 4–14.

Abedi, J., Courtney, M., Mirocha, J., Leon, S. and Goldberg, J. (2000). Language accommodation for large-scale assessment in science: assessing English language learners. Draft Deliverable to Office of Bilingual Education and Minority Language Affairs, OBEMLA, Contract No. R305B60002. Los Angeles, CA: University of California, National Center for Research on Evaluation, Standards, and Student Testing (CRESST).

Alderson, J. C., Clapham, C. and Wall, D. (1995). *Language Test Construction and Evaluation*. Cambridge: Cambridge University Press.

Alderson, J. C. (1991). Bands and scores. In J. C. Alderson and B. North (eds.), *Language Testing in the 1990s* (pp. 71–86). London: Modern English Publications and the British Council.

Alderson, J. C. (2000). *Assessing Reading*. Cambridge: Cambridge University Press.

Alderson, J. C. and Wall, D. (1993). Does washback exist? *Applied Linguistics 14*, 115–29.

Alexander, R. (2000). *Culture and Pedagogy*. Oxford: Blackwell.

August, D. and Hakuta, K. (1997). *Improving Schooling for Language-Minority Children*. Washington, DC: National Academic Press.

Australian Council of Educational Research. (2004). *The Australian Language Certificates*. Retrieved September, 2004, from http://www.acer.edu.au/tests/schools/alc/intro/html

Bachman, L. F. (2002). Alternative interpretations of alternative assessments: some validity issues in educational performance assessments. *Educational Measurement: Issues and Practices 21*(3), 5–19.

Bachman, L. F. (2004). *Statistical Analyses for Language Assessment*. Cambridge: Cambridge University Press.

Bachman, L. F. and Palmer, A. S. (1996). *Language Testing in Practice.* Oxford: Oxford University Press.

Bailey, A. L. (in press). From *Lambie to Lambaste:* the conceptualization, operationalization and use of academic language in the assessment of ELL students. In T. Wiley and K. Rolstad (eds.), *Rethinking School Language.* Mahway, NJ: LEA.

Bailey, A. L. and Butler, F. A. (2002). *An Evidentiary Framework for Operationalizing Academic Language for Broad Application to K-12 Education: A Design Document (CSE Tech. Rep. No. 611).* Los Angeles: University of California, National Center for Research on Evaluation, Standards, and Student Testing (CRESST).

Bailey, A. L. and Butler, F. A. (2003). *An Evidentiary Framework for Operationalizing Academic Language for Broad Application to K-12 Education: A Design Document (CSE Tech. Rep. No. 611).* Los Angeles: University of California, National Center for Research on Evaluation, Standards, and Student Testing (CRESST).

Bailey, A. L., Butler, F. A., LaFramenta, C. and Ong, C. (2004). *Towards the Characterization of Academic Language in Upper Elementary Science Classrooms (CSE Tech. Rep. No. 621).* Los Angeles: University of California, National Center for Research on Evaluation, Standards, and Student Testing (CRESST).

Baker, C. and Hornberger, N. H. (2001). *An Introductory Reader to the Writings of Jim Cummins.* Clevedon, Avon: Multilingual Matters.

Ball, F. and Wilson, J. (2002). Research projects relating to YLE speaking tests. In *Research Notes 7* (pp. 8–11). Cambridge: University of Cambridge Local Examinations Syndicate.

Barnes, D., Britton, J. and Torbe, M. (1986). *Language, the Learner and the School.* Harmondsworth: Penguin.

Bartlett, R. (2001). *Secret Codes: Hiragana Instruction in Year Six* M.Ed. thesis. Queensland University of Technology, Brisbane.

Berwick, R. (1993). Towards an educational framework for teacher-led tasks. In G. Crookes and S. M. Gass (eds.), *Tasks in a Pedagogical Context: Integrating Theory and Practice* (pp. 97–124). Clevedon, Avon: Multilingual Matters.

Bialystok, E. (2001). *Bilingualism in Development.* Cambridge: Cambridge University Press.

Bialystok, E. and Hakuta, K. (1999). Confounded age: linguistic and cognitive factors in age differences for second language acquisition. In D. Birdsong (ed.), *Second Language Acquisition and the Critical Period Hypothesis* (pp. 61–81). Mahwah, NJ: Lawrance Erlbaum.

Bielby, A. (2002). Unpublished term paper, M.Ed. (TESOL), Queensland University of Technology.

Bills, D. (1995). *Now You're Talking.* Adelaide: Department of Education and Children's Services. South Australian Education Video Unit/Department of Employment, Education and Training.

Black, P. and Wiliam, D. (1998). Assessment and classroom learning. *Assessment in Education 5*(1), 1–74.

Breen, M. P. (1997). The relationship between assessment frameworks and classroom pedagogy. In M. P. Breen, C. Barratt-Pugh, B. Derewianka, H. House, C. Hudson, T. Lumley and M. Rohl (eds.), *Profiling ESL Children. How Teachers Interpret and Use National and State Assessment Frameworks*, Vol. I (pp. 91–128). Canberra: Department of Employment, Education, Training and Youth Affairs.

Breen, M. P., Barratt-Pugh, C., Derewianka, B., House, H., Hudson, C., Lumley, T. and Rohl, M. (eds.), (1997). *Profiling ESL Children: How Teachers Interpret and Use National and State Assessment Frameworks*, Vol. I. Canberra: Department of Employment, Education, Training and Youth Affairs.

Brewster, J. (1984). Listening and the young learner. In C. Brumfit, J. Moon and R. Tongue (eds.), *Teaching English to Children* (pp. 158–77). Harlow, Essex: Longman.

Brindley, G. (1998). Outcomes-based assessment and reporting in language learning progammes: a review of the issues. *Language Testing* (15), 45–85.

Brindley, G. (2001). Outcomes-based assessment in practice: some examples, and emerging insights. *Language Testing 18*(4), 393–408.

Brookhart, S. M. (2003). Developing measurement theory for classroom assessment purposes and uses. *Educational Measurement: Issues and Practices 22*(4), 5–12.

Brown, G. and Yule, G. (1983). *Discourse Analysis*. Cambridge: Cambridge University Press.

Brown, J. D. (1994). *Teaching by Principles: An Interactive Approach to Language Pedagogy*. Englewood Cliffs, NJ: Prentice-Hall Regents.

Brown, J. D. and Hudson, T. (1998). The alternatives in language assessment. *TESOL Quarterly 32*(4), 633–75.

Brown, K. (1999). *Monitoring Learner Progress*. Sydney: National Centre for English Language Teaching and Research.

Brumfit, C., Moon, J. and Tongue, R. (eds.), (1995). *Teaching English to Children*. Harlow, Essex: Longman.

Buck, G. (2002). *Assessing Listening*. Cambridge: Cambridge University Press.

Butler, F. A. and Bailey, A. L. (2002). Equity in the assessment of English Language learners K-12. *Idiom 32*(1), 1.3.

Butler, F. A., Lord, C., Stevens, R., Borrego, M. and Bailey, A. L. (2004). *An Approach to Operationalizing Academic Language for Language Test Development Purposes: Evidence from Fifth-grade Science and Math (CSE Tech. Rep. No. 626)*. Los Angeles: University of California, National Center for Research on Evaluation, Standards, and Student Testing (CRESST).

Butler, F. A. and Stevens, R. (1997). *Accommodation Strategies for English Language Learners on Large-Scale Assessments: Student Characteristics and Other Considerations (CSE Tech. Rep. No. 448)*. Los Angeles: University of California,

National Center for Research on Evaluation, Standards, and Student Testing (CRESST).

Butler, F. A. and Stevens, R. (1998). *Initial Steps in the Validation of the Second Language Proficiency Descriptors for Public High Schools, Colleges, and Universities in California: Writing.* Los Angeles: Center for the Study of Evaluation, Graduate School of Education and Information Studies, University of California, Los Angeles.

Butler, F. A. and Stevens, R. (2001). Standardised assessment of the content knowledge of English language learners K-12: current trends and old dilemmas. *Language Testing 18*(4), 409–27.

Butler, F. A., Weigle, S., Kahn, A. B. and Sato, E. (1996). *California Department of Education Adult English-as-a-Second-Language Assessment Project: Test Development Plan with Specifications for Placement Instruments Anchored to the Model Standards.* Los Angeles: University of California, Center for the Study of Evaluation (CSE).

California Department of Education. (2003). *Targeted Standards for Foreign Languages Years 1–4: Draft Interim Standards.* Retrieved September, 2003, http://www.cde ca.gov/challenge fmlog.pdf.

Cameron, L. (2001). *Teaching Languages to Young Learners.* Cambridge: Cambridge University Press.

Candlin, C. (1987). Towards task-based learning. In C. Candlin & D. Murphy (eds.), *Language learning tasks* (pp. 5–22). Englewood Cliffs, NJ: Prentice-Hall.

Carle, E. (1974). *The Very Hungry Caterpillar.* Middlesex, England: Puffin.

Carless, D. R. and Wong, P. M. J. (2000). Teaching English to young learners in Hong Kong. In M. Nikolov and H. Curtain (eds.), *An Early Start: Young Learners and Modern Languages in Europe and Beyond* (pp. 209–24). Strasbourg: European Centre for Modern Languages. Council of Europe.

Carpenter, K., Fujii, N. and Kataoka, H. (1995). An oral interview procedure for assessing second language abilities in children. *Language Testing 12*(2), 157–75.

Carr, J. (2003). Culture through the looking glass: an intercultural experiment in sociolinguistics. In A. Liddicoat, J. Eisenchlas and S. Trevaskes (eds.), *Internationalising Education* (pp. 75–86). Melbourne: Language Australia.

Carrell, P. L., Devine, J. and Eskey, D. (eds.), (1991). *Interactive Approaches to Second-Language Reading.* Cambridge: Cambridge University Press.

Carson, J. G. (2000). Reading and writing for academic purposes. In M. Pally (ed.), *Sustained Content Teaching in Academic ESL/EFL* (pp. 19–34). Boston: Houghton-Mifflin.

Chalhoub-Deville, M. (1995). Deriving oral assessment scales across different tests and rater groups. *Language Testing 12*(1), 16–33.

Chamot, A. U. and O'Malley, J. M. (1994). *The CALLA Handbook: Implementing the Cognitive Academic Language Learning Approach.* Reading, MA: Addison-Wesley Publishing Company.

Clair, N., Adger, C. T., Short, D. and Millen, E. (1998). *Implementing Standards with English Language Learners: Initial Findings from Four Middle Schools.* Providence, RI: Northeast and Islands Regional Education Laboratory at Brown University.

Clay, M. (2000). *Running Records for Classroom Teachers.* Heinemann.

Coles, M. and Jenkins, R. (1998). *Assessing Reading,* Vol. II. London: Routledge.

Collier, V. (1992). A synthesis of studies examining long-term language minority students' data on academic achievement. *Bilingual Education Research Journal, 16,* 187–212.

Cope, B., Kalantzis, M. and Wignell, P. (1993). The language of social studies: using texts of society and culture in the primary school. In L. Unsworth (ed.), *Literacy, Learning and Teaching: Language as Social Practice in the Primary School* (pp. 297–348). South Melbourne: MacMillan Education.

Corson, D. (1988). *Oral Language Across the Curriculum.* Clevedon, Avon: Multilingual Matters.

Council of Europe. (2001). *Common European Framework of Reference for Languages: Learning, Teaching, Assessment.* Cambridge: Cambridge University Press.

Crozet, C. (2001). Part 2: A framework to identify cultural and some linguistic characteristics of indigenous languages. *Australian Language Matters,* Jan/Feb/ Mar 2001, 3–5, 10.

Cummins, J. (1979). Linguistic interdependence and the educational development of bilingual children. *Review of Educational Research 49,* 222–51.

Cummins, J. (1980). The construct of proficiency in bilingual education. In J. E. Alatis (ed.), *Georgetown University Round Table on Languages and Linguistics: Current Issues in Bilingual Education* (pp. 81–103). Georgetown.

Cummins, J. (1981). The role of primary language in promoting educational success for language minority students. In *Schooling and Language Minority Students: A Theoretical Framework* (pp 3–49). Los Angeles: California State University, Evaluation, Dissemination and Assessment Center.

Cummins, J. (1983). Language proficiency and academic achievement. In J. W. Oller (ed.), *Issues in Language Testing Research* (pp. 108–26). Rowley, MA: Newbury House.

Cummins, J. (1984). *Bilingualism and Special Education: Issues in Assessment and Pedagogy.* San Diego, CA: College-Hill Press.

Cummins, J. (2000). *Language, Power and Pedagogy.* Clevedon, Avon: Multilingual Matters.

Cummins, J. (2001a). The influence of bilingualism on cognitive growth: a synthesis of research findings and explanatory hypotheses. In C. Baker and N. H. Hornberger (eds.), *An Introductory Reader to the Writings of Jim Cummins* (pp. 1–43). Clevedon, Avon: Multilingual Matters.

Cummins, J. (2001b). Tests, achievement and bilingual students. In C. Baker and N. H. Hornberger (eds.), *An Introductory Reader to the Writings of Jim Cummins* (pp. 26–55). Clevedon, Avon: Multilingual Matters.

Davidson, F. and Lynch, B. K. (2002). *Testcraft*. New Haven: Yale University Press.

Davies, F. (1995). *Introducing Reading*. London: Penguin.

Davison, C. (1999). Missing the mark: The Problem with the Benchmarking of ESL students in Australian schools. *Prospect 14*(2), 66–76.

Davison, C. and McKay, P. (2002). Counting and dis-counting learner group variation: English language and literacy standards in Australia. *Journal of Asian-Pacific Communications 14*(2), 66–76.

Davison, C. and Williams, A. (2002). *Learning from Each Other: Critical Connections. Studies of English Language and Literacy Development*, Vol. I. Melbourne: Language Australia. Victorian Child Literacy and ESL Research Centre.

de la Luz Reyes, M. (1987). Comprehension of content area passages: a study of Spanish/English Readers in third and fourth grade. In S. R. Goldman and H. T. Trueba (eds.), *Becoming Literate in English as a Second Language* (pp. 107–26). Norwood, NJ: Ablex.

Derewianka, B. (1992). Assessing oral language. In B. Derewianka (ed.), *Language Assessment in Primary Classrooms* (pp.68–102). Marrickville, NSW: Harcourt Brace Jovanovich.

Des-Fountain, J. and Howe, A. (1992). Pupils working together on understanding. In K. Norman (ed.), *Thinking Voices*. London: Hodder and Stoughton.

Dodd, C. and Butler, C. (2002). Unpublished data on teacher ratings of outcomes. Brisbane.

Edelenbos, P. and Johnstone, R. (eds.), (1996). *Researching Languages at Primary School*. London: CILT.

Education Department of South Australia. (1973). *Resource Book on the Development of Reading Skills*. Adelaide: South Australia.

Education Department of South Australia. (1990). *ESL Student Needs Assessment Procedures R-10*. Adelaide: Education Department of South Australia.

Education Department of Western Australia. (1997a). *First Steps Reading Resource Book*. Perth: Rigby Heinemann.

Education Department of Western Australia. (1997b). *First Steps. Oral Language Resource Book*. Perth: Rigby Heinemann/Education Department of Western Australia.

Education Department of Western Australia. (1997c). *First Steps. Reading Developmental Continuum*. Perth: Rigby Heinemann.

Education Department of Western Australia. (1997d). *First Steps. Writing Resource Book*. Perth: Rigby Heinemann.

Education Department of Western Australia. (1997e). *First Steps: Spelling Developmental Continuum*. Perth: Rigby Heinemann.

Fairclough, N. (1989). *Language and Power*. London: Longman.

Falvey, P. and Kennedy, P. (eds.), (1997). *Learning Language through Literature*. Hong Kong: Hong Kong University Press.

Feeney, S. (1992). *Early Childhood Education in Asia and the Pacific*. New York: Garland Publishing.

Foster, J. and Lewis, J. I. (1996). *You Little Monkey and Other Poems for Young Children*. Oxford: Oxford University Press.

Foucault, M. (1979). *Discipline and Punishment*. New York: Vintage Books.

Freebody, P. and Austin, H. (1992). Assessing reading comprehension. In B. Derewianka (ed.), *Language Assessment in Primary Classrooms* (pp. 139–80). Marrickville, NSW: Harcourt Brace Jovanovich.

Freire, P. (1972). *Pedagogy of the Oppressed*. Kibdib: Penguin.

Fullan, M. (1993). *Change Forces: Probing the Depths of Educational Reform*. Bristol, PA: Falmer Press.

Garcia, G. E. (1991). Factors influencing the English reading test performance of Spanish speaking Hispanic students. *Reading Research Quarterly 26*, 371–92.

Garcia, G. E. and Pearson, P. D. (1994). Assessment and diversity. In L. Darling-Hammond (ed.), *Review of Research in Education 20* (pp. 337–92). Washington: American Educational Research Association.

Gardner, H. (1993). *Multiple intelligences: The theory in practice*. New York: Basic Books.

Gardner, S. and Rea-Dickins, P. (2001). Conglomeration or chameleon? Teachers' representation of language in the assessment of learners with English as an additional language. *Language Awareness 10*(2 and 3), 161–77.

Gatullo, F. (2000). Formative assessment in ELT primary (elementary) classrooms: an Italian case study. *Language Testing 17*(2), 278–88.

Gee, J. P. (1996). *Social Linguistics and Literacies*. London: Falmer Press.

Genesee, F. and Hamayan, E. V. (1994). Classroom-based assessment. In F. Genesee (ed.), *Educating Second Language Children* (pp. 212–39). Cambridge: Cambridge University Press.

Genesee, F. and Upshur, J. A. (1996). *Classroom Evaluation in Second Language Education*. Cambridge: Cambridge University Press.

Genishi, C. and Brainard, M. B. (1995). Assessment of bilingual children: a dilemma seeking solutions. In G. E. Garcia and B. McLaughlin (eds.), *Meeting the Challenge of Linguistic and Cultural Diversity in Early Childhood Education* (pp. 49–63). New York: Teachers College, Columbia University.

Gipps, C. V. (1994). *Beyond Testing. Towards a Theory of Educational Assessment*. London: Falmer Press.

Gottlieb, M. (2003). *Large-Scale Assessment of English Language Learners. Addressing Educational Accountability in K-12 Settings*. Alexandria, Virginia: Teachers of English to Speakers of Other Languages.

Greatorex, J. (2003). Developing and applying level descriptors. *Westminster Studies in Education 26*(2), 125–33.

Hall, D. (1995). *Assessing the Needs of Bilingual Pupils*. London: David Fulton Publishers.

Halliday, M. A. K. (1975). *Learning how to Mean: Explorations in the Development of Language*. New York: Elsevier.

Halliday, M. A. K. (1994). *An Introduction to Functional Grammar*. London: Edward Arnold.

Halliwell, S. (1992). *Teaching English in the Primary Classroom*. Harlow, Essex: Longman.

Hamp-Lyons, L. (1991). Pre-text: task-related influences on the writer. In L. Hamp-Lyons (ed.), *Assessing Second Language Writing in Academic Contexts* (pp. 87–107). Norwood, NJ: Ablex.

Hargreaves, A. (1994). *Changing Teachers, Changing Times: Teachers' Work and Culture in the Postmodern Age*. New York: Teachers College Press.

Harklau, L. (1994). ESL versus mainstream classes: contrasting L2 learning environments. *TESOL Quarterly 28*(2), 241–79.

Hasselgren, A. (2000). The assessment of the English ability of young learners in Norwegian schools: an innovative approach. *Language Testing 17*(2), 261–77.

Hasselgren, A. (2005). *Language Testing, 22*(3), 337–54.

Heath, S. B. (1983). *Ways with Words: Language, Life and Work in Communities and Classrooms*. Cambridge: Cambridge University Press.

Herman, J. L., Aschbacher, P. R. and Winters, L. (1992). *A Practical Guide to Alternative Assessment*. Alexandria, VA: Association for Supervision and Curriculum Development.

Hester, H. (1996). The stages of English Learning: the context. In *Invitational Conference on Teaching and Learning English as an Additional Language* (pp. 182–87). London: School Curriculum and Assessment Authority.

Hill, D. A. (2000). Adding foreign languages to the elementary school curriculum: the Italian experience. In J. Moon and M. Nikolov (eds.), *Research into Teaching English to Young Learners* (pp. 137–52). Pecs: University Press Pecs.

Huerta-Macias, A. (1995). Alternative assessment: responses to commonly asked questions. *TESOL Journal* (Autumn), 8–11.

Hughes, A. (2003). *Testing for Language Teachers*. Cambridge: Cambridge University Press.

Illinois State Board of Education. (2003). *Foreign Language Standards*. Retrieved 15 August 2003, from http://www.isbe.net/ils/foreignlanguage/fog28.html.

Ingeborg, P. (1998). European Language Portfolio. *Language Teaching* (October, 1998).

Jalongo, M. R. (2000). *Early Childhood Language Arts*. Boston: Allyn and Bacon.

Jantscher, E. and Landsiedler, I. (2000). Foreign language education at Austrian primary. In M. Nikolov and H. Curtain (eds.), *An Early Start: Young Learners and Modern Languages in Europe and Beyond* (pp. 13–27). Strasbourg Cedex: Council of Europe.

Johnstone, R. (2000). Context-sensitive assessment of modern languages in primary (elementary) and early secondary education: Scotland and the European experience. *Language Testing 17*(2), 123–43.

Kershner, R. (2000). Recognising and responding to children as individuals. In D. Whitebread (ed.), *The Psychology of Teaching and Learning in the Primary School.* London: Routledge-Falmer (pp. 235–55).

Koenig, J. A. and Bachman, L. F. (2004). *Keeping Score for All: The Effects of Inclusion and Accommodation Policies on Large-Scale Educational Assessment.* Washington, DC: National Research Council, National Academies Press.

Law, B. and Eckes, M. (1995). *Assessment and ESL.* Winnipeg: Peguis.

Leung, C. (1996). English as an additional language within the National Curriculum: a study of assessment practices. *Prospect 11*(2), 58–68.

Leung, C. (2004). Developing teacher assessment: knowledge, practice and change. *Language Assessment Quarterly 1*(1), 19–41.

Leung, C. (2005). Classroom teacher assessment of second language development: construct as practice. In E. Hinkel (ed.), *Handbook of Research in Second Language Learning and Teaching.* Mahwah, NJ: Lawrence Erlbaum Associates (869–88).

Leung, C. and Teasdale, A. (1997). What do teachers mean by speaking and listening? A contextualised study of assessment in multilingual classrooms in the English National Curriculum. In A. Huhta, V. Kohonen, L. Kurki-Suonio and S. Louma (eds.), *New Contexts, Goals and Alternatives in Language Assessment* (pp. 291–324). Jyvaskyla: University of Jyvaskyla.

Liddicoat, A. J. (1997). *Communicating in LOTE. Writing and Oral Interaction.* Canberra: Modern Language Teachers' Association of the Australian Capital Territory.

Lippi-Green, R. (1997). *English with an Accent: Language, Ideology and Discrimination in the United States.* London: Routledge.

Lloyd-Jones, R. (1997). Primary trait scoring. In C. R. Cooper and L. Odell (eds.), *Evaluating Writing* (pp. 33–69). New York: National Council of Teachers of English.

Losardo, A. and Notari-Syverson, A. (2001). *Alternative Approaches to Assessing Young Children.* New York: Paul H. Brookes.

Low, L., Brown, S., Johnstone, R. and Pirrie, A. (1995). *Foreign Languages in Primary Schools.* Stirling: Scottish Centre for Information on Language Teaching and Research, University of Stirling.

Luke, A. and Freebody, P. (1990). Literacies' programs: debate and demand in cultural context. *Prospect, 5*(3), 7–16.

Lumley, T., Mincham, L. and Raso, E. (1994). Exemplar assessment activities, observation guidelines and reporting formats. In P. McKay (ed.), *The NLLIA ESL Development: Language and Literacy in Schools,* Vol. I: *Teachers' Manual* (pp. E1–F18). Canberra: National Languages and Literacy Institute of Australia.

Luoma, S. (2004). *Assessing Speaking.* Cambridge: Cambridge University Press.

Mahon, T. (1994). *Focus on Reading and Writing*. Hong Kong: Hong Kong Language Development Fund/Institute of Language in Education.

Markee, N. (1993). The diffusion of innovation in language teaching. *Annual Review of Applied Linguistics, 13,* 229–43.

Marshall, H. and Gutteridge, M. (2002). Candidate performance in the Young Learner English Tests in 2000. In *Research Notes 7*. Cambridge: University of Cambridge Local Examinations Syndicate.

Mason, J. (1992). Assessing early literacy development. In B. Derewianka (ed.), *Language Assessment in Primary Classrooms* (pp. 103–38). Marrickville, NSW: Harcourt Brace Jovanovich.

Masters, G. N. and Forster, M. (1997). *Mapping Literacy Achievement: Results of the 1996 National School English Literacy Survey*. Canberra: Department of Education, Employment, Training and Youth Affairs.

Maybin, J., Mercer, N. and Stierer, B. (1992). 'Scaffolding' learning in the classroom. In K. Norman (ed.), *Thinking Voices: The Work of the National Curriculum Project* (pp. 142–52). London: Hodder and Stoughton for the National Curriculum Council.

McKay, P. (1998). Discriminatory features for ESL learners in the literacy benchmarks. In *Australian Language Matters Background Papers No. 2* (pp. 27–29). Melbourne: Australian Council of TESOL Associations.

McKay, P. (2000). On ESL standards for school-age learners. *Language Testing* 17(2), 185–214.

McKay, P. (2001). National literacy benchmarks and the outstreaming of learners in ESL. In J. Lo Bianco and R. Wickert (eds.), *Australian Policy Activism in Language and Literacy* (pp. 223–39). Melbourne: Language Australia.

McKay, P. (2004). *Do Standards Have Something to Answer For? A Pedagogic Response to Standards. Plenary Address. TESOL Arabia. Dubai. March, 2004.*

McKay, P. (forthcoming). Classroom second language assessment in Australian schools: new roles and new tensions under educational reform. *Language Assessment Quarterly.*

McKay, P., Hudson, C. and Sapuppo, M. (1994). NLLIA ESL Bandscales. In P. McKay (ed.), *NLLIA ESL Development: Language and Literacy in Schools*, Vol. I (pp. B1–D52). Canberra: National Languages and Literacy Institute of Australia.

McKee, L. P. (1999). Thursday Island State School Case Study. (Unpublished MEd (TESOL) Coursework assignment). Brisbane: Queensland University of Technology.

McMillan, J. H. (2003). Understanding and improving teachers' classroom assessment decision making: implications for theory and practice. *Educational Measurement: Issues and Practices* 22(4), 34–44.

McMillan, J. H. and Nash, S. (2000). Teacher classroom assessment and grading practices decision making.

McNamara, T. F. (1996). *Measuring Second Language Performance.* London: Longman.

Meadows, S. (1993). *The Child as Thinker.* London: Routledge.

Meister, D. G. (2000). Teachers and Change: Examining the Literature. Unpublished manuscript.

Mercer, N. (1994). Neo-Vygotskian theory and classroom education. In B. Stierer and J. Maybin (eds.), *Language, Literacy and Learning in Educational Practice* (pp. 92–109). Clevedon, Avon: Multilingual Matters/Open University.

Miller, J. (2003). *Audible Difference ESL and Social Identity in Schools.* Clevedon, Avon: Multilingual Matters.

Mincham, L. (1985). ESL student needs procedures: an approach to language assessment in primary and secondary school contexts. In G. Brindley (ed.), *Language Assessment in Action* (pp. 65–91). Sydney: National Centre for English Language Teaching and Research.

Mislevy, R. J., Steinberg, L. S. and Almond, R. G. (2002). Design and analysis in task-based language assessment. *Language Testing 19*(4), 477–96.

Mohan, B. A. (1986). *Language and Content.* New York: Addison-Wesley Publishing Company.

Mohan, B. A. and Slater, T. (2004). The evaluation of causal discourse and language as a resource for meaning. In J. Foley (ed.), *Functional Perspectives on Education and Discourse.* London: Continuum.

Morris, P., Lo, M.-l., Chik, P.-M. and Chan, K.-k. (2000). One function, two systems: changing assessment in Hong Kong's primary schools. In B. Adamson, T. Kwan and K.-k. Chan (eds.), *Changing the Curriculum. The Impact of Reform on Primary Schooling in Hong Kong* (pp.195–215). Hong Kong: Hong Kong University.

Moya, S. S. and O'Malley, M. (1994). A portfolio assessment model for ESL. *Journal of Educational Issues of Language Minority Students 13*, 13–36.

National Standards in Foreign Language Education Project. (1996). *Standards for Foreign Language Learning: Preparing for the 21st Century.* Lawrence, KS: Allen Press.

Nicholas, H. (1999). Comparing developments in Oral and Written English in the lower primary school. In C. Davison and A. Williams (eds.), *Learning from Each Other: Studies of English Language and Literacy Development 1995–1998,* Vol. II. Melbourne: Language Australia's Victorian Child Literacy and ESL Research Network.

Nikolov, M. (2000). Teaching foreign languages to young learners in Hungary. In *An Early Start: Young Learners and Modern Languages in Europe and Beyond* (pp. 29–40). Strasbourg: European Centre for Modern Languages, Council of Europe.

North, B. (1993). *The Development of Descriptors on Scales of Language Proficiency.* Washington, DC: National Foreign Language Center.

North, B. (1995). The development of a common framework scale of descriptors of language proficiency based on a theory of measurement. *System 23*(4), 445–65.

Northern Territory Board of Studies. (1995). *Walking Talking Texts. A Program of Teaching and Learning for English as a Second Language.* Darwin: Northern Territory Board of Studies.

Notari-Syverson, A., O'Connor, R. E. and Vadasy, P. F. (1998). *Ladders to literacy: A Preschool Activity Book.* Baltimore: Paul H. Brookes.

Nunan, D. (1989). *Designing Tasks for the Communicative Classroom.* Cambridge: Cambridge University Press.

Nunan, D. (1993). Task-based syllabus design: selecting, grading and sequencing tasks. In G. Crookes and S. M. Gass (eds.), *Tasks in a Pedagogical Context: Integrating Theory and Practice* (pp. 55–68). Clevedon, Avon: Multilingual Matters.

O'Malley, J. M. and Valdez Pierce, L. (1996). *Authentic Assessment for English Language Learners.* USA: Addison-Wesley.

Pavlenko, A. and Lantolf, J. P. (2000). Second language learning as participation and the (re)construction of selves. In J. P. Lantolf (ed.), *Sociocultural Theory and Second Language Learning.* Oxford: Oxford University Press.

Pennycook, A. (2000). The social politics and the cultural politics of the language classroom. In J. K. Hall and W. G. Eggington (eds.), *The Sociopolitics of English Language Teaching.* Clevedon, Avon: Multilingual Matters.

Phang, E. (2001a). *Primary 4 English Exam Papers.* Singapore: Educational Publishing House.

Phang, E. (2001b). *Primary 5 English Exam Papers.* Singapore: Educational Publishing House.

Phillips, S. (1993). *Young Learners.* Oxford: Oxford University Press.

Piaget, J. (1930). *The Child's Conception of Physical Causality.* London: Routledge and Kegan Paul.

Pinter, A. (1999). Investigations into task-related strategy use with young learners of English. In S. Rixon (ed.), *Young Learners of English: Some Research Perspectives.* Harlow, Essex: Longman.

Puckett, M. B. and Black, J. K. (2000). *Authentic Assessment of the Young Child.* Upper Saddle River, NJ: Prentice-Hall.

Purpura, J. (2004). *Assessing Grammar.* Cambridge: Cambridge University Press.

Pye, J. (1988). *Invisible Children: Who Are the Real Losers at School?* Oxford: Oxford University Press.

Qualifications and Curriculum Authority *National Curriculum in Action. Modern Foreign Language Levels,* from http://www.ncaction.org.uk/subjects/mfl/index/htm.

Queensland Schools Curriculum Council. (2000). *Languages Other than English. Years 1 to 3 Curriculum Guidelines.* Brisbane: State of Queensland.

Read, J. (2000). *Assessing Vocabulary.* Cambridge: Cambridge University Press.

Rea-Dickins, P. (2001). Mirror, mirror on the wall: identifying processes of classroom assessment. *Language Testing, 18*(4), 429–62.

Rea-Dickins, P. and Gardner, S. (2000). Snares and silver bullets. Disentangling the construct of formative assessment. *Language Testing 17*(2), 217–44.

Rea-Dickins, P. and Rixon, S. (1997). The assessment of young learners of English as a foreign language. In C. Clapham and D. Corson (eds.), *The Encyclopaedia of Language and Education, Volume 7: Language Testing and Assessment* (151–61). Netherlands: Kluwer Academic Publishers.

Rea-Dickins, P. and Rixon, S. (1999). Assessment of young learners' English: reasons and means. In S. Rixon (ed.), *Young Learners of English: Some Research Perspectives* (pp. 89–101). Harlow, Essex: Longman.

Reilly, V. and Ward, S. M. (2000). *Very Young Learners.* Oxford: Oxford University Press.

Rhodes, N. and Thomas, L. (1990). An oral assessment instrument for immersing students. In A. Padilla, H. Fairchild and C. Valdez (eds.), *Issues and Strategies.* Newbury Park, CA: Sage.

Richards, J., Platt, J. and Weber, H. (1985). *Longman Dictionary of Applied Linguistics.* Harlow, Essex: Longman.

Rivalland, J. (1992). Building profiles. In B. Derewianka (ed.), *Language Assessment in Primary Schools* (pp. 18–67). Sydney: Harcourt Brace Jovanovich.

Rixon, S. (ed.). (1999). *Young Learners of English: Some Research Perspectives.* London: Longman.

Sadler, R. (1987). Specifying and promulgating achievement standards. *Oxford Review of Education 13*(2), 191–209.

Salinger, T. (1998). Developing an early literacy portfolio. In M. Coles and R. Jenkins (eds.), *Assessing Reading,* Vol. II. London: Routledge.

Scarino, A., Vale, D., McKay, P. and Clark, J. L. (1988). *The Australian Language Levels Guidelines (Books 1–4).* Canberra: Curriculum Development Centre.

Schmidt, R. (1990). The role of consciousness in second language learning. *Applied Linguistics 11*(2), 129–58.

Schumann, J. H. (1997). *The Neurobiology of Affect in Language.* Malden, MA: Blackwell.

Selly, N. J. (1999). *The Art of Constructivist Teaching in the Primary School.* London: David Fulton Publishers.

Shohamy, E. (1993). *The Power of Tests: The Impact of Language Tests in Teaching and Learning.* Washington, DC: National Foreign Language Centre.

Shohamy, E. (2001). *The Power of Tests: Critical Perspectives on the Uses of Language Tests.* Harlow, England: Longman.

Shorrocks, D. (1995). The development of children's thinking and understanding. In C. Brumfit, J. Moon and R. Tongue (eds.), *Teaching English to Children.* Harlow, Essex: Longman.

Skehan, P. (1998). *A Cognitive Approach to Language Learning.* Oxford: Oxford University Press.

Slavin, R. E. (1994). *Educational Psychology.* Boston: Allyn and Bacon.

Smallwood, B. A. (ed.). (2001). *Integrating the ESL Standards into Classroom Practice. Grades Pre-K-2*: TESOL.

Smith, J. K. (2003). Reconsidering reliability in classroom assessment and grading. *Educational measurement: Issues and Practices 22*(4), 26–34.

Solano-Flores, G. and Trumbull, E. (2003). Examining language in context: the need for new research and practice paradigms in the testing of English-language learners. *Educational Researcher 32*, 3–14.

Stevens, R. A., Butler, F. A. and Castellon-Wellington, M. (2000). *Academic Language and Content Assessment: Measuring the Progress of ELLs (CSE Tech. Rep. No. 552)*. Los Angeles: University of Los Angeles, National Center for Research on Evaluation, Standards and Testing.

Swain, M. (1985). Large-scale communicative language testing: A case study. In Y. P. Lee, A. C. Y. Fok, G. Lord and G. Low (eds.), *New Directions in Language Testing* (pp. 35–46). Oxford: Pergamon Press.

Swain, M. and Lapkin, S. (1998). Interaction and second language learning: two adolescent French immersion students working together. *Modern Language Journal 82*(3), 320–7.

Taylor, L. and Saville, N. (2002). Developing English language tests for young learners. In University of Cambridge Local Examinations Syndicate. *Research Notes 7* (pp. 2–5). Cambridge: Cambridge University Press.

Teasdale, A. and Leung, C. (2000). Teacher assessment and psychometric theory: a case of paradigm crossing? *Language Testing 17*(2), 163–84.

TESOL. (1997). *ESL Standards for Pre-K-12 Students*. Alexandria, VA: Teachers of English to Speakers of Other Languages.

Thompson, L. (1997). *Foreign Language Assessment in Grades K-8. An Annotated Bibliography of Assessment Instruments*. Washington, DC: Center for Applied Linguistics and Delta Systems.

Toohey, K. (2000). *Learning English at School. Identity, Social Relations and Classroom Practice*. Clevedon, Avon: Multilingual Matters.

Torrance, H. and Pryor, J. (1998). *Investigating Formative Assessment*. Buckingham: Open University Press.

University of Cambridge ESOL Examinations. (2002). *Cambridge Young Learners English Tests Sample Papers*. Cambridge: University of Cambridge Local Examinations Syndicate.

University of Cambridge ESOL Examinations. (2003). *Cambridge Young Learners Handbook*. Cambridge: University of Cambridge ESOL Examinations.

Ur, P. (1994). *Teaching Listening Comprehension*. Cambridge: Cambridge University Press.

Urquhart, I. (2000). Communicating well with children. In D. Whitebread (ed.), *The Psychology of Teaching and Learning in the Primary School*. London: Routledge/Falmer (pp. 57–77).

Valdes, G. and Figueroa, R. (1994). *Bilingualism and Testing a Special Case of Bias*. Norwood, NJ: Ablex.

Valdez Pierce, L. (2001). Assessment of reading comprehension strategies for intermediate bilingual learners. In S. R. Hurley and J. V. Tinajero (eds.), *Literacy Assessment of Second Language Learners*. Boston: Allyn and Bacon.

Vygotsky, L. (1962). *Thought and language* (E. Hanfmann and G. Vakar, Trans).

Warwick, U. O. (2000). *Analysis and Evaluation of the Current Situation relating to the Teaching of Modern Foreign Languages at Key Stage 2 in England*: University of Warwick. Report commissioned by Qualifications and Curriculum Authority.

Weigle, S. (2002). *Assessing Writing*. Cambridge: Cambridge University Press.

Wells, G. (1989). Language in the classroom: literacy and collaborative talk. *Language and Education 3*(4251–273).

Whitebread, D. (2000). Organising activity to help children remember and understand. In D. Whitebread (ed.), *The Psychology of Teaching and Learning in the Primary School*. London: Routledge/Falmer (pp. 119–139).

WIDA Consortium. (2004). *English Language Proficiency Standards for English Language Learners in Kindergarten through Grade 12: Frameworks for Large-Scale State and Classroom Assessment. Overview Document:* State of Wisconsin.

Wiliam, D. (2001). An overview of the relationship between assessment and the curriculum. In D. Scott (ed.), *Curriculum and Assessment* (pp. 165–81). Westport, CT: Ablex.

Williams, M. (1984). A framework for teaching English to young learners. In C. Brumfit, J. Moon and R. Tongue (eds.), *Teaching English to Children*. Harlow, Essex: Longman.

Wong Fillmore, L. (1976). *The Second Time Around: Cognitive and Social Strategies in Second Language Acquisition*, Stanford University.

Wong Fillmore, L. (1991). Second-language learning in children: a model of language learning in social context. In E. Bialystok (ed.), *Language Processing in Bilingual Children*. Cambridge: Cambridge University Press.

Wood, D. (1992). Teacher talk: How modes of teacher talk affect pupil participation. In K. Norman (ed.), *Thinking Voices. The Work of the National Oracy Project*. London: Hodder and Stoughton.

Yat, K. (2001). *Primary 1, 2 & 3 English Exam Papers*. Singapore: Educational Publishing House.

Zangl, R. (2000). Monitoring language skills in Austrian primary (elementary) schools: a case study. *Language Testing 17*(2), 250–60.

Index

Publishers' acknowledgments

The author and publishers are grateful to those authors, publishers and others who have given permission for the use of copyright material identified in the text. It has not always been possible to identify the source of material used or to contact the copyright holders and in such cases the publishers would welcome information from the copyright owners.

Table 1.1 (page 12) Widely Held Expectations of Literacy Development by Puckett and Black in *Authentic Assessment of the Young Child: Celebrating Development and Learning*, 2nd edition, © 2000; Table 8.4 (page 289) Example of an analytic rating scale; Table 8.3 (page 287) Sample of holistic rating scales for writing samples by O'Malley and Pierce in *Authentic Assessment for English Language Learners*, © 1996. Reprinted by permission of Pearson Education Inc. Upper Saddle River, NJ.

Page 30 Four areas to identify cultural codes by C. Crozet in *Australian Language Matters, Jan/Feb/March 2001*; Figure 5.1 (page 149) Example of assessment embedded in a teaching cycle by T. Lumley, L. Mincham and E. Raso in *The NLLIA ESL Development: Language and Literacy in Schools. Volume 1: Teachers' Manual* © 1994; Figure 8.9 (page 311) The three levels of the Australian (NLLIA) ESL Bandscales; Figure 8.10 (page 312) Extract from the Australian (NLLIA) ESL Bandscales (Junior Primary Listening Levels 4 and 5) by P. McKay, C. Hudson and M. Sapuppo in *NLLIA ESL Development: Language and Literacy in Schools*, Vol 1 © 1994. By permission of CAE Press, Melbourne.

Page 45 TESOL Standards, in TESOL 1997 © Teachers of English to Speakers of Other Languages, Inc. (TESOL). Reprinted with permission.

Table 2.2 (page 50) Curriculum goals for language learning for years 1 to 3 (adapted from *Years 1 to 3 Curriculum Guidelines, LOTE Syllabus*) published by the Queensland Studies Authority, Brisbane.

Table 2.3 (page 52) Areas of language knowledge; Table 4.4 (page 135) Template for checking task characteristics for young learners; Figure 9.1 (page 320) Model of test development by Lyle F. Bachman and Adrian S. Palmer in *Language Testing in Practice* © 1996; Figure 6.7 (page 211) Suggestions for total physical response by S. Phillips in *Young Learners* © 1993. Reproduced by permission of Oxford University Press.

Page 56 Growth of learners' knowledge, by Billows: Table 3.2 (page 81) Factors influencing response difficulty in tasks (adapted); Figure 5.12 (page 167) Peer evaluation (adapted) in *The Australian Language Levels Guidelines* by Scarino, Vale, McKay and Clark, © 1988; page 72 Assessment framework by Breen in *Profiling ESL Children: How Teachers Interpret and Use National and State Assessment Frameworks*, Vol 1 © 1997. Reproduced by permission of The Australian Government, Department of Education, Science and Training.

Page 69 Different stages in teacher assessment process; Figure 5.2 (page 150) Processes and strategies in instruction-embedded classroom assessment by P. Rea-Dickins in *Mirror, mirror on the wall: identifying processes of classroom assessment*, © 2001; page 353 P. Rea-Dickins and S. Rixon, Assessment of young learners' English: reasons and means in *Young Learners of English: Some Research Perspectives* © 1999. By permission of the author.

Page 80 Assessment procedure by A. Hasselgren in The assessment of the English ability of young learners in Norwegian schools: an innovative approach *Language Testing 17(2) 261–277* © 2000; page 85 Warm-up activities by K. Carpenter, N. Fujii and H. Kataoka, in An oral interview procedure for assessing second language abilities in children *Language Testing 12(2)157–175* © 1995; Table 9.4 (page 340) Two categories of accommodations for English language learners by Butler and Stevens in Standardised assessment of the content knowledge of English language learners K-12: current trends and old dilemmas, *Language Testing 18(4) 409–427* © 2001. By permission of Edward Arnold (Publishers) Ltd.

Table 3.1 (page 77) Extract from Elementary Written Language Assessment Criteria for a Persuasive Argument by L. Mincham from ESL student needs procedures: an approach to language assessment in primary and secondary school contexts in *Language Assessment in Action* by Geoff Brindley (1995) with permission from the National Centre for English Language Teaching and Research. Copyright © Macquarie University.

Figure 4.4 (page 104) 'I'm painting a picture' © John Foster 1996 from *You Little Monkey* (Oxford University Press), by permission of the author.

Figure 4.5 (page 105) An example of an embedded language use assessment task in a classroom teaching task, and pages 115 and 224 *Teaching Languages to Young Learners* by L. Cameron © 2001; Figure 10.1 (page 361) The hierarchy of interrelating subsystems in which an innovation has to operate by Kennedy 1998 cited in N. Markee The diffusion of innovation in language teaching. *Annual Review of Applied Linguistics 13, 229–43*. By permission of Cambridge University Press.

Figure 4.6 (page 107, also page 241) Example of a listening assessment task; Figure 9.2 (page 329) Movers Reading and Writing Task, Part 5; Figure 9.3 (page 330) Marking Key for Flyers Reading and Writing, Part 1 taken from University of Cambridge ESOL Examinations 2002; Table 9.1 (page 325) Extract from Starters Structure List; Table 9.2 (page 327) Summary of Starters Listening Test Components; Table 9.3 (page 328) Components for Movers Speaking Component taken from University of Cambridge ESOL Examinations 2003, By permission of University of Cambridge ESOL Examinations.

Table 6.5 (page 204) Types of oral information-gap tasks (adapted); Figure 7.1 (page 235) Working with smaller groups in the classroom to observe reading; page 236 A miscue and its explanation; page 246 Major forms of writing, all taken from *First Steps Reading Resource Book* © 1997 Steps Professional Development, Swindon.

Figure 7.2 (page 239) Example of a 'read-and-do task' requiring a short answer; Figure 7.5 (page 242) Example of a multiple-choice vocabulary item; Figure 7.9 (pages 260–1) Example of picture-stimulated writing by K. Yat in *Primary 1, 2 & 3 English Exam Papers*, © 2001; Figure 7.7 (page 243) Example of a gap-filling task adapted from E. Phang in *Primary 5*

English Exam Papers © 2001. Published with permission from Educational Publishing House (S) Pte Ltd. [????]

Figure 8.3 (pages 283–4) A task-based criteria sheet for a report on a written process (based on the genre approach) by L. Mincham in *ESL Student Needs Assessment Procedures R-10*. Copyright © 1990 The Minister for Education and Children's Services for the State of South Australia.

Page 293 Low- and high- stakes assessment by J. L. Herman, P. R. Aschbacher and L. Winters in *A Practical Guide to Alternative Assessment* © 1992. By permission of The Association for Supervision and Curriculum Development, www.ascd.org.

Table 8.6 (page 303) Illinois Foreign Language Learning Standards: Standards under Goal 28 Communication, available from www.isbe.net/ils/foreignlanguage/fog28.html Copyright © 2001, Illinois State Board of Education, reprinted by permission. All rights reserved.

Figure 8.7 (page 308) First three levels of Common Reference Levels: global scale; Figure 8.8 (page 309) example of the levels A1–B1 of an illustrative scale: interviewing and being interviewed in *Common European Framework of Reference for Languages: Learning, Teaching, Assessment* © 2001 Council of Europe. The copyright of the text is held by the Council of Europe exclusively.

Table 9.5 (page 346) Example of test specification components allied to a draft prototype academic language proficiency task by A. L. Bailey and F. A. Butler in *Language Demands of Students Learning English in School: Putting academic language to the test*. New Haven CT. © Yale University Press.